Integrated Performance Management

A Guide to Strategy Implementation

D0609624

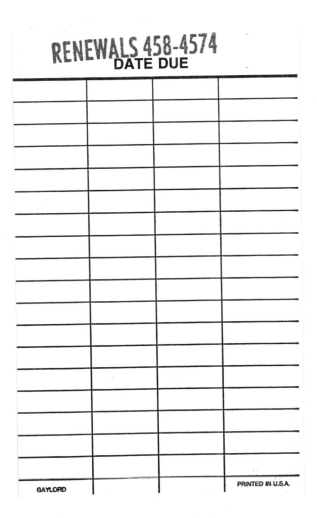

Integrated Performance Management

A Guide to Strategy Implementation

Edited by
KURT VERWEIRE AND
LUTGART VAN DEN BERGHE

 SAGE Publications
London • Thousand Oaks • New Delhi

First published 2004

SAGE Publications Ltd
1 Oliver's Yard
55 City Road
London EC1Y 1SP

SAGE Publications Inc
2455 Teller Road
Thousand Oaks, California 91320

SAGE Publications India Pvt Ltd
B-42 Panchsheel Enclave
Post Box 4109
New Delhi 110 017

British Library Cataloguing in Publication data
A catalogue record for this book is available from the British Library

ISBN 1 4129 0154 5
ISBN 1 4129 0155 3 (pbk)

Library of Congress Control Number available

Typeset by M Rules
Printed and bound in India by Gopsons Papers, Noida

Contents

PART III – ADDING A NEW DIMENSION TO INTEGRATED PERFORMANCE MANAGEMENT: INTRODUCING THE CONCEPT OF MATURITY ALIGNMENT

Preface

The management literature brings us many new concepts, cases, and experiences. However, companies struggle to implement, nor do they succeed in implementing, their strategy effectively. Introducing new management concepts by motivated managers often fails to deliver the expected improvements, sometimes resulting in worse performance and disappointed employees and customers.

The Integrated Performance Management Framework helped me to understand the levers of an organization and the need for their integration and balance. Many management publications describe situations and offer solutions that are almost impossible to apply in our business. In reality, most companies are far away from the ideal situations described in most management books. And sometimes a description of these ideal states can be misleading, rather than instrumental to get your business back on the right track.

This book clearly describes what a balanced and integrated approach towards performance management is all about. The Integrated Performance Management Framework is *really* integrated, and it allows us to position other management frameworks in a new, holistic context. It provides a very good reference base for all our activities and performance improvement initiatives. The maturity dimension, which is described in Part III of the book, is innovative and helpful in getting the business under control. Changes in the business environment forced us to rethink the way in which we manage our organization. Through a better understanding of the maturity of Electrabel, Tractebel, Suez and their various departments, we were able to make better decisions and to communicate and explain more clearly the change processes that occurred in our organization.

We are very happy that – with the help of Vlerick Leuven Gent Management School – we have contributed to a book that contains messages not only relevant for our company, but also offers new ideas and concepts that will be relevant for many other organizations as well, whether a multinational or a small local player. Our experiences linked to the inputs of various professors of the Vlerick Leuven Gent Management School have proven that the academic world can meet the business world in a way that is enriching for both.

I hope you find this interesting reading and that you will try the concepts described in *Integrated Performance Management* in your own organization.

Dirk Beeuwsaert

Brussels (Belgium), December 2003

Editors' Preface

This book is the result of an intensive dialogue between academicians and business people. About three years ago, some managers at Electrabel, Belgium's largest utility company, asked us at the Vlerick Leuven Gent Management School to provide the academic foundations for a management model they used within their organization. This management model incorporated aspects of strategy, operations, management control, risk management and leadership issues. It took some time before we accepted the challenge – the topic was too broad for each of our specialties – but once accepted, we started an extremely interesting, sometimes confronting, but enriching journey through the various disciplines of management.

Rather soon, we decided to link this model to the topic of performance management. Performance management is a booming topic both in the academic and the business worlds and addresses how organizations can improve their performance. Both academicians and consultants have responded with an immense and rapidly changing set of tools and frameworks. We feel, however, that managers get confused and lose sight of all these different performance management developments. In Implementing Strategy through *Integrated Performance Management*, we want to provide an answer to this challenge and develop an Integrated Performance Management Framework that presents the broader picture of performance management.

Writing about strategy, operations, human resources, leadership, organizational design, and control is a challenging task. Linking all these various disciplines and 'pushing' them into one overall framework is even more challenging. But we have made an attempt and have tried to identify the major challenges for organizations managing their performance. Although much more research is needed to develop and test new hypotheses in this field, we believe that our Integrated Performance Management Framework is relevant for the academic world and helpful for the business community.

One of the major strengths of this book is that it clearly specifies what 'integrated' really means. In this way, we provide the reader with a concrete framework incorporating the dimensions that need to be managed for organizations to be successful. Furthermore, we have identified two types of alignment – strategic and maturity alignment – that provide the reader with some solid guidelines on how to manage the organization in a more integrated way. The first concept – strategic alignment – is quite popular nowadays in management; the second concept – maturity alignment – is new, but we believe vital in successfully launching performance management initiatives.

The second major strength of *Integrated Performance Management* is that it is the result of an intense dialogue between academicians and business managers. The academic world has provided the academic rigour; the business world has taken care of the relevance and usefulness of the concepts described in the book. The models and frameworks we have presented have been used in practice for many years. The answers we have provided to the performance management challenges do work, if used appropriately, and have proven to be of great value for the managers who used them.

Of course, the scope of the topic is very broad. This makes it impossible to provide a detailed overview of each topic under study. Rather, we want to provide an introduction to the various themes and show how they are related to the topic of performance management. In this way, we provide you with a more global overview on how the various topics are linked. The interested reader can then dive into the more specialized literature for more information on the more specific topics.

This book would never have been published in its current form without the contributions, support and help of the following people:

- Ian McKillop, Professor in the School of Business and Economics at Wilfrid Laurier University in Waterloo, Canada.
- Marc Buelens, Professor, Vlerick Leuven Gent Management School, Belgium.
- Werner Bruggeman, Professor, Vlerick Leuven Gent Management School, Belgium.
- Paul Gemmel, Professor, Vlerick Leuven Gent Management School, Belgium.
- Wil Koning, Chief Risk Officer, Eureko Group, The Netherlands.
- Dirk Deschoolmeester, Professor, Vlerick Leuven Gent Management School, Belgium.
- Xavier Baeten, Professor, Vlerick Leuven Gent Management School, Belgium.
- Herman Van den Broeck, Professor, Vlerick Leuven Gent Management School, Belgium.
- Dirk Buyens, Professor, Vlerick Leuven Gent Management School, Belgium.
- Steven Mestdagh, Researcher, Vlerick Leuven Gent Management School, Belgium.
- Bart Malfliet, Researcher, Vlerick Leuven Gent Management School, Belgium.
- Olivier Braet, Researcher, Ghent University, Belgium.
- Ann Vereecke, Professor, Vlerick Leuven Gent Management School, Belgium.

- Lieven Somers, Researcher, Vlerick Leuven Gent Management School, Belgium.
- Ans De Vos, Professor, Vlerick Leuven Gent Management School, Belgium.

They all have helped us not only by writing various chapters of the book, but by shaping our ideas and stimulating the discussion on this vivid topic.

Special thanks go to our 'sparring partners' from Electrabel. The numerous discussions we had were very enriching and stimulating, and ultimately provided the basis for this book. The commitment of the steering committee was huge, and at every meeting new challenges popped up. Others seemed unresolved. Thank you for all your patience, and creative support throughout this whole project:

- Bernard Hindryckx, Corporate Chief Quality Coordinator, Tractebel, Belgium, and Quality and Audit Manager Generation, Electrabel (Belgium & Luxembourg), Belgium.
- Philip De Cnudde, Executive Vice President Business Control, Tractebel EGI, Belgium.
- Mario Bauwens, Head Finance and Control Generation, Electrabel, Belgium.
- Bernard Carrette, Head of Corporate Audit, Electrabel, Belgium.

Apart from all the creative input, we have received other support as well. First, we would like to thank Electrabel and the Suez Group for their financial backing throughout the project. We also received a lot of support from within our School to get the book ready for publication. We would like to thank Veerle Panis, who managed the administrative process, including the copyrights. Special thanks go to Sage Publications, and especially to Delia Martinez Alfonso, our commissioning editor, who guided us through the review and publication process. Without her support, this book would never have been published.

Kurt Verweire and Lutgart Van den Berghe
Gent (Belgium), August 2003

Acknowledgements

Every effort has been made to trace all the copyright holders, but if any have been inadvertently overlooked, the publishers will be pleased to make the necessary arrangement at the first opportunity.

Figures

Fig. 1.1   Strategos Institute (2001)

Fig. 1.2   Gates, S. (1999) 'Aligning strategic performance measures and results', *Research Report - The Conference Board*, 1261-99-RR, New York.

Fig. 2.1   Hennell, A. and Warner, A. (1998) *Financial performance measurement and shareholder value explained*, Financial Times Management, London.

Fig 2.2   Kennerley, M. and Neely, A. (2002) 'Performance measurement frameworks: A review', in Neely, A. (ed.), *Business performance measurement: Theory and practice*, Cambridge University Press, Cambridge.

Fig 2.4   Johnson, G. and Scholes, K. (1999) *Exploring corporate strategy* (5th edition), Prentice-Hall, London.

Fig. 4.1   Hayes, R. H. and Wheelwright, S. (1984) *Restoring our competitive edge*, Wiley, London and New York.

Fig. 4.2   European Foundation for Quality Management (1999) *The EQFM Excellence Model*, Pabo Prestige Press, Tilbury.

Fig 4.3   European Foundation for Quality Management (2001) 'ISO 9001: 2000: A new stage on the journey to excellence', Excellence Network, *European Foundation for Quality Management*, 1(2): February–March: 4–7.

Figs 5.3, 5.4, 5.5   DeLoach, J. (2000) *Enterprise-wide Risk Management: strategies for linking risk and opportunity*, Arthur Andersen, Financial Times Prentice Hall, London.

Fig. 6.1   Simons, R. (2000) *Performance Measurement & Control Systems for Implementing Strategy: text and cases*, Prentice Hall: New Jersey.

Fig. 6.2   Treacy, M. and Wiersema, F. (1995) *The discipline of market leaders*, Perseus Books, Reading, MA.

Fig. 6.3   Chakravarthy, B.S. & White, R.E. (2002) 'Strategy process: forming, implementing and changing strategies', in Pettigrew, A., Thomas, H. & Whittington, R. (eds), *Handbook of strategy and management*, Sage Publications, London.

Fig. 7.2   Shostack, G. L. (1985) 'Planning the service encounter', in Czepiel, J.A., Solomon, M.A. and Surprenant, C.F. (eds) *The service encounter: Managing employee-customer interactions in service businesses*, copyright © 1985 by Jossey-Bass Inc., Publishers. First published by Lexington Books. All rights reserved.

Fig. 8.1   Leavitt, H.J. (1965) 'Applied organizational change in industry: structural, technological and humanistic approaches", in March, J.G. (ed.), *Handbook of organizations*, Rand McNally, Chicago.

Fig. 8.2   Henderson, J. and Venkatraman, N. (1993) 'Strategic alignment: Leveraging information technology for transforming organizations', *IBM Systems Journal*, 32(1): 472-84.

Fig. 8.3   Weill, P. and Broadbent, M. (1998) *Leveraging the New Infrastructure: How market leaders capitalize on information technology*, Harvard Business School Press, Boston, MA.

Fig. 8.4   McFarlan, F.W. (1984) 'Information technology changes the way you compete', *Harvard Business Review*, May-June, pp. 98-103.

Fig. 8.5   Luftman, J. (2001) 'Strategy formulation: The roles of conversation and design', in Hitt, M.A., Freeman, R.E. and Harrison, J.S. (eds), *The Blackwell handbook of strategic management*, Blackwell, Oxford.

Figs 9.1, 9.2   Simons, R. (1995) *Levers of control: How managers use innovative control systems to drive strategic renewal*, Harvard Business School Press, Boston, MA.

Figs 9.4, 9.5   Kotter, J. P. and Heskett, J. L. (1992) *Corporate culture and performance*, The Free Press, New York.

Figs 11.2, 11.3   Ulrich, D. (1997) *Human resource champions: the next agenda for adding value to HR practices*, Harvard Business School Press, Boston

Fig. 11.4   Curtis, B., Hefley, W.E. and Miller, S. (1995) 'People Capability Maturity Model™', *Report Software Engineering Institute (Carnegie Mellon University)*, CMU/SE-95–MM-02, Pittsburgh, PA.

Fig. 12.1   Reprinted with permission from Dr. Paul Hersey (1984). The Management of Organizational Behavior, The Centre for Leadership Studies: Escondido, CA. All rights reserved.

Figure 15.1   Labovitch, G. & Rosansky, V. (1997) *The power of alignment: How great companies stay centered and accomplish extraordinary things*, John Wiley & Sons: New York.

Tables

Table 2.1   Money.cnn.com (2002)

Table 2.2   Jorissen, A. and Bruggeman, W. (1999) *De Balanced Scorecard in de praktijk: Een leidraad voor strategische prestatiemeting*, Maklu, Antwerpen-Apeldoorn.

Table 4.1   Buttle (1996) 'Servqual: review, critique, research agenda', *European Journal of Marketing*, 3 (1).

Table 4.3   Stalk, G. and Hout, T. (1990) *Competing against time: How time-based competition is reshaping global markets*, The Free Press, New York.

Table 6.1   Hart, S.L. (1992) 'An integrative framework for strategy-making processes', *The Academy of Management Review*, 17 (2): 327-51.

Table 17.2   Angel, LC. and Chandra, M.J. (2001) 'Performance implications of investments in continuous quality improvement', *International Journal of Operations & Production Management*, 21 (1/2).

Contributors

Xavier Baeten holds university degrees in Applied Economics (Ghent University) and in Tax (Vlerick Leuven Gent Management School). He started his career at the Vlerick Leuven Gent Management School at the end of 1994. He currently is responsible for the Strategic Rewards Research Centre, which aims at developing the strategic importance of rewarding. His main interests are reward management, employee benefits, strategic management, corporate citizenship and stakeholder management.

Mario Bauwens graduated as a civil engineer from Ghent University. He has a degree in Management from the Vlerick Leuven Gent Management School and followed the Advanced Development Programme at the London Business School. He started his career at a Belgian bank and also worked for an international consulting company. In 1989 he joined Electrabel, where he occupied different functions, mainly in the area of finance. In 1992 he worked for the Tractebel group at Northern Ireland Generation. He is currently manager of the Finance, Control and Information Department of the business unit Generation Belux at Electrabel.

Olivier Braet holds a university degree in Sociology and is assistant at the Department of Management and Organization (Faculty of Economics and Business Administration) at Ghent University. He currently examines how IT systems can be successfully implemented when organizations adopt new technologies.

Werner Bruggeman is Doctor in Economics (Ghent University) and specialization in Industrial Engineering at the Georgia Institute of Technology (USA). He is a professor at the Faculty of Economics and Business Administration (Ghent University) and head of the Competence Centre Management Accounting and Finance of Vlerick Leuven Gent Management School. He is Partner of Vlerick Leuven Gent Management School and Managing Partner of B&M consulting. Research interests include the Balanced Scorecard, Value-Based Management, target costing, and Activity-Based Costing.

Marc Buelens is Doctor in Industrial Psychology (Ghent University). He worked as a scientific staff member (Ghent University), and then for the Artois breweries. He was the General Manager and Managing Director of Vlerick Leuven Gent Management School. He is also Partner of Vlerick

Leuven Gent Management School. He gave lectures at the universities of Leuven, Antwerp, Moscow and Bandung (Indonesia) and now teaches General Management and Organization at Ghent University and at Vlerick Leuven Gent Management School. His research interests include: organizational behaviour, negotiation, executive decision-making, workaholism, management and social skills – emotional intelligence and knowledge management.

Dirk Buyens is Doctor in Industrial and Organizational Psychology (Ghent University) and Master of Business Administration (Katholieke Universiteit Leuven). He was doctoral fellow at the IR Center of the Graduate School of Management at the University of Minnesota (USA). He is currently Academic Dean and Partner of Vlerick Leuven Gent Management School and Programme Director of the part-time international MBA programmes. He is also Professor at Ghent University. He specializes in the following disciplines: competency management, human resource management, strategic HRM and lifelong learning.

Bernard Carrette graduated as an Engineer from the University of Brussels (VUB) in 1979. He joined Electrabel in 1981, and has occupied several management positions in the various departments of the company (electricity and gas distribution). In 2000, he became responsible for the business reporting (controlling) and process monitoring in the Marketing & Sales Industry business unit. He was appointed head of the internal audit in 2002. He followed the general management programme at Cedep/Insead in 2002.

Philip De Cnudde graduated from Ghent University as a civil engineer in electronics in 1983 and as a civil engineer in operations management in 1986. He followed the general management programme at Cedep/Insead in 2000. He started his career in 1985 with Santens Engineering Services, an EPC (Engineering Procurement Construction) contractor for internal transportation and automation. He became General Manager of Santens of America in 1989, an integrated terry textiles manufacturer in the USA. He moved in 1993 to Electrabel, a Belgian utility company, where he was responsible for process re-engineering and ERP (Enterprise-wide Resource Planning) implementation in the Generation business unit. In 1998 he became Director of Internal Audit. Since 2001 he is Executive Vice President responsible for Business Control in the international Electricity and Gas division of the Suez/Tractebel Group.

Dirk Deschoolmeester is a civil engineer, has an MBA and a Doctorate in Applied Sciences (Ghent University). He participated in the International Teachers Programme at Harvard and MIT (USA) and was visiting professor at the Asian Institute for Technology and the China–EEC Management Programme. He is professor and Partner of Vlerick Leuven Gent

Management School and Ghent University. His research domains include e-business and start-ups.

Ans De Vos is Doctor in Applied Economic Sciences (Ghent University) and licentiate in Psychology (KU Leuven). She also holds a postgraduate degree in Personnel Management Sciences (Universiteit Antwerpen). Her doctoral research focused on newcomer psychological contract development during the socialization process. During her doctoral studies, she was a doctoral fellow at Tilburg University (The Netherlands). She is currently an Assistant Professor at the Human Resource Management Centre of Vlerick Leuven Gent Management School. Her research interests include psychological contracts, newcomer socialization, career management and strategic human resource management.

Paul Gemmel is Doctor in Applied Economic Sciences (Ghent University). He was visiting research fellow at the College of Business of Arizona State University, Arizona, USA (1992–93). He is a professor at the Faculty of Economics and Business Administration of Ghent University and at Vlerick Leuven Gent Management School. Paul Gemmel is Director of the MINOZ Research Centre for Hospital Management of Vlerick Leuven Gent Management School. He develops activities in the area of service (operations) management, but also focuses on capacity management and efficiency benchmarking in service organizations.

Bernard Hindryckx graduated as a civil engineer at Ghent University in 1977. After three years of academic research in Physics and a short span at Siemens Telephony, he joined Electrabel in 1981. He has worked both in the Generation department (Operations, Maintenance and Care) and in the Marketing & Sales department (Contracts, After sales, Controlling). From 1994 to 1997 he worked as Corporate Auditor in the field of environmental management, business risk management, IT security and accounting. In that function, he introduced the Integrated Performance Management System (IPMS) concept in Electrabel in 1995. Since 1997 he has been further developing the concept with colleagues within the company. He is responsible for process performance management in Generation Belgium/Luxembourg and is currently involved in quality and knowledge management. He followed the General Management Programme at the Vlerick Leuven Gent Management School in 1993 and at Cedep/Insead in 2002.

Bart Malfliet is licentiate and a qualified teacher in Germanic Philology (Ghent University). He used to be National President of the Katholieke Landelijke Jeugd before he joined the HRM Centre of Vlerick Leuven Gent Management School. Currently he is senior scientific staff member and is responsible for the Competency Management Research Centre (CMC²) and for the development of the organization counselling activities of the

HRM Centre. Recently he has also been appointed Programme Manager of the pilot 'Investors in People' in Flanders (Belgium), aiming to introduce this strategic HRM label in the Flemish market. Bart teaches the Masters and Executive programmes of Vlerick Leuven Gent Management School and often speaks on HRM topics in organizations. His research interests are strategic HRM linked with performance management, lifelong learning, human resource development and competency management.

Steven Mestdagh graduated in Psychology in 2000 and has been working at the Department of Organizational Behaviour at Vlerick Leuven Gent Management School ever since. He is the co-author of a successful book on change management. His current research activities focus on organizational applications of social and cognitive psychology, more specifically in the fields of behavioural decision-making, negotiation, conflict resolution and emotion. He is particularly fascinated by the frontiers of human rationality and adaptability as they occur both in business and everyday life.

Lieven Somers obtained his degree in Applied Economics at Ghent University. Since September 2000, he has been working at the Impulse Centre Business in Society, a department within the Vlerick Leuven Gent Management School. He focuses on the link between stakeholder management and the strategic management process of the company.

Lutgart Van den Berghe is Doctor in Economics (Ghent University). She is Partner at the Vlerick Leuven Gent Management School and head of the Competence Centre Entrepreneurship, Governance and Strategy of the School. She is also a part-time professor at Ghent University (domain of corporate governance). She serves as a non-executive director in a number of listed and non-listed multinational companies. She has been a visiting or part-time professor at the universities of Rotterdam (Netherlands), Antwerp (Belgium), Lille (France), Bocconi (Italy), Vienna (Austria) and at the Georgia State University (USA). Her research interests focus on corporate governance, institutional investors and financial conglomerates. She functions as academic director of the Belgian Directors' Institute.

Herman Van den Broeck is Doctor in Pedagogical Sciences. He is Partner and professor of Vlerick Leuven Gent Management School, and head of the Competence Centre People and Organization. He is professor at the Faculty of Economics and Business Administration (Ghent University). He teaches Educational Interaction and Communication at the Teacher Training Department of Ghent University. His main interests are social skills, emotional intelligence and change.

Ann Vereecke is a civil engineer and Doctor in Management (Ghent University). In 1993–94 she followed the doctoral programme at Insead

(France). She lectures at the Faculty of Economics and Business Administration (Ghent University) and at Vlerick Leuven Gent Management School, where she is also the Programme Director of the Master in General Management and head of the Operations and Technology Management Centre. Her main interests are production planning, inventory management systems and production strategy. She specializes in global manufacturing strategy and supply chain management.

Kurt Verweire is Doctor in Economics (Erasmus University Rotterdam). He is Assistant Professor at Vlerick Leuven Gent Management School and is Programme Director of the MBA in Financial Services and Insurance (MBA-FSI). His main topics of interest are strategic issues for the financial services industry, financial conglomeration and financial convergence (diversification in the financial services industry) and Integrated Performance Management.

1 Integrated Performance Management: New Hype or New Paradigm?

KURT VERWEIRE AND LUTGART VAN DEN BERGHE

A new world with new challenges . . .

The business world is changing at an ever-increasing pace. The globalization of markets, the revolution in information and communication technologies, the increasing importance (and volatility) of financial markets, and the war for talent are only a few of the change drivers in our current business climate. In this ever-changing world, today's managers are confronted with a number of daunting challenges in their quest for creating value. Business is becoming more and more complex. Newly trained and empowered employees have implemented many innovative practices, including continuous improvement, empowerment, Activity-Based Costing, re-engineering and quality management. Companies are looking for new forms of relationships with customers, suppliers, employees and other stakeholders. Intangible assets have become the major source of competitive advantage. As a reaction, companies have been changing their operating assumptions to include the development of closer value chain relationships, customization of products and services, reliance on knowledge workers, and an intense focus on innovation. At the same time, companies have been downsizing, de-layering and outsourcing strategically non-relevant activities. And all these new trends are occurring against a background of intensified competition.

Managers are thus confronted with greater uncertainty and unpredictability, leading to greater risk in decision-making. In such a rapidly changing and complex environment, past performance becomes less valuable for guiding future strategic options. Furthermore, the consequences of making 'wrong' decisions can be disastrous. Effective risk management is becoming increasingly key to successful business. In the current Information Age, the rising activism of all kinds of stakeholder puts further pressure on managers, and new codes for corporate governance create additional responsibilities for the directors and managers. The management of any organization (whether private or public, for-profit or non-profit) is held accountable for more than just financial bottom-line results.

All these changes in the business context impose new challenges on the management of today's organizations. Academic and consulting professionals are responding with an ever-expanding range of new tools, usually encapsulated in nice three-letter acronyms (BPR, TQM, EVA®, and many others). In many cases, the results have been disappointing – particularly when the initiatives have been attempted without linking them to corporate strategy (Stivers and Joyce, 2000). Research at the Strategos Institute, Gary Hamel's international consulting company, has shown that only a small number of companies were able to provide sustained high returns to their shareholders in the last decade (Figure 1.1).

The research indicates that not even 20 US companies were able to provide high shareholder returns for five consecutive years. Only four companies were able to show these returns for seven consecutive years.[1] Why do so many organizations have difficulty delivering sustained performance?

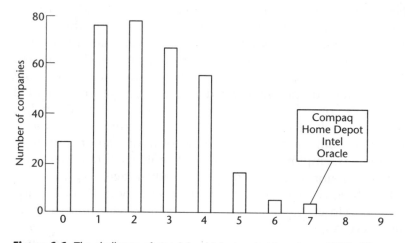

Figure 1.1 The challenge of sustaining high shareholder returns (1990–99)
Source: Strategos Institute (2001)

What is lacking?

There are, of course, many reasons why organizations are not able to meet their performance expectations. One of the most obvious reasons is the inability of companies to efficiently and effectively define and create customer (and hence, shareholder) value. The idea that companies succeed by selling value is not new. But companies find it extremely difficult to define a unique strategic position in an ever-changing competitive arena.

However, having a clear vision and a well-defined strategy are not enough. Business observers are more and more convinced that the ability to *execute* strategy is more important than the quality of the strategy itself.

In their most recent book, *The Strategy-Focused Organization: How Balanced Scorecard Companies Thrive in the New Business Environment*, Robert Kaplan and David Norton (2001) see the ability to execute the strategy as an even bigger management challenge than determining the right vision and strategy in the first place. Kaplan and Norton point to the importance of adequate *performance management systems* as a critical success factor for implementing strategy: 'Strategies are changing, but the tools for measuring strategies have not kept pace' (2001: 2).

Consultants and academicians are aware of this and have started a quest for the appropriate performance measures. For a long time, companies have used financial accounting-based performance measures to track how well the organization is doing. Financial control systems emerged when international conglomerates were created at the end of the previous century. The managers of these conglomerates focused on controlling costs and installing efficient production processes. These financial control systems were adequate for such industrial economies. The picture changed when new elements, such as quality and service, started to determine the competitive advantage of firms and when the Total Quality movement conquered the world. However, the management control systems did not change and financial control systems stayed in place (although some of them captured some aspects of quality as well).

Criticism of conventional performance measurement systems grew in the mid-1980s. Critics charged that financial performance measures lack the requisite variety to give decision-makers the range of information they need to manage processes. Performance measurement systems based primarily on financial performance measures lack the focus and robustness needed for internal management and control (Atkinson et al., 1997). Andy Neely and Rob Austin (2002) have called this first measurement crisis *measurement myopia*, which essentially stems from the fact that the wrong things were being measured.

Hence, the call for more strategic types of management control. One of the first definitions of *strategic control* goes as follows: 'Strategic control focuses on the dual questions of whether: (1) the strategy is being implemented as planned; and (2) the results produced by the strategy are those intended' (Schendel and Hofer, 1979). According to this definition of strategic control (and other, similar definitions), there should be a clear link between an organization's strategy and its performance measures. Good performance measures should predict the long-term financial success of the business. More and more companies are acknowledging that performance measurement systems need focus by linking them to the strategy of the organization. Often, managers are confused by changing priorities. This year, a company may focus on Business Process Re-engineering (BPR), next year on capabilities enhancement, and the year after that on Total Quality Management (TQM). Without a clear strategy, managers will remain confused and sceptical about new strategic initiatives. An international survey by The Conference Board of 113 chief financial officers (CFOs) and corporate strategists revealed that the lack of organizational focus is the major reason for having a formal strategic performance measurement system. Furthermore, the respondents believe that strategic performance measurement systems could be very helpful for implementing strategy more effectively (Gates, 1999), as is shown in Figure 1.2.

Many academicians and performance management consultants see a solution in new performance measurement systems, as demonstrated in the following statement:

> The global market and its rapid pace of change have increased the demand on measurement systems in modern corporations. The 'command and control' function (previously served by performance measurement systems) has been transformed into a need to 'predict and prepare' the organization to meet the next challenge and to create the next opportunity. Changes to the business context are also changing the nature of measurement. Process management emphasizing value and service to the customer is replacing traditional vertical and functional structures. Decision-making is increasingly being moved lower in the organization; self-directed teams rather than individual managers now make decisions. Virtual corporate structures are creating the need to manage and measure performance across the value chain. Each of these shifts has implications for the performance management system and its ability to effectively serve the organization and its stakeholders. (Institute of Management Accountants and Arthur Andersen LLP, 1998: 1–2)

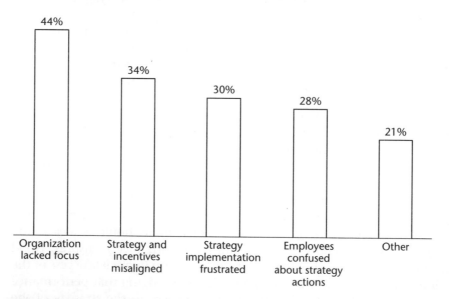

Figure 1.2 Reasons cited for introducing strategic performance measurement systems
Source: Gates (1999)

However, according to Andy Neely and Rob Austin, this quest for more appropriate performance measures (and measurement systems) has resulted in a real *'measurement madness'*:

[S]ociety is obsessed with measurement. The desire to measure and quantify has become overwhelming. . . . Organizations are seeking to value their intellectual assets, their brands, their innovative potential, in addition to their operating efficiency, their economic profit, and the satisfaction of their employees, customers, and shareholders. Today the old adage, 'if you can't measure it, you can't manage it,' has been taken to a new extreme and in many organizations the result is confusion. (Neely and Austin, 2002: 42–3).

Therefore, rather than developing new performance measures or measurement systems, we need a more integrated approach towards performance management. In this book, we will present such an integrated approach. But before we outline the building blocks of our new framework, we will first explain how we define the concept of Integrated Performance Management.

Integrated Performance Management: what's in a name?

Integrated Performance Management or IPM (a new three-letter acronym indeed) is not a new term. It is being used with increasing frequency in the performance management literature but, as is the case with many widespread management concepts, there is confusion about what it exactly stands for. This can partly be ascribed to the fact that performance management processes manifest themselves in many different ways and that contributions to performance management come from many different angles: strategy, finance, management accounting and control, operations management, and human resource management (HRM).

Still, the concept has great potential for helping to solve some of the issues we have been discussing. But then we need to define what we mean by 'performance' and 'performance management', and we should explain what makes performance management really 'integrated'.

A definition of performance

'Performance' is a term used in a variety of disciplines. For example, athletes out-perform the field when they jump the highest or run the fastest. In other sports disciplines – in team sports or gymnastics, for example – performance evaluation becomes somewhat more complicated. In these sports disciplines, athletes or teams are usually evaluated along composite 'performance' measures, such as technical difficulty, originality or a creativity criterion. The personal experience and intuition of the jury plays an important role in their rating. In the field of biology, Darwin introduced his ideas of variation, specialization and collaboration as tactics for survival in a complex and uncertain environment. Those species that manage to adapt to their environment ultimately survive. The ability to adapt, and the speed and method of adaptation, can be seen as forms of out-performance.

In this book, we focus on organizational performance. *Organizational performance* is at the heart of strategic management and accounting disciplines (Venkatraman and Ramanujam, 1986). Although widely used in theoretical and empirical research, the notion of organizational performance remains largely unexplained and recourse is taken to commonly used operationalizations of performance. There is relatively little agreement about which definitions are 'best' and which criteria should be used to judge the definitions (Barney, 1997). Moreover, many definitions capture the notion of performance only partially. The reason why organizational performance is so difficult to define is to be found in the multidimensionality of the performance concept. For example, performance can be defined in financial terms (e.g., market value, profitability, value-at-risk), but it is often used in other environments, such as operations (e.g., efficiency, effectiveness, number of outputs, throughput-time, product or service quality), marketing (e.g., customer satisfaction, number of customers retained over a certain period), and others.

A conceptual definition of organizational performance was forwarded by Jay Barney, a strategy professor at Ohio State University. The starting point for Barney's (1997) conceptualization is that an organization is an association of productive assets which come together to obtain economic advantages. For an organization to continue to exist, the owners of these productive assets must be satisfied with their use. The owners will only be inclined to provide these assets if they are satisfied with the returns they are receiving. So, organizational performance is defined in terms of the value that an organization creates using its productive assets in comparison with the value that the owners of these assets expect to obtain. If the value that is created is at least as large as the expected value, then it is likely that the owners of these assets will make them available to the organization. On the other hand, if the value created is less than expected, the owners might look for other alternatives and withdraw their support.

A definition of performance management

Apart from the multidimensional nature of the performance concept, the performance management literature also suffers from concentrating too much on finding the appropriate performance measures. That is, there is too much focus on *performance measurement*. In general, performance measurement can be viewed as the process of quantifying the efficiency and effectiveness of purposeful action and decision-making (Waggoner et al., 1999). Performance measurement should provide the data that will be collected, analysed, reported and, ultimately, used to make sound business decisions. As such, performance measurement is a process of monitoring and reporting on how well someone or something is doing. In theory, it is a broad concept applicable to people, things, situations, activities and organizations. Strategic performance measurement is defined as the measurement and reporting system that quantifies the degree to which managers achieve their objectives.

However, driving a car entails much more than looking at the dashboard indicators. Today's managers have more trouble managing their business than finding optimal performance measures (and measurement frameworks). Therefore, more attention should be paid to *performance management*, which we define as *a process that helps an organization to formulate, implement, and change its strategy in order to satisfy its stakeholders' needs*.[2] In other words, performance management is 'a comprehensive management process framing the continuous improvement journey, by ensuring that everyone understands where the organization is and where it needs to go to meet stakeholder needs' (Institute of Management Accountants and Arthur Andersen LLP, 1998: 3). The ultimate goal of performance management is to achieve sustainable organizational performance.

Most definitions stress the importance of having formulated goals, objectives and strategies, primarily at the organizational or corporate level. Then, the purpose of performance management is to achieve organizational effectiveness and 'to get better results'. Important aspects of performance management are setting performance goals, developing strategies, and translating them into concrete guidelines for action (i.e., making the strategies operational). Performance management is also about creating commitment and motivation to realize the proposed goals. Communication plays an important role in this process. All this goes to say that performance management is much more than merely measuring performance.

The evolution from performance measurement to performance management is perfectly illustrated by the evolution of the Balanced Scorecard, as explained by Robert Kaplan and David Norton:

> The Balanced Scorecard has evolved since we first developed and introduced the concept as a new framework for measuring organizational performance. It was originally proposed to overcome the limitations of managing only with financial measures. . . .
>
> We quickly learned that measurement has consequences beyond just reporting on the past. Measurement creates focus for the future because the measures chosen by managers communicate to the organization what is important. To take full advantage of this power, measurement should be integrated into a management system. Thus we refined the Balanced Scorecard concept and showed how it could move beyond a performance measurement system to become the organizing framework for a strategic management system. A strategy scorecard replaced the budget as the center for management processes. In effect, the Balanced Scorecard became the operating system for a new strategic management process. (Kaplan and Norton, 2001: 23)

Thus, Kaplan and Norton see the Balanced Scorecard as a central management concept for the whole organization. This requires a totally different management approach, and a huge organizational transformation:

As organizations managed with the scorecard, they made further discoveries. The speed and magnitude of the results achieved by the early adopters revealed the power of the Balanced Scorecard management system to focus the entire organization on strategy. To achieve such intense strategic focus the organizations had instituted comprehensive, transformational change. They redefined their relationships with the customer, reengineered fundamental business processes, taught their workforces new skills, and deployed a new technology infrastructure. Also, a new culture emerged, centered not on traditional functional silos but on the team effort required to support the strategy. The management system provided the mechanism to mobilize and guide the process of change. But this new culture involved even more than a management system. Companies created a new kind of organization based on the requirements of their strategy – hence the term Strategy-Focused Organization. ... By clearly defining the strategy, communicating it consistently, and linking it to the drivers of change, a performance-based culture emerged that linked everyone and every unit to the unique features of the strategy. (Kaplan and Norton, 2001: 23–5)

Performance management is about 'running the business'. Performance management practices must derive from and be tailored to fit each organization's changing requirements (Armstrong and Baron, 1998). It is about doing the right things, and doing the things right. What this means in practice can differ from organization to organization: there is no one way of managing performance. In some companies performance management is very informal; other companies need more formal performance management systems. All too often, consultants and academicians propose the latter as the ultimate tool for success. Good examples are the many books and tools on the Balanced Scorecard and *Value-Based Management*. One of the major lessons that we have learned is that these tools and frameworks can be very helpful for some companies, but they are totally inappropriate for others.

Performance management: why integrated?

Performance management will only deliver sustained success if it is integrated. The current literature defines integrated as *strategically aligned*. This means that all (performance management) processes and activities should be linked to the organization's *strategy*. Integrated Performance Management systems should *focus* attention on those critical activities that, if done well, will lead to competitive advantage and long-term growth. Thus, strategy is a central element for every performance management system. This might seem obvious, but practice shows that this is not always the case. In many organizations, the formulation and implementation of strategy are two separate activities. However, achieving integration between the long-term strategy and operational performance is crucial. Therefore, strategy has to be made operational! Many scholars and business people have pointed to the important roles of evaluating and controlling, but we will show throughout this book that other (management) aspects are equally important.

Integrated Performance Management is not only about focus, but also about *alignment*. Integrated Performance Management is only beneficial if the different components of performance management are aligned. All too often, management receives conflicting signals from the performance measures used in each of the various management processes. For example, strategic planning emphasizes growth in a particular market, reporting focuses on the profitability per product line, and compensation is based on still other criteria. Many consultants see alignment as a straightforward process. First, decide on clear strategic priorities; second, translate these priorities into appropriate measures; third, incorporate and integrate them into current management processes, such as strategic planning, compensation and reward.

Practice shows that implementing these basic rules is more difficult and often requires a totally different attitude from management and employees. That is why many performance management projects become change management projects affecting the entire organization. We strongly believe in a more focused and aligned approach towards performance management, but acknowledge that implementing Integrated Performance Management is a long and difficult road. Many companies do not know where to start and do not know which elements to consider.

Therefore, the purpose of this book is to present an Integrated Performance Management framework that provides concrete guidelines and practical recommendations to put the entire organization on the right track. The framework is new and provides a different way of looking at how to manage an organization. We will compare our framework with existing performance management frameworks, and explain what makes ours more integrated than the current models (which most often focus on only a small part of the overall performance challenge).

Structure of this book

Integrated Performance Management is a hot topic at the moment but it is still surrounded with too much fuzz and hype. Many attempts have been undertaken to develop tools and frameworks for effectively (formulating and) implementing strategy. Yet, often these attempts are too fragmentary in approach and focus only on a minor aspect of the overall performance management challenge. Andy Neely and Chris Adams (2000) have recognized this as well:

> Interest in performance measurement and management has rocketed during the last few years. Frameworks and methodologies – such as the Balanced Scorecard, the Business Excellence Model, Shareholder Value Added, Activity-Based Costing, cost of quality, and competitive benchmarking – have each generated vast interest, activity and consulting revenues, but not always success. Yet therein lies a paradox. For one might reasonably ask, how can multiple, and

seemingly inconsistent, business performance frameworks and measurement methodologies exist? Each framework purports to be unique. And each appears to claim comprehensiveness. Yet each offers a different perspective on performance. (Neely and Adams, 2000: 2)

Integrated Performance Management must become more integrated if it wants to be more than just the next management fad! Therefore, we provide a broader and more comprehensive framework for Integrated Performance Management. At the same time, we introduce some new insights on how to initiate and implement performance management processes within an organization. We are aware that these are quite ambitious goals. How will we tackle them?

As Figure 1.3 shows, this book is composed of three major parts. Part I provides an *overview of the main performance measures and performance management frameworks*. This part offers the reader who is unfamiliar with the literature a first glimpse of what performance measurement and performance management are all about. As performance is a multidimensional concept, it has been tackled from many different perspectives. The contributions to this field come from various management disciplines, such as corporate finance, management control, operations management and risk management. Each of these contributions has focused on different dimensions of the performance challenge. Managing performance in an integrated way requires that we understand the nature and scope of these different contributions. In Part I, we investigate how the following academic management disciplines have tackled the performance challenge and what particular performance management frameworks have been developed:

- Performance management from a *finance* perspective (Value-Based Management);
- Performance management from a *management control* perspective (the Balanced Scorecard);
- Performance management from an *operations* perspective (European Foundation for Quality Management (EFQM) Excellence Model);

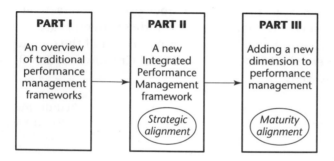

Figure 1.3 Structure of *Integrated Performance Management*

- Performance management from a *risk* perspective (Integrated Risk Management).

In Part II, we develop *a new framework for Integrated Performance Management* and identify its *constituent elements*, which we call the *Integrated Performance Management Framework* (see Figure 1.4). This framework is composed of five main building blocks:

- The organization's direction and goal-setting processes;
- Operational processes;
- Support processes;
- Evaluation and control processes;
- Processes, systems and structures that create commitment and motivation (this is the organizational behaviour component of our framework).

INTEGRATED PERFORMANCE MANAGEMENT FRAMEWORK				
Direction and goal-setting objectives	Operational processes	Support processes	Evaluation and control	Organizational behaviour • Organizational design • HRM systems • Leadership skills • Reward systems

Figure 1.4 Components of the Integrated Performance Management Framework

As Figure 1.4 shows, the organizational behaviour component consists of four elements: (a) organizational design; (b) HRM systems; (c) leadership skills; and (d) reward systems. This second part of the book provides an introduction to each of these management disciplines.

Our framework can be used to position the various performance management frameworks in their broader context, and gives us a better view on the scope of Integrated Performance Management. Successful performance management requires that attention be paid to all components of this framework. This is what makes performance management 'integrated'. In line with current publications in the field, we also investigate how the Integrated Performance Management Framework can be linked to an organization's strategy. Although the concept of *strategic alignment* is not entirely new, little is known about how (difficult it is) to create this alignment. Therefore, we also pay attention to how each component of our Integrated Performance Management Framework contributes to an effective strategy implementation. The literature is not conclusive in this respect, and one of the main challenges in performance management is to come to an integrated concept of strategic alignment. By presenting these various perspectives on strategic alignment, we hope we have begun to approach the concept in a more integrated way.

Part III introduces *a new dimension to Integrated Performance Management*, which we call *maturity alignment* (see Figure 1.5). Strategic alignment is a necessary aspect of Integrated Performance Management but, unfortunately, it is not sufficient. Many companies have the tools to create strategic alignment and have still met with mediocre success. We believe that the problems in the performance management process are caused by a lack of maturity alignment.

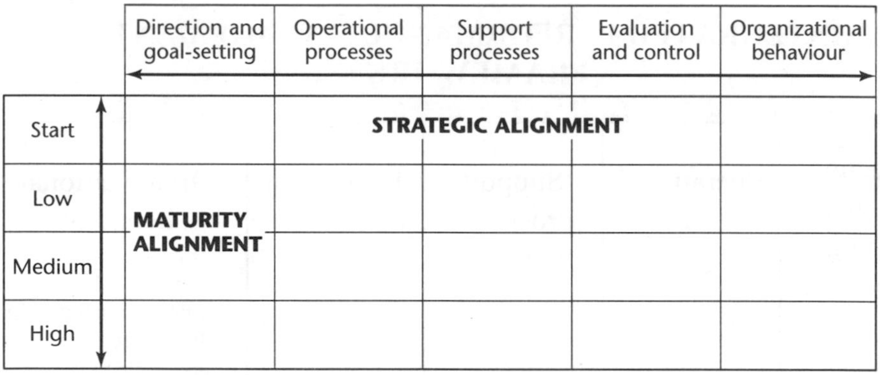

	Direction and goal-setting	Operational processes	Support processes	Evaluation and control	Organizational behaviour
Start		STRATEGIC ALIGNMENT			
Low	**MATURITY ALIGNMENT**				
Medium					
High					

Figure 1.5 Introducing maturity alignment: a new dimension to Integrated Performance Management

Maturity alignment focuses on the process side of the performance management trajectory and describes how well the Integrated Performance Management process has been developed. Maturity alignment requires that each of the five components of the Integrated Performance Management Framework be positioned at about the same maturity level. If there is no maturity alignment, either the managers or the employees get frustrated, and the performance initiatives fail. Therefore, the concept of maturity alignment provides the reader with a number of guidelines for successfully introducing Integrated Performance Management. The concept of maturity alignment was originally developed within Electrabel, a global and customized energy solutions provider. Electrabel is a subsidiary of Tractebel, which is the energy arm of the Suez Group. The maturity alignment framework is a basic concept in their Integrated Performance Management System. It is now increasingly used in other companies as well.

How to read this book?

Integrated Performance Management has become an extensive book, with 17 chapters structured in three major parts. The message that we bring is rather straightforward: 'Organizations need both strategic alignment and maturity alignment to get on the right track!' But what this means in practice is difficult to explain in a couple of paragraphs. Indeed, developing an integrated approach towards performance management and strategy implementation is a very ambitious task. It requires that we gain an understanding of the state of the art in each management discipline, and that we then try to combine these insights in a coherent and systematic way.

This implies that this book consists of many literature overviews of the various management disciplines, such as strategy, operations, leadership, management control, human resources, organizational design, etc. This is especially the case for the chapters of Part II, where we present the building blocks of our Integrated Performance Management Framework. Each of these literature reviews addresses two major questions: What are these various management disciplines all about? And how do they contribute to an effective strategy implementation? This is one of the major strengths of *Integrated Performance Management*. It provides good – albeit some personal – introductions to most management disciplines in one book. Specialists in the field will probably not learn from the literature reviews in their discipline, but will rather learn from what other management disciplines tell us.

But it is clear that we have more ambitious goals with this publication. Our major purpose is to present a real *Integrated* Performance Management Framework, and to start developing an integrated approach towards strategic and maturity alignment. Strategic alignment is a central concept in the performance management literature, but we are still far away from an integrated approach towards strategic alignment! For example, finance people look at the appropriate performance measures and add some strategic frameworks that should help to achieve the financial goals. Management controllers have investigated how to align control systems with strategy. Operations researchers have identified operations strategies and how to implement them. In Part II, we present the building blocks for such an integrated approach towards strategic alignment. However, more research and deeper insights are needed to develop tools and frameworks for strategic alignment that can be used by both academicians and practising managers.

Nevertheless, this book presents a new framework that opens up many opportunities to look at the concept of strategic alignment in a more integrated way. We hope that this multidisciplinary team effort offers you as reader, regardless of your background, some new ideas, maybe some which you already knew about but that never were formalized in this particular way.

We have also introduced a new concept, called maturity alignment. This framework also builds on our Integrated Performance Management Framework and some concepts defined in Part II. However, this does not mean that the reader has to go through all chapters of Part II to understand what maturity alignment is about. Reading the introductions to Parts I, II and III should provide the reader with the necessary insights to catch up and to learn about this new concept.

The introductions to the three parts should guide you all the way from the introduction to the final part of the book. They contain the main messages of this book and explain the structure of the three parts. At the same time, they provide a 'red wire' for the book and indicate clearly how the various chapters contribute to our overall goals.

We hope that *Integrated Performance Management* stimulates you to look out of your traditional box and to adopt a more 'broadening' perspective towards performance management, and strategy formulation and implementation.

Notes

1 These figures were presented by Gary Hamel at the 21st Annual International Conference of the Strategic Management Society in his presentation 'Building the Post-Industrial Firm' (San Francisco, 22 October 2001). The figures were based on S&P Compustat and Strategos calculations.
2 Although the focus of many performance management initiatives is on implementing the organization's strategy, introducing these initiatives often leads to questioning what the strategy of the organization is, and should be. Therefore, we have also added the concept of strategy formulation in the definition of performance management.

PART I

An Overview of Traditional Performance Management Frameworks

Performance management approached from different perspectives

If we want to develop a good understanding of the scope of Integrated Performance Management and its implications for an organization, we must understand the different dimensions of performance and evaluate the strengths and weaknesses of the different contributions in these areas. However, this multidimensionality of performance has not been sufficiently acknowledged in the existing literature. Different frameworks have been developed, which all have contributed to our understanding of performance. Each of these frameworks purports to be unique and comprehensive, but each offers a different perspective on performance (Neely and Adams, 2000). These differences have mainly been caused by the different functional backgrounds of the researchers. The different chapters of Part I all focus on performance as viewed from a particular functional area.

Evaluating the corporate performance of firms is a central theme in *corporate finance*. One of the central ideas in corporate finance is that the firm's performance depends on the value it creates for its shareholders. Whether the company is listed or not, managers must ensure that the financial returns created by the sustained profitability of their business are meeting the expectations of owners and potential owners. In Chapter 2, we examine these ideas in greater detail. First, we describe the traditional financial performance measures. Then attention is paid to the concepts of shareholder value and Value-Based Management (VBM). Finally, we broaden the concept of shareholder value towards stakeholder value and describe how a stakeholder-oriented management approach can contribute to Integrated Performance Management.

In Chapter 3, we present the *management accounting and control* perspective on Integrated Performance Management. This is one of the most developed perspectives in the field. The measurement of firm performance has always occupied a central place in the management accounting and control literature. The development of the Balanced Scorecard, by Robert Kaplan and David Norton, has further boosted the interest in this theme. The Balanced Scorecard is a very popular measurement and management framework, originally aimed at offering a more integrated view on business unit performance. Nowadays, it is translated to the corporate ('corporate scorecard') and the individual level ('individual scorecard') as well. Chapter 3 offers an overview of the literature on the Balanced Scorecard.

Chapter 4 elaborates on the different performance objectives of the *operations* function. The operations function has always paid particular attention to the performance of products, services and processes. Quality is a central concept in this literature and many of the principles of Total Quality and components of organizational infrastructure can be found in integrating frameworks for achieving Total Quality and Performance Excellence, such as the European Foundation for Quality Management (EFQM) Excellence Model and the ISO quality systems.

In Chapter 5, we investigate how *risk management* can contribute to Integrated Performance Management. Managers are increasingly aware that managing (shareholder) value also implies managing risk. A company can create value by controlling or significantly reducing the possibility that harmful events occur. This is the more traditional definition of risk management. Risk management has increasingly been approached from a more opportunistic perspective. It is shown that a company's share price is significantly influenced by the way it is able to anticipate and to manage an uncertain future. The new trend towards strategic risk management adopts this point of view. In Chapter 5, we describe both the traditional and the modern approaches towards risk management.

Performance at different organizational levels

We have already argued that performance management has been approached from different angles. These differences reflect the different functional backgrounds of the researchers in the field. It is worth mentioning that the different definitions of performance and the different performance management frameworks to a large extent correspond with the definition of performance at different organizational levels.

Generally, we distinguish between three main levels in large organizations: the corporate, the business unit and the functional level. Managers at each of these organizational levels face different challenges. For example, management at the *corporate level* seeks to find an answer to the question: In what industries and markets do we have to compete? Managers at the *business unit level* are concerned how the firm competes within a particular industry: How can the firm achieve a competitive advantage in a given market? What new opportunities can be identified or created in markets? Which products or services should be developed in which markets? In smaller companies, the corporate and the business unit levels are often integrated, but in larger international multi-business companies, there is a clear distinction between the two. The third level within an organization is the *functional (or operational) level*. Functional strategies are concerned with the detailed deployment of resources at the operational level. This level constitutes policies towards R&D, human resources management, marketing, operational and finance issues.

Performance measurement and performance management take place at all three organizational levels. However, the nature of the performance measures (and hence the focus of the performance management frameworks) differs according to the level in the organization. Typically, managers at the corporate level are more concerned with financial data; functional managers mainly use non-financial data (inventory turnover, delivery cycle time, material as percentage of total cost, among many others) to evaluate the department's performance. This explains why contributions on corporate performance mainly come from the corporate finance angle. On the other hand, performance at the functional level has mainly been approached from an operations perspective. With the development of the Balanced Scorecard in the early 1990s, management accountants and controllers have claimed the field of business unit performance. This is graphically represented in Figure I.1.[1]

This picture looks very nice but might be somewhat misleading. One can rightly argue that Figure I.1 captures the situation of about five years ago. At that time, each of these models focused on one particular

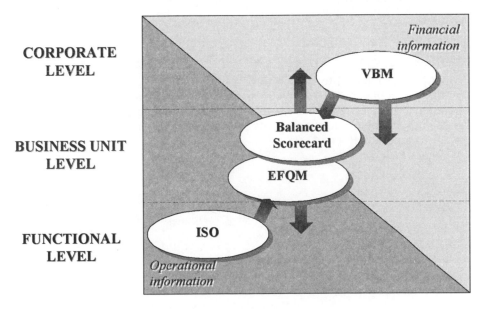

Figure I.1 Overview of the main performance management models

organizational level. For example, Value-Based Management was a pure corporate issue, while the Balanced Scorecard and the EFQM Excellence Model were the performance management frameworks developed for the business units. At the operations level, ISO was the appropriate standard. We are aware that the content and the use of these different frameworks has changed over time (as is indicated by the different arrows in our figure). For instance, the Balanced Scorecard is now increasingly used at both the corporate and the functional levels. Kaplan and Norton introduced the concept of the corporate-level scorecard, extending the use of the Balanced Scorecard to the corporate level. At the same time, the principles of the Balanced Scorecard have been translated down in the organization. Functional, and even individual, scorecards are introduced to monitor and control the performance of departments and individual employees. Similarly, we see that newer ISO versions are developed with a broader focus, moving up in the direction of the EFQM Excellence Model.

Despite these remarks, we believe that Figure I.1 is a good reference when discussing the different performance models. It shows that these frameworks are to some extent complementary in nature, as is also acknowledged by some of the authors. It also shows the 'roots' of each performance management framework. These roots still significantly determine the actual focus of the models and explain why the performance management literature is still so fragmented and why there are hardly any attempts to integrate the different ideas and frameworks into one coherent and logical framework. Unfortunately, functional thinking is not only the 'privilege' of the business world, but also prevails in the academic world.

Note

1   Figure I.1 is less relevant to explain the different dimensions of risk management. The different elements of traditional risk management are mainly situated on the functional level. The new trend towards strategic (or integrated) risk management tries to integrate these different elements and brings risk management to the business unit (and corporate) level.

2 Performance from a Finance Perspective: Shareholder Value and Beyond

KURT VERWEIRE, XAVIER BAETEN,
LIEVEN SOMERS AND LUTGART VAN DEN BERGHE

Performance measurement and performance management are vivid topics among finance people. Finance people are mainly concerned how the outside world sees and values the long-term performance of an organization.[1] *Corporate performance* measures indicate how the successful organization can allocate its resources over different product markets. In specialized firms, the resources are devoted to a single product market (and in these cases, corporate and business unit performance are the same). In order to operationalize the concept of corporate performance in greater detail, we go back to the basic definition of the corporation: an organization is an association of productive assets which come together to obtain economic advantages. For an organization to continue to exist, the owners of these productive assets must be satisfied with their use. Then, corporate performance can be defined as a firm's level of achievement in creating value for *market constituents*.

Robert Simons (2000), a well-known Harvard professor, identifies three key constituents of value creation from a corporate performance perspective: (1) customers; (2) suppliers; and (3) owners and creditors. He sees these three groups of stakeholders transacting with the organization through different markets. Customers buy goods and services through *product markets*; suppliers sell products and services to an organization through *supply markets*; and owners and creditors buy and sell ownership claims – shares of stock in the company – or debt instruments through *financial markets*.

In this chapter, we investigate how the concept of performance is considered at financial markets. Whether the company is listed or not, managers must ensure that the financial returns created by the sustained profitability of their business are meeting the expectations of owners and potential owners. The quest for value creation from a financial market perspective has received most attention and dominates the Anglo-Saxon (and increasingly the global) world. The starting points for this chapter are the performance measurement and performance management frameworks, developed for this particular category of stakeholders, i.e., the *shareholders*.

First, we look at the traditional (financial) measures of corporate performance. We then focus on shareholder value and Value-Based Management. These performance measurement and management frameworks have been developed as a reaction against the traditional performance measurement frameworks. However, the new corporate performance measures, focusing on shareholder value, have been attacked as well. Nowadays, there is an increasing demand for *stakeholder value*. Therefore, we also pay attention to this concept and to the concept of stakeholder management. We will define these concepts and describe their implications for performance management in the last paragraph of this chapter.

Traditional measures of corporate (financial) performance

Traditionally, corporate performance is defined in financial terms. Consequently, financial information is the most widely available information source on companies. This is mainly due to requirements imposed by regulators and supervisors to disclose certain financial information. The extent to which this financial information must be disclosed is dependent upon the public or private character of the company, its size, or whether the company is listed or not. The financial performance measures can be divided into two main types: (1) measures based on accounting data; and (2) market-based measures derived from stock market values. In this section, we briefly describe these two types of measure. We refer to the more specialized literature for an extensive review of these various performance measures.

Accounting-based performance measures

The validity of accounting-based performance measures has been extensively examined. The focus has been on *profitability measures*, such as *Return on Investment* (ROI) and *Return on Sales* (ROS). The interest in profitability as the ultimate performance measure is not that strange. Neo-classical economists and classical management theorists consider profit maximization as the legitimate objective of all private organizations. But, as we will see later in this chapter, this assumption has more recently come under attack from other economists and management theorists.

Apart from more philosophical reasons, Balaji Chakravarthy (1986), a strategy professor at IMD, concluded that traditional profitability measures are inadequate for evaluating a firm's strategic importance. Despite the criticisms on these financial performance measures, they still play – and will continue to play – a central role in corporate life. Whatever their limitations, they are far too deeply linked to the legal and regulatory side of business to be completely replaced by new approaches (Hennell and Warner, 1998).

The most frequently used accounting-based measures are:

- Return on equity: earnings over shareholder's equity;
- Earnings per share: earnings over average shares in issue during the year;
- Pay-out ratio: defined as dividends over earnings;
- Cash flow: usually defined as earnings plus depreciations.

All these different financial measures paint a picture of the performance of the companies over the financial year, and over a longer period of time when compared with earlier accounts. Yet, herein lies one of the major criticisms of accounting-based performance measures: they merely reflect the firm's past performance, which is not always useful to monitor and guide future performance.

There are other drawbacks associated with accounting measures. One of the main drawbacks is that accounting measures can be misleading if they have been manipulated or massaged in such a way as to present a spurious reflection of the firm's performance. It is logical that the figures paint a façade of the company in the colours that the company wants (Brown and Laverick, 1994). Other critiques of accounting measures concern differences in accounting principles. With the General Accepted Accounting Principles (GAAP) varying significantly from country to country, it is possible for the same company, using the same figures, to declare a profit in one country and a loss in another. This is because of different treatments of goodwill, taxation, valuation of inventories, capitalization of costs, provisions, among others.

Market-based performance measures

Market-based performance measures are completely different from accounting-based performance measures. While accounting-based performance measures are thought to reflect a firm's past performance, market-based measures reflect the present value of future streams of income. They vary from day to day, and incorporate evolutions in accounting profits, as well as external factors.

A central concept here is *market capitalization*, which is defined as the total value of all shares in the stock market. If the market capitalization is higher than the shareholders' equity, the management has created value. This value added is called *market value added* (MVA), and is the difference between the company's market capitalization and the shareholders' equity. Equity is made up of share capital plus retained profits. Consequently, MVA tells us how much net value has been created for the owners of the company, i.e. the shareholders (see Figure 2.1).

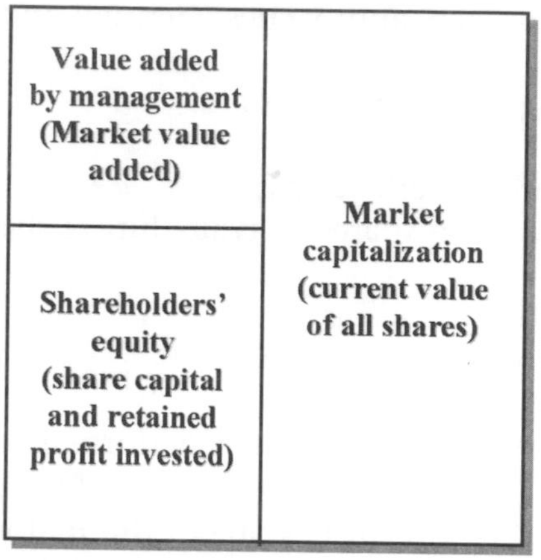

Value added by management (Market value added)	**Market capitalization (current value of all shares)**
Shareholders' equity (share capital and retained profit invested)	

Figure 2.1 Relationship between equity and market capitalization
Source: Hennell and Warner (1998: 39)

Based on these different concepts, different market-based performance measures can be computed. The most common measures are:

- Price-to-book ratio: defined as the market capitalization over the shareholders' equity;
- Price-to-earnings ratio (P/E ratio): current share price over earnings per share;
- Dividend yield: dividend per share over current share price.

In general, high measures indicate well-performing firms. But this is not always the case. For example, a high P/E ratio can be a sign of the quality of the management, but might also reflect the poor quality of present performance. Furthermore, it is better to consider market-based performance measures in relation to the whole stock market, or against an industry average, or a subset of companies in a particular industry (peer groups).

Accounting and market-based performance measures: a preliminary conclusion

This overview of both accounting-based and market-based performance measures has made clear that you need multiple performance measures to evaluate a firm's financial performance. It is also important to consider several years and, if possible, to benchmark with similar companies. We have collected some common key ratios for five major US companies and Suez. These figures are presented in Table 2.1.

Table 2.1 Common key ratios and statistics for major US companies and Suez *(pricing and volume data as of 1 March 2002)*

	ROE (%)	EPS ($)	Market capital ($bn)	Price/ Book	P/E	Dividend yield (%)
Microsoft Corp.	12.57	1.10	332.30	6.43	56.05	0.00
Wal-Mart Stores Inc.	20.12	1.49	279.9	7.97	42.15	0.45
General Electric Co.	27.27	1.41	391.8	7.31	28.04	1.83
The Coca-Cola Co.	39.00	1.60	120.4	10.86	30.22	1.65
Citigroup Inc.	20.52	2.75	235.6	3.08	16.63	1.40
Suez	15.76	1.80	29.0	2.36	15.73	0.00

Source: Money.cnn.com (2002)

Towards shareholder value and economic value added (EVA®) – the emergence of Value-Based Management

The traditional financial performance measures have been subject to growing criticism. One of the major critiques has come from the accounting and financial corner. In the beginning of the 1980s, researchers detected that there was little correlation between historical accounting earnings and shareholder value, the latter becoming increasingly important in a global world dominated by the capital markets. Shareholder value is – as the word describes – the value created for the shareholder and is composed of two basic elements: (1) capital gains; and (2) dividends. This sum is often referred to as *total shareholder return* (TSR). The lack of correlation between shareholder value and accounting measures shows that profit is clearly not the only driver of stock market performance.

In order to cope with these criticisms, analysts, consultants and managers have been searching for performance measures that are more closely aligned with corporate strategies and long-term value creation. One of the solutions forwarded was the concept of *shareholder value*. The basic idea of shareholder value is simple: measure the value that firms create or destroy by subtracting a capital charge from the cash returns they generate on invested capital. The objective is to get decision-makers think about the *economic profit* that is generated when they evaluate new business opportunities. Economic profit means that a business generates returns similar to an investment in the stock market. Economic profit is different from accounting profit because the latter does not take into account the opportunity cost of the capital employed.

Some history

Theories of shareholder value are rooted in the history of corporate finance. According to Andrew Black and his colleagues (1998), the concept of shareholder value started to take on a life of its own as a result of the work done by Harry Markowitz and William Sharpe, and John Lintner and Jan Mossin on the *Capital Asset Pricing Model* (CAPM). This model gives a precise prediction of the relationship between the risk of an asset and its expected return. Generally stated, the higher the risk the greater the return should be. The key insight of the CAPM model – one that is central to the shareholder value view of the world – is that there is a risk-weighted discount factor which allows you to assess the value today of tomorrow's developments, profits and cash flows. This discount rate is derived from observations of capital markets and defines what the opportunity cost of equity to an investor in the market is. It states what the company has to earn in order to justify the use of the capital resources tied up in the business (Black et al., 1998).

These insights have been applied to the corporate world in the late 1970s and the early 1980s and gained prominence with Alfred Rappaport's *Creating Shareholder Value* (1986). Other publications followed and software products, which helped managers in achieving the goals of shareholder value, were created. Since then, the concept has gained more and more attention and, from the 1990s on, the idea that business existed only to increase shareholder wealth has dominated significant parts of the corporate world, especially in the USA and the UK. In fact, shareholder value became so popular among analysts that the mere announcement of its introduction could cause a share price to rise.[2]

In an article in the *Financial Times*, Anjan Thakor, Jeff DeGraff and Robert Quinn (2000) see two major reasons why CEOs are worshipping at the altar of shareholder value. The first one is corporate control pressures. During the 1980s and 1990s, corporate control contests in the US often resulted in the removal of CEOs whose companies failed to deliver adequate shareholder value. A second important reason is executive compensation. Large institutional investors are increasingly influencing corporate policies and are creating a heightened awareness of the role of compensation-based incentives in focusing executive efforts on creating shareholder value (Thakor et al., 2000).

What is new about shareholder value and EVA®?

As we already mentioned, the basic idea associated with shareholder value is that a company only adds value for its shareholders when equity returns exceed equity cost. There are different metrics available to calculate shareholder value. One of the most famous ones is *economic value added* (EVA®), a concept that is registered by Stern Stewart & Co., a consulting firm based in New York.

The basic idea of EVA traces back to the concept of *residual income*, which was first used by General Motors earlier this century. Residual income is a measure of how much additional profit remains for investment in the business or distribution to owners after allowing for normal (expected) returns on investment. It is defined as the accounting profit minus a charge for capital used to generate profit. A positive residual income should correlate with increases in the market value of the firm because positive residual income indicates that a business is accumulating net resources at a rate greater than is needed to satisfy the providers of capital (Simons, 2000). As such, the residual income concept has shifted the paradigm from a focus on growth to a focus on good growth.

EVA builds further on the concept of residual income, as it tries to measure the difference between the sales made in a period and the real up-to-date cost of all resources consumed in that same period. Ideally, these resources should be valued in true economic terms, reflecting the current rather than historic costs. Stern Stewart has identified a possible 164 adjustments which can be applied to the profit or capital employed numbers before arriving at EVA. The differences in the approaches towards shareholder value are situated in which adjustments are made. However, all measures of shareholder value (whether it is EVA or another measure) have some elements in common. Hennell and Warner (1998) clearly describe what makes EVA (and other metrics of shareholder value) different from the traditional performance measures:

> It is, however, in its treatment of the economic cost of using assets within the business that EVA is significantly different from the [traditional performance] measures. . . . The key feature of EVA is that it brings balance sheet and therefore cash flow variables into the profit and loss account in a way which achieves the benefits of ROCE (Return on Capital Employed) without some of the problems. It does this by charging the company's cost of capital as a percentage of assets employed in the business as a final entry before the bottom-line profit.
>
> Another important feature of EVA is its emphasis on post-tax profit rather than profit at the operating level, encouraging managers to take a proactive approach to the management of this line of the profit and loss account. Not every company may wish to take this approach and we have seen companies adopt measures for their business units which are otherwise similar to EVA but at the pre-tax level. Their view is that it is better to encourage operating managers to leave tax issues to the specialists in the center. . . .
>
> The post-tax profit number is not as easy to extract as it may seem and this is one of the practical complexities of arriving at a true EVA number. The normal accounting definition of post-tax profit – the earnings number in the profit and loss account – is after the deduction of interest costs. As the above average on capital employed includes the cost of interest in the overall cost of capital calculation, an adjustment has to be made to avoid double counting. The actual interest cost is therefore added back and a new calculation of tax is made on the adjusted profit. The resulting number is often called NOPAT – net operating profit after tax. This adding back of interest may be an area of complexity but it illustrates a very important point. Interest on borrowing is not the only element of cost of capital, which has to be charged to arrive at a true definition of economic profit. There is also the required return for shareholders and any inclusion of a charge for capital must reflect both elements. Thus interest is added back only to be included as part of the composite cost of capital figure. (Hennell and Warner, 1998: 49–50)

Table 2.2 compares the traditional profit calculation with the EVA-based profit calculation.

Table 2.2 Comparison between traditional profit calculation and EVA®

Traditional profit calculation	EVA-based profit calculation
Revenues − Operational costs	Revenues − Operational costs
= Earnings before interest and taxes (EBIT) − Interest	= Earnings before interest and taxes (EBIT) − Taxes
= Earnings before taxes − Taxes	= Net operating profit after taxes (NOPAT) − Capital charge
= Profit after taxes	= Economic value added (EVA)

Source: Jorissen and Bruggeman (1999)

Shareholder value and EVA: pros and cons

Shareholder value and EVA have increased in importance over the last years. In this paragraph, we focus on EVA since it is the best known of the shareholder value metrics (Brown et al., 2000).

Both academicians and practitioners point out numerous benefits of EVA. Because it is a single-period measure, it allows for an annual measurement of actual, not-estimated or forecasted, value created performance (Armitage and Fog, 1996). Others refer to the fact that it corresponds more closely to economic profit than accounting earnings do and, as an objective, is consistent with the pursuit of shareholder interest. Claims have also been made that EVA can drive behavioural change by providing the incentive for managers to promote shareholder wealth as the primary objective (Dodd and Chen, 1996).

Although some research indicates that EVA, indeed, is quite well correlated with stock price performance (Lehn and Makhija, 1996; O'Byrne, 1996; Bacidore et al., 1997), other research points out that EVA does not dominate earnings in association with stock market returns (Dodd and Chen, 1996; Biddle et al., 1997; Günther et al., 1999). The implied effectiveness of EVA as a performance measure based on the association between EVA and stock return is therefore at least ambiguous.

Moreover, EVA, being a single period measure, does not address the problem of the time period over which profits are to be maximized, nor does it deal with issues over short-termism. Furthermore, the EVA practice of 'decoupling' performance measures from GAAP while having significant incentive benefits also induces potential costs in the form of increased auditing requirements. Due to the fact that EVA is a monetary measure, Stewart (1999) proposes to standardize the metric on business unit level to reflect a common level of capital employed. Finally, because EVA assesses the capital charge on the firm's economic book value rather than on its market value, next to the fact that the adjusted capital represents only the values of the physical assets in place and not the strategy, some authors suggest using total market value of the firm's assets instead of the adjusted book value (Badicore et al., 1997).

A final drawback of EVA and shareholder value is their financial focus. Shareholder value measures fail to consider the industry and competitive context in which firms compete. They give no clear answers on how firms can create sustainable wealth from a more strategic perspective. As we will see later, other performance measures, such as the Balanced Scorecard, are more helpful in providing these answers. We will come back to this issue in Chapter 3.

Shareholder value and Value-Based Management

The discussion of shareholder value has mainly focused on which metrics to use – and perhaps even more who can claim the copyright on them. Out of this discussion some new performance measurement (and management) frameworks emerged. These frameworks combine the performance measures discussed above with a specific management technique, which is labelled *Value-Based Management*. Value-Based Management is defined as 'a formal, systematic approach to managing companies to achieve the governing objective of maximizing wealth and shareholder value over time' (McTaggart et al., 1994: 367). How this is done is not agreed upon yet. Value-Based Management as a practice emerged from the experience and fieldwork of different professionals and consultants. Well-known Value-Based Management frameworks are Stern Stewart's EVA Financial Management System, Marakon's Managing for Value framework, McKinsey's Valuation framework, and PricewaterhouseCoopers' ValueBuilder.

The concept of Value-Based Management is very interesting from an Integrated Performance Management perspective. The main idea here is that adopting a Value-Based Management programme is more than simply altering the performance measures. It is not enough that a management accounting system is set up to capture business profitability by adjusting for a true cost of capital instead of measuring and reporting traditional return on income. Almost every consulting firm warns companies not to adopt only a performance measure change. Value-Based Management requires a fundamental change in the management processes adopted by an organization to interpret strategy, develop plans and budgets, measure performance and take decisions. Furthermore, all Value-Based Management frameworks stress the importance of an adequate and aligned reward and compensation system (Ameels et al., 2002). So far, consultants agree. However, there is less agreement on the format of the management system. It is beyond the scope of this book to give a detailed explanation of the differences between the main Value-Based Management frameworks of the four consulting firms. We will restrict ourselves to presenting the main steps in a Value-Based Management approach. Generally, Value-Based Management can be thought of as a three-stage process:

- Gain understanding of value creation in each business;
- Transform the company to align it with the ultimate goal of shareholder value maximization;
- Communicate, both internally and externally (Black et al., 1998).

Value creation is central in Value-Based Management. Shareholder value is created when a strategy is developed which generates future cash flows with positive present value that exceeds expectations. The whole organization needs to focus on the *value drivers* which ultimately generate the shareholder value of the organization. These value drivers are often defined in financial terms (e.g., revenue growth, profit margins, working capital, cost of equity, etc.). The management should set clear targets for each of these value drivers, which must then be cascaded down to the managers who exercise day-to-day control. As such, every aspect of the organization has to adopt an approach consistent with the overall goal of shareholder value maximization.

After the analysis phase, action must be undertaken to create and *preserve* shareholder wealth. 'Creating and sustaining value is not merely an analytical or planning exercise', says James Knight (1998: 3): 'To build long-term sustainable value in your organization you must transform its people, culture and processes to drive for shareholder wealth.' Clearly, this is the management component of the Value-Based Management process. Many consultants use some well-known strategy frameworks (such as portfolio management and competitive advantage frameworks) to back this part of the process. Many add a specific section on how to reward and compensate managers. We elaborate in greater detail on these and other (often neglected) issues in the second part of this book.

Communication is the third step in a Value-Based Management approach. Some frameworks focus on the internal communication within the company. The purpose is to stress the importance of Value-Based Management to the whole company and to specify how everybody can contribute to this overarching goal. Communication efforts need to go outside the company as well. This is the *value realization* process.

The final step, value realization, is often neglected by corporations. Investors realize value through capital appreciation of their stock and dividend pay-outs. In most cases, the bulk of shareholder returns comes through capital appreciation. Since markets are only as efficient as the information available, investors will not benefit unless the market understands the value created by your company and the strategies in place to build and preserve that value. Companies that deliver credible and relevant information to the market in a timely fashion, and are recognized for effectively managing value expectations, are much more likely to maintain a market value that reflects their true value than businesses with poor communication programs. (Black et al., 1998: 78)

Internal communication is a central element in the Integrated Performance Management literature, and the corporate governance literature tells us that a good and clear communication to the financial markets is crucial.

All in all, the philosophy that is promoted by Value-Based Management is fully in line with the philosophy behind Integrated Performance Management, as presented in Chapter 1. Value-Based management favours a more integrated management approach and goes beyond just measuring performance, although the measurement aspect receives most of the attention. How the management part is given shape remains controversial and open for discussion. So far there is no generally accepted framework. Even the well-developed financial measures are being attacked. In the remainder of this chapter, we challenge one of the basic principles on shareholder value in greater detail, i.e., the maximization of shareholder value as the ultimate goal for a company.

Broadening the financial concept: from shareholder value to stakeholder value

The purpose of each company is to create value. The question then arises: for whom? So far there is no consensus about the answer. Two, seemingly contradictory, perspectives have been taken: the shareholder perspective versus the stakeholder perspective.

It was Milton Friedman who stated that the only social responsibility of the firm was the maximization of profits. Profit is a surplus that is created by the firm's activities and is thus a signal that value is created (Henderson, 2001). The shareholder should then be the constituent for whom value is created. The strongest argument for this idea is based on the principle of private property. The shareholders are considered as the owners of the company and therefore have the right to control corporate resources so as to make sure that they are used in the shareholders' best interests.

This argument has been countered by several authors, who have introduced the stakeholder concept, arguing that the company is no longer the private property of one or a small group of owners, and hence should create value for all stakeholders (Figge and Schaltegger, 2000). Stakeholders can be defined as individuals or groups who have a direct or indirect stake in the company's activities. This means that the stakeholder approach is broader than the shareholder approach, the latter focusing only on one stakeholder. More and more managers are convinced that the corporation should be regarded as a coalition of interest groups with a stake. Charles Handy (1994a), for instance, is convinced that the immediate interests of shareholders have been given too much attention. He is convinced that their interests should be more balanced with the interests of other claimants. In their book, *The Performance Prism*, Neely, Adams and Kennerley (2002) have presented many examples that prove that there is a growing trend that executives across the world recognize and accept that the business empires they manage have a broader role to play in the twenty-first century than simply delivering value to their shareholders: 'For companies to be successful over time they must address multiple constituencies. If companies do not give each of them the right level of focus, both their corporate reputation and their market capitalization are likely to suffer' (Neely et al., 2002: 4–5). In the meantime, stakeholder management has been further developed, and a stakeholder view of the corporation has emerged (Post et al., 2002).

In what follows we will briefly present the most important stakeholder theories, and address the concept of stakeholder value. Finally, we present a framework for stakeholder-driven management.

Stakeholder theories

From a business perspective, there are several arguments why companies should adopt a broader perspective, focusing on stakeholders. Donaldson and Preston (1995) consider three stakeholder theories. We will briefly discuss two of them: the normative stakeholder theory and the instrumental stakeholder theory.[3] According to the *normative stakeholder theory*, which has a more philosophical background, a company should address its stakeholders because it is the only right thing to do. *The instrumental stakeholder theory* proposes that stakeholder-oriented companies perform better than companies that do not address their stakeholders. Potential reasons for this relationship are:

- Not establishing stakeholder relations could lead to a rise in stakeholder risk;
- Strong relationships with the business partners can stimulate innovation;
- Networks of relationships provide resources and knowledge for the development of new markets and opportunities;
- Relationships are the source of an excellent reputation, which in turn decreases the franchise risk and increases the *brand* value (Svendsen et al., 2000).

Thus, there are several theoretical arguments for why stakeholder management might affect performance. But what does academic research reveal in this respect? Post, Preston and Sachs (2002: 28) have examined the most important studies in the field and conclude that 'the empirical studies do not prove that corporations can "do well by doing good," but neither do they disprove that view, and there is no substantial evidence that corporations can "do well by doing harm".'

Stakeholder value versus shareholder value

It is clear that there is still a vast debate concerning the question for whom value should be created. This is not the only question that evokes a lot of discussion. Another equally important question is: 'What is stakeholder value? And how can we measure it?' Unlike shareholder value, stakeholder value is not a univocal concept, and there are many operationalizations for it.

John Elkington presented in *Cannibals with Forks* (1997) the concept of the *Triple Bottom Line*. The Triple Bottom Line is a more integrated performance measure, giving equal weight to the economic, social and ecological dimensions of corporate performance. It is true that these three dimensions should be managed properly, but it is our belief that it is not efficient to manage these dimensions (and the associated stakeholders) as if they were equally important. Therefore, it is very important to identify the expectations of different types of stakeholder. They are not all equally important, and it would be naive to suppose that all stakeholders should and will benefit all the time (Freeman and McVea, 2001). This is one of the first steps in the stakeholder management process. We will come back to this process in the next paragraph. Another drawback of this measure is that it does not help managers to understand and respond to what stakeholders want and expect. Svendsen et al. (2000) call for new stakeholder value measures that incorporate the quality of the relationships with different stakeholders. They consider this as a key, but still underdeveloped, territory in the field of stakeholder management.

Recently, Andy Neely, Chris Adams and Mike Kennerley (2002) have developed the *Performance Prism*, a more comprehensive and comprehensible measurement framework, built around five major interrelated perspectives on performance that pose specific vital questions (see Figure 2.2):

- Stakeholder satisfaction: who are our key stakeholders and what do they want and need?
- Stakeholder contribution: what do we want and need from our stakeholders on a reciprocal basis?
- Strategies: what strategies do we need to put in place to satisfy the wants and needs of our stakeholders while satisfying our own requirements too?
- Processes: what processes do we need to put in place to enable us to execute our strategies?
- Capabilities: what capabilities do we need to put in place to allow us to operate our processes? (Neely et al., 2002: 160).

Neely and his colleagues define strategy and strategic objectives in terms of stakeholders. The central question becomes: How can our stakeholders help us to realize our strategy, and thus to achieve our organizational

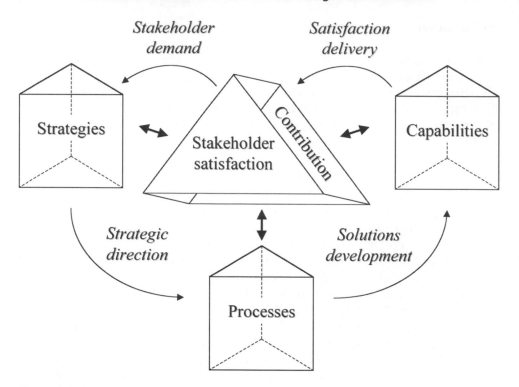

Figure 2.2 The five dimensions of the Performance Prism
Source: Kennerley and Neely (2002: 153)

objectives? In their book *The Performance Prism* (2002), they present some relevant ideas and new performance measures to manage the following stakeholder categories:

- Investors (including shareholders, bankers and other capital providers);
- Customers and intermediaries;
- Employees (including labour unions);
- Suppliers and alliance partners;
- Regulators, pressure groups, communities and the media.

A framework for stakeholder-driven management

In the previous paragraphs, we defined stakeholder value and described why it is important to incorporate an increasing number of stakeholders in the strategy process. We define *stakeholder-driven management* as a goal-setting process, not limiting the organization's purpose to the sole creation of shareholder value, but broadening it to creating societal value for all those who have a direct or an indirect interest (stake) in the company's functioning. It should be made clear that it can by no means be the intention to manage the stakeholders (i.e., trying to convince stakeholders without taking their needs into account) or to have the company managed by its stakeholders.

Stakeholder value can only be realized if a company has a clear understanding of what stakeholders want and how they can contribute to the company's objectives. Therefore they need an open stakeholder dialogue to identify stakeholders and issues and to integrate this into the company's strategy, its management style and daily operations. A much more open and collaborative relationship between the company and its stakeholders is a key success factor. We are convinced that stakeholder dialogue is one of the most essential elements for creating stakeholder value. The framework, presented in Figure 2.3, gives an overview of the main steps of a stakeholder-driven management approach.

The stakeholder management process consists of a defined number of recurrent steps. The first step is the *identification and mapping* of the stakeholders. Stakeholders are abundant. They are not limited to

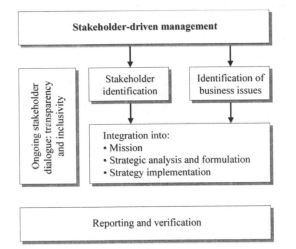

Figure 2.3 The business framework for stakeholder-driven management (and CSR)

shareholders, customers and employees. For example, suppliers, authorities, local communities can also play a significant role in formulating and implementing the firm's strategy. It will also become clear that the stakeholders will differ depending upon the level of analysis. A multinational organization will consider national governments as a very important stakeholder. When we look at the business unit level of that multinational company, more local stakeholders will become relevant. Therefore, before engaging in the process of stakeholder management, the level of analysis, or scope, should be defined.

Every stakeholder has his or her own interests and issues to be addressed. However, not all issues are equally urgent or important. A company must set priorities on which issues to solve. It is therefore necessary to segment the generic stakeholder groups into different subgroups. Stakeholder mapping is a tool that helps companies looking for common denominators among stakeholders to categorize them and to approach them in similar ways. The stakeholder identification model of Mitchell, Agle and Wood (1997) uses three variables – urgency, legitimacy and power – to group stakeholders into nine different categories. Johnson and Scholes (1999) identified the power/interest matrix to map the different types of stakeholder (see Figure 2.4). It is important to detect gaps between the current status and future stakeholder expectations and to study the actual quality of the relationships with these different stakeholders. Some variables that can help to do this are communication flows, personal relationships, problems that have occurred in the past, etc. The next step consists of making an inventory of *business issues*, i.e., environmental issues, changing values and needs, etc. It is extremely interesting to link these issues to the relevant stakeholders.

Stakeholder dialogue is the second step in the stakeholder management process and is the most crucial one. The purpose of the stakeholder dialogue is to find a balance between the expectations of the company and

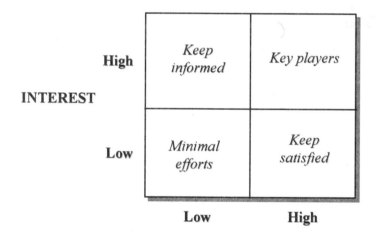

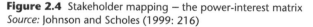

Figure 2.4 Stakeholder mapping – the power-interest matrix
Source: Johnson and Scholes (1999: 216)

its stakeholders. A stakeholder dialogue requires efforts from both sides and is not free of engagement. Expectations will rise and it is very important to be aware of the expectations of the stakeholders before engaging in dialogue. These expectations have to be in line with the expectations of the company. Another important aspect of the stakeholder dialogue is the knowledge level of both parties. When a company wants to dialogue with its stakeholders and it expects input from the stakeholders on a particular issue, the company must be sure that stakeholders are sufficiently informed and understand the issues at hand. Otherwise, stakeholders might lose their trust in the dialogue process, which might even lead to adverse effects!

Once the expectations of both parties are known, the adequate dialogue technique must be selected. It is obvious that, depending on the purpose and the number of stakeholders involved, different techniques should be used. Examples of dialogue techniques are: focus groups, surveys, group meetings, information sessions, etc.

The information obtained during the stakeholder dialogue will be used in the strategy formation process. As we said before, stakeholders have interests and want those interests to be served. In other words, they expect a certain degree of progress. To express this progress, performance indicators will have to be identified, calculated and reported. *Identifying these performance indicators* is the third step in the stakeholder management process.

Reporting and verification is the final step in the stakeholder management cycle. It is the end of a cycle and, at the same time, provides the input for the next cycle. It is a very important step because the company indicates to the stakeholders that it has taken actions, as agreed upon in the stakeholder dialogue. Credibility is a critical issue. It is a challenge to build credibility into stakeholder management reports. One way to do this is to have the report externally verified by a trusted independent organization. Another method for building credibility is to follow a reporting standard such as the *Global Reporting Initiative* (GRI), although these guidelines also suggest an external verification.[4] Several companies publish a stakeholder report without passing the previous steps of the stakeholder management cycle. Those reports are easily dismissed by stakeholders as public relations efforts.

Many companies have started the process of stakeholder management. Case studies show that it is far from easy to establish solid relationships. Stakeholder management is a gradual and a continuous approach. The aim of the process cannot be reached by having a single dialogue or by publishing a report.

We acknowledge that other stakeholder models exist that were not discussed in this publication. Most of them focus on identifying relevant performance measures for an extended group of stakeholders. But more is needed to redefine the corporation, and to convince people that stakeholder management can be the driving force of organizational wealth.

Conclusion

This overview has shown that the concept of corporate performance is multidimensional in nature. Within corporate performance, the focus has always been on the financial side, but this encompasses a broad range of elements. For a long time, accounting measures and market-based measures have been the most important measures to evaluate a company's overall performance. Now the concept of shareholder value is dominating large parts of the corporate world. This concept has evoked a new set of management tools, commonly referred to as Value-Based Management. Value-Based Management incorporates some aspects of Integrated Performance Management, but is restricted to developing strategies, rewards and the appropriate communication.

Furthermore, in Value-Based Management the focus is too much on the shareholder. Other stakeholders are important in the strategy formulation and implementation process. Here we introduced the concept of stakeholder-driven management. It was defined as a goal-setting process, not limiting the organization's purpose to the sole creation of shareholder value, but broadening it to creating societal value for all those who have a direct or an indirect interest (stake) in the functioning of the company.

Notes

1 In this book, we use the terms 'organization', 'corporation', 'firm' and 'company' as synonyms.
2 Famous examples in this respect were Coca-Cola and Quaker. Their moves to performance systems based on shareholder value had a direct and positive impact on their share price: they went up merely on the announcement of such a move (Hennell and Warner, 1998: 4).
3 The third one is the descriptive stakeholder theory, which describes how companies consider their stakeholders. This theory is less relevant in explaining why companies should address their stakeholders.
4 The Global Reporting Initiative (GRI) was established in 1997 with the mission of designing globally applicable guidelines for preparing enterprise-level sustainability reports. GRI is one of the better-known reporting standards for Triple Bottom Line performance.

3 Performance Management from a Control Perspective: Introducing the Balanced Scorecard

WERNER BRUGGEMAN

The 1990s literature on performance measurement created the awareness that most companies' performance measurement and reporting systems focus too much on financial performance. On a corporate and business unit level many executives now understand that traditional financial accounting measures (like return on investment (ROI), earnings per share and unit cost per product) can give misleading signals for continuous improvement, innovation and competence-building activities. They feel a need to improve financial control systems and to supplement them with *strategic performance measures*. To be effective these measures must be aligned with the company's mission, goals and strategy.

In order to be able to better align performance measures to strategy Robert Kaplan and David Norton developed the Balanced Scorecard. This chapter describes the basic concepts and techniques in developing a Balanced Scorecard. It also shows how a company can use the Balanced Scorecard as a central element in its performance management process to become a *Strategy-Focused Organization*. In the final section of this chapter, we compare the Balanced Scorecard with some other accounting and control frameworks.

Defining The Balanced Scorecard

The Balanced Scorecard, a framework introduced by Kaplan and Norton, offers a methodology to develop a set of measures that gives top managers a fast but comprehensive view of the business (Kaplan and Norton, 1992, 1993, 1996a, 1996b, 2000, 2001). It helps managers translate the company's mission, goals and strategies into measures. It complements the financial measures with operational measures on customer satisfaction, internal processes and the organization's innovation, learning and improvement activities – operational measures that are the drivers of future financial performance (see Figure 3.1). The Balanced Scorecard provides a framework to describe, communicate and manage the strategy in a consistent and explicit way.

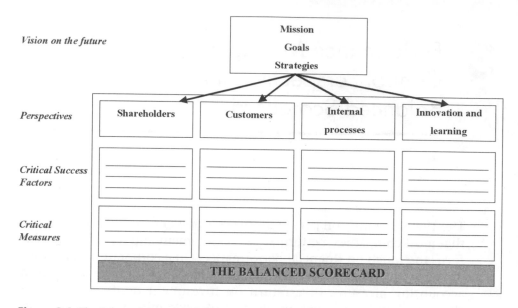

Figure 3.1 The Balanced Scorecard linking measurement to strategy
Source: Adapted from Kaplan and Norton (1992)

The four perspectives of the scorecard permit a balance between short-term and long-term objectives, between desired outcomes and the performance drivers of those outcomes, and between hard objective measures and softer, more subjective measures. The Balanced Scorecard distinguishes between four main performance measures (Kaplan and Norton, 1992).

- According to Kaplan and Norton, *financial performance measures* define the long-term objectives of the business unit. Apart from profitability measures (see Chapter 2), other financial measures are possible, such as sales growth, cash flow, cost reduction measures, etc.
- In the *customer perspective*, managers identify the customer and market segments in which the business unit competes and the measures of the business unit's performance in these targeted segments. Generic outcome measures include: customer satisfaction, customer retention, new customer acquisition and customer profitability. More specific measures should focus on the different value propositions that are offered to the customer, such as convenience, uniqueness, functionality, price, quality, service level, etc.
- In the *internal business process perspective*, managers identify the critical internal processes in which the organization must excel. Internal processes should deliver the value propositions for the customers, and this should be done in the most efficient and effective way. Managers should not only look at the existing processes, but identify new processes if necessary. (Operational) innovation is a crucial point, and should be measured.

- *Learning and growth* is the fourth Balanced Scorecard dimension and identifies the infrastructure that organizations must build to create long-term growth and improvement. The organizational learning and growth come from three principal resources: people, systems and procedures. For each of these different resources, appropriate measures need to be developed, in line with the strategic objectives of the firm. Reskilling employees, developing appropriate information technology and systems, and aligning organizational procedures should help companies to cope with a fast-changing environment.

These four perspectives of the Balanced Scorecard should be considered as a template, not as a 'straitjacket'. No mathematical theorem exists to prove that four perspectives are both necessary and sufficient (Simons, 2000). But the perspectives identified by Kaplan and Norton make sense for many companies: shareholders, customers and employees are very important stakeholders in each and every company.[1] Depending on industry circumstances and the strategy, one or more additional perspectives may be needed to incorporate the interests of other important stakeholders (e.g., suppliers, the community, the environment).

Figure 3.2 shows the Balanced Scorecard of a company where the ambition of the management is to become the market leader and to be an excellent company for the shareholders by implementing a strategy of high-quality products, on-time delivery and lean manufacturing in an organization with strong employee involvement.

Although the Balanced Scorecard was originally devised as a measure to

---

Long-term goals: become the market leader; be an excellent company for our shareholders.
Strategy: high-quality products, on-time delivery and lean manufacturing
Organization: create a working environment stimulating employee involvement

CRITICAL SUCCESS FACTORS	STRATEGIC OBJECTIVES	MEASURES
Financial		
Market leadership	Increase market share	Market share
Excellence for the shareholder	Create more shareholder value	EVA® increase
Customer		
High-quality products	Improve quality	Number of complaints
On-time delivery	Improve delivery reliability	Percentage of orders on time
Processes		
Lean manufacturing	Shorten cycle time	Cycle time
	Reduce work in process	Days work in process
Innovations and learning		
Employee involvement	Improve employee involvement	Number of suggestions

Figure 3.2 The Balanced Scorecard – an example

'tell the story of the business unit's strategy', it can be implemented at the corporate and the functional levels, and on the level of corporate support functions and shared services as well. A functional scorecard translates the functional strategy (e.g., marketing, manufacturing, Human Resources, ICT strategy) into a coherent set of performance measures. A Balanced Scorecard of a corporate or a shared service links the performance measures of the service unit with its mission, its goals and its strategies and aligns them with the corporate strategy in order to offset the problems of facing different or even conflicting goals and strategies on the different organizational levels.

Important steps in developing a Balanced Scorecard are: clarification of the mission, goals and strategy of the entity under focus, identification of the critical success factors (or the strategic objectives), translating the critical success factors into measures, designing the necessary data collection systems and channelling the right data into each of the four quadrants of the scorecard. In some cases the Balanced Scorecard requires the implementation of a data warehouse.

From vision to strategy maps

In many companies or business units and organizational units, the mission, the goals and the strategies are not clearly defined. In this case the management team should spend more time in clarifying their *strategic vision*. That is, the management team should clearly indicate where the organization (or the unit of analysis) wants to go. To make this process more effective, Kaplan and Norton offer an analytical framework, called the *strategy map*, which is a logical and comprehensive architecture for describing the strategy. When building a strategy map a management team should first make explicit its long-term performance goals. Then one reflects on the hypothesized key drivers of the future performance. Figure 3.3 shows an example of a strategy map of a Divisional Balanced Scorecard.

The long-term goals are to become the market leader and to be an excellent company for the shareholder. The perceived key driver of these performances is new customer acquisition, customer loyalty and overhead cost management. The drivers of new customer acquisition are sales and marketing skills and customer satisfaction. Customer satisfaction is driven by product innovation, service quality and the delivery of total problem solutions. Total solutions delivery is driven by experience and expertise, which is determined by employee satisfaction. The strategy map shows the causal relationships between the critical success factors. For each factor one can determine one or more performance indicators and fit them into a Balanced Scorecard (see Figure 3.4).

This can also be done for various functional levels within organizations. As such, Balanced Scorecards and strategy maps can also be developed for the HR department, for the IT department, and so on.

Figure 3.3 The cause and effect chain

Integrating sustainability goals into the Balanced Scorecard

Most strategy maps focus on shareholder value creation, growth and market share as the main long-term company goals. Some authors argue that the Balanced Scorecard implicitly considers the shareholder as the only stakeholder (Otley, 1999). The financial perspective measures shareholder value creation; the customer, the internal and the learning and growth perspective contain measures of the drivers of future financial performance. This is a typical example of an instrumental stakeholder approach, as defined in Chapter 2.

Some people argue that following an instrumental stakeholder approach, one might not consider the needs of other stakeholders, such as employees and their families, the national and international society at large, local communities, suppliers and the future generations. Modern

CRITICAL SUCCESS FACTORS	MEASURES
Financial	
Market share	Revenue growth rate
Excellence for the shareholder	EVA®
Growth through new customer acquisition	Revenue from new customers
Growth through customer loyalty	Revenue from existing customers
Customer	
Customer satisfaction	Customer satisfaction index
Total solution provider	Number of complaints
	Percentage of revenue from total solution projects
Service quality	Percentage of due dates met
Processes	
Account management	Percentage of revenue under account management
Lean overhead services	Overhead costs/revenue
Innovations and learning	
Sales and marketing skills	Number of days training
Expertise and experience	Average number of years seniority of employees
Satisfaction employees	Satisfaction index (survey)
Product innovation	Number of free leaves
	Percentage of revenue from products < 3 years
R&D investment	R&D budget

Figure 3.4 Critical success factors derived from the example Strategy Map

performance management pays more and more attention to sustainability management and defines goals and strategies in the area of social responsibility and ecological sustainability (see also Chapter 2). In implementing the Balanced Scorecard one can take full advantage of the opportunity to develop a performance measurement system that contains measures linked to the key sustainability goals and strategies. Thus the Balanced Scorecard may contain measures of environmental performance and satisfaction measures of regulators, communities and suppliers. In this case the Balanced Scorecard becomes an all-stakeholder model of performance measurement.

Benefits of using the Balanced Scorecard

The Balanced Scorecard helps companies to design an integrated performance measurement system. The Balanced Scorecard project invites top management to develop a clear strategy and build a consensus around it. The process of translating the strategy into measures also gives middle managers a clear understanding of what the strategy really means for them. As such the scorecard project helps to communicate the strategy throughout the company, align unit and individual goals with the company strategy, link strategic objectives to long-term targets and identify cause-and-effect relationships between performance measures.

For the (corporate) staff functions, shared services and coordination centres, the Balanced Scorecard contributes to the alignment of the goals, the strategies and the actions of the corporate centres with the corporate and the business unit strategies. With the scorecard, top and functional management have a tool to monitor continuously the degree to which strategies are implemented. The use of the Balanced Scorecard strongly affects the behaviour of managers. They show a stronger motivation to implement the organization's strategy. Recall the statement: 'What you get is what you measure.'

From a measurement to a management instrument: towards a Strategy-Focused Organization

In the introductory chapter, we described that the use of the Balanced Scorecard has evolved over time. For some years, the Balanced Scorecard has been considered a performance measurement instrument; nowadays, Kaplan and Norton (2001) see the Balanced Scorecard as the central element in a 'new approach to implementing strategy'. Unlike traditional management programmes, which link performance to financial frameworks, budgets or even new shareholder value approaches, companies which successfully implement Balanced Scorecards reinvent part of their management systems to focus on strategy.

A number of companies (Mobil Oil, Cigna Insurance, and the former Chemical Retail Bank) have shown remarkable performance improvements only three years after the introduction of the Balanced Scorecard. According to Kaplan and Norton, the success of these companies was due to the successful implementation of their strategy: 'these executive teams successfully executed their strategies when the majority of their colleagues could not' (2001: 13).

> Strategy must be understood and executed by everyone. The organization must be aligned around its strategy, and performance management systems help create that alignment. Herein lies one of the major causes of poor strategic management. Most performance management systems are designed around the annual budget and operating plan. They promote short-term, incremental, tactical behavior. While this is a necessary part of management, it is not enough. You cannot manage strategy with a system designed for tactics. It is our belief that it is this need – the need for strategic enterprise management – that has been driving the widespread adoption of the Balanced Scorecard. (Kaplan and Norton, 2001: 12–13)

This alignment and focus on the strategy of the organization can create breakthrough performance. Recall from Chapter 1 that 'alignment' and 'focus' are two central concepts in the performance management literature. This is the main message from Kaplan and Norton's most recent book, *The Strategy-Focused Organization: How Balanced Scorecard Companies Thrive in the New Business Environment* (2001). In this book, they argue that successful organizations create a performance management programme that puts strategy at the centre of its management processes. They detected five principles that permit organizations to become strategy-focused, enabling them to execute their strategies rapidly and effectively.

Mobilize change through executive leadership

Balanced Scorecard programmes are not about metrics, but about change. Therefore, the single most important condition for success is the ownership and active involvement of the executive team. As strategy must be understood and executed by everyone in the organization, change must come from every part of the organization. If those at the top are not energetic leaders of the process, change will not take place and the opportunity will be missed. In order to run the change project successfully, it is necessary to establish a sense of urgency and to create the leadership team. Establishing a sense of urgency is about creating mobilization and creating momentum. Once the organization is mobilized, the process must be governed, with emphasis on fluid, team-based approaches to deal with the unstructured nature of the transition to a new performance management model. According to Kaplan and Norton, the creation of a shared vision and strategy was an effective way to build an executive leadership team (in contrast to a collection of individual business unit heads who met periodically to discuss business issues).

Translate strategy into operating terms

The Balanced Scorecard approach can only be successful if the mission, the vision, the goals of the company and the strategy (i.e., how the vision and goals can be achieved) are clearly defined. Unfortunately, there are no standards for strategy-making. *Developing* and *crafting* a strategy remain an art, says Mintzberg (1987). However, there is nothing 'arty' about *describing* the strategy. Nevertheless, describing the strategy is of utmost importance.

Kaplan and Norton argue that the Balanced Scorecard provides the discipline for describing the strategy of the organization reliably and consistently. In addition to building scorecards, the Balanced Scorecard approach helps executive teams to better understand and articulate their strategies. The foundation of the design is the 'Strategy Map', which we described earlier in this chapter. Strategy scorecards, along with their graphical representations on Strategy Maps, should provide a logical and comprehensive tool to describe strategy. It communicates clearly the organization's desired outcomes and its hypotheses about how these outcomes can be achieved (Kaplan and Norton, 2001: 9–11).

Align the organization with the strategy

The Balanced Scorecard is a powerful tool to describe a business unit's strategy. But organizations consist of numerous sectors, business units and specialized departments, each with its own operations and often its own strategy. In order to be really successful, synergies should be created and the strategies across these units should be coordinated.

Kaplan and Norton are convinced that the Balanced Scorecard can and should be used to define the strategic linkages that integrate the performance of multiple organizations. In this way, individual strategies are linked and integrated. It requires that the goals and strategies at the corporate level are clearly formulated and articulated. The high-level strategic themes should then be translated to the business unit level. As such, the Corporate Scorecard provides the communication and coordination mechanisms across business unit scorecards. Beyond aligning the business units, organizations must also align their staff functions and shared service units, such as Human Resources, IT, finance, etc.

Make strategy everyone's everyday job

Strategy cannot be limited to a few people at the top of an organization. This is especially the case in 'modern firms', where decision-making is increasingly being moved lower in the organization and where self-directed teams rather than individual managers now make decisions. Kaplan and Norton showed that successful Balanced Scorecard users took steps to ensure that everyone in the organization understood the strategy, was aligned with it, and was capable of executing it.

This was done in several ways. Communication is clearly one of the most important processes in this respect. Organizational alignment can only be achieved if the programme is conveyed in all communication media and if it is reinforced by the personal behaviour of executives. Some companies developed personal scorecards, to align individuals with the company's strategy.[2] Another major instrument to bring down the strategy to the individual level is to link incentive compensation to targeted scorecard measures. This is often done at the managerial level. Rewarding managers on the basis of the Balanced Scorecard is consistent with the goal of creating a better 'strategic alignment'. Kaplan and Norton (2000) refer to a study of the Hay Group which stipulates that of 15 companies using the Balanced Scorecard 13 have linked their remuneration system to the Balanced Scorecard, which they call 'the Balanced Paycheck'. They describe a number of case studies and already give a few practical recommendations for implementation. Their experience is that:

- It might be a good idea to link the remuneration of managers not too quickly to the Balanced Scorecard, due to the fact that the first scorecards are only preliminary and the reported performance data are still insufficiently reliable in a first phase;

- It might be a good idea to base the remuneration of managers especially on objective (output) measures instead of subjective (behavioural) measures;
- Some companies link the remuneration of their managers to a limited number of Balanced Scorecard measures;
- A balance needs to be found between measures for individual performance and team performance;
- It is difficult to link remuneration to the Balanced Scorecard if the measures need to be frequently adapted in a fast-changing environment.

Linking remuneration and reward systems to the Balanced Scorecard is, however, a delicate and complicated issue. It is not only important to determine which performance measures to use as the basis for the reward system, but also to decide how the performance targets are set. The target-setting literature suggests that performance control should be based on challenging but attainable targets. The performance targets set by the Balanced Scorecard are sometimes considered 'unattainable'. Thus, the motivation impact of Balanced Scorecard-based variable remuneration should not be overestimated. This finding was also supported by academic research. One study examined how the introduction of a Balanced Scorecard affected the motivation of managers of a manufacturing division of a Danish petrochemical company (Bruggeman et al., 2001). The general idea was that the managers perceived that the implementation of the Balanced Scorecard had positively affected their motivation. However, the positive motivational effect had mainly come from the *visioning process* and from the design and the use of the Balanced Scorecard as a tool to monitor the implementation of strategy and to measure the departmental progress. The effect of linking the variable pay system to the Balanced Scorecard had only a minor impact – and in some cases even a negative one – on the motivation of the operating managers. On the one hand, when the performance targets were met, they considered it as fair to receive a bonus but, as stated before, the variable pay was not their major source of motivation. Some managers felt that the percentage of variable pay was set too low. However, not paying the bonus when targets were not met was considered as unfair and caused significant demotivation and frustration. In such cases the following reasons were mentioned:

- Some performance measures in the Balanced Scorecard were not precise measures of the objectives to be realized;
- Some important performance measures in the Balanced Scorecard could hardly be influenced by the managers.

Make formulating strategy a continual process

Just like change projects, Balanced Scorecard projects should become continual processes. Kaplan and Norton propose to use the Balanced Scorecard as the central element in management meetings, instead of the traditional budget and operating plans: 'Companies with the Balanced Scorecard adopt a new "double-loop process". The process integrates the management of tactics with the management of strategy' (Kaplan and Norton, 2001: 13–15). This is done in three ways.

Strategy-Focused Organizations should link the strategy to the budgeting process. The Balanced Scorecard is used as a screen for evaluating potential investments and initiatives. Strategy budgets are introduced. These strategy budgets are used to fund all types of strategic innovation initiative, which should guarantee the long-term performance of the organization. The Balanced Scorecard has also become the instrument on which management meetings are based. Management meetings are scheduled on a monthly or quarterly basis to discuss the Balanced Scorecard: are performance targets reached? Are strategic initiatives implemented properly and timely? According to Kaplan and Norton, the process creates a focus on strategy that did not exist before.

Finally, a process for learning and adapting the strategy evolved. The Balanced Scorecard and the strategy maps make the strategy explicit and formulate hypotheses and links between different value drivers, which ultimately result in long-term financial success. As the scorecard is put into action and feedback systems begin their reporting on actual results, an organization can test the hypotheses of its strategy to see whether its strategy is working. This is where organizational learning can begin.

The Balanced Scorecard and other performance measurement models

Without any doubt the Balanced Scorecard has been the most popular performance management framework that originated from the accounting and control world. However, many other initiatives were undertaken to develop new tools and frameworks for performance measurement and management. In this section, we briefly introduce some other well-known frameworks.

All these frameworks aim to address some of the weaknesses of traditional performance measurement approaches (just like the Balanced Scorecard did):

- The cost focus of traditional performance measures gives little indication of future performance and encourages short-termism (Bruns, 1998). The traditional methods of performance measurement review results instead of the causes for those results.

- Traditional performance measures fail to reflect changes in the competitive circumstances and strategies of modern organizations (Johnson and Kaplan, 1987; Kennerley and Neely, 2002).
- There is too much focus on financial measures, which leads to an unbalanced performance measurement system.

The performance measurement revolution in the 1980s and 1990s brought widespread acceptance of the need for organizations to take a more balanced approach to performance measurement. Many performance measurement frameworks emerged and a huge discussion started on what exactly 'balanced' meant. For example, Keegan, Eiler and Jones (1989) proposed a performance measurement matrix that categorized measures as being 'cost', 'non-cost', 'external' or 'internal'. They argued that the performance measurement system should consist of measures along all these dimensions. The SMART (Strategic Measurement and Reporting Technique), developed by Wang Laboratories (Lynch and Cross, 1991), also started from this idea and included internal and external performance measures. However, the notion of cascading measures down the organization was added so that the departments' objectives were aligned with the organization's objectives. This is an idea that we find was used in the Tableau de Bord, a tool that was developed in France in the early twentieth century (Kennerley and Neely, 2002).

Other researchers identified other dimensions of 'balance'. Fitzgerald and colleagues (1991) proposed a framework that distinguished between: measures that related to results and measures that focus on determinants of those results. This is an element that comes back in Kaplan and Norton's Balanced Scorecard as well. Brown (1996) developed the concept of linking measures through cause-and-effect relationships further. Kaplan and Norton's strategy maps clearly incorporate this particular aspect.

Identifying relevant performance measures is one thing, developing and implementing Integrated Performance Management Systems is another. But here again, there is a lot of material available in addition to Kaplan and Norton's work on the Balanced Scorecard. There is one publication that we thought was very useful because it provides concrete tools and techniques for setting up Integrated Performance Management systems. The Institute of Management Accountants and Arthur Andersen LLP (1998) published a document called *Tools and Techniques for Implementing Integrated Performance Measurement Systems: Statement on Management Accounting 4DD*, where they describe a three-phase approach to designing and implementing integrated performance management systems:

- The conceptual design phase is an analysis phase where attention is paid to understanding and identifying the organization's goals and strategies, and the way the organization operates. From these goals and strategies, critical success factors and key performance indicators are deducted. This phase consists of both top-down and bottom-up analyses, and of the creation of a steering team that has the (active) support of the top management team to develop consensus and assess the gaps between 'as is' and 'to be' environments.

- In the detailed design and implementation phase, the system is made operational and is integrated in the current management system. The costs and benefits of running the system are analysed, training and education is planned, and efforts are made to flesh out the details of the Integrated Performance Management System design, architecture and technology. This phase includes pilot projects and the ultimate system conversion.
- The ongoing support phase focuses on realizing the full benefits of implementation by supporting and fine-tuning the newly changed environment, and by facilitating continuous improvement in systems and performance (Institute of Management Accountants and Arthur Andersen LLP, 1998).

Conclusion

This chapter illustrates how the Balanced Scorecard can be a basis for developing an effective performance measurement and management system. The Balanced Scorecard presents significant opportunities to develop, communicate and implement the strategy of the organization. Managers respond positively to the Balanced Scorecard and use it as a device to monitor strategy, to set targets, to benchmark and to plan strategic initiatives. Some remarkable examples have shown that the Balanced Scorecard can be used as a central tool in the strategy implementation process. These companies have realized breakthrough performance by organizing their management system around the Balanced Scorecard. However, more research is necessary to investigate exactly how the Balanced Scorecard can create this breakthrough performance. For example, recent research has shown that linking the Balanced Scorecard to the reward system does not always yield the expected results. We have also briefly presented some other accounting and control models that are very useful when setting up integrated performance management systems.

Notes

1   There has been some debate where to position employee-related items in the Balanced Scorecard: either in the internal business process perspective or in the learning and growth perspective. In our opinion, this is a meaningless debate. The Balanced Scorecard is a means to an end. The ultimate purpose is to track your performance along several dimensions. If employees are considered vital to the success of the company, then appropriate measures should be developed. Where you position them in the Balanced Scorecard is less relevant.

2   According to Kaplan and Norton (2001), the individual scorecards differ from the more traditional Management-by-Objectives approach. The objectives in an MBO system are established within the structure of the individual's organizational unit, reinforcing narrow, functional thinking. The individual objectives established within the framework of the Balanced Scorecard are cross-functional, longer-term and strategic.

4 Performance at the Operational Level: Quality- and Time-Based Competition

PAUL GEMMEL

Performance from an operations perspective: a general overview

In the previous chapter we looked at performance from a corporate and business unit perspective. Performance can also be approached from an operations perspective. There, one looks at how inputs such as people, materials and machines are transformed into outputs such as finished goods and satisfied customers. The key focus is the process of transformation.

One example of a process transforming 'goods' is an assembly line of cars. A key issue in such an assembly line is the balancing of lines so that there is a smooth throughput with an adequate utilization of the work station. In an insurance company, the process transforms a request for underwriting into an insurance policy. The main challenge here is to keep the turnaround time between request and written policy low. In a hospital, patients are flowing from one department to another (such as the pre-operative care department, the operating theatre, intensive care and the post-operative care department), but not all patients follow the same sequence. The main task of the operations function here is to combine a smooth throughput with a high utilization of the medical equipment. Based on these examples, some fundamental differences between the transformation processes can be observed:

- The 'subject' of the transformation can be materials, such as in the example of the car, information, such as in the insurance company, or people such as in a hospital.
- The way the transformation is organized can be different. Cars are assembled using a product-line approach, while a hospital works rather as a job shop. Generally, processes can be organized in different ways: project, job shop, batch production, assembly line and continuous flow. There is an evolution from low volume/low standardization (often one of a kind) products to high volume/high standardization commodity products.
- The operations management function is different depending on the subject of transformation and the organization of the transformation

process. The scheduling task is fundamentally different when people are involved than when machines and materials are involved.

In summary, measuring performance at an operational level requires making a distinction between manufacturing companies, service companies and information companies. Because of the particularity of the latter one, this chapter mainly focuses on manufacturing and service companies.

The operations function is not an isolated part of the company. As with many other functions, it must be linked to business strategy. Hayes and Wheelwright's (1984) four-stage model holds that the strategic contribution of an operations function can be judged by its aspirations (see Figure 4.1).

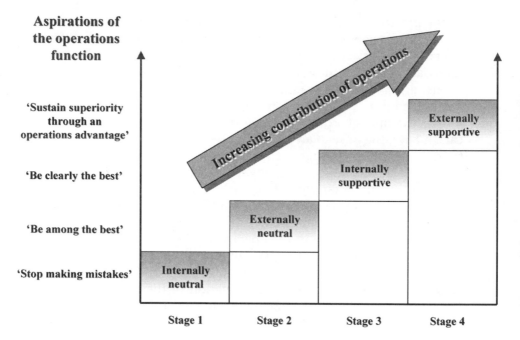

Figure 4.1 Different stages in the aspiration of the operations function
Source: Hayes and Wheelwright (1984: 8)

In the first stage, the contribution of operations is considered as a necessary evil, trying to avoid bigger mistakes. In a second stage, the operations function is looking at other companies and tries to adopt best practices from its competitors. In the internally supportive stage, the operations function is aiming at becoming one of the best in the market and further tries to integrate itself with the strategy of the firm. While in this stage, the operations function is rather supportive for the strategy; in the last stage, the operations function is providing the foundation for its future competitive success (see discussion in Slack et al., 1995: 49–52). In the third and fourth stage, firms are formulating an operations strategy as 'the total pattern of decisions and actions which set the role, objectives and activities of the operation so that they contribute to and support the organization's business strategy' (Slack et al., 1995: 83).

The operations function contributes and supports the organization's business strategy through five performance objectives:

- The quality objective – doing the things right;
- The dependability objective – doing things on time;
- The speed objective – doing things fast;
- The flexibility objective – changing what you do;
- The cost objective – doing things cheap (Slack et al., 1995: 53).

In this chapter we elaborate on these different performance objectives of the operations function. We regroup them into three categories: the quality objective, the time-based objective and the cost objective. Speed and flexibility are all aspects of what is called time-based competition. Dependability is closely linked to quality. The cost objective will only be discussed in relation to the other two performance objectives. However, costing methods (such as Activity-Based Costing) have played an important role in shaping work systems. That is why we focus very briefly on the role of Activity-Based Management in Chapter 7.

Quality-based competition

Some definitions of quality

Quality has been studied for years. The great Greek philosophers Socrates, Plato and Artistotle mention '*excellence*' as the absolute ideal to strive for (Reeves and Bednar, 1994). Since then there have been many publications on quality in books, academic journals and trade journals, resulting in many different definitions of quality, which are not always consistent or coherent. In a review article on the definitions of quality, Reeves and Bednar (1994) recognize four categories, based on what concept is behind them:

- Quality is excellence;
- Quality is value;
- Quality is conformance to specification;
- Quality is meeting and exceeding customers' expectations.

Quality is excellence Although the real root of this category of 'quality' definition lies in Ancient Greece, it is now very popular again. For instance, the European Foundation for Quality Management (EFQM) has developed a framework for business excellence. It describes 'essence of excellence' as being when a company is aware of competition, survives in the long term through changing and improving, satisfies customers, shares knowledge and experiences, develops leadership and is aware that its people are its greatest asset (European Foundation for Quality Management, 1999a). Based on this description of excellence, one can conclude that a company must excel in everything it does, without knowing the limits. Excellence means that the sky is the limit. Although striving for excellence is always a good attitude in any firm, it gives only very limited guidance to managers on how to reach quality (Reeves and Bednar, 1994).

Quality is value From an economic point of view, value can be seen as the incorporation of features and benefits of products or services for the customer, as compared with the price (or cost) of obtaining this product or service. Feigenbaum (1951) introduced the idea that value must be included in any definition of quality:

> Quality does not have the popular meaning of 'best' in any absolute sense. It means 'best for certain customer conditions'. These conditions are (a) the actual use and (b) the selling price of the product. Product quality cannot be thought of apart from the product cost. (Feigenbaum, 1951: 14)

Value is a very popular managerial concept. For instance our definition of performance, outlined in Chapter 1, is based on the comparison of the value generated by the firm and the value expected by the stakeholders. In the same chapter value is defined in the Service Profit Chain as a comparison of the results the customers receive and their total costs, including the price and other costs the customers incur in acquiring services. Value is often a perception-based measure: customers and stakeholders perceive value.

Quality is conformance to specifications While the previous definitions of quality are subjective, Shewhart (1931), and later Juran (1988), introduce a more objective way of looking at quality. This more engineering point of view includes two important steps. The first one is to translate the 'wants' of the customer into 'physical' characteristics of the manufactured product (Shewhart, 1931). *Quality Function Deployment* (QFD) has been proposed as a technique for translating customer requirements into the product design as well as in the design and operation of production systems (Evans and Dean, 2000: 98). QFD is successfully used by manufacturers of clothing, electronics, electrical appliances and construction equipment, and is increasingly used in the service sector.

The second step is to 'set up ways and means of obtaining a product which will differ from the arbitrarily set standards from these quality characteristics (Shewhart, 1931: 53–4). This gave birth to more statistically oriented techniques such as *Statistical Process Control* (SPC). The purpose of Statistical Process Control is to try to keep the variation of processes under control by detecting assignable causes (as opposed to common or unassignable causes) (Liberators, 2001). Such thinking has led to the still very popular *Six Sigma* programmes, originally developed by Motorola. The basic idea behind Six Sigma is to limit the number of defects as much as possible. Six Sigma programmes have combined statistical and non-statistical methods in order to improve businesses (Pearson, 2001). The main distinctive feature in Six Sigma programmes is the focus on measurement, data-driven analysis and control. This kind of statistical thinking is extremely useful when a tangible product is produced. Conformance to specification is rather inappropriate in a high-contact service environment because it is very difficult (and in many cases impossible) to specify standards (Reeves and Bednar, 1994).

Quality is meeting and exceeding customer expectations Quality defined as conformance to specifications is sometimes considered as a more inward-looking definition of quality. According to Berry, Parasuraman and Zeithaml (1988), this definition of quality is misleading because it is the customer who defines the specifications. Although Shewhart and Juran also recognized the importance of customer wants in defining quality, they gave no advice on how to assess these wants. As to Berry and his colleagues, customers assess service quality 'by comparing what they want or expect and what they actually get or perceive they are getting' (Berry et al., 1988: 37). So quality has something to do with expectations and performance as actually perceived by the customer. This definition of quality is based on the so-called '*Paradigm of Disconfirmation*' (De Carvalho and Leite, 1999). A customer is only satisfied when the actual performance is equal or better than expected.[1] Of course, an important question is to identify the components (called service quality dimensions) for which customers have expectations and perceive performance. (These service quality dimensions will be discussed later in this chapter.) In trying to explain the gap between customer expectations and customer performance, Parasuraman, Zeithaml and Berry (1985) came up with a '*gap model*' consisting of four causes leading to the gap in expectations and performance.

- The gap between management perception of consumer expectations and expected service by the customer. For instance, a field service engineer sometimes knows very well what their customers want. This kind of information is not always fed back to the company. In the longer term this may lead to role conflict. Market research can help close this gap.
- The gap between management perception of consumer expectations and the translation of those perceptions into service quality specifications. The quality specifications (which can be set in quality

systems such as ISO 9000 are not fine-tuned on the customer expectations. Quality Function Deployment can be very useful in closing this gap. Refer to Chapter 7 for more details on Quality Function Deployment (QFD).

- The gap between service quality specifications and the actual service delivery. Lack of resources can make it impossible for employees to work up to the quality specifications. Other factors contributing to the closing of this gap are teamwork, employee–job fit, technology–job fit, perceived control, supervisory control systems, role conflict and role ambiguity (Zeithaml et al., 1988).
- The gap between the actual service delivery and the way the organization communicates about it. External communication of what the customer can expect through advertising can be important in reducing this gap.

The gap model shows that quality, defined as meeting or exceeding expectations, is a complex construct which is difficult to operationalize and to measure because expectations and perceptions are not easy to measure.

Different definitions of quality: summary The different definitions of quality can be positioned in a historical perspective (Walburg, 1997). The conformance to specifications of Shewhart and others fits well in an industrial world where quality inspection was the main area of attention. The next era is that of quality assurance, where the customer comes into the story and where quality is expanded from the production function to all different functional areas in a company. Deming, Crosby, Juran and Feigenbaum are the protagonists of this stage.[2] The last stage is that of *Total Quality Management*. The value-based definition can be positioned here, certainly when values of all different stakeholders are taken into account. Total Quality Management implies that quality is a matter for everyone involved with the company. Quality is completely integrated in the operational, tactical and strategic management. A last stage is that of continuous improving, innovating and learning in order to strive for excellence.

Quality in manufacturing and services

Based on the previous discussion, it also becomes clear that manufacturing companies and service firms (certainly those firms with a lot of interactions with customers) are confronted with different quality issues. For instance, quality in manufacturing revolves around the design of the tangible product and one of the big quality issues is the conformance of this product to the predetermined specifications. Quality control is an important tool in guaranteeing this conformance. One essential goal of quality control is to avoid what the customer perceives as non-conformance and errors. In the delivery of services where the customer is often present during the 'production', errors cannot be hidden. Moreover, an error in one aspect of service delivery can have a much larger impact on the perceived service quality than another one. This is especially the case when the transaction is not tangible.

In *manufacturing*, the following quality dimensions are recognized:

- Performance – a product's primary operating characteristics;
- Features – the 'bells and whistles' of a product;
- Reliability – the probability of a product's surviving over a specified period of time under stated conditions of use;
- Conformance – the degree to which physical and performance characteristics of a product match pre-established standards;
- Durability – the amount of use one gets from a product before it physically deteriorates or until replacement is necessary;
- Serviceability – the ability to repair a product quickly and easily;
- Aesthetics – how a product looks, feels, sounds, tastes and smells;
- Perceived quality – subjective assessment resulting from image, advertising or brand names (Garvin, 1984; Evans and Dean, 2000).

Several authors have tried to identify the *service quality* dimensions. Parasuraman and his colleagues (1985) originally listed ten determinants or dimensions of service quality (see Table 4.1). This list was made up as a result of focus group studies with service providers and customers. Later, they found a high degree of correlation between communication, competence, courtesy, credibility and security, and therefore merged them into one dimension, which they called 'assurance'. Similarly, they found a high correlation between access and understanding which they merged into 'empathy'. The researchers claimed that the dimensions are sufficiently generic that they could cover a wide spectrum of service sectors (Van Ossel, 1998). Using the expectation–performance gap and these dimensions, they developed an instrument to measure service quality, the so-called *Servqual* tool. Although a lot of critique has been formulated on this tool (Buttle, 1996), a wealth of empirical studies show that Servqual can be used in many different service situations such as health care, banks, and many others. However, the five basic dimensions are not always recognized.

Table 4.1 An overview of service quality dimensions

1. Reliability involves consistency of performance and dependability. It also means that the firm performs the service right first time and honours its promises. Specifically, it may involve:
   - accuracy in billing;
   - performing the service at the designated time.

2. Responsiveness concerns the willingness or readiness of employees to provide service. It may involve:

- mailing a transaction slip immediately;
- calling the customer back quickly;
- giving prompt service (e.g., setting up appointments quickly).

3. Competence means possession of the required skills and knowledge to perform the service. It involves:
   - knowledge and skill of the contact personnel;
   - knowledge and skill of operational support personnel;
   - research capability of the organization.

4. Access involves approachability and ease of contact. It may mean:
   - the service is easily accessible by telephone;
   - waiting time to receive service is not extensive;
   - convenient hours of operation and convenient location of service facility.

5. Courtesy involves politeness, respect, consideration and friendliness of contact personnel (including receptionists, telephone operators, etc.). It includes:
   - consideration for the consumers property;
   - clean and neat appearance of public contact personnel.

6. Communication means keeping customers informed in language they can understand and listening to them. It may mean that the company has to adjust its language for different customers. It may involve:
   - explaining the service itself and how much the service will cost;
   - explaining the trade-offs between service and cost;
   - assuring the consumer that a problem will be handled.

7. Credibility involves trustworthiness, believability and honesty. It involves having the customer's best interests at heart. Contributing to credibility are:
   - company name and reputation;
   - personal characteristics of the contact personnel;
   - the degree of hard sell involved in interactions with the customer.

8. Security is the freedom from danger, risk or doubt. It may involve:
   - physical safety;
   - financial security and confidentiality.

9. Understanding/knowing the customer involves making the effort to understand the customer's needs. It involves:
   - learning the customer's specific requirements;
   - providing individualized attention.

10. Tangibles include the physical evidence of the service:
    - physical facilities and appearance of personnel;
    - tools or equipment used to provide the service;
    - physical representations of the service, such as a plastic credit card.

Source: Buttle (1996)

Principles of Total Quality

As said before, *Total Quality* means that the value of all stakeholders involved in the company is maximized. 'Total Quality works across functions and departments, involves all employees, top to bottom, and extends backward and forward to include the supply chain and the customer chain' (Evans and Dean, 2000: 13). There are some fundamental principles underlying Total Quality, which can be found in many studies:

- Customer focus;
- Participation and teamwork;
- Continuous improvement and learning (Evans and Lindsay, 1999).

These three basic principles of TQ are further supported by an integrated organizational infrastructure, a set of management practices and a wide variety of tools and techniques. Important components of the organizational infrastructure are:

- Leadership;
- Strategic planning;
- Human resources management;
- Process management;
- Data and information management.

Many of these principles of Total Quality and components of organizational infrastructure can be found in the integrating frameworks for achieving Total Quality and Performance Excellence.

Frameworks for achieving Total Quality and Performance Excellence

Totally in line with the 'quality is excellence' definition, the *European Foundation for Quality Management* (EFQM) was founded in 1988 by the presidents of 14 major European countries, with the endorsement of the European Commission. The main aim of EFQM was to apply principles of Total Quality Management in European business to make it more competitive (Jackson, 1999). Following the successes of the Deming Prize in Japan and the Malcolm Baldrige National Quality Award (MBNQA) in the USA, EFQM adopted the principle of self-assessment and introduced a European Quality Award (EQA). EFQM defined self-assessment as '. . . a comprehensive, systematic and regular review of an organization's activities and results referenced against the EFQM Excellence Model. The self-assessment process allows the organization to discern clearly its strengths and areas in which improvements can be made and culminates in planned improvement actions which are then monitored for progress' (European Foundation for Quality Management, 1994). The *EFQM Excellence Model* (Figure 4.2) provides a tried-and-tested framework, an accepted basis for evaluation and a means to facilitate comparisons both internally and externally.

The EFQM Excellence Model is based on nine criteria, grouped into two parts: enabler criteria and results criteria (see Table 4.2). The five enabler criteria are Leadership, Policy and Strategy, People, Partnerships and Resources, and Processes. Central to the use of the enablers in the EFQM Excellence Model is the RADAR approach. In this four-step approach an

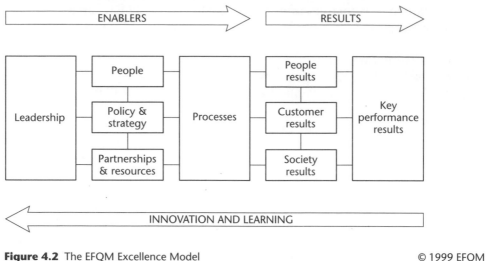

Figure 4.2 The EFQM Excellence Model   © 1999 EFQM
Source: European Foundation for Quality Management (1999b)

organization needs to determine the Results it is looking for, plan and develop sound Approaches to attain the results, Deploy the approaches in a proper way and finally Assess and Review the approaches. This is very similar to the Plan, Do, Check, Act cycle of Deming. The four results criteria are Customer results, People results, Society results and Key performance results.

In terms of the results, the questions of the EFQM Excellence Model aim at defining the organization's actual performance, the organization's performance against its own targets and, if possible, the performance compared to competitors and 'best in class' organizations (Porter and Tanner, 1996; European Foundation for Quality Management, 1999b).

There is a dynamic relationship between the enablers and the results: excellence in the enablers will be visible in the results. An organization using the scoring profile of the EFQM Excellence Model can earn up to 1,000 points distributed among the nine categories.

The EFQM Excellence Model is a non-prescriptive framework of criteria. In other words, it recognizes that there are many approaches to achieving excellence. In line with this observation that organizations can follow a different path to excellence, EFQM introduced in 2001 different levels of recognition of the efforts and progress of organizations towards quality management. While before only the European and National Quality Awards were available, now organizations can apply for the 'Recognition of Achievement in Excellence' and the 'Recognition of Commitment in Excellence' (European Foundation for Quality Management, 2001a). The European Quality Award is the key stimulator of excellence for role model organizations. The Recognition of Achievement in Excellence is designed for organizations that aspire to become best in class. The application for this recognition scheme is shorter and the assessment is modified. Finally, the recognition of commitment is designed for organizations at the

Table 4.2 A description of the nine criteria areas of EFQM

The Criteria

Enablers	Results
1. Leadership **How** leaders develop and facilitate the achievement of the mission and vision, develop values required for long-term success and implement these via appropriate actions and behaviours, and are personally involved in ensuring that the organization's management system is developed and implemented.	**6. Customer results** **What** the organization is achieving in relation to its external customers.
2. Policy and strategy **How** the organization implements its mission and vision via a clear stakeholder-focused strategy, supported by relevant policies, plans, objectives, targets and processes.	**7. People results** What the organization is achieving in relation to its people. **8. Society results** **What** the organization is achieving in relation to local, national and international society as appropriate.
3. People **How** the organization manages, develops and releases the knowledge and full potential of its people at an individual, team-based and organization-wide level, and plans these activities in order to support its policy and strategy and the effective operation of its processes.	**9. Key performance results** **What** the organization is achieving in relation to its planned performance.
4. Partnerships and resources **How** the organization plans and manages its external partnerships and internal resources in order to support its policy and strategy and the effective operation of its processes.	
5. Processes **How** the organization designs, manages and improves its processes in order to support its policy and strategy and fully satisfy, and generate increasing value for, its customers and other stakeholders.	

Source: European Foundation for Quality Management (1999b)

beginning of the path to excellence. The emphasis is on helping organizations to understand their current level of performance and to establish improvement priorities.

During the development of the EFQM Excellence Model, several questions were raised about the relationship of this model with other 'models' such as the Balanced Scorecard and ISO 9000. While the Balanced Scorecard is designed to communicate and assess strategic performance, the EFQM Excellence Model focuses on encouraging the adoption of good practice across all management activities of the organization (Lamotte and Carter, 2000).

A self-assessment by the EFQM Excellence Model seeks to establish how well an organization defines and manages the process of strategic planning. The Scorecard, on the other hand, tests the validity of the strategy and monitors the organization's performance against its delivery on regular and frequent basis. (Nilsson and Samuelsson, 2000: 2)

While self-assessment based on EFQM looks at the management of Total Quality, ISO asks more for a quality assurance assessment or audit. An audit confirms (or not) that the requirements in the standard are being met. A *standard* is a quality system standard that guides a company's performance of specified requirements in the areas of design/development, production, installation and service (Evans and Lindsay, 1999). It must be recognized that over the last 15 years, ISO has gradually become the *de facto* quality (system) standard worldwide. To stay competitive, organizations need ISO certification.

Traditionally, ISO is very much oriented on the process area of the EFQM Excellence Model. The major differences between ISO and EFQM is that the former is prescriptive and the latter is not. The openness of the EFQM Excellence Model introduces more room for creativity and its holistic approach makes it more complex. In contrast, ISO procedures can be deployed without the complexity of a holistic approach (European Foundation for Quality Management, 2001b). In business practice, EFQM and ISO are considered complementary, since they are both used as management tools. ISO enables better management of production processes, while the Excellence Model is used for self-assessments and long-term orientation.

The new ISO 9001:2000 includes some major new features also covered by the EFQM Excellence Model. These new features include customer feedback, business improvement, ideas from the Deming Cycle (Plan–Do–Check–Act) and new requirements for management when dealing with customers and suppliers (European Foundation for Quality Management, 2001b). As such, the new ISO 9001:2000 is going a step further towards the excellence idea. This is even more true for the ISO 9004:2000. It is considered as a guide for organizations that want to expand further and improve the quality system after implementing ISO 9001. It is possible to position ISO 9000, ISO 9001:2000 and EFQM as stages on the journey to excellence (see Figure 4.3).

[Figure 4.3] shows where an organization stands in its journey to excellence. In a first phase, organizations tend to focus only on product conformity in order to obtain basic ISO certification (ISO 9001 version 1994). In the second phase, organizations start paying attention to customer satisfaction (ISO 9000 version 2000). The third phase sees organizations becoming mature enough to be interested in the EFQM methodology with its broader focus on customer and stakeholder satisfaction. The graph also shows that ISO versions are gradually moving up the scale. The new EFQM Recognition and Advice Scheme creates a new low-end emphasis for EFQM methodologies. The two methods are getting closer to one another. ISO 9004 looks certain to continue this trend by

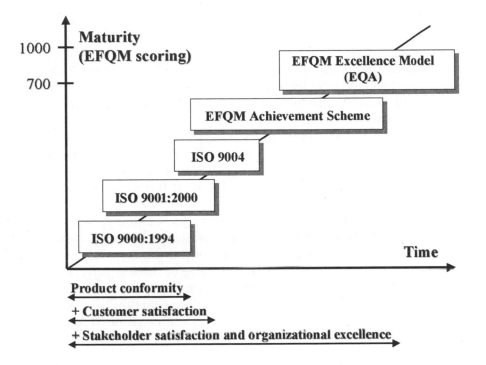

Figure 4.3 EFQM and ISO 9001:2000 – Different stages on the journey to excellence
Source: European Foundation for Quality Management (2001b)

including self-assessment of quality and management systems. The range of methodologies is becoming more complete. Whatever the maturity of an organization, there will always be a logical next step for implementing excellence. (European Foundation for Quality Management, 2001b: 4)

The different stages in Figure 4.3 can also be described using our different definitions of quality. The first stage is the 'quality to conformance to specification' stage where ISO 9001 is a useful tool to attain this kind of quality. The idea of 'quality is meeting and exceeding customer expectations' is the characteristic of the second stage. This is an important characteristic of the ISO 9001:2000. In the third stage satisfaction of all stakeholders is introduced. This is reflected in the ISO 9004 and the EFQM Recognition and Advice Scheme. Finally, the EFQM Excellence Model supports the achievement of quality as excellence. How organizations look at quality and which models they use depend on the maturity of this company on the journey to excellence.[3]

Time-Based Competition

Time-Based Competition: what's in a name?

The expression 'Time-Based Competition' (TBC) was invented by George Stalk and his colleagues from the Boston Consulting Group. George Stalk and James Abegglen first observed the evolution of Just-In-Time (JIT) production systems in Japanese companies, such as Toyota (Stalk and Abegglen, 1985). They learned how these JIT companies reduced throughput time in production and how they developed JIT to an organization-wide management philosophy. These JIT companies were the first time-based competitors of the world. Based on their observations, Stalk and Abegglen (1985) defined Time-Based Competition as 'the extension of JIT principles into every facet of value delivery cycle, from research and development through marketing and distribution'.

Both concepts, JIT and TBC, have the same goals: eliminate waste in the production or the service delivery process. Waste is anything that does not add value to a product or a service. In many instances, waste involves activities which do not contribute to the value of the company. Through the elimination of waste time, more time can be spent on value-added activities. While JIT looks more at the operations function, TBC considers the whole value chain and focuses on the total time required to produce and deliver products and services (Blackburn, 1991).

Principles of Time-Based Competition

The basic principle of Time-Based Competition is to react faster on changes in the environment and to be more flexible than competitors in order to grow faster. One of the key issues in Time-Based Competition is to reduce the development time of new products and services. A flexible operations process, a fast reaction and innovation are the key elements in order to attract profitable customers. The new company strategy is 'the highest value for the lowest cost in the shortest time'.

Time in itself is not necessarily the only driver for Time-Based Competition. Shorter lead times generate many secondary effects, such as higher efficiency, higher supplier reliability and flexibility. Figure 4.4 summarizes how total lead time can be reduced and why it should be reduced.

A first step in Time-Based Competition is to eliminate non-value-added activities. For example, one study found that for each dollar spent in the hospital, 60 cents are 'wasted' on non-value-added activities such as coordination, planning, communication and documentation. Another study found that barely 25 per cent of the total available time of a CT-scan in a hospital was used for investigations. The other 75 per cent of the time was spent on waiting for patients, set-up, etc. In the same way, one can wonder why a request for underwriting an insurance policy requires two or three weeks while no more than a couple of hours is needed to produce a written policy.

One of the major causes of the long lead times is the bad or difficult

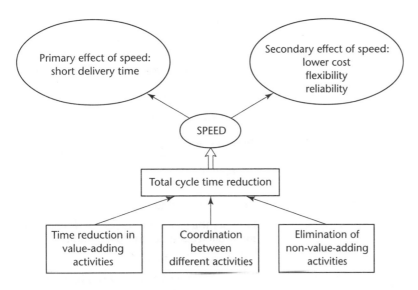

Figure 4.4 The causes and effects of speed

coordination between different activities. For instance, in the insurance example a request for underwriting is going through different workstations such as distribution clerks, underwriting teams, rating agents and policy writers. The probability is high that one of the workstations is a bottleneck, slowing down the whole process. In a manufacturing company, the relationship between the R&D department and the production department is crucial in the time required to bring innovations to the market.

Finally, the value-added activities are not always performed in an efficient way. For example, sometimes work needs to be redone because the product does not satisfy the standards. It is quite clear that here quality and Total Quality are coming in. If the photos are not clear after a CT-scan, the procedure must be repeated, leading to a longer throughput for the patient and taking away time for other investigations.

Besides the primary effect of being faster, Time-Based Competition also generates secondary effects in costs and quality. This will be explored in the next section.

Quality, time and cost

Eliminating non-value-adding activities or preventing rework in order to work faster are strategies totally in line with quality management. There is a bi-directional relationship between speed and quality. Speed is a component of quality because it contributes to the satisfaction of customers; at the same time, quality is a necessary condition in order to produce or deliver goods or services quickly (Stalk and Hout, 1990).

Becoming a time-based competitor is a strategy that goes arm in arm with Total Quality Management. This can be seen in Table 4.3 where a traditional company is compared with a time-based competitor. Based on these comparisons, it can be said that a time-based competitor is one of the ultimate stages on the path to excellence.

Table 4.3 Comparing a traditional company and a time-based competitor

Traditional companies	Time-based competitors
Improve one function a time.	Improve the whole system and focus on core activities.
Work in departments and batches.	Generate a continuous stream of work.
Eliminate bottlenecks to speed up work.	Evaluate the whole design of the system and the organization before speeding up work.
Invest to reduce cost.	Invest to reduce time.
Information is created and diffused by specialist.	Information is created and used by teams.
Managers build information bridges throughout the organization.	Multifunctional groups build their own sources of information to do the daily work.
Central handling, slow feedback.	Local handling and fast feedback.

Source: Stalk and Hout (1990)

In looking at the relationship between cost and quality, one must be aware of the 'old' misconception that improving quality is expensive (DeFeo, 2001). Of course engaging in activities such as self-assessment or introducing Six Sigma programmes costs money, without, at first glance, short-term benefits. The problem is that the cost of poor quality is often hidden and not quantified. As Feigenbaum states: 'Quality costs mean the cost of delivering complete customer satisfaction through accounting for quality in a way that links quality and business improvement. It helps provide increased customer value capability.' (Feigenbaum, 2001: 26)

The cost of quality has two primary components. The first component is the *cost of quality disconnects*. This includes internal and external failure costs. Internal failure costs are the result of unsatisfactory quality found before the delivery of a product or service to the customer, for example, the cost of rework. The external failure costs relate to the costs associated with customers being exposed to poor quality. The cost of customers who complain and ask for recovery is an example in this latter category (Evans and Lindsay, 1999). The second component comprises the *cost of quality investment*, including prevention and assessment. Prevention costs are those that stop non-conforming products from occurring and reaching the customer. The salaries of people involved in quality planning is an example of a prevention cost. Appraisal costs are those associated with efforts to ensure conformance to requirements, for example the costs of inspection and testing (Evans and Lindsay, 1999).

It is important to measure failure cost (certainly when it becomes external) in the right way. These costs can lead to customer deficiencies and unsatisfied customers can become 'terrorists' for the company. In this case the tree of excellence will no longer have leaves. In contrast, an organization can show (just as the foliage of the tree) how well it performs by doing it right the first time and by avoiding external failures. This kind of image can attract new customers or make existing customers loyal. In other words, striving for excellence is not only a matter of cost, but also a matter of business.

Conclusion

We conclude by linking the many different concepts introduced in this chapter. The alert reader has discovered that at several points in this chapter, four stages on the path to excellence are recognized. Table 4.4 summarizes the characteristics of these four stages. In Chapter 7, we will use this four-stage approach to position different quality management tools and techniques. The core assumption is that each stage requires specific ways to deal with quality and that a firm needs to determine carefully at which stage it is positioned before engaging in the quality journey.

Table 4.4 Four stages in the journey to quality excellence

	Stage 1	Stage 2	Stage 3	Stage 4
Aspiration of the operations function	Internally neutral	Externally neutral	Internally supportive	Externally supportive
Definition of quality	Quality is conformance to specifications	Quality is meeting and exceeding customer expectations	Quality is value	Quality is excellence
The (self-) assessment framework	ISO 9001	ISO 9001:2000 and EFQM Commitment to Excellence Scheme	ISO 9004 and EFQM Achievement of Excellence Scheme	EFQM Quality Award Scheme
Strategy based on	Costs and quality, as defined in stage 1	Costs and quality, as defined in stages 1 and 2	Costs and quality, as defined in stage 3	Time and quality, as defined in stages 3 and 4

Notes

1 Service quality and customer satisfaction are very closely related concepts. In the literature both have been defined as the degree and direction of discrepancy between expectations and perceptions. The difference (suggested by some authors) is that *satisfaction* describes expectations as predictions made by customers while *quality*

views expectations as desires or wants of consumers (Reeves and Bednar, 1994: 435).

2   Their key works are: Deming, W.E. (1986) *Out of Crisis*, MIT Center for Engineering Study, Cambridge, MA; Crosby, P.B. (1979) *Quality is Free*, McGraw-Hill, New York; Juran, J.M. and F.M. Gryna (1988) *Juran's Quality Control Handbook*, 4th edn, McGraw-Hill, New York; Feigenbaum, A.V. (1991) *Total Quality Control*, 3rd edn revised, McGraw-Hill, New York.

3   This maturity can be defined in terms of EFQM scoring on 1,000 points.

5 Managing Risk, Managing Value

KURT VERWEIRE AND LUTGART
VAN DEN BERGHE

'Managing risk, managing value' is the title of an executive briefing on enterprise-wide risk management, written by James DeLoach.[1] The statement reflects very well the importance of new approaches to risk management when formulating and implementing a company's strategy. In a more volatile world, the challenge for companies is increasingly to take a proactive approach and to understand better the odds of the game. A company's share price is significantly influenced by the way it is able to anticipate and to manage an uncertain future. Some corporations have boosted their market value by carefully developing risk management strategies. Others have destroyed it by a lack of adequate risk management procedures. Risk management is becoming important in boardrooms as well. For example, the Turnbull Report tries to establish best governance practices by adopting a risk-based approach to designing, operating and maintaining a sound system of internal control.[2] Therefore, a book on Integrated Performance Management should at least offer an overview of the new developments in the risk management field.

In this chapter, we start with a definition and description of some basic concepts on risk and risk management. We then focus on the traditional approaches towards risk management and explore the new developments towards strategic risk management.[3]

(Strategic) risk and risk management: some introductory concepts

Risk and strategic risk defined

As the statement above indicates, risk is central in our daily lives. Although everyone has a notion of the concept of *risk*, no universally accepted definition exists. Often associations are made between risk and uncertainty, risk and danger, risk and damage, and risk and the probability of profit (speculative risks). According to Harold Skipper (1998), professor of risk management and insurance at Georgia State University, risk is commonly used to refer to insured items ('that building is a poor risk'), to causes of loss ('we insure against the risks of fire, windstorm . . .'), and to the chance of loss ('the risk of loss is high').

Statisticians and economists associate risk with variability. A commonly found definition of risk is: 'the relative variation of the actual from the expected outcome'. Or put differently: 'a situation is risky if a range of outcomes exists and the actual outcome is not known in advance' (Skipper, 1998: 6). This last definition of risk can also be translated to the strategic context: we can use the term *strategic risk* to indicate 'unpredictability or down-side unpredictability of business outcome variables such as revenues, costs, profit, market share, and so forth' (Bromiley et al., 2001: 261). Strategic risk can also be defined as the probability of not realizing the intended goals and targets. Along similar lines, James DeLoach defines *business risk* as 'the level of exposure to uncertainties that the enterprise must understand and effectively manage as it executes its strategies to achieve its business objectives and create value' (2000: 50). From these definitions, it is clear that strategic risk and business risk can be used as synonyms to denote overall organizational risk. In the remainder of this chapter, we focus our attention on strategic (or business) risk.

Sources of strategic risk

There are various sources of organizational (and strategic) risk and various ways to classify them.[4] *Operations risk*, one of the main internal risks, is the risk of a defect in one of the core operating or processing activities (or capabilities). For most companies, the management of operations risks is where the action is. *Competitive risk*, or external risk, is the risk associated with changes in the competitive environment that could impair the business's ability to create value successfully. *Asset impairment risk* is a third source of risk. An asset becomes impaired when it loses a significant portion of its current value due to a reduction in the likelihood of receiving those future cash flows. Market and credit risk, as defined in the financial services industry, are good examples of this risk category. The impairment of intellectual property rights is another example in this respect (Simons, 2000). DeLoach (2000) adds another category of risks: *information for decision-making risks*. These risks arise when information used to support business decisions is incomplete, out of date, inaccurate, late or irrelevant to the decision-making process.

One special category of risk deserves some specific attention: *misrepresentation and fraud*. This risk can be considered as an internal risk, but is different in nature from the operations risk or the information for decision-making risk. Misrepresentation and fraud generally occur because employees are put under pressure (e.g., to show increased profits in periods of economic downturn). Then, they may misrepresent their performance or that of their business, or misappropriate company assets. Bad decisions can be covered up and expose the firm to the loss of valuable assets, or might even destroy the business. Of course, in many cases the management itself gets caught in this web. Examples are numerous, but the Enron case – for a long time considered to be one of the best managed companies in the risk management literature – is perhaps the most painful one.

All these different sources of risk ultimately influence the *franchise (or reputation) risk*. This is the risk that the value of the entire business erodes due to a loss of confidence by critical stakeholders. As such, it is a measure of *stakeholder vulnerability*. The franchise risk is not a source of risk, rather it is a consequence of excessive risk in one of the sources of risk (Simons, 2000: 262).

There are many other typologies of 'organizational risk', and there is great confusion about the terminology as well. For example, in Figure 5.1, the term 'business risk' is used in a more specific context than we have done so far.

Risk has also been investigated in great detail in the finance and insurance world. Figure 5.1 distinguishes between market risk, credit risk and liquidity risk. In finance books, you will also find other risks (such as default risk, interest rate risk, exchange rate risks, etc.). Another common classification that finance researchers make is between systematic risk and non-systematic risk (or firm-specific risk). *Systematic risk* is the risk that is attributable to macro-economic factors (e.g., political risks). *Firm-specific risk* reflects risks peculiar to an individual firm that is independent of market risk (Bodie et al., 1999). If we talk about strategic and business risk, we mainly focus on the firm-specific risks.

The finance people have significantly contributed to new insights in the risk management field, and have developed new tools and

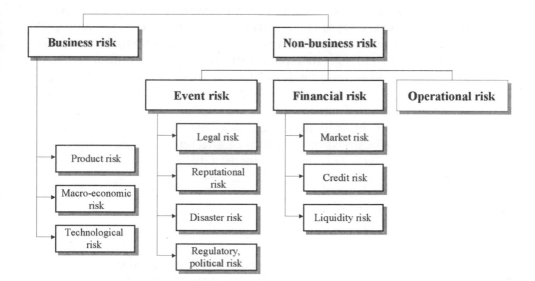

Figure 5.1 Another classification of 'organizational risks'
Source: Adapted from Jorion (2001: 120)

techniques to monitor and manage financial risk. Financial risk management has been developed since the early 1970s when new risks, such as floating currencies, soaring oil prices and spiking interest rates, emerged. In order to cope with the increased volatility, corporate risk managers have used *derivatives* to handle fluctuations in exchange rates, interest rates and commodity prices. These derivatives are powerful tools for managing financial risks and continue to play an extremely important role, despite some well-known disasters (e.g., Metallgesellschaft, Orange County, Procter & Gamble). The insights developed in the finance literature have been applied to the analysis of non-financial, or real, assets. *Real option theory* is now used to evaluate investment projects that have important follow-on opportunities that the firm may or may not exploit subsequently. Another important development in the field of financial risk management is situated in the reporting on financial risk. *Value at Risk (VaR)* has become a popular standard benchmark for measuring financial risk. This measure has been widely accepted in the financial sector, but major companies (such as Microsoft and Philip Morris) now report their VaR calculations in their annual reports. We refer to the specialized literature for more information on these and other developments in the financial risk management field.

An organization's sensitivity to risk

It is not only important to understand the different sources of risk, but also the sensitivity of the organization to these risks (on whatever level). The organization's sensitivity to risk is a function of three components. The first is the significance or *impact* of the enterprise's exposures *(I)*. This is the impact of an event/set of conditions that could harm the company or the realization of an intended strategy. This impact can be financial or non-financial (e.g., damage to reputation). The second component is the probability (or likelihood) of those different events occurring *(P)*. In many publications on risk and risk management, attention is paid to these two elements.

An organization's sensitivity to risk is also determined by its ability to manage the business implications of different possible future events, if they occur *(M)*. The *residual risk* is a function of these different elements:

$$RISK_{residential} = \frac{I \times P}{M}$$

There will always be some residual risk (sometimes called basis risk), either voluntarily (e.g., because the company has not the appropriate resources to do so or because there is no viable business reason to do so) or involuntarily.

Risk management: what is it all about?

Given the many definitions and sources of risk, it is no wonder that there exist many definitions of risk management. Matthias Haller, professor for risk management and insurance economics at the University of St Gallen in Switzerland, defines risk management as 'an overall concept of thought and action with the following purposes:

- To recognize and assess essential risks in systems threatened by risks, such as families, companies, social institutions;
- To tackle these risks systematically with the use of suitable instruments;
- To draw conclusions for the management and the organization' (Haller, 1999: 16).

Other definitions of risk management are similar: 'risk management is any set of actions taken by individuals or corporations in an effort to alter the risk arising from their primary line(s) of business' (Cummins et al., 1998: 30). The purpose is to reduce the possibility or impact of future events harming an organization or to control the probability that results will deviate from the expected (Zech, 2001). Risk management is performed at different organizational levels. This might explain why risk management means different things to different people. The functional level is more concerned with the operations risks. If we go higher in the organization, then we talk about *strategic risk management* (other terms are: integrated risk management, holistic risk management or enterprise-wide risk management).

Modern risk management has its roots in a number of unrelated disciplines, all of which have contributed to our understanding of the concept. Christopher Clarke and Suvir Varma describe it this way:

Military risk analysis led to the evolution of operational research. Personal and commercial risks generated the insurance and actuarial approach to risk management. Strategic risk analysis and the recognition that the future may not be like the past gave birth to scenario planning. Another approach is the use of option pricing theory to view different alternatives. Currency, interest and credit risks generated a banking approach to risk management and various hedging instruments. Operational and environmental risk management gave rise to contingency planning approaches. (Clarke and Varma, 1999: 415)

In the remainder of this chapter, we discuss some new trends in risk management in greater detail. But first, we describe the traditional approach towards risk management. All this can be summarized in Figure 5.2.

Traditional risk management approaches

According to David Laster, senior economist at Swiss Re, a firm has four possible approaches to managing a given risk: (1) risk avoidance; (2) risk

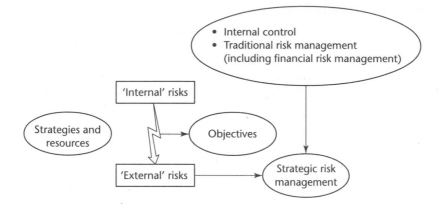

Figure 5.2 Evolutions in risk management

reduction; (3) risk transfer; and (4) risk retention. The first two approaches minimize a firm's exposure to risk and are sometimes referred to as *risk control*. The latter two approaches are known as *risk financing*. The goal of risk financing is to fund losses arising from risks that remain after the risk control (Laster, 1999).

Risk avoidance

Risk avoidance is the first risk management technique. If the pay-offs of a strategy or investment are too uncertain, a firm can choose to abstain from that strategy or investment. In this respect, the firm considers that particular risk unacceptable. What is acceptable or unacceptable depends on combinations of both internal and external factors. A firm might set for itself risk tolerance levels. Once these tolerance levels are exceeded, the firm might decide not to continue with a particular strategy, investment or activity. The firm must also take industry practices and market realities into account. For example, a firm that is unwilling to tolerate major risks and ambiguities cannot hope for much success in rapidly changing fields like pharmaceuticals, biotechnology or electronic commerce (Laster, 1999).

Risk reduction

Every firm faces core risks fundamental to its business that it cannot avoid. There are three ways this core risk can be reduced: (1) loss prevention; (2) loss control; and (3) diversification.

Loss prevention seeks to reduce the likelihood of a given type of risk occurring. The standard examples of loss prevention measures are security devices (e.g., smoke detectors, burglar alarms, airbags or security guards). As with any risk management technique, loss prevention has its limits.

Loss control techniques are designed to reduce the severity of a loss (i.e., the impact of the risk) should it occur. Firewalls and sprinkler systems are loss control techniques in the case of a fire. Stop-loss orders, which automatically trigger a sell order once the value of a stock falls below a certain threshold are a control technique for equity investors.

Diversification is a third risk reduction technique and is about putting your eggs in different baskets. Diversifying product lines across different sectors or countries might reduce the overall risk of a company. According to portfolio theory, a diversified investment portfolio yields a better risk/return profile than a non-diversified one.

Risk transfer

When risks cannot be avoided or retained, they can be transferred to one party who is better equipped or more willing to bear them. Risks can be transferred to *insurance companies*: in exchange for an agreed-upon premium the insurer agrees to indemnify its client, up to a specific limit, in the event of a loss.

Another way that management can transfer risks is through *hedging*, which is the purchase or sale of goods or services for future delivery. Hedging converts an uncertain event into a certain one. For example, consider a French firm that exports most of its product to Great Britain. The firm is vulnerable to the fluctuations in the Euro/pound exchange rate. To offset its foreign exchange exposure, the firm might engage in transactions that bring it profits when the pound depreciates. Then the lost profits from business operations due to a depreciation of the pound will be offset by gains on its financial transactions.[5]

Risk retention

Companies can also retain a variety of risks, whether voluntarily or involuntarily. Voluntary risk retention reflects a conscious decision to absorb certain risk exposures internally, because it is the most cost-effective way of addressing the risk. That is why many large companies have set up captives, which they use as an instrument of self-insurance. Involuntary risk retention occurs when a business fails to identify a given risk exposure and therefore bears the risk unknowingly. Be careful: a risk neglected is a risk retained!

Risk control and internal control

What is the role of internal control in the traditional risk management process? To answer this question, it is necessary to reflect on what is internal control. There are many definitions of internal control. One of the most comprehensive frameworks on internal control was developed by the Committee of Sponsoring Organizations of the Treadway Commission (COSO). They define internal control as 'a process, effected by an entity's board of directors, management and other personnel, designed to provide reasonable assurance regarding the achievement of objectives in the following categories:

- Effectiveness and efficiency of operations;
- Reliability of financial reporting;
- Compliance with applicable laws and regulations' (Committee of Sponsoring Organizations of the Treadway Commission, 1992: 1).

Thus, the goal of an internal control system is to protect assets and to remove the opportunity for inadvertent error or wilful violations in transaction processing and performance measurement (Simons, 2000). The purpose of internal control, as described in this definition, is closely related to the goals of risk management. This is also acknowledged by the Canadian Institute of Chartered Accountants (1995). It argues that the effectiveness of control is dependent upon the extent that risk management goals are achieved: 'Control is effective to the extent that the remaining (uncontrolled) risks of the organization failing to achieve its objectives are deemed acceptable. Control therefore includes the identification and mitigation of risks' (Canadian Institute of Chartered Accountants, 1995: 2).

This means that internal control focuses on risk control, i.e., the avoidance and reduction of organizational risks. Risk assessment is one of the five components of internal control, as identified by COSO. These components should be present in every control framework, whether it is for a large multinational or for a small company. They are derived from the way management runs a business, and are integrated with the management process. COSO describes the five components as follows:

- *The control environment* sets the tone of an organization and influences the control consciousness of its people. It includes integrity, ethical values and competences of the people.
- *Risk assessment* is defined as the identification and analysis of relevant risks to the achievement of an entity's objectives. Based on this analysis, the entity can decide how to manage the risks.
- *Control activities* are the policies and procedures that help ensure management directives are carried out. They help ensure that necessary actions are taken to address risks to the achievement of the entity's objectives. These activities occur throughout the whole organization, at all levels and functions, and include segregation of duties, audits, authorizations, adequate resources, reports . . .[6]
- *Information and communication* is a fourth component of internal control. Pertinent information must be identified, captured and communicated in a form and timeframe that enables people to carry out their responsibilities and to run and control the business.
- *Monitoring* is the process of assessing the quality of the internal control

system's performance over time. It is the control of the control system. This is accomplished through ongoing monitoring activities, separate evaluations or a combination of the two (Committee of Sponsoring Organizations of the Treadway Commission, 1992: 2).

These five components are interrelated, forming an integrated system that reacts dynamically to changing conditions. The internal control system should be intertwined with the entity's operating activities and is most effective when controls are built into the entity's infrastructure and are part of the enterprise.

Towards strategic (or integrated) risk management

Strategic (or integrated) risk management: what is it all about?

The traditional risk management approaches are increasingly being incorporated in the organization's management. However, during the last couple of years a more integrated view on risk management has emerged. This new approach has been labelled either 'integrated risk management', 'strategic risk management', 'holistic risk management' or 'enterprise-wide risk management'. All approaches have in common that they aim at measuring, controlling and managing the overall risk of a company across all risk categories and business lines, using a consistent methodology. Integrated risk management is a 'structured and disciplined approach that aligns strategy, processes, people, technology and knowledge with the purpose of evaluating and managing the uncertainties the enterprise faces as it creates value' (DeLoach, 2000: 5).

Traditional risk management in large corporations is fragmented and compartmentalized. Risk management resides with different people: the risk manager is responsible for pure risks, the treasurer manages financial risks and the chief financial officer tries to achieve an optimal capital structure. Each of these disciplines has its own techniques and its own language, which in turn reinforces specialization and fragmentation. The new approach aims at integration and addresses overall business risk. This requires coordination between the different risk management disciplines. Even if the individual managers are all masters of their respective specialties, their failure to communicate and coordinate with one another will result in a sub-optimal mix of financing, hedging and insurance. The example, described by David Laster, gives a good view on what risk management currently means in practice:

> Consider how risk is often managed within a firm. The CFO determines the optimal capital structure with respect to debt and equity financing. Taking the structure as a given, the treasurer then devises a strategy for raising capital and

hedging financial risks. Meanwhile, in a separate department, the risk manager determines the most expedient way of protecting against accidental and operational risks.

This conventional approach leaves ample room for improvements through coordination. A firm might, for example, be spending hundreds of thousands of dollars to insure its plant and equipment against accidental losses that would be far less devastating than a shift in exchange rates, against which it has little protection. By retaining additional hazard risk and using the savings in premiums to hedge some of its currency exposure, the firm can reduce its overall level of risk. Alternatively, if the insurance market is particularly soft, it might pay for a firm to increase its property/casualty coverage.

To make such decisions in a coherent manner, a firm must have a unified framework with which to view all of its risks. This will enable it to identify and measure its chief risks, or at least get a clear sense of risk management priorities and how much it should be prepared to spend to address them. (Laster, 1999: 26)

As the focus of integrated risk management is on the enterprise-wide risk, it considers not only the negative side of the risk spectrum but also the positive side. Every company faces risks as it tries to capture the opportunities available in the environment. In fact, the business risks are those that the corporation willingly assumes to create a competitive advantage. The new approach towards risk management should provide the organization with the processes and tools they need to become more anticipatory and effective at evaluating, embracing and managing the uncertainties they face. Integrated risk management should enable the company to pursue strategic growth opportunities with greater speed, skill and confidence (Jorion, 2001).

Financial institutions have also noticed this shift in corporate risk management, and are developing new integrated solutions. These new solutions bring risk and capital together. Capital management has always focused on balance sheet optimization in order to minimize the cost of capital; risk management has focused on ensuring that cash flows are regular, predictable and as risk-free as possible, also with the purpose to minimize the cost of capital. Thus, risk management and capital management are two sides of the same coin. These new solutions, called Alternative Risk Transfer solutions, rely on more traditional risk mitigation and risk transfer approaches, but also take advantage of any internal risk hedging opportunities.

New risk management philosophies: higher value added

By setting these purposes, integrated risk management is approached from a totally different perspective: it becomes a tool for management to develop and assess the strategy of the organization. Furthermore, the focus now is on how to create value, rather than on risk control and loss prevention. This is perfectly illustrated in Figure 5.3.

James DeLoach (2000) sees different stages in the risk management perspective, with an associated value added for each step. *Risk management*

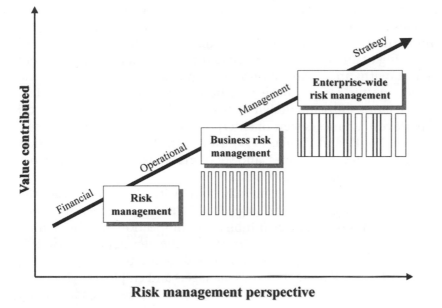

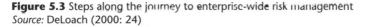

Figure 5.3 Steps along the journey to enterprise-wide risk management
Source: DeLoach (2000: 24)

is a first stage and focuses on financial and hazard risks and internal controls. The focus is more on risk control and loss prevention, and it involves people from treasury, insurance and operations. Risk management tries to minimize unpleasant surprises (risk control and loss prevention) but pays no attention to the positive side of the risk spectrum. This changes when firms have reached the *business risk management* stage. The focus is now on the business risk and the linkage to the opportunity side is much clearer. The business managers are accountable risk by risk. In the last stage, which is labelled the *enterprise-wide risk management* stage, every decision that is made is meant to improve the organization as a whole. Enterprise-wide risk management becomes a disciplined and rational process of pursuing opportunities which can eventually lead to a greater exposure to performance variability, depending on the nature of the firm's business model.

The different steps in the strategic risk management process

It is quite clear that this new philosophy is not created overnight. Building capabilities in risk management is a continuous process, consisting of different steps. For the moment, there is no uniform framework of what the ideal integrated risk management process should look like. However, DeLoach's *Enterprise-wide Risk Management* (2000) provides some valuable lessons and useful ideas for companies which see enterprise-wide risk management as a powerful management process.

Figure 5.4 presents strategic (or integrated) risk management as a continuous process, which should ultimately result in better communication within the company, improved strategy formation and the leveraging of an organization's capabilities. Risk management should be aligned with an organization's strategy and processes. The best companies in this respect have specific and well-defined tasks, clear reporting relationships and designate risk-owners. Many publications on this topic favour a process view of enterprise-wide risk management (see, for instance, Clarke and Varma, 1999). However, DeLoach's framework is one of the most developed ones, and we therefore rely on his framework to explore the process in greater detail.

Strategic risk management generally starts with *developing a common business risk language* and *setting clear goals, objectives and oversight structures.* The lack of a common language inhibits communication and the sharing of best practices. Communication is central in the new approach towards risk management. Adopting a common language is a tool for facilitating an ongoing dialogue among the firm's managers and employees about risk and the processes affected by risk. The classification schemes, identifying

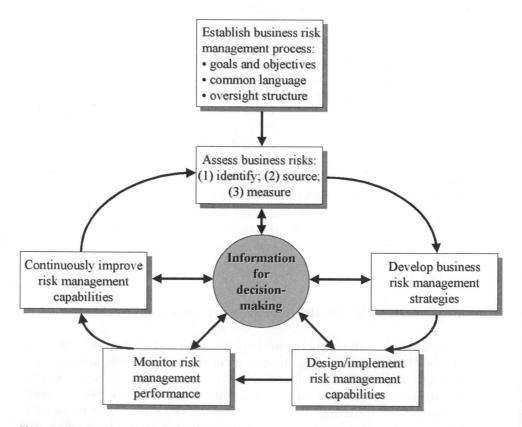

Figure 5.4 The Arthur Andersen enterprise-wide risk management process
Source: DeLoach (2000: 116)

the different sources of risk, are helpful instruments in developing a more systematic understanding of the risks of an organization. Apart from developing a common language, the top management should set clear goals and objectives for the risk management process. Business strategies should provide the context for understanding the risks the organization desires to take. Business policies add the tactical details to the implementation of strategies, and are useful in delineating desired and undesired risks. Top management should also set up clear and effective oversight structures and risk responsibilities. These might include: senior management working committees, a senior executive responsible for the overall organizational risk, job descriptions, authorization levels, clear reporting lines, and so on. In companies with an enterprise-wide risk management strategy, risk management structures go as high as to the board of directors, and the CEO is seen as the 'comprehensive risk executive'.

A second step in the risk management process is to *assess the risk* and to *develop risk strategies*. Assessing risks includes: (1) identifying the risk; (2) sourcing why, how and where the risks originate; and (3) measuring the severity, likelihood and financial impact of the risk. Risk mapping is often used when assessing risks. The focus should be on the risks with a high impact and a high probability of occurring.

For the most important risks, the company should decide the appropriate risk strategy, as identified in traditional risk management: (1) risk avoidance; (2) risk reduction; (3) risk transfer; and (4) risk retention. It is clear that for some risks a company might choose to combine several of these different risk strategies.

After the risk management strategies have been developed, a company needs to design and implement risk management capabilities. Capabilities include the processes, the people, reports, methodologies and technologies (both systems and data) needed to implement a particular strategy. All these different components should be aligned with each other.

The risk management process described so far needs to be *monitored* on an ongoing basis by using metrics, communications and periodic audits and evaluations. This monitoring should indicate where *improvements* are necessary and possible. This, in turn, should lead to improved risk management capabilities. The ultimate goal of this exercise is to *develop information for better decision-making*. In the ideal state, an enterprise-wide view ultimately leads the firm to integrating its business risk management information for decision-making with other information used in the business. The firm measures and reports what matters: all critical information relating to quality, cost, time and risk should be integrated in the performance management framework. In this way, risk management strategies have different functions:

- They support the firm's value creation objectives by reducing the performance variability inherent in its normal future operations;

- They protect accumulated wealth from unacceptable losses;
- They leverage the firm's core competences to produce greater value.

Strategic risk management: a continuous process

The process as presented here describes an ideal state of enterprise-wide risk management. Hardly any company has reached this stage, either because of a lack of vision, resources or capabilities. Arthur Andersen is aware that developing enterprise-wide risk management does not happen overnight. The process described here is an iterative process, where an organization continuously improves its risk strategies. The higher the focus on improving performance, the more organizations will try to remove all significant inefficiencies, including in their risk management practices.

For each type (or group) of risk, the management must evaluate the relative maturity of the firm's risk management capabilities (for the most important risks the company is facing). This maturity model (see Figure

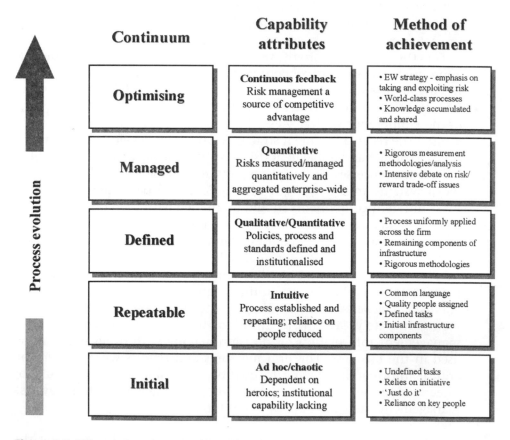

Figure 5.5 Different stages in a maturity continuum
Source: DeLoach (2000) Adapted from Carnegie Mellon University Capability Maturity Model

5.5) was originally developed for software development by the Software Engineering Institute (SEI) and Carnegie Mellon University, but it is an effective framework for discerning risk management capabilities and targeting desired capabilities. (We will again refer to this model in Part III of this book.) The management must make a conscious decision about how much capability is needed to continuously achieve its business objectives. Of course, management must also consider the costs and benefits of increased risk management capabilities.

Once these issues have been addressed, each firm must then decide where on the continuum it wants to be with respect to each type of risk that it intends to manage. Some risks are more important than others. Different risks require different degrees of capability to accomplish management objectives.

Conclusion

In this chapter, we have presented an overview of the most recent trends in risk management. It has become clear that (strategic) risk is a multidimensional concept and risk management has its root in a number of different disciplines. Here too, integration is increasingly becoming important. The new trend towards strategic (or integrated) risk management is the most prominent example in this respect. We have described the Arthur Andersen approach in greater detail, as it is one of the most extensive approaches found in the risk management literature. One of their main conclusions is that integrated risk management should be an integral part of Integrated Performance Management. It has to become more integral to the process of managing a business, not some appendage whose relevance is questioned (DeLoach, 2000: 209).

Notes

1 This executive briefing is based on one of the best publications on strategic (or integrated) risk management we have met so far: James DeLoach (2000). This publication offers valuable insights and frameworks for an innovative risk management approach.

2 The Turnbull Report is the abbreviated name given to guidance provided by the Institute of Chartered Accountants in England and Wales to enable UK companies to implement the internal controls required by the Combined Code on Corporate Governance.

3 We know that the term *strategic risk management* is sometimes used to indicate the management of external risks. We use the term more broadly and see it as a synonym of *integrated* or *enterprise-wide risk management.*

4 Useful classifications can be found in Simons (2000) (where distinction is made between operations risk, asset impairment risk, competitive risk and fraud and misrepresentation); DeLoach (2000) (where distinction is made between externally-driven risk, internally-driven risk and decision-driven risk); and Shimpi (1999)

(which classifies financial/market risk, operational risk, political risk and legal liability risk).

5 Hedging is a common financial instrument. Consequently, all financial textbooks devote sections on this concept. We found a good overview in Bodie, Kane and Marcus (1999).

6 For a good overview of different internal control categories, we refer to Simons (2000), who distinguishes between structural safeguards (segregation of duties, defined levels of authorization and independent audits), systems safeguards (accurate and complete records, secure databases and timely management reports) and staff safeguards (adequate expertise for accounting and control staff, rotation in key jobs and sufficient resources).

PART II

The Integrated Performance Management Framework: Constituent Elements

Integrated Performance Management: towards a more integrated framework

In Part I, we have presented several performance management frameworks that have received a lot of attention in the management literature. All these frameworks have the common aim of increasing the performance of the organization (or department under study), but they differ in how to tackle this overall goal.

In some organizations, these different performance management frameworks compete for the managers' attention and organizational resources. This situation occurs when the organization is structured along the traditional functional silos: control, marketing, finance, risk management, strategic planning, etc. This is an unhealthy situation, where many resources are wasted and employees are frustrated. In fact, this proves the need for a more integrated approach to performance management – to leverage the tools and techniques that have emerged over the last couple of years.

In Part II of this book, we develop a more integrated framework for performance management. Several authors have criticized the fragmentary approach of the publications in this field. The various frameworks that were presented in Part I have focused on different dimensions of the performance concept, but no real, holistic framework has emerged. The purpose of this book is to position all these different frameworks in their broader context. This allows us to better understand their added value.

The overall picture

In order to develop this more integrated framework, we return to the concept of Integrated Performance Management, which we defined as the process that helps an organization to formulate, implement and change its strategy to satisfy its stakeholders' needs. Our starting point is that

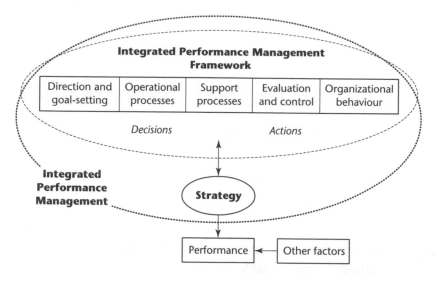

Figure II.1 Integrated Performance Management positioned in a broader context

organizations that develop good strategies and implement them properly will achieve superior long-term performance for their various stakeholders.

As Figure II.1 indicates, achieving superior *performance* is the ultimate goal of every (performance) management system. The success of an organization depends on the presence of a sound, well-formulated and effectively implemented *strategy*. This does not necessarily mean that the strategy has to be written down in detailed plans, but an organization needs to develop a 'consistency of direction, based upon a clear view of the "game" being played and guidelines for competing in order to achieve a position of advantage' (Grant, 1995: 10). Good strategies yield a unique strategic position in the market. Companies that are successful in the long run choose a strategic position that differs from that of their competitors. This unique position allows the companies to charge better prices for their products and services, resulting in superior performance. In the short term, performance is also influenced by other factors (such as general economic conditions or unexpected economic shocks). We believe that these factors have only a modest impact on long-term performance, hence our focus on strategy as the major determinant of an organization's performance.

There is often the misconception that a strategy is the result of a rational decision-making process, whereby the managers of an organization first decide on the best strategy and then take actions to implement the strategy. However, this rational decision-making process is not always observed in practice. In many cases, managers or employees undertake actions that, over time, evolve into some form of strategy. In this situation, organizations formulate strategy after they implement it, not before. They undertake a number of actions, then look back over them and conclude that what they have implemented is a strategy. Strategic planning and strategic exercises are then used to discern a pattern in past actions which is called the strategy (Chakravarthy and White, 2002).

However, whichever come first – decisions or actions – these two elements are viewed as the core elements of the strategy-making and implementation process. Thus, the strategy grows out of the interplay between decisions made and actions taken in *all* the components of the *Integrated Performance Management Framework*. This framework consists of the organization's:

- Direction and goal-setting processes;
- Operational processes;
- Support processes;
- Evaluation (monitoring) and control processes;
- The processes, systems and structures that create commitment and motivation (which is the organizational behaviour component).

The Integrated Performance Management Framework: five major components

Before we investigate the role of Integrated Performance Management in this broader context, it is necessary to study the Integrated Performance Management Framework in greater detail. The five components of the model are presented in Figure II.2.

- *Direction and goal-setting* involves all processes and actions that lead to the formulation and communication of the organization's mission and vision, and their translation into concrete strategies and performance

INTEGRATED PERFORMANCE MANAGEMENT FRAMEWORK				
Direction and goal setting / Objectives	Operational processes	Support processes	Evaluation and control	Organizational behavior • Organizational design • HRM systems • Leadership skills • Reward systems

Figure II.2 Components of the Integrated Performance Management Framework

goals. Direction setting is the most widely recognized managerial activity and involves charting an organization's course, mobilizing support and ensuring alignment with stated goals (Garvin, 1998). It is intuitively clear that at the business unit level, strategy development is an important aspect of direction and goal-setting. But direction and goal-setting is broader because it also involves translating the strategy into concrete goals and targets, communicating these goals, mobilizing support and allocating resources.

- *Operational processes* are those activities and processes that are concerned with the creation or delivery of a product or service. Operations are more than just production activities, they also include logistics, marketing and sales, and service activities. Michael Porter has called these operational processes 'primary activities'. These activities/processes produce goods and services that external customers consume, and they generate the revenues for an organization (Porter, 1985).

- *Support processes* help to improve the effectiveness and efficiency of the operational processes. They do not produce output for external customers, but are necessary to running the business. Support activities include purchasing and procurement, technology development (to improve the products and the processes), finance, accounting, legal and governmental affairs, etc.

- *Evaluation (monitoring) and control processes* are designed to ensure that the organization is performing as planned. These processes detect perturbations, initiate corrective action and restore the organization to its previous equilibrium (Garvin, 1998). Audit, risk management and management control are examples of these types of process. It is worth mentioning that the new view on control also attributes a more proactive approach to the controlling function. As we have said in Chapter 1, the 'command and control' function, previously served by performance measurement systems, has been transformed into a need to 'predict and prepare' the organization to meet the next challenge and to create the next opportunity (Institute of Management Accountants and Arthur Andersen LLP, 1998).

- *Organizational behaviour* is the last component of the Integrated Performance Management Framework. This component aims to create commitment and motivation across all employees and managers within the organization. The organizational behaviour component not only consists of processes but also encompasses structural elements. For example, the organizational design is an important determinant of organizational behaviour, yet this is often overlooked in the performance management literature. In addition, we include HR systems, reward systems and leadership issues in this component.

Figure II.1 suggests that the new framework is designed for business unit managers who are responsible for developing a strategy that is in line with the overall goals, mission and vision of the entire organization. They need to develop more concrete goals and targets, and allocate their resources to realize these goals. The business unit manager is responsible for the operations and support processes (although he or she does not always have full control over some of them) and has to ensure that the business unit performs as planned. The manager has an arsenal of organizational behaviour tools to motivate his or her subordinates and employees and to create commitment to reach the stated goals.

This framework, however, is also useful to corporate managers. Of course, their focus is less on the operational (and support) function and more on direction-setting and monitoring and control. That is, corporate management is involved in developing the overall mission and vision, preparing the business unit plans, and monitoring and controlling these business units. A major task of corporate management is to stimulate business unit managers to act in accordance with the corporate goals. Organizational design, HR practices and reward systems are important tools for creating this goal congruence. It is clear that leadership skills are equally essential.

This framework can also be applied to the functional level in the organization. Functional managers are more involved with operational (and/or support) processes and activities. Their goals are derived from the business unit strategy, and they have to verify whether or not the process yields the expected results. Their arsenal of motivation tools is more limited, but functional managers can and must create the necessary commitment from their employees, and their leadership skills are very important.

Structure of Part II

The purpose of the second part of this book is to develop a more integrated framework for performance management. The first thing that is needed is to identify the constituent elements of such a framework. The Integrated Performance Management Framework, with its five major components, will serve as our guide. In each chapter of Part II, we will explore one of the constituent elements of this business model in greater detail. We will summarize what the management literature tells us about each of these particular components and investigate how to align your strategy with it.

Obviously, strategy is a central concept when striving for strategic alignment. Unfortunately, 'strategy' has become a catchall concept that is used to mean whatever one wants it to mean (Hambrick and Fredrickson, 2001). Therefore, we start the second part of this book with a chapter on strategy. That is, we present an overview of the various performance goals and how they influence an organization's strategy, and explain how these goals and strategies are set and developed.

Chapter 7 moves to the second component of our framework and tackles the operational processes. It addresses how companies can obtain better performance through Business Process Orientation. Business Process Orientation is seen as an answer to the challenge for firms to become more quality-oriented (see Chapter 4). Throughout this process, organizations look differently at the role of operations. In Chapter 7, we explain the different roles companies have to go through in their journey to World-Class Manufacturing.

Chapter 8 focuses on a particular support domain: information technology. This chapter investigates how information technology (IT) and information systems (IS) contribute to an effective strategy implementation. It illustrates how to align support processes with your strategy and how to manage this process.

Chapter 9 tackles the evaluation and control component of our framework: we describe how management control systems can be used to manage company and business performance effectively. Attention is paid to the three major elements of a management control system: (1) the management control structure; (2) the management control process; and (3) the management control culture (beliefs systems).

From then on, we explore the various building blocks of the organizational behaviour component. Organizational design is a hot topic in management and managers are struggling with it. Chapter 10 starts with a discussion of the basic elements of organizational design and how they fit together. We present three 'generation' designs and discuss the implications of these designs for implementing strategy.

Chapter 11 focuses on the new function attributed to human resources management (HRM). The HRM function is increasingly seen as one of the key functions in the development and implementation of a strategic response to the new competitive environment. To make the shift to a strategic partner, HRM faces some new challenges. Chapter 11 will outline them and present some frameworks that show how HRM can become critical to organizational effectiveness.

Chapter 12 is about leadership. It explores how leadership can contribute to the development of superior strategies and their fast and skilful execution. We present a rather personal view on what leadership is, and describe some of the leading theories on leadership.

Reward systems are the last element of the organizational behaviour component. Although they are often considered a major strategy implementation tool, there is still much confusion about what rewarding really is and how it motivates (and often demotivates) people to achieve organizational goals. Chapter 13 explains what reward is all about, how it can become strategic and also how to manage (i.e., formulate and implement) a reward strategy.

When managers talk about performance management, the aspect of organizational change is a major issue in their discussions. In Chapter 14, we will outline how the performance management concept can be translated into a change management approach and how change, learning and performance are inextricably intertwined. We will present some new ideas on the context in which changes take place and learn how 'change-friendly' organizations can boost themselves to maximum performance, thereby illustrating how two eternal enemies – chaos and order – can be structurally reconciled.

Chapter 15 concludes Part II. In this chapter, we reflect on all the different chapters from Part II and make recommendations to integrate the lessons that can be learned from those chapters. This is not an easy task, and we do not pretend that we have an integrated approach towards performance management yet. However, we will show that our Integrated Performance Management Framework is a useful framework that opens many opportunities to guide further research in this new direction.

6 Performance Goals and the Strategy Formation Process

KURT VERWEIRE AND LUTGART
VAN DEN BERGHE

In many organizations, setting clear goals and objectives is the starting point for the strategy formulation and strategy implementation process. Providing a sense of purpose plays an extremely important role in shaping the behaviours of people within an organization, and it is an important lever that top management can use in the Integrated Performance Management process (Chakravarthy and White, 2002). That is why many definitions of strategy and management pay explicit attention to the role of setting performance goals and objectives, often referred to as 'planning'.

In this chapter, we tackle two major questions: (1) What are the performance goals for an organization; and (2) How are these goals set and how are strategies developed? The first question is tackled in the first and second sections of this chapter. We start with a discussion of the organizational purposes of the company as defined in its vision and mission. These can be considered as the performance goals at the corporate level. The mission and vision must then be translated into concrete strategies and actions, which serve as guidelines and benchmarks for the business unit and functional levels.

Given our interest in the process side of the performance management trajectory, we investigate the goal-setting and strategy formation process in the second part of this chapter. There, we also discuss the role of strategic planning in the strategy formation process.

Organizational purpose: what is (the use of) it?

Mission and vision

In Chapter 2, we have already raised the question: What is the purpose of the company, and for whom should value be realized? Companies significantly differ in the goals they set for themselves. At one extreme, there are organizations that have taken the view that the only responsibility of business is *short-term interests of shareholders*. These organizations meet the minimum obligations imposed by the government but no more. At the other end of the spectrum, organizations have purposes that are concerned with *shaping society*, and financial considerations are regarded as of secondary importance or as constraints. Many companies fall somewhere in between and address the interests and expectations of (a larger or smaller number of) stakeholders.

Whatever perspective is chosen, it is very important that it is integrated into the organization's *'sense of purpose.'* Given the many different perspectives that can be adopted, we see that organizations formulate many different goals, ranging from 'becoming the largest company in a particular industry' to 'delivering maximal shareholder value' to 'earning a living for the founder and his family.' Goals can also be defined for different stakeholders. For example, the Co-operative Bank aims at 'delivering value to all its Partners in an equitable manner'. The Co-operative Bank has identified seven partners and for each of them it has developed specific targets and appropriate performance measures.[1]

Many people see growth as one of the main goals of a business company. Clearly, growth is necessary to become the largest player in an industry, and profitable growth is necessary to increase shareholder value. However, not all companies go for growth. For example, growth might be less of an issue when the purpose of the company is to provide financial (and possibly other) means to the founder or his family.

The ultimate goal of any organization should be reflected in the organization's mission and vision. Traditionally, developing the mission and vision of the company is the starting point in the strategic management process. The *mission* outlines the broad directions that the organization should and will follow and briefly summarizes the reasoning and values that lie behind them. These values are often rooted in the personal values of the founders and provide guidance about responsibilities to customers, employees, local communities, shareholders and other important stakeholders. *Core values* explicitly define top management's view of trade-offs (such as short-term performance versus long-term responsibilities) and provide guidance to employees where rules and standard operating procedures alone cannot suffice (Simons, 2000).

In their book *Built to Last*, Jim Collins and Jerry Porras (1994) have demonstrated the role of an *enduring guiding philosophy* in achieving superior performance. They identified 18 'visionary companies', which they define as companies that are premier institutions in their industries, widely admired by their peers, and having a long track record of making a significant impact on the world around them (e.g., Boeing, Ford, Motorola, Walt Disney). Collins and Porras have figured out why these companies have separated themselves into the visionary category. One of the striking characteristics that visionary companies share is that they all pursue a cluster of objectives, of which making money is only one and not necessarily the primary one. Equally important is that these companies are guided by a *core ideology* – or *core values* – and a sense of purpose beyond just making money. Yet, paradoxically, the visionary companies make more money than the purely profit-driven comparison companies. It is not so much the content of this ideology that matters to the company, 'but how deeply it believes its ideology and how consistently it lives, breathes, and expresses it in all that it does' (Collins and Porras, 1995: 21). Furthermore, visionary companies almost religiously preserve these core ideologies, and hardly ever change them. The values survive the trends and fashions of the day, and some of them have even remained intact for well over 100 years. At the same time, visionary companies display a powerful drive for progress which enables them to change and adapt without compromising their cherished goals.

Although there are no good or bad missions, there are good and bad *mission statements*. These are the formal statements in which the mission of a company is written down. A mission statement is a text containing the goals and objectives, the strategic choices and the values of an organization. They exist in all forms and formats and most of them are written in some awfully dreary corporate prose. But there are some exceptions – some mission statements prove to be very powerful and inspiring:

> BancOne Corporation: 'We'll deal with you straight, no fluff and no excuses. . . . We also know that was then and this is now.'

> Microsoft Corporation: 'One vision drives everything we do: a computer on every desk and in every home using great software as an empowering tool.'

Mission statements have become very popular; in some cases, they have even been considered as a cure-all for stuck-in-the-mud businesses. Of course, companies need more than just a good mission statement to achieve good performance. This has also been noted by Collins and Porras: visionary companies have not become visionary through mission statements:

> The visionary companies attained their stature not so much because they made visionary pronouncements (although they often did make such pronouncements). Nor did they rise to greatness because they wrote one of the vision, values, purpose, mission, or aspiration statements that have become popular in management today (although they wrote such statements more frequently than the comparison companies and decades before it became fashionable). Creating a statement can be a helpful step in building a visionary company, but it is only one of the thousands of steps in a never-ending process of expressing the fundamental characteristics we identified across the visionary companies. (Collins and Porras, 1995: 23)

Well-conceived mission statements make sense, as is also acknowledged by Peter Drucker, one of the most influential management gurus of the last decades. He acknowledges that defining the purpose and mission of the organization is difficult, painful and risky, but he considers it crucial to enable the organization to set objectives, to develop strategies and to manage an organization for performance (Drucker, 1974: 94). Good mission statements, which are actively communicated, can give employees a sense of pride, purpose and direction. This sense of direction is often called the *vision* of the organization. It paints a picture of the future that clarifies the direction of the organization ('a possible and desirable future state') and helps individuals to understand why and how they should support the organization. C.K. Prahalad and Gary Hamel (1989) use the term *'strategic intent'* to denominate the desired future state or aspiration of an organization. For Prahalad and Hamel, strategic intent is about creating an obsession to win at all levels within the organization, and then sustaining it over 10 to 20 years. One of the best examples comes from outside the business world: the 'Apollo programme' – landing a man on the moon ahead of the Soviets – was a real strategic intent for Americans in the 1950s and 1960s.[2]

In summary, the vision, the mission and the accompanying core values and beliefs can provide a compass for action and a sense of direction for employees. At the same time, these elements can also be considered part of the control system. In *Levers of Control*, Robert Simons (1995) develops the concept of *beliefs systems*, which he defines as the explicit set of organizational definitions that senior managers communicate formally and reinforce systematically to provide basic values, purpose, and direction for the organization. If expressed vividly and actively, beliefs systems motivate organizational participants to search for and create opportunities to accomplish the overall mission and vision of the firm. We come back to these beliefs systems and other levers of control in Chapter 9.

Influences on organizational purposes

Setting the goals and objectives of a company does not happen in a vacuum. Instead of being independent, self-standing entities, companies are part of a much larger network. We have identified four main influences on organizational purposes: (1) corporate governance; (2) stakeholders; (3) business ethics; and (4) the cultural context. These influences together shape the purposes of an organization at any given time.

According to Johnson and Scholes (1999), *corporate governance* tries to provide an answer to the following questions: (1) Who should the organization serve? and (2) How should the direction and purposes of an organization be determined? In its simplest definition, corporate governance is defined in terms of good and decent management. More complex definitions take into account the tasks directors should perform and pay attention to the 'division of labour' between shareholders, managers and the board of directors. Still others broaden the discussion and take *all* factors into account (e.g., environmental factors) that could influence the goals of the organization. Finally, the more normative definitions provide a framework that can be used to consider and balance the interests of various groups of stakeholders (Van den Berghe and Levrau, 2000).

Stakeholders are the second category of 'influences' on organizational goals. Companies are increasingly adopting a broader perspective, focusing on stakeholders rather than on shareholders. Managers are becoming aware that they need to understand the concerns of shareholders, employees, customers, suppliers, lenders, and society at large, when developing the objectives and the business strategies of the organization. Only in this way will the firm be able to survive in the longer term. Such a stakeholder approach emphasizes actively managing the business environment, relationships and the promotion of shared interests. Furthermore, the interests of key stakeholders must be integrated into the very purpose of the firm, and stakeholder relationships must be managed in a coherent and strategic fashion (Freeman and McVea, 2001). How this can be done has already been described in greater detail in Chapter 2, where we introduced the concept of stakeholder-driven management.

So far, we have viewed organizational purposes as being concerned with the expectations of stakeholders – in particular, those who have formal rights through the corporate governance framework and those stakeholders who are most interested and powerful in other ways. Johnson and Scholes (1999) complete their framework by providing answers to the following questions:

- Which purposes *should* be prioritized? And why?
- Which purposes *are* prioritized? Why?

Ethical considerations are the main guidelines for answering the first question. Ethical issues can be found on several levels. On the macro level, ethics define the extent to which an organization will strive to exceed its minimum obligations to stakeholders. The concept of business ethics is also relevant on the individual level, where it can be applied to both employees and managers.

The question 'Which purposes *are actually* prioritized above others?' is related to a variety of factors in the *cultural context* of the organization. Power and stakeholders are not the only influences on the mission and objectives: company culture – 'the way we do things around here' – is a more subtle, but equally important, issue. Therefore, it is important to understand an organization's culture, since it is the filter and shaper through which all employees develop and implement their strategies (Lynch, 1997).

From mission and vision to strategy and action

Joel Arthur Baker (1991) once said: 'Vision without action is merely a dream. Action without vision just passes the time. Vision with action can change the world.' In his outstanding book, *Performance Measurement and Control Systems for Implementing Strategy*, Robert Simons (2000) clearly summarizes the steps necessary to go from vision to action. Because missions and vision are designed to appeal to all levels of the organization, they must be written with a high degree of abstraction and generality. These inspirational beliefs are typically too vague to provide much concrete guidance and need to be translated into more concrete business objectives. Business strategy and strategic management play a crucial role in this process. As you can see in Figure 6.1, Simons relied on four (of the five) *Ps of strategy*, as identified by Henry Mintzberg.[3] In order to provide further insights on how the process of moving from vision to action can be improved, we need to outline very briefly what strategy and strategic management are all about.

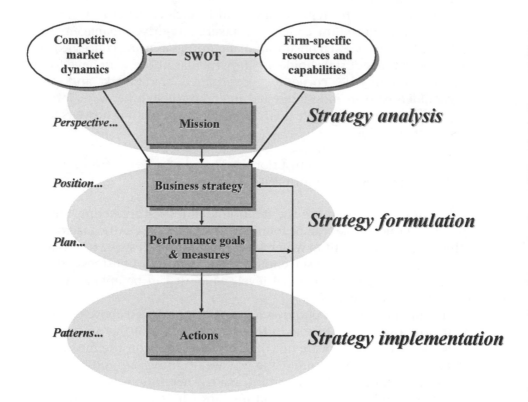

Figure 6.1 Hierarchy of business strategy
Source: Adapted from Simons (2000: 18)

Strategy analysis

Figure 6.1 indicates that a firm's mission (and vision) provides the overarching 'perspective' for the business strategy and all the firm's activities. The strategy of the company and its business units flows directly from its mission but is also influenced by the external and internal environment in which the firm and its business units operate. The analysis of the competitive market dynamics (*external analysis*) seeks to formulate an answer to the following question: What changes are going on in the environment, and how will they affect the organization and its activities? The *internal analysis* identifies firm-specific resources and capabilities, which should provide special advantages or yield new opportunities. The analysis of the external environment should identify Opportunities and Threats for the company; the internal analysis should identify internal Strengths and Weaknesses. The SWOT analysis combines all these elements and provides the context within which successful strategies can be developed.

Strategy formulation

In the *strategy formulation* (sometimes referred to as the *strategy development*) *phase*, the strategist seeks to formulate different strategic options and courses of action to reach the vision and the objectives formulated in the strategy analysis phase. With the mission and vision providing the overall perspective, and the SWOT analysis providing the context, the next step is to focus on how to 'position' the company (and its main business units) in the market.

The question of how to compete and where to position the company in the market is a central point of discussion in strategic management. Most companies and their business units compete with a variety of players in a particular industry. In every industry, there are viable positions that companies can occupy. According to Constantinos Markides (1999b), a strategy professor at the London Business School, the essence of strategy is selecting one position that a company can claim as its own. A strategic position is the sum of a company's answers to the following questions:

- Whom should the company target as customers?
- What products or services should the company offer the targeted customers?
- How can the company do this efficiently? (Abell, 1980)

Although these questions are straightforward, the answers most often are not. Strategy involves making tough choices in these three different dimensions. Successful companies choose a strategic position that differs from that of its competitors. According to Markides, the most common source of strategic failure is the inability to make clear and explicit choices in these three dimensions. These ideas are clearly in line with Michael Porter's theory of generic competitive strategy: 'the essence of strategy is choosing to perform activities differently in a sustainable way' (Porter, 1985: 12). Competitive strategy is about being different. A company must either deliver greater value to customers (differentiation strategy) or create comparable value at a lower cost (cost leadership). A failure to choose between cost leadership or differentiation will result in inferior performance, which is the so-called *stuck-in-the-middle* hypothesis.

Porter's generic strategies have been regarded as the dominant paradigm for a long time. In the early 1990s, Michael Treacy and Fred Wiersema (1993, 1995) developed a somewhat similar framework based on how value is created for customers. Like Porter, Treacy and Wiersema argue that companies become successful by narrowing their business focus, not by broadening it. The market leaders have focused on delivering superior customer value in line with one of the following three value disciplines: operational excellence, customer intimacy or product leadership (see Figure 6.2). Treacy and Wiersema define customer value as the sum of the benefits minus the costs incurred by the customer from the product ('what we sell') and the service ('how we do business') that are provided.[4] Their research has shown that customers can be classified in three clusters according to the type of customer value they prefer: best total cost, best products and best total solution. They also found that market leaders focus their strategy and align their whole organization on one of these three value disciplines.

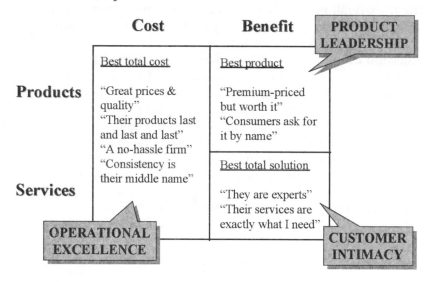

Figure 6.2 Customer value and market leadership
Source: Treacy and Wiersema (1995: 21)

- *Operational excellence* describes a specific strategic approach to the production and delivery of products and services. The objective of a company following this strategy is to lead its industry in price and convenience. Companies pursuing operational excellence are indefatigable in seeking ways to minimize overhead costs, to eliminate intermediate production steps, to reduce transaction and other friction costs and to optimize business processes across functional and organizational boundaries.

The standard example is Dell Computer, the market leader in the personal computer industry. Dell Computer invented a totally different and far more efficient operating model than competitors, such as Compaq and IBM. By selling to customers directly and cutting dealers out of the distribution process, Dell has been able to undercut Compaq and other PC makers and still provides high-quality products and service. In addition, Dell has created a disciplined, extremely low-cost culture, which stresses its position as an operational excellence company. (Treacy and Wiersema, 1993: 85–6)

- *Customer intimacy* describes a strategy in which a company continually tailors and shapes products and services to fit an increasingly fine definition of the customer. This might be more expensive, but customer-intimate companies are willing to make investments in order to build customer loyalty for the long term. These companies look at the customer's lifetime value to the company, not at the value of any single transaction. Customer-intimate companies have decentralized marketing operations in order to increase the responsiveness of the various stores or distribution centres. MLP, a German financial services provider, is a very good example.

  MLP Holding, as the company is known today, started its business activities as a trading company in 1971 focusing on the lucrative target group of academics (doctors, economists, engineers, natural scientists, and lawyers) as an independent insurance broker. MLP has achieved a very good position in this market, because it has developed distinct know-how in these occupational groups. MLP consultants must complete a strict assessment exam prior to starting with MLP. 94 percent of MLP consultants have a university or college degree, and more than half of them are economists. This means that the consultant has the same (or similar) education as his client, so it is easy for him to put himself in his client's position and recognize both his requirements and his problems. The MLP consultant is the reflection of his customer – he is of a similar age as well. This means that he advises many clients when they are in a situation similar to his own: e.g., starting a career, safeguarding against risks, building up a capital stock, investing in property and/or career, forming assets, and providing for a pension. As a result, he accompanies his client and his target group for a lifetime. This successful concept guarantees long-term customer relationships and that new clients can be won continually. (Lautenschläger, 1999: 8)

- The third value discipline, *product leadership*, is about producing a continuous stream of state-of-the-art products and services. Product leaders focus on their innovation potential and try to minimize time-to-market. Speed is central and marketing new ideas is core. Product leaders must relentlessly pursue new solutions to the problems that their own latest product or service has just solved. Johnson & Johnson, a pharmaceutical company, is a good example, as is illustrated by this story:

In 1983, the president of Johnson & Johnson's subsidiary Vistakon, Inc., a maker of specialty contact lenses, heard about a Copenhagen ophthalmologist who had conceived of a way of manufacturing disposable contact lenses inexpensively. What was unusual was the way Vistakon's president got his tip. It came from a J&J employee whom he had never met who worked in an entirely different subsidiary in Denmark. The employee, an executive for Janssen Pharmaceutica, a J&J European drug subsidiary, phoned Vistakon's president to pass along the news of the Danish innovation. Instead of dismissing the ophthalmologist as a mere tinkerer, these two executives speedily bought the rights to the technology, assembled a management team to oversee the product's development, and built a state-of-the-art facility in Florida to manufacture disposable contact lenses called Acuvue. (Treacy and Wiersema, 1993: 90)

After determining the mission, vision and desired strategic positioning, the preparation of 'plans' and *performance goals* (or objectives) represent the formal means by which managers communicate the strategy throughout the organization and coordinate internal resources to ensure that the strategy is achieved. These strategic plans indicate the destinations or ends that the organization seeks to achieve. Objectives and performance goals tell *where* the company or the strategic business unit (SBU) is going and *when* it wants to get there. Performance goals denote a desired level of accomplishment against which actual results can be measured (Simons, 2000). A clear financial objective, for example, reads as follows: 'The company (or SBU) has as its objective 25 per cent profit before tax and 15 per cent return on stockholders' equity and long-term debt.' Objectives can be set in two areas:

- Financial objectives (e.g., earnings per share, return on investment, cash flow). These objectives are usually quantified.
- Strategic objectives (e.g., greater customer satisfaction, employee job satisfaction). Some of these objectives are more difficult to quantify.

Strategy implementation

Next, the performance goals and plans should be translated into concrete *actions*. This is the domain of the functional managers: they develop new products, expand the operating capacity, introduce new marketing initiatives and develop appropriate human resources programmes.

However, in the traditional strategy books, the strategy implementation phase is the least developed one. Most textbooks pay attention to the importance of having the right organizational structures ('Structure follows strategy'), strategic planning (including the resource allocation process) and strategic control, some people issues (covering commitment, culture and leadership), and they introduce a chapter on 'change'. Then the work of the strategist is finished and it is up to the marketer, the operations manager and the controller to finish the job. In many companies this is still the way that people look at strategy and its implementation. Later in this chapter, we show that there are other ways to look at this process.

The corporate level

The discussion of SWOT and strategy formulation has focused on the business unit level. Recall that at this level, managers are concerned with how to compete in a particular industry and how to position the business in the competitive arena. Corporate strategy is relevant when an organization has several business units, competing in different product or geographic markets. Managers at the corporate level are concerned with the strategic scope of the organization, and corporate strategy addresses the main concerns of the multidivisional firm. Diversification, the use of mergers and acquisitions versus internal development and the development of organization-wide competences are all issues that need to be addressed by the managers at the corporate level. One of the central discussions at the corporate parent is how to coordinate and stimulate cooperation between the various business units and how to create synergies.

Setting goals at the corporate level is important for two reasons. First of all, it is at the corporate level that the broad goals are defined. Traditionally, these goals have been more financial in nature. They define the boundaries for the performance goals at the business unit level. For example, Jack Welch, CEO of General Electric, has communicated clearly to his employees that he will not support investments in any business that cannot attain a number one or number two position in its market. As such, these corporate goals can be considered as strategic boundaries for the strategic business units. (We discuss these *boundary systems* in greater detail in Chapter 9.)

Second, specific goals must be developed to evaluate the value of the corporate centre. Nowadays, we see the corporate centre being put under increasing pressure to provide *parenting value* for its business units. Michael Goold and Andrew Campbell, professors at Ashridge College, have developed the concept of 'parenting advantage' and have clearly explained how corporate value can be created (Goold et al., 1994; Goold and Campbell, 1998). Then, clear and well-specified goals for concrete actions at the corporate centre should be formulated.

The strategy formation process

The vision and the mission, the strategy, and the performance goals should direct a company towards the path of sustainable performance. All these concepts describe attractive destinations but do not tell how to get there. Given our focus on Integrated Performance Management and how this can affect the strategy formulation and implementation process, we think it necessary to dwell a little longer on the strategy formation process.

Phases in the strategic planning process

The process we described in the previous section of this chapter starts with the strategy analysis and strategy formulation phase, and results in concrete plans ready for implementation. This process is often referred to as the *strategic planning process*.[5] However, this representation does not always describe how the strategy formation process works in practice.

In general, firms pass through several stages in their planning processes, in response to increasing size, diversity and environmental complexity. Jeffrey Harrison and Caron St John (1998), both well-known strategy professors, see firms pass through four stages:

- Phase 1 – *Basic financial planning*: in this phase, organizations focus on meeting budgets and developing financial plans.
- Phase 2 – *Forecast-based planning*: organizations start to look outward to the external environment for trends and developments that may impact on the future. SWOT analyses are popular strategy tools in this particular phase.
- Phase 3 – *Externally-oriented planning*: it is only in this phase that organizations start to think strategically. That is, they devise strategies in response to markets and competitors.
- Phase 4 – *Strategic management*: in the final phase, organizations manage all their resources and take into account their stakeholders in an attempt to develop sustainable competitive advantage and to 'create the future'.

Start-up firms seldom exhibit the 'strategic management' planning process associated with phase 4. These firms generally start with an entrepreneur who sees an opportunity to successfully launch a product or service in the market. This entrepreneur might develop an informal sense of direction and only a few, short-term goals, but probably neglects the rest of the strategic planning process. It is only after the firm has become successful and has grown larger that the entrepreneur (or his/her successor) may attempt to formalize various aspects of strategic planning. Many companies stick to the second phase. They perform many 'strategic' exercises – a SWOT analysis is one of their favourites – to examine some general environmental trends and to analyse their particular strengths and weaknesses. But these exercises often lead to strategic reports that are never consulted. In the 'externally-oriented planning' phase, firms begin to think strategically. They understand what kind of value they deliver to the customers and analyse how they compete in the market. They are aware that they need to position themselves in the market and that the organization should support this positioning. That is, they try to align their strategy with their managerial and operational processes. In the final phase, companies know well what makes them successful, and they manage their core assets, core processes and competences in such a way that they foresee and 'proact' rather than react to competitors' moves. Or, to put it into Gary Hamel's (2000) words, these companies are able to 'lead the revolution'.

Strategic planning and the formation of strategies

Strategic planners primarily pay attention to the strategy analysis and the strategy formulation phases. Strategy implementation is often considered to be the major responsibility of the functional managers. This explains why academicians separate the strategy formulation phase (including strategy analysis) from the strategy implementation phase. This separation is often found in companies as well, where the strategy staff (the 'thinkers') report and operate – somewhat disconnectedly – from the line and operational managers (the 'doers').

Strategic planning reached its heyday in the 1960s when the industrial conglomerates started to emerge, but it fell into disrepute in the 1970s and 1980s. After all, people wondered whether strategic planning resulted in better strategies. Not everybody was convinced of that. One of the most famous opponents of this strategic planning approach is Henry Mintzberg (1994; Mintzberg et al., 1998). Strategic planning, he argues, is an analytical process aimed at programming already identified strategies. Its outcome is a plan, not a strategy. He continues: 'Nobody in the history of the world has ever created a strategy through an analytical process' (Mintzberg et al., 1998: 12). Constantinos Markides (1999b) partially agrees with Mintzberg's statement: 'Behind every successful company, there is a superior strategy. The company may have developed this strategy through formal analysis, trial and error, intuition, or even pure luck' (1999b: 6). Markides believes that strategic planning can yield good strategies, but he is convinced that there are many other ways in which appropriate strategies can be developed.

One reason for the negative connotations of strategic planning is the fact that these planning exercises easily degenerate into rather mechanical long-term extrapolation exercises. A typical reaction is to consider strategy as an annual event: 'It's September, it must be time for strategy.' Of course, if strategy is such a routine procedure, routine results will be obtained, and the basic ingredient of a good strategy – insight into how to build a competitive advantage – rarely emerges from formal planning procedures and planning meetings. Henry Mintzberg even claims that formalized strategic procedures have in fact often 'ruined strategic thinking'.

Formulating and planning strategies can be very relevant, but this ignores the importance of spontaneous strategy development. Many successful strategies arise from local experimentation and from grabbing unexpected opportunities. McCarthy, Mintzberg and Markides formulate this as follows:

> Good strategies grow out of ideas that have been kicking around the company, and initiatives that have been taken by all sorts of people in the company. It's not just the great, brilliant coup all the time. That means that a lot of very effective, so-called strategists or chief executives don't come up with the brilliant new strategy. They bring out the energy in people by creating systems that encourage and stimulate people. (McCarthy et al., 2000: 35)

Every manager sets some direction and some performance goals. Some of these goals are realized, others are not. Intentions that are fully realized are called *deliberate strategies*; those that are not realized are *unrealized strategies*. However, some of the realized strategies were not intended at all; these are called *emergent strategies*. Henry Mintzberg believes in a balance between deliberate and emergent strategies:

> Few, if any, strategies are purely deliberate, just as few are purely emergent. One means no learning, the other means no control. All real-world strategies need to mix these in some way: to exercise control while fostering learning. Strategies, in other words, have to form (emergent strategies) as well as be formulated (deliberate strategies) . . .
>   For, after all, perfect realization implies brilliant foresight, not to mention an unwillingness to adapt to unexpected events, while no realization at all suggests a certain mindlessness. The real world inevitably involves some thinking ahead as well as some adaptation *en route*. (Mintzberg et al., 1998: 11)

An effective strategy must not only seek to *exploit* the firm's external opportunities and internal competences creatively, but it must also endeavour to strengthen its business context by *exploring* for new opportunities and renewing its competences (Chakravarthy and White, 2002). For a long time, strategy researchers have focused on the exploitation side: strategy in the traditional view has been about closing the gap and creating a fit between external demands and internal capabilities. The emergence of the *Resource-Based View* in the mid-1990s has made academicians pay attention to the exploration side of management. According to this new stream of strategic thinking, the source of competitive advantage comes from selecting and developing the appropriate capabilities (Prahalad and Hamel (1989) call these capabilities *core competences*). Capabilities are developed by opening the gap between the current reality and some future vision. This calls for planning processes capable of greater creativity and flexibility, capitalizing more quickly on opportunities and more rapid implementation (Liedtka, 2001).

Exploration and exploitation require two different mindsets and different management processes. These differences can create tensions within an organization. To become successful, firms need to balance these two approaches. Therefore, we completely agree with the following statement by Jeanne Liedtka, a strategy professor at the University of Virginia:

Closing the gap, correcting the lack of alignment, is necessary for increasing stability and efficiency and fostering high performance. Yet we know that disequilibrium is the driver of learning and innovation. When we reduce variation, we increase the performance of the system in the short term. In the long term, we risk depriving the system of the new information that it needs to move forward. This is the 'adaptation paradox' – or as Karl Weick explains it, the observation that 'adaptation precludes adaptability' . . .

In this view, strategy-making is ideally a process of continuous adaptation that straddles the tension between offering too much or too little direction, between relying too heavily on or disrupting too precipitously the *status quo*, between collaborating to create new value systems and competing for a larger piece of the system's profits, and between reaping the benefits of autonomy and losing the benefits of scale and scope. (Liedtka, 2001: 77)

In this short overview, we have approached the strategy process from both a *rational* and an *evolutionary* perspective. In the rational approach, the focus is on planning and decision-making (not tackled here in this section). In the evolutionary perspective, action-taking is the driver of strategy. Strategy process researchers also look at the strategy process from two additional perspectives. In the *political perspective*, researchers investigate the roles of power and politics (defined very broadly here) in resolving goal conflicts. The *administrative perspective* on strategy process focuses on how the organizational context of a firm influences its decision-making and action-taking (Chakravarthy and White, 2002). We will not discuss the political perspective for the rest of this book. But, as outlined in the introduction to the second part of this book, we will discuss extensively how the administrative context influences the Integrated Performance Management and the strategy process.

Integrated Performance Management, the strategy formation process and strategy dynamics

In today's environment, where everything evolves and changes so quickly, integrating strategy formulation with managing its execution is critical. This is at the core of the Integrated Performance Management process. Ultimately, Integrated Performance Management (and a good strategy formation process) should help companies to improve, consolidate or change their strategic position. If this is the case, we are convinced that the company will be able to survive in the longer term and satisfy all the stakeholders' needs. Many strategy process researchers have tried to link the strategy process with financial performance. However, the financial performance of a company is influenced not only by its strategy, but also by its business context. At times, the general macro-economic climate and the industry context are thought to explain more of the variance of stock prices than the strategy itself.

We believe that successful firms are those that *continuously* develop and implement good strategies. Unfortunately, a position's uniqueness does not last forever. Competitors will imitate attractive positions, others will develop new and even better positions (e.g., by developing a better substitute product or by improving the operations capabilities). This calls for a dynamic view of Integrated Performance Management and the strategy process – they should arm companies against their competitors' moves.

There are several frameworks that show how companies react in a changing competitive environment. The typology developed by Raymond Miles and Charles Snow (1978) is one of the more famous ones in the strategy literature. Their typology is based on how companies respond to a changing environment and align environment with their organization.

- *Defenders* are organizations with a narrow business scope. Top managers in this type of organization are highly expert in their organization's limited area of operation but tend not to search outside their domains for new opportunities. Consequently, they seldom need to make major adjustments in their methods of operation and their structure. They devote primary attention to improving the efficiency of their existing operations.
- *Prospectors* are organizations that almost continually search for market opportunities, and they regularly experiment with potential responses to emerging environmental trends. Because of their strong concern for product and market innovation, these organizations are usually not completely efficient.
- *Analysers* are organizations that operate in two types of product–market domain, one relatively stable, the other changing. In their stable areas, these organizations operate routinely and efficiently through the use of formalized structures and processes. In the turbulent areas, top managers watch their competitors closely for new ideas and then rapidly adopt those that appear to be the most promising.
- Finally, *reactors* are organizations in which the top management frequently perceives change and uncertainty occurring in their organizational environments but is unable to respond effectively. According to Miles and Snow, these organizations lack a consistent strategy–structure relationship, and therefore seldom make adjustments of any sort until environmental pressures force them to do so (Miles and Snow, 1978: 29).

In an outstanding article on strategy process research, Bali Chakravarthy and Roderick White (2002) have come up with a new typology that classifies firms according to their strategy formation process. Imagine that a firm operates in a two-dimensional strategy space: S_1 and S_2, for example, defined in terms of 'cost leadership' and 'differentiation' (see Figure 6.3). The curved solid line represents a hypothetical *strategy frontier*, where those firms with the current best practice are positioned. Using this framework, Chakravarthy and White have identified four types of strategy dynamic or strategy outcome: (1) improving/imitating, (2) consolidating, (3) innovating, and (4) migrating.

- If a firm is not on the strategy frontier, *improving/imitating* advances the firm's strategic position towards the strategy frontier. Other firms that are on the strategy frontier, or those closer to it, provide the firm seeking improvement with ready benchmarks to follow.
- Firms that have reached the strategy frontier can start *consolidating* and maintaining this position by monitoring their competitors and making incremental improvements.
- Firms can also start *innovating*, i.e., moving beyond established best practices and advancing the strategy frontier.
- *Migrating* is the fourth option and involves a change in a firm's position along the existing frontier. While this is a significant change for a firm, it differs from innovating. According to Chakravarthy and White, a firm migrating from one generic strategy to another has exemplars: the position it seeks is not new. Other firms, elsewhere on the strategy frontier, provide benchmarks. This is a luxury that innovators do not have.

It is intuitively clear that migrating and innovating are the more risky strategy dynamics, compared to improving, imitating and consolidating. Or, in the words of the two authors: 'These two dynamics place the current

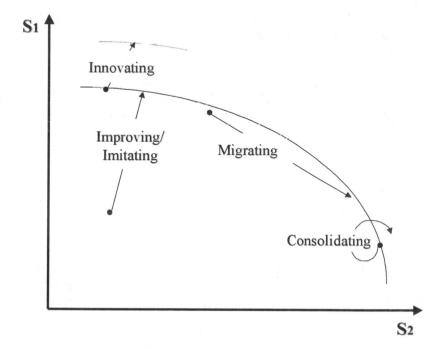

Figure 6.3 Strategy dynamics
Source: Chakravarthy and White (2002: 186)

success of the firm at risk, in their search for greener pastures. Firms opting for innovation and migration not only seek a different market opportunity, they are also willing to redo their competence base' (Chakravarthy and White, 2002: 186). They argue that different types of strategy process and different organizational contexts are required to drive these four strategy dynamics. As this chapter focuses on the goal-setting and strategy formation process, we investigate what types of strategy formation process have been recognized in the strategy literature. In the other chapters of Part II, we will focus on the various components of the organizational context.

Different types of strategy formation process

Different types of strategy formation process will emerge, depending upon the strategy dynamics that companies want to achieve. Companies that aim to consolidate their current position will have a totally different strategy process from companies that want to innovate and explore new territories. Are there any frameworks in the literature that has documented differences in the strategy-making process? And is there a link with the strategy dynamics developed by Chakravarthy and White?

The answer to the first question is definitely 'yes'. Several authors have developed frameworks and typologies of strategy formation (or strategy-making) processes (Dess and Lumpkin, 2001). Stuart Hart (1992) has developed an integrative framework for strategy-making processes where he identified five modes of strategy formation processes. Hart's framework is built around who is involved in the strategy-making process and in what manner. It is integrative because he looks at these different elements of the strategy formation process:

- The *rationality* in the strategy formation process, i.e., the extent to which the strategic process is comprehensive, exhaustive and analytical;
- The *symbolic role of top managers* in the strategy process: i.e., the extent to which leaders can articulate a clear strategic vision and motivate organizational members to adopt it;
- The extent and type of *involvement* of organizational members in the strategy-making process.

These five modes of strategy-making can be described as follows (Hart, 1992).

- In the *command mode*, a strong individual leader or a few top managers exercise total control over the firm. Strategy-making is a conscious, controlled process that is centralized at the very top of the organization. The strategic situation is analysed, alternatives are considered, and the appropriate course of strategic action is decided upon. Strategies are deliberate, fully formed and ready to be implemented. The top manager is the commander, and the organization's members are good soldiers (somewhat further in his article, Hart calls them 'sheep') who execute the strategy as it is articulated by the top.

- The second mode is the *symbolic mode*, which involves the creation by top management of a compelling vision and a clear corporate mission. This corporate vision defines the basic philosophy and values of the firm. The role of top management is to motivate and inspire organizational members, and to provide the necessary focus (e.g., by means of slogans, persuasion, new projects) to guide the creative actions of the organizational players.

- The *rational mode* seeks to be comprehensive in scope (unlike the two previous modes). Strategy is developed through formal analysis (and thus information processing) and strategic planning, involving written strategic and operating plans. Organizational members participate in a formal system requiring the upward sharing of data and information. The result is a detailed plan of action. To ensure effective implementation, top management carefully monitors and controls the activities of subordinates who are held accountable for performance benchmarked against the plan. Through structure and formal systems, organizational members are induced to behave in desired ways.

- In the *transactive mode*, strategy-making is based on interaction and learning, rather than on the execution of a predetermined plan. Top management is aware that it is difficult to separate the formulation of strategy from its implementation (e.g., because of the uncertainty in the environment). Strategy is crafted based upon an ongoing dialogue with key stakeholders/employees, suppliers, customers, governments. Cross-functional communication among organizational members is very important in this mode. Feedback and learning necessitate an iterative approach to strategy-making. Here, top management is concerned with facilitating a process for transacting with key stakeholders and linking the outcomes of those processes together over time to determine the strategic direction. For example, initiatives such as just-in-time management or quality circles are perfect examples of outcomes in the transactive strategy-making mode.

- The last mode of strategy formation is the *generative mode*. This mode depends on the autonomous behaviour of the organization's members. A central concept in this mode is 'intrapreneurship': new product ideas emerge upwards, and employee initiatives shape the firm's strategic direction. Top managers are seen as 'sponsors'; they are primarily involved in selecting and nurturing high-potential proposals that emerge from below. Established firms make innovations by behaving more like small entrepreneurial ventures. New strategies are germinated by separating innovating activity from the day-to-day work of the operating organization. Hart sees benefits in this mode of strategy-making, but he sees disadvantages as well: in his eyes, strategy here results from the action of 'wild ducks' (i.e., the independent initiatives of internal entrepreneurs).

Each of these strategy modes represents a type of 'pure' process. Some firms might combine several of these modes into their strategy formation process. In fact, this is recommended in order to integrate the benefits of each of these modes. Nevertheless, it is clear that, in some circumstances, firms will exhibit more of one particular strategy formation mode. For example, the command mode will be found more frequently in smaller companies, where one person can still maintain effective control. On the other hand, firms that operate in environments characterized by high levels of complexity and heterogeneity will favour a transactive mode of making strategy. Such an approach may be necessary to gain adequate knowledge about, and consensus among, key stakeholders.

Apart from the external environment and the development stage of the firm (see Table 6.1), we argue that strategy dynamics will also influence the choice of strategy mode. The strategy process for innovating companies will probably benefit more from a generative approach than from a command approach, while firms aiming to consolidate their strategic position might benefit from a more rational mode of strategy-making. Clearly, more research is necessary to determine under which conditions each strategy mode yields the best strategies.

Table 6.1 Strategy-making modes and contingency factors

Contingency factors	Command	Symbolic	Rational	Transactive	Generative
Environment	Simple; low-level complexity	Dynamic; high velocity or radical change	Stable; low degree of change	Complex; many stakeholders	Turbulent; dynamic and complex
Firm size	Small	Medium–large	Medium–large	Large	No relation
Stage of firm development	No relation	Rapid growth; reorientation	Steady growth	Mature	No relation
Strategic orientation	No relation	Proactive change (Prospector/ analyser)	Solidify position (Defender)	Continuous improvement (Analyser)	Innovator (Prospector)

Source: Hart (1992: 342)

We found some interesting similarities with a benchmark framework for performance management, developed by Rupert Booth. This framework is presented in Figure 6.4. It shows that the involvement of organizational members in the strategy-making process – Booth calls this 'decision rights' – differs according to the stage in the performance management journey. Booth also sees different types (and an increased effectiveness) of strategic planning (see 'norms and values').

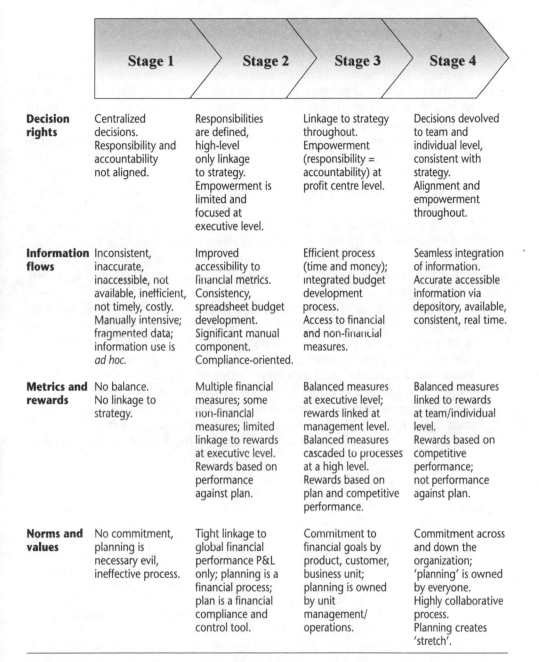

	Stage 1	Stage 2	Stage 3	Stage 4
Decision rights	Centralized decisions. Responsibility and accountability not aligned.	Responsibilities are defined, high-level only linkage to strategy. Empowerment is limited and focused at executive level.	Linkage to strategy throughout. Empowerment (responsibility = accountability) at profit centre level.	Decisions devolved to team and individual level, consistent with strategy. Alignment and empowerment throughout.
Information flows	Inconsistent, inaccurate, inaccessible, not available, inefficient, not timely, costly. Manually intensive; fragmented data; information use is *ad hoc*.	Improved accessibility to financial metrics. Consistency, spreadsheet budget development. Significant manual component. Compliance-oriented.	Efficient process (time and money); integrated budget development process. Access to financial and non-financial measures.	Seamless integration of information. Accurate accessible information via depository, available, consistent, real time.
Metrics and rewards	No balance. No linkage to strategy.	Multiple financial measures; some non-financial measures; limited linkage to rewards at executive level. Rewards based on performance against plan.	Balanced measures at executive level; rewards linked at management level. Balanced measures cascaded to processes at a high level. Rewards based on plan and competitive performance.	Balanced measures linked to rewards at team/individual level. Rewards based on competitive performance; not performance against plan.
Norms and values	No commitment, planning is necessary evil, ineffective process.	Tight linkage to global financial performance P&L only; planning is a financial process; plan is a financial compliance and control tool.	Commitment to financial goals by product, customer, business unit; planning is owned by unit management/ operations.	Commitment across and down the organization; 'planning' is owned by everyone. Highly collaborative process. Planning creates 'stretch'.

Figure 6.4 Progress in performance management
Source: Adapted from Booth (1997: 30)

Conclusion

Setting goals and developing strategies is an important step in the Integrated Performance Management process. Effective organizations need a sense of direction at every level in the organization. This explains why the first component of our Integrated Performance Management Framework addresses the *direction and goal-setting* process.

In this chapter, we have looked at two major questions: (1) *What* are the performance goals for an organization; and (2) *How* are these goals set, and how are strategies developed? These are two very important questions in the context of our Integrated Performance Management journey. Formulating an answer to the first question is crucial: many publications have demonstrated the importance of formulating an inspiring mission and vision, and a specific and clear strategy which provides guidance for the whole organization. No *strategic alignment* can be achieved if strategies are vague, hollow marketing slogans that can be interpreted in many different ways.

We have also paid significant attention to the question: How are goals set and strategies developed? We started with an overview of different strategic planning processes. Strategy formation, however, is not always the result of a rigid planning process. A good strategy formation process yields both intended and emergent strategies. Hart has shown that, in reality, it is difficult to find a balance between these two different strategy formation processes. In some situations, we find a focus on intended strategies, in others the focus is on emergent strategies. In Part III, we will explain that this focus also depends on the 'maturity' of the goal and strategy formation process.

Notes

1   The Co-operative Bank is a UK bank and its products are only available to UK residents and British expatriates overseas. The Co-operative Bank profiles itself as the ethical bank of the UK. In 1997 the bank celebrated its 125th anniversary by launching its Partnership approach, becoming the first company in the UK to produce a 'warts and all' social report involving all of the seven partners involved in the bank's activities. These partners are: (1) shareholders; (2) customers; (3) staff and their families; (4) suppliers; (5) local communities; (6) national and international society; and (7) past and future generations of cooperators (Co-operative Bank, 2001; see also website: www.co-operativebank.co.uk).

2   A good business example of strategic intent is Honda. When Honda attacked the leaders in the motorcycle industry, it began with products that were just outside the conventional definition of the leaders' product–market domains. As a result, it could build a base of operations in under-defended territory and then use that base to launch an expanded attack. These moves were largely unnoticed by the main competitors, who failed to see Honda's strategic intent and its growing competence in engines and power trains. And even as Honda was selling 50cc motorcycles in the USA, it was already racing larger bikes in Europe – assembling the design skills and

technology it would need for a systematic expansion across the entire spectrum of motor-related businesses. In their article 'Strategic intent', Prahalad and Hamel (1989) cite examples from other industries that adopted a similar strategic intent (Canon, Komatsu, NEC).

3   In fact, Henry Mintzberg and his colleagues argued that the concept of 'strategy' requires a number of definitions – five in particular. Clearly, strategy is one of those words that is defined in one way yet often used in another. The first definition is: strategy is top management's plans to attain outcomes consistent with the organization's mission and goals. This is the normal definition of strategy. However, strategy is often defined as a pattern, that is, consistency in behaviour over time. This is especially the case if you ask someone: What has been your strategy over the last five years? The plan might not always correspond with the actual behaviour of the organization.

To some people, strategy is a position, namely, locating particular products in particular markets. Porter's (1985) definition starts from this perspective. Still others see strategy as a perspective, that is, an organization's fundamental way of doing things. Mintzberg also has a fifth definition of strategy: strategy as a ploy. Here, strategy is a specific 'manoeuvre' intended to outwit an opponent or competitor (e.g., a 'dumping strategy') (Mintzberg et al., 1998).

4   Treacy and Wiersema make this definition more explicit by illustrating the dimensions of value.

> *Costs* include both the money spent on purchase and maintenance, and the time spent on basic service errors, delays, and inconvenience. Both tangible and intangible costs reduce value. *Product benefits* build value to the extent that the product has features that improve the customer's performance or experience. *Service* can also add value when it provides expert advice, personalized service, or other benefits that exceed basic service expectations. (Treacy and Wiersema, 1995: 20, emphasis added).

5   Megginson and his colleagues define strategic planning as '(1) choosing or setting an organization's mission, or purpose, and objectives; and then (2) determining the policies, projects, programs, procedures, methods, systems, budgets, standards, and strategies needed to achieve them' (Megginson et al., 1989: 27).

7 Obtaining Better Performance through Business Process Orientation

PAUL GEMMEL AND ANN VEREECKE

As a conclusion to Chapter 4, we introduced four stages on the path to operational excellence:

- In the first stage, a company tries to stop making mistakes. Quality is defined as conformance to specifications and ISO 9000 is recognized as an important quality framework.
- In the second stage, the focus is more externally oriented and the operations function incorporates the customer's expectations. A company aspires to be among the best.
- In the third stage, a company is giving more attention to the relationship between the performance at the operational level and the strategic performance. Management understands that the operations function is the implementer of the company's strategy. This is the stage where a comprehensive framework such as EFQM becomes very popular, because the strategic links between process performance and many of the other management areas are made clear.
- In the fourth stage, the operations function is not only a basic element of strategy implementation, but is seen as the foundation of the company's competitive success. The operations function is considered to be the long-term driver of the strategy. In this stage, Time-Based Competition is a very important issue.

Organizations going through the evolution from stage 1 to stage 4 look differently at the role of operations. Our central hypothesis is that an evolving company puts increasing emphasis on the importance of business process orientation. This will be further explained in the first section of this chapter. In the remainder of this chapter, we will develop three major topics which are related to maturity in Business Process Orientation:

- Process management (stage 2);
- Supply chain management (stage 3);
- World-Class Manufacturing (stage 4).

Maturity in the operations function: an evolution towards more business process orientation

Organizations going through the evolution from stage 1 to stage 4 look differently at the role of operations. In the first stage, *operations* is considered *as one of the functional areas* among others (such as marketing, research and development, human resources, accounting, etc.). In this stage, the biggest challenge is to manage the interface between the various functional areas. The greatest opportunity for performance improvements lies 'in the points where the "baton" is being passed from one function to another' (McCormack and Johnson, 2001: 17). In this stage, the major focus of many scientific research projects is on how to improve the relationship between the operations function and other functions, such as marketing. In this functional approach, processes are unstructured and ill-defined.

The first scholars to take on a *more business process orientation* were Edward Deming and Michael Porter in the 1980s. The Deming (1986) flow diagram maps the process from supplier to customer, and Deming's 14 points and seven deadly diseases describe strategies for optimizing the flow diagram (Walton, 1986). Deming used this flow diagram in his presentations at every conference with top management in Japan. It was one of the basic tools in the *Kaizen* toolbox. *Kaizen* adds the dimension of continuous improvement of everything, every day. The *Kaizen* tools are various methods and techniques to design, monitor, and evaluate processes. Michael Porter's (1985) value chain puts a lot of emphasis on linkages, i.e., relationships between the way one value activity is performed and the cost of performance of another. One example is the linkage between the supplier and customer value chain. Optimizing these linkages can create a competitive advantage for the firm.

In the same years, Peter Drucker (1988) pointed out the growing importance of knowledge and information technology in firms, and this led to a shift towards an 'information-based organization'. Central concepts in this information-based organization are process-orientation, customer focus, and teamwork among empowered specialists. These are the major characteristics of the second stage in our four-stage model. The basic processes are defined, documented and available in flow-charts. There is a lot of coordination or linkage between the various functional areas.

In the 1990s, the importance of processes is further underlined with the coming of the concept of *re-engineering*. Re-engineering is described as 'the fundamental rethinking and radical redesign of business processes to achieve dramatic improvements in critical, contemporary measures of performance, such as cost, quality, service and speed' (Hammer and Champy, 1993: 32). According to Hammer and Champy, the major elements of rethinking processes are:

- Work units change from functional departments to process teams;
- Jobs change from simple tasks to multidimensional work;
- People's roles change from controlled to empowered;
- Job preparation changes from training to education;
- The focus of performance measures and compensation shifts from activity to results;
- Advancement criteria change from performance to ability;
- Values change from protective to productive;
- Managers change from supervisors to coaches;
- Organizational structures change from hierarchical to flat;
- Executives change from scorekeepers to leaders.

Other authors further developed and operationalized the idea of *process re-engineering* and introduced the enabling role of information technology (IT). The focus in this third stage is no longer on optimizing functions within the organization, but on ways of understanding and managing the horizontal flows within and between organizations. This is called the horizontal organization as opposed to the vertical organization (Byrne, 1993). Managers employ process management with strategic intent and results. This is the stage where companies recognize that something like 'operations strategy' exists.

In the last stage, process measures and management systems are deeply imbedded in the organization. The company and its suppliers and customers work together from a process point of view. In the digital, Internet age, competition will be based on cross-company process integration across a network of companies (McCormack and Johnson, 2001). In this fourth stage, the *World-Class Manufacturing* (or World-Class Operations) firm emerges:

> A symbol of the level of manufacturing performance that is being exhibited by the top manufacturers in the world. This is a precursor of the standard performance that will be expected of all who are to continue as manufacturers in the future. (Roth and Griffith, 1990)

Process management

When we talk about processes in this chapter, we are primarily focusing on work processes as opposed to behavioural processes or change processes. A work process can be defined as: 'a specific ordering of work activities across time and place, with a beginning and end, and clearly defined inputs and outputs: a structure for action' (Davenport, 1993: 5). Approaches based on work processes draw heavily on the principles of quality management and re-engineering, both of which equate process improvement with process management. Process management means that processes are defined, documented, implemented and measured such that they can be improved in a structured way. In this part of the chapter, we further describe the basic building blocks of process management:

- *Process choice:* Not all processes are equal. We have already made a distinction between material, information and people processes. Further characterization is necessary to manage these processes in an adequate way.
- *The 'as is' process:* The starting point in process management is to draw a flow chart of the existing process. This allows one to analyse processes and to evaluate the 'as is' situation, which can lead to suggestions for improvement.
- *The 'to be' process:* In this stage, the 'to be' situation is formulated. This 'to be' situation can be an incremental improvement of the existing process (as suggested by Total Quality Management) or, instead, a radical change (as suggested by re-engineering scholars).

Process choice

A three-star French restaurant looks quite different from a fast-food restaurant (such as McDonald's) for a variety of reasons, and both of these restaurants are quite different from a Benihana restaurant, a Japanese-style restaurant where the meal is prepared in front of the customers on a hibachi cooking table (Benihana case, 1972). One of the major differences is the type of process. The French restaurant has many characteristics of a so-called *'job shop process'* and has a functional layout. The fast-food restaurant has many characteristics of a *'line process'* and has a line layout. The Benihana restaurant, with its insistence on grouping customers in 'batches' of eight in the bar before preparing and serving the meal, seems more like a *'batch process'*.

In manufacturing firms as well as in service firms, the main determinant of the type of process is the transaction volume. The higher the volume, the more a line process will be appropriate; the lower the volume, the more a job shop process will be used. In extreme cases, such as management consulting, a project approach might be desired. This relationship between process type and volume is illustrated in Figure 7.1.

The matrix in Figure 7.1 has the process type as a multidimensional construct – several different manufacturing dimensions are combined. Correlated with process type are such variables as:

- Product range (from narrow to broad);
- Size of the (customer) order (from large to small);
- Degree of product change accommodated (from standardized products to completely customized products);
- Degree of innovativeness (from low to high);
- Degree of automation (from highly automatic to purely manual work); and
- Capital intensity *versus* labour intensity.

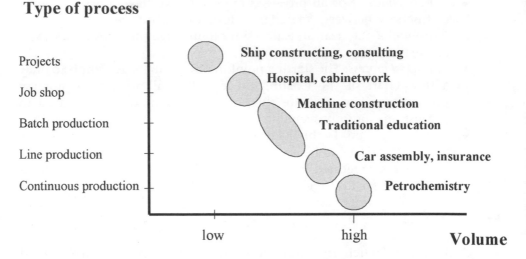

Type of process

Projects — Ship constructing, consulting

Job shop — Hospital, cabinetwork

Batch production — Machine construction

Traditional education

Line production — Car assembly, insurance

Continuous production — Petrochemistry

low   high   **Volume**

Figure 7.1 The relationship between process type and transaction volume

The choice of production process is also determined by the competitive strategy of the organization. A firm will select a certain type of process depending on whether the emphasis is on cost-effectiveness, flexibility, innovation or delivery speed. For example, Volvo makes cars on movable pallets rather than on an assembly line. Thus, in Figure 7.1, this process would be at the intersection of the line and batch production processes. Volvo's production rate is lower than that of its competitors because it is sacrificing the speed and efficiency of the line. However, the Volvo system is more flexible because it uses multi-skilled workers who are not paced by a mechanical assembly line (Chase et al., 1995).

The choice of process type also limits the strategic options. Therefore, we can state that the choice of process is probably the most important variable in strategic operations management.

The 'as is' process

A process (as a sequence of activities) must deliver the expected outcomes in a reliable way and at a satisfactory level of quality. In manufacturing, systematic analytical methodologies are used to design processes that are reliable and satisfactory. In services, it is much less common to design processes in a systematic way. Services are put together haphazardly, relying on a mixture of judgement and past experience (Ramaswamy, 1996).

One of the most important basic techniques in process management is *flowcharting*. Although flowcharting is a rather straightforward technique in manufacturing, it must be adapted in a service situation to bring in the customer interaction. Shostack extended the existing process mapping techniques by explicitly taking into account the interaction with the customer in what is called 'blueprinting' (Shostack, 1984). Blueprinting makes the process visible and distinguishes between front- and back-office. Blueprinting allows focus on the crucial points of interaction and can be used as a tool in service positioning (Shostack, 1987). To illustrate this, consider the example in Figure 7.2 of a financial service process for discount brokerage (Shostack, 1985).[1]

The first step is to identify the various activities that together constitute the service process. The customer makes a telephone call, asking to open an account. The back-office then processes that request and decides to grant or deny an account. If accepted, the customer can place various

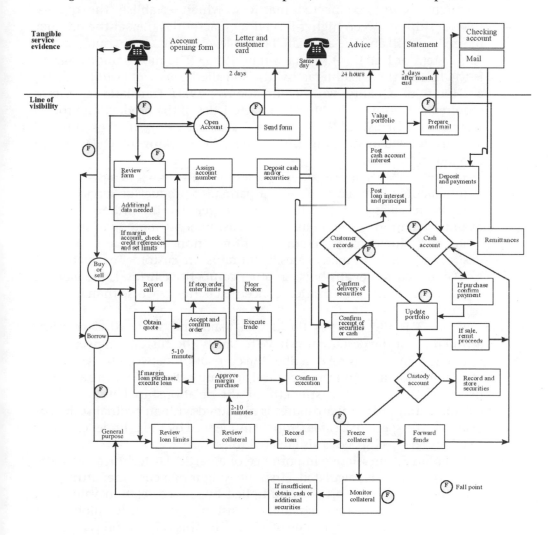

Figure 7.2 The service encounter: a blueprint for discount brokerage
Copyright © 1985 by Jossey-Bass Inc., Publishers. First published by Lexington Books. All rights reserved.
Source: Shostack (1985: 94)

orders, obtain advice and receive a monthly financial statement. All activities should be mapped – the activities that the customer actually sees (front-office), as well as the back-office activities. Front- and back-office activities are separated in this approach by a *line of visibility*, indicating where the customer intervenes in the service delivery process.

Increasingly, scholars are proposing the use of more systematic approaches to designing customer needs into processes. One of these approaches is *Quality Function Deployment* (QFD), which translates customer needs and preferences into operational goals for the firm. In a manufacturing context, QFD is very popular because it creates a bridge between the engineer and the customer. The QFD methodology uses a hierarchy of interconnected matrices, which establish the quality relationships between higher-level design activities (i.e., at the product or service level) and the associated lower-level activities (i.e., sub-process, sub-system or function) (Ramaswamy, 1996). The most famous matrix is the first in the QFD hierarchy, the so-called '*House of Quality*'. Using a 'House of Quality with eight rooms', QFD translates customer requirements into the technical characteristics of the production process (Hauser and Clausing, 1988). Figure 7.3 shows a simplified example of a House of Quality. Using this house, the working of QFD can be explained.

Room 1 shows a list of the customer attributes. These are the requirements of the customer for a particular product or service. Each attribute receives a weight indicating its relative importance. In this example, comfort is a more important customer attribute than speed.

Room 2 shows more descriptive information about the customer's desires and needs. In many cases, it contains the customer evaluation of each of the customer attributes in other competitive firms. Is the score of the attribute in the organization concerned better or worse than in other organizations?

Room 3 is the voice of the design team and shows the technical attributes that the design must have to satisfy the customer's needs.

Room 4 (in the centre) describes the correlation between the customer attributes (Room 1) and the technical attributes (Room 3) using a matrix diagram. Generally, the strength of the relationship between these customer and technical attributes is measured with an ordinal scale. For example, the speed of a car is strongly influenced by the cylinder capacity; to a lesser degree, speed is also related to car size.

In Room 5, the relative importance of a particular technical attribute (e.g., accessories) is calculated. First, the weight of a customer attribute – 5 in the case of comfort – is multiplied by the correlation value of a technical attribute (accessories) and the customer attribute (comfort). This multiplication results in a value of 15 (5×3). This calculation is repeated for each customer attribute that is correlated with that particular technical attribute. In this case, accessories is also correlated with attributes such as price level and safety. The scores here are 27 for price and 12 for safety. The

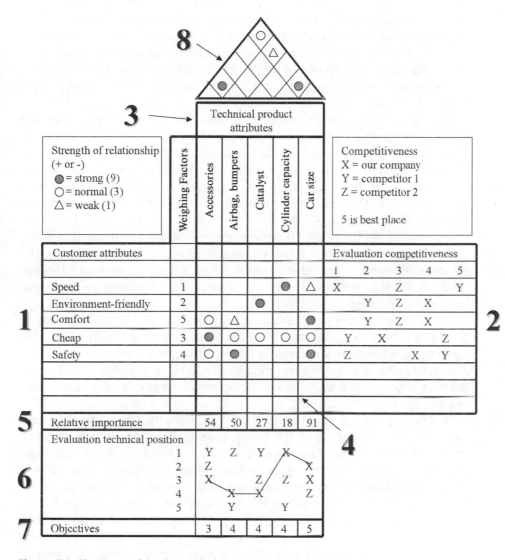

Figure 7.3 The House of Quality applied to cars

total value of the technical attribute 'accessories' is therefore: 15 + 27 + 12 = 54 (taking into account the relative importance of each customer attribute, as long as it is correlated with it). The importance of the technical attributes are compared one to another. In our example, car size is the most important technical attribute to satisfy the customer's needs.

Room 6 shows more descriptive information about the quality of the performance of the competitors' designs. As company X, we have rather small cars compared to our competitors Y and Z. So, we have a clear disadvantage in satisfying the desires of our customers.

In Room 7, we define target values (based on the figures obtained from Rooms 5 and 6). These objectives teach us more about the future direction of the company in improving the design function. In the example, it is important that the company improves its technical attribute 'car size'.

Room 8 (the roof) shows which technical attributes are compatible (or not) with each other. In our example, there is a strong correlation between cylinder capacity and car size. A higher cylinder capacity requires a larger engine block, which in turn requires a larger car.

The QFD methodology has been applied in many different business environments (both in manufacturing and in services). Applications of QFD have been reported in car manufacturing, the computer and electronics fields, machine construction, software development, education, and the transport and distribution industry. The service applications of QFD are rather limited, but nevertheless are promising (Dubé et al., 1999).

The main benefits of the QFD method are cost reduction and increasing returns. Cost reduction is achieved through more standardization in the production process and the availability of a tool to evaluate interim changes in the project. Increased returns are obtained because the products or processes incorporate the customer's requirements. QFD also leads to reducing time for designing, developing, producing and selling products or services (Cohen, 1995). Since its first introduction, QFD has evolved from simply an engineering technique to an overall quality management technique. In this perspective, QFD is not only useful in the first stage of the life cycle model of operations functions, but it is also relevant in the later stages.

A key aspect in the analysis of processes is the detection and explanation of variation in the process. Basically, a distinction must be made between *common causes* and *special causes* of variation. Only special causes of variation lead to a process that is 'out of control'. To be able to make a distinction between common and special causes of variation, control limits can be introduced. Control limits represent the range within which all points are expected to fall when the process is in control (i.e., when only common causes of variation are present). *Statistical Process Control* (SPC), using control charts, is a very common way to monitor variation in processes. We refer to the specialized literature for more explanation about the working of SPC.[2]

In some situations, especially in the service sector, SPC and similar tools cannot be used to detect process variation. In order to understand process variations in these cases, it is helpful to look at the relative performance of similar processes (or part of processes) in different organizations. One technique that can be used in this case is Activity-Based Management (ABM).

Activity-Based Management originated out of Activity-Based Costing (ABC), which itself originated out of a growing dissatisfaction with the traditional cost accounting systems. With the traditional systems, the rather arbitrary allocation of overhead costs often led to distorted cost information. With Activity-Based Costing approaches, it is the amount of resources used by the activities during the transformation process that determines the allocation of overhead costs to products or services. For instance, instead of allocating the cost of invoices to different sales departments based on the sales volume of each department – an approximate indicator – a company starts to use the actual number of invoices as this is the real cost driver. ABC implies that the relevant cost drivers are established for the activity invoicing; the major cost driver is without doubt the number of invoices. This driver indicates what is causing the consumption of resources for that activity and hence the cost of that activity.

ABM starts from the same basic ideas as ABC (Rotch, 1990; Antos, 1992). It extends the ABC logic to an overall management approach that focuses on influencing underlying activities and their dynamics (Campi, 1992; Roberts and Silvester, 1996). Applying activity-based management principles requires a thorough knowledge of the activities and the drivers underlying the service delivery process. If we want to link the consumption of resources with a specific activity, we have to know which activities make up the service delivery process. Process mapping has an important role to play in this respect.

Once the different activities have been distinguished and mapped within the process, drivers can be identified for each activity. Indicators of productivity are then derived by relating the resources spent on each activity with the appropriate driver. For example, if we know that three people (= the resources) are continuously handling invoices and we know the number of invoices (= the driver), a performance indicator can be derived for this activity by dividing the number of invoices by the number of resources. If all three people work eight hours and the daily number of invoices is 500, the performance indicator for productivity relating to this task shows that handling one invoice takes approximately three minutes.[3]

The final outcome of the process design stage is a very clear map of the 'as is' process, including a determination of problems and the root causes of these problems.

The 'to be' process

In this stage, a 'to be' process is designed. Depending on the kind of philosophy being followed (Total Quality Management versus re-engineering), this can be an incremental change of the process or a radical change. In this section, using a process of CT scanning of patients in a hospital as an example, we illustrate how processes can be re-engineered.[4] The particularity of the situation is that time is a very important performance measure in this case.

A company that wants to re-engineer processes has to walk through the six Rs: Realization, Requirements, Rethink, Redesign, Retool, and Re-evaluate (Edosomwan, 1996). The requirements and the rethink stages are based on the 'as is' process description (see previous section).

Realization In the realization phase, a company must become aware that continuous and radical improvement of processes is a condition *sine qua non* for survival in a competitive environment. Data must be captured to convince decision-makers to start up a re-engineering process. It is impossible to re-engineer without the support of the whole company. For example, referral physicians are a very important customer group in the case of CT scanning. Getting quick access to the facilities and receiving fast feedback after investigation are important basic needs for these physicians. Data on these needs must be collected.

Requirements Before changing the processes, it is important to define clearly the mission, vision, values, and the most important requirements for meeting (and even exceeding) customer expectations. The customer voice must be brought in and criteria for measuring process performance must be defined. These performance criteria must be in line with the strategy of the firm. The Balanced Scorecard (see Chapter 3) is often used to define these performance measures.

In our CT scanning example, ROI, cash flow, reliability, quality of the medical diagnosis, patient satisfaction, process innovation, utilization rate, throughput time and waiting time are all examples of performance measures, reflecting the financial perspective, the customer perspective, the internal process perspective, and the innovation and learning perspective (as identified by the Balanced Scorecard). Table 7.1 shows examples of some operational performance measures of the CT scanning process in two different hospitals. Hospital B is able to serve customers more quickly than hospital A and, at the same time, has a higher utilization rate.

Table 7.1 A comparison of operational performance measures for two hospitals

	Hospital A	Hospital B
Utilization rate CT scan	81%	91%
Ratio of real investigation time to total throughput time	23%	34%
Total throughput time (room out – room in)	66 minutes	43 minutes
Average waiting time before CT	23 minutes	13 minutes
Set-up times	2.48 minutes	1.25 minutes

Rethink In the rethink stage, we examine the existing working conditions of the organization. The current processes are evaluated and compared with the objectives and expectations. The causes of the operational weaknesses in the organization and the variability in these processes are further investigated. Every activity or process that does not add value in the realization of the product or service is labelled as waste.

Figure 7.4 shows the relationships between different time components in the CT scanning process and the factors driving time (Gemmel, 2000). It is important to study the non-value-adding activities in greater detail. These are 'waiting' and 'transport'. One of the important drivers of the

Drivers	Waiting on transport	Transport time	Waiting before preparation	Preparation time	Investigation time	Transport time
Architecture		X				X
Preparation room				X	X	
Appointment system			X			
Communication system	X					
Transport time			X			

Figure 7.4 Time drivers in the CT scanning process

transport time is the architecture of the building and, more particularly, the presence (or absence) of an elevator. In a tall building, where patients and employees need an elevator to go to the radiology department, there seems to be no relationship between the distance (from the room to the department) and the total transport time. Because of the unpredictability of the transport time, patients are transferred earlier to the radiology department (to make sure that they arrive in time).

Redesign A process is a set of logical, related tasks which are executed to bring forth a predetermined output. Every task is analysed in the function of redesigning the most important processes. This redesign can be radical, i.e., old processes are substituted by totally new processes.

When analysing the CT scanning process, it was found that in several hospitals patients were prepared for CT when already lying on the CT scanner. This preparation seemed to be the most variable time component of the whole investigation. One possible solution is to install a separate room where patients can be prepared before entering the CT scanner room. Because the variability of the time on the CT scanner reduces remarkably, a higher utilization can be achieved without substantially increasing the waiting time.

Retool Radical change is not possible without having the right tools (equipment, machines, and other critical instruments). It is quite clear that the creation of a separate preparation room for CT scanning takes hospital space (which is often very scarce). Another way to solve the problem is to think about the layout of the radiology department. This layout is crucial to using the CT scanners efficiently. Having a working room in between two rooms with scanners is much more interesting than having two scanner rooms in separate locations.

In our example, it is possible to simulate the proposed changes and to get some insights into the change in performance before implementing the changes in reality. *Computer simulation* is a tool that allows one to imitate the behaviour of production or service systems to compare several designs of the processes. For example, in production, the layout of warehouses can be investigated before changes are implemented. In the CT scanning example, the effect of introducing a preparation room can be simulated before implementation. Computer simulation has been described in a variety of books and is extremely useful in those situations where a buffer exists – a queue in a service situation or an inventory in a production situation.[5]

Re-evaluate After redesigning and retooling, the complete process is re-evaluated to find out whether or not this has led to better performance. This assumes the availability of evaluation criteria such as throughput time, quality, productivity, customer satisfaction, employee satisfaction, market share, profitability, and other measures.

After implementing the changes (e.g., installing an investigation room), it is important to re-evaluate the performance of the new process.

Supply chain management[6]

The philosophies of Total Quality Management (TQM), and particularly Just-in-Time (JIT), emphasize the fact that the logistics chain does not end at the door of the firm. Better relationships with suppliers are considered crucial to process management across organizations. This might be the involvement of suppliers in product development, the development of long-term relationships with an intensive exchange of information, and even impact of the customer on the design of the supplier's production process. In the consumer business, producers are increasingly taking into account the desires of the distributors and the final points of sale.

Supply chain management (SCM) is the management of the entire chain: from the supply of raw materials, through the distinct production and distribution phases, to the final customer. Figure 7.5 shows the supply chain of a producer of watches. The fundamental principle of supply chain management is that through effective information exchange between the various links in the chain, and through striving for a win-win relationship, a better supply of products is generated for the customer.

There are various driving forces behind the growing importance of supply chain management:

- *The shortening of the product lifecycles.* While in the past, the clothing industry considered it good practice to introduce a new collection two times per year, today – to be competitive – a clothing firm needs to introduce at least four new collections per year. This means that time-to-market is becoming a very crucial performance measure.

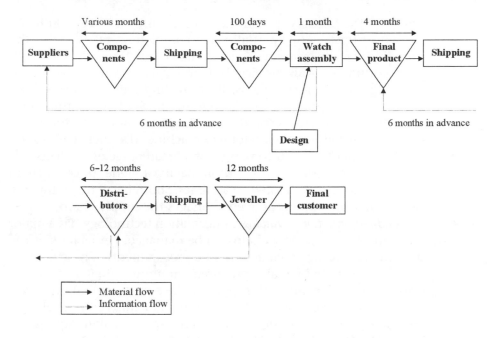

Figure 7.5 The supply chain of a producer of watches

- *The focus on core activities.* In line with the idea of focus on core competences, firms are starting to outsource activities with greater frequency. Most often, these are secondary activities, such as maintenance, distribution and product development. But primary activities, such as production and packaging, are also outsourced. This makes the supply chain much more complex.
- *The virtual factory.* A virtual factory is a factory that attains its target of transforming materials and components into value for the customer by using resources outside the manufacturing function proper. If the service component of the offering represents the core of the company's competitive advantage, then traditional manufacturing companies may ultimately subcontract the tangible part and concentrate entirely on the service component. For example, E&J Gallo Winery, the largest wine producer and distributor in the USA, outsources the growing of specialized grapes for its wines. Gallo devotes its resources and management attention to the marketing and sales functions (Quinn et al., 1998).
- *Towards 'servitization'.* Competitive pressures force firms to differentiate their product offering. This is achieved by enhancing the product. The product offering can be decomposed into a hardware core, traditional components of service such as installation, after-sales services, repair and payment arrangements, and finally all kinds of services that are necessary to offer a solution to the customer's problem. Consider the

example of the full service contracts at Asea Brown Boveri (ABB). In such a contract, ABB partially or completely takes over the responsibility of its customer's maintenance function. With its 'Full-service contracts', ABB Service is being paid for its expertise in optimizing a customer's process. By providing guidance during the design and development stage, by offering preventive maintenance, and so on, ABB Services creates value for the customer, resulting in increased availability of the customer's machines (Desmet et al., 1998).

- *Towards more flexibility*. Customers want a broad range of products – or products that are customized – without paying a higher price for them or being confronted with longer lead times. Shorter lead times are only possible when a company actively manages the supply chain.
- *Evolution in information technology*. Information technology has a major impact on how the supply chain can be managed. Let us look at the example of electronic procurement (or e-procurement). E-procurement applications can help make procurement more efficient and can enhance the relationship with suppliers. The e-procurement evolution promises to redefine buyer and supplier relationships completely, yet many enterprises simply implement Web e-procurement software – without rethinking the processes needed to transform the procurement cycle (Reilly et al., 2000). This common, but short-sighted, practice again emphasizes the need to rethink or redesign the current logistic system. E-procurement can take a variety of forms, such as electronic data interchange, Internet, Intranet, Extranet, electronic catalogue ordering, e-mail, etc. The increased popularity of e-procurement is due to the multitude of operational benefits that it can bring to purchasing practices (Min and Galle, 1999).

Successful supply chain management assumes a radical rethinking of the supply chain. SCM is not just the automation of the existing production and distribution processes. Processes, roles and responsibilities sometimes must be changed drastically. This can lead to the elimination or substitution of a link in the chain. This rethinking of the supply chain can be based on the same steps as in process re-engineering. The supply chain must be mapped and the added value of each step in the chain must be evaluated.

A crucial element in successful SCM is the link between the material process and the information process. For instance, it is important for a component supplier to have fast access to information about the final consumption of the product in which his component is placed. Better information can significantly reduce inventories because these inventories are safety stocks against uncertainty. This leads to so-called lean production, an approach to managing operations without massive buffers of inventory.

Successful SCM also requires the shift from a vertical organization to a horizontal organization. More than that, it is important that there is some concordance in the degree of process orientation of the various companies in the supply chain. This also means that the performance measurement systems must be redesigned: existing systems are too focused on optimizing one department or one firm. SCM requires achieving a win-win situation in the whole chain (as in the example of ABB Services). In such a setting, the emphasis is much more on lead-time performance. It is important to point out that performance measures must relate not only to traditional logistical elements but also to the impact of the supply chain on the bottom line of the business.

World-Class Manufacturing[7]

World-Class Manufacturing (WCM) can be regarded as an objective, something like manufacturing excellence. It is a precursor of the standard performance for all firms that want to compete globally. WCM firms are better than almost every other company in their industry in at least one aspect of manufacturing. They have workers and managers who are so skilled that other companies are trying to attract them away. They are able to react quickly and adequately to market changes (Hayes et al., 1988). They foster continuous improvements in human assets, technology, materials and information flows. These are the kinds of firm that are able to break through the classical 'trade-off' between low-cost producer and differentiator. They excel in every kind of operating performance at the same time: quality, dependability, speed, flexibility and price (see Chapter 4).

An example of such a firm is Southwest Airlines, which is able to deliver low cost without giving up great service. Southwest Airline planes typically spend much more time in the air than planes in the more traditional airline companies – 70 per cent of their flights have a turnaround time of less than 15 minutes at the terminal. Their planes are in the air 11 hours per day, as compared to the industry average of eight hours. Their pilots fly many more hours for lower wages than pilots in other airline companies. At the same time, they have a very good record of on-time performance and very few lost bags.

A key element in their success is selecting their employees carefully and training them to be customer-oriented. It is interesting to read the comments of a Burger King manager after visiting Southwest Airlines.

> For me, I know a company has it right when the front line people actually do and say what management values. Any company can teach customer service, but only companies that have systems in place that reward great service will demonstrate it in practice. Very few companies treat people as their most important asset, especially the people that count the most – the ones that deal with the customer. For me, the lesson learned is that it is possible to be the low cost and high service leader. The key is to invest heavily in training, staffing, and reward systems for your people that are aligned with the values of the company. (Southwest Airlines (A–1) case, 1995: 3)

Many of these WCM firms very clearly understand that customers from different market segments cannot be served with the same delivery or production system. Therefore, they focus on one specific segment and are able to develop excellent performance in all areas. One other example is the Canadian hospital 'Shouldice', which performs much better than a traditional general hospital in terms of cost, quality, service, speed and customer orientation. So, it can be said that WCM firms have a very clear manufacturing strategy, which assumes a bi-directional relationship between the strategy of the firm and the production system.

The main secret of WCM firms is that they are based on dynamic processes that allow them to change and improve in a continuous way. These processes further explain why such firms are able to be active on these different performance fronts simultaneously:

- Customer orientation;
- Continuous improvement;
- Lead-time performance (Sweeney, 1991).

Customer orientation

WCM firms understand very well that the production function must be externally oriented and, more specifically, customer-oriented. The message of Jan Carlzon, president of the Scandinavian airline company SAS, very clearly illustrates this idea: 'We fly people, not airplanes' (Carlzon, 1987). Bringing in the voice of the customer, servitization and a horizontal organization are the core elements in obtaining customer orientation.

Continuous improvement

WCM firms apply the principles of continuous improvement (*Kaizen*). This starts with reliability of processes and products. Employees are considered as the main source of new ideas and are empowered to implement changes. Sometimes this leads to radical changes (re-engineering) to obtain seamless processes.

The results of the changes or the progress in the company are measured and made explicit. Then, at a certain moment, a quality assurance system (such as ISO 9000) must consolidate the progress of the company. Otherwise, there is a danger of regression.

Lead-time performance: high throughput

WCM firms put the emphasis on the maximization of throughput. In other words, they believe in Time-Based Competition (see Chapter 4). The reduction of throughput times in production, administrative processes, purchasing, distribution and in product development generate an important leverage effect on performance.

WCM firms apply the concepts of Just-In-Time (JIT) to their internal production processes as well as to their relationships with suppliers. JIT teaches that inventories often hide many operational problems. Inventory reduction requires a fundamental strategy to cope with these problems – leading to better performance in terms of quality, productivity, lead-time reliability and flexibility.

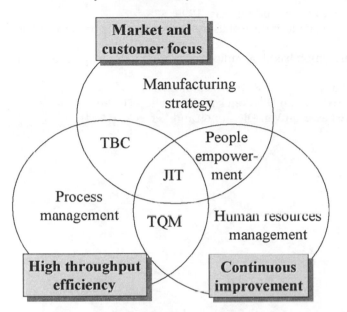

Figure 7.6 The simultaneous interaction of performance processes that lead to WCM

Conclusion

In Chapter 4, we proposed a relationship between the various definitions of quality and the 'maturity' of the firm in terms of quality experience. In this chapter, we have further developed the idea that becoming more mature in terms of quality experiences means becoming more business process oriented. This also means that organizations going through the evolution from stage 1 to stage 4 look in a different way at the role of operations. In the first stage, we recognize the traditional functional department where the biggest challenge is the collaboration between the different departments. In the second stage, process management plays a greater role. The basic processes are defined and documented. The 'as is' process is described and evaluated. The 'to be' process is proposed. In the third stage, this process orientation is extended further towards relationships with suppliers and customers. This results in what is called management of the supply chain. In the last stage, firms are fully integrated in terms of functions and processes within and across the company. These are the firms that excel in the global economy and establish benchmarks for other firms. They are the so-called World-Class Manufacturing firms.

Notes

1   Many process mapping techniques exist, and process mapping has many other purposes which go beyond the scope of this book. The reader interested in learning more about process mapping may refer to, for instance, the structured analysis and design technique and the service logic map (see Congram and Epelman, 1995; Kingman-Brundge et al., 1995).
2   SPC is discussed in detail in Evans and Lindsay, 1999: 528.
3   The technique of ABM and an illustration of its use have been described in Van Looy et al., 1998.
4   CT scanning is an investigation based on radiology in order to look into the human body.
5   See, for example, Van Looy et al., 1998: Technical note 3.
6   This part is partially based on Van Dierdonck and Busschop (1996).
7   Parts of this chapter are based on Van Dierdonck and Vereecke (1994).

8   Strategic Information Systems Alignment

DIRK DESCHOOLMEESTER AND OLIVIER BRAET

In general, IT (information technology) and IS (information systems) are considered important support functions in an organization. This is a domain that is well documented in the management literature. One of the main considerations is to demonstrate how IT and IS can contribute to strategy implementation, and thus increase the image of IT within the organization.

In this chapter, we start by outlining the strategic role of information and information systems. Then we focus on the concept of strategic IS alignment, which seeks to link business strategies to IT strategies. We will rely on a framework, presented by Henderson and Venkatraman (1993), which is considered one of the fundamental frameworks in this respect. In a next step, we will describe the necessary steps for strategic IS alignment. Finally, we will link strategic IS alignment to the maturity concept.

The strategic role of information and information systems

Everybody agrees about the critical role of information and knowledge in our current (business) society. Knowledge is information that can be used in all types of managerial decision-making and action-taking. Most of the information and knowledge that an organization needs is drawn from inside (business processes, structure and culture) as well as from outside the organization (i.e., the competitive environment in which the organization operates). Collecting information about markets, market trends, competitors' actions, general economic trends and legislation is a critical step in every strategic analysis. Information systems that fail to provide access to internal or external sources of information and knowledge can diminish the performance of an organization.

Qualitative information is essential for the improvement of organizational performance and for the realization of strategic goals. The aim of strategic information systems management is to get the right information in the right context to the right person at the right time. O'Brien (1997) extends this basic insight into a more detailed description of what information quality should entail. He distinguishes three dimensions that, taken together, describe information quality: time, content and form.

In the *time* dimension, O'Brien points to the following elements:

- *Timeliness* (information should be provided when it is needed);
- *Currency* (information should be up to date when it is provided);
- *Frequency* (information should be provided as often as needed); and
- *Time period* (information can be provided about past, present and future time periods).

The *content* dimension amounts to:

- *Accuracy* (information should be free from errors, bias and noise);
- *Relevance* (information should be related to the information needs of a specific recipient for a specific situation);
- *Completeness* (all the information that is needed should be provided);
- *Conciseness* (only the information that is needed should be provided);
- *Scope* (information broad or narrow in scope); and
- *Performance* (information can reveal performance by measuring activities accomplished, progress made, etc.).

Finally, the *form* entails:

- *Clarity* (information should be provided in a form that is easy to understand);
- *Detail* (information can be provided in detailed or summary form);
- *Order* (information can be arranged in predetermined sequences);
- *Presentation and media* (information can be provided in the form of printed paper documents, videos or other media).

These basic principles concerning the quality of information and the role of strategic information systems management apply regardless of the technologies used in an organization. Even as we are witnessing an evolution from information technology (IT) towards information communication technology (ICT, or IT that makes use of modern telecommunication networks, such as the Internet or wireless communication networks), the basic definitions of information systems management still apply.

To understand the potential impact of ICT and IT on organizational performance, it is necessary to look at IT holistically (i.e., in relation to the organization and its processes) rather than to consider IT as a function separate from other organizational processes. Almost 40 years ago, Harold Leavitt (1965) emphasized that an organization's structure, the tasks or processes at hand, the people and its technology are intimately intertwined (see Figure 8.1).

The message of Leavitt's diamond was simple. Every element of organizational life affects every other element. Change the technology and you change the tasks, which in turn causes changes in the organizational structure and in the workforce. Change the people and they will find new ways of performing tasks, which requires adjusting the technology.

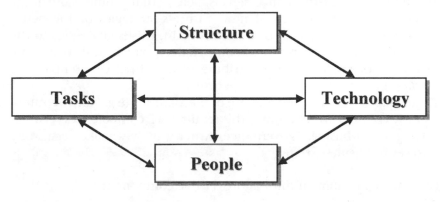

Figure 8.1 Leavitt's diamond
Source: Leavitt (1965)

Strategic Information Systems alignment

When we consider the IT function more holistically, we see that it is necessary to improve the fit between the IT infrastructure and the IT processes and the strategy. This is called *Strategic Information Systems alignment*. Strategic IS alignment aims to develop a strategic consensus about the strategic business and related IT priorities, the contribution of IT to the company strategy, and the impact of IT on the business operations and results. Strategic IS alignment amounts to linking an organization's IS plans with the business plans of distinct business units or product lines. By aligning these plans, information resources support business objectives, which is a necessary condition for effective strategic control and use of IT.

Henderson and Venkatraman (1993) have developed a strategic alignment model, based on two building blocks: strategic fit and functional integration. *Strategic fit* is about creating alignment between the external and internal environments. They also translate these general strategic principles to the IT domain: 'IT strategy should be articulated in terms of an external domain – how the firm is positioned in the IT marketplace – and an internal domain – how the Information Systems infrastructure should be configured and managed' (Henderson and Venkatraman, 1993: 474). According to the authors, the *position* of the organization *in the IT marketplace* involves three sets of choices:

* *Information technology scope*: those specific information technologies (e.g., electronic imaging, expert systems, robotics, networks) that support current business strategy initiatives or could shape new

business strategy initiatives. (Note that this is analogous to business scope, which deals with choices pertaining to product–market offerings in the output market.)

- *Systemic competences*: those attributes of IT strategy (e.g., system reliability, cost–performance levels, etc.) that could contribute positively to the creation of new business strategies or the better support of existing business strategy. (Again, this is analogous to the concept of distinctive business competences, which deal with those attributes of strategy that contribute to a distinctive, comparative advantage of a firm over its competitors.)
- *IT governance*: the selection and use of mechanisms (e.g., joint ventures, joint R&D, etc.) for obtaining the required IT competences. (This is analogous to business governance, which involves make-versus-buy choices in business strategy.)

The internal IS domain must address three components:

- *IS architecture*: the choices that define the portfolio of applications, the configurations of hardware and software, and communication and the data architecture that collectively define the technical infrastructure. (This is analogous to the choices within the internal business strategy arena to articulate the administrative structure of the firm dealing with roles, responsibilities and authority structures.)
- *IS processes*: those choices that define the work processes central to the operations of the IS infrastructure, such as systems development, maintenance, and monitoring and control systems. (This is analogous to the need for designing the business processes that support and shape the ability of the firm to execute business strategies.)
- *IS skills*: those choices pertaining to the acquisition, training and development of the knowledge and capabilities that individuals need to manage and operate the IS infrastructure effectively within the organization. (This is analogous to the skills needed to execute a given strategy.)

According to Henderson and Venkatraman (1993), managers think of IT strategy in terms of the latter three components, which reflect the internal orientation. When managers consider only the internal orientation, IT is often viewed as a 'cost of doing business' and is rarely seen as a strategic investment. If IT emerges as a critical enabler of business transformation with capabilities to deliver firm-level advantages, firms need to address the three external components of IT strategy as well. Moreover, realizing a fit between the internal and external domains of IT is a key success factor for deriving benefits from IT investments.

Strategic fit is one element; *functional integration* is the second building block of the strategic alignment model. Functional integration means that the IT strategy is aligned with the business strategy. It considers how choices made in the IT domain impact – enhance or threaten – those made in the business domain, and vice versa (Figure 8.2).

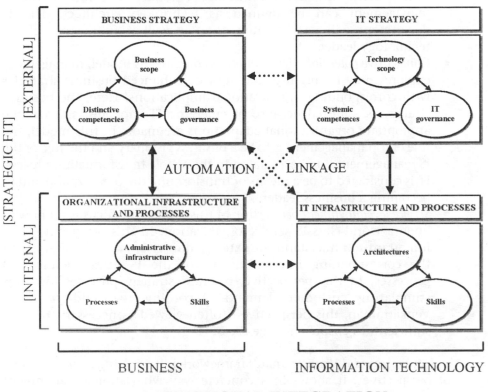

Figure 8.2 Strategic alignment model
Source: Henderson and Venkatraman (1993: 476)

Henderson and Venkatraman (1993) have identified four different ways that strategic alignment can be achieved:

- *Strategy execution alignment perspective*: in this model, the business strategy is articulated and drives both organizational design choices and the design of the IS infrastructure. Top management formulates the strategy and the role of the IS management is to implement the strategy. The IS department is seen as a cost/service centre, and will be evaluated on how well it fulfils this function.
- *Technology transformation alignment perspective*: this model involves the assessment of implementing the chosen business strategy through appropriate IT strategy and the articulation of the required IS infrastructure and processes. Organizational design is not so much of

a restriction and the organization seeks to identify the best possible IT competences through appropriate positioning in the IT marketplace. Since technology is crucial for the success of the company, top management should be technology visionary. The role of the IS management can be defined as technology architect. The IS department will be evaluated on how well it fulfils the role of technology leader.

- *Competitive potential alignment perspective*: in this model, management explores how IT might enable new or enhanced business strategies with corresponding organizational implications. Here, the business strategy is adjusted because of emerging IT capabilities. Then the appropriate organizational adaptations are made. In this model, the role of top management is to be a business visionary and the role of the IS management is to be a catalyst in this whole transformation process. IT is considered to be a means of transforming the organization and to becoming a business leader.
- *Service level alignment perspective*: in this model, the focus is on how to build a world-class IS service organization. In this perspective, it is important to understand the external dimensions of IT strategy with the corresponding internal design of the IS infrastructure and processes. In this perspective, business strategy provides ideas for stimulating customer demand. According to Henderson and Venkatraman, this perspective is often viewed as necessary, but not sufficient, to ensure effective use of IT.

Henderson and Venkatraman's framework is interesting from a number of perspectives. It shows in a concrete way what strategic alignment means: it involves both strategic fit and functional integration. The framework is also useful because it points to different ways IT and IS can be approached when aligning them with the business strategy. The four different perspectives take various aspects of strategy formation into account (see also Chapter 6), identify various roles for top management and IS management, and suggest several performance criteria.

How to create Strategic Information Systems alignment?

Senior management's awareness of IT

The implementation of a model for strategic IS alignment (such as the one proposed by Henderson and Venkatraman) will remain hampered if the gap between *perceiving* the potential benefits of IT and *realizing* these benefits is not closed. Without awareness of the potential benefits, the subsequent necessary steps – evaluation – remain aimless.

Kaplan and Norton (2001) see the development of an understanding of the business strategy throughout the organization as a first step towards the creation of strategic awareness. Similarly, insight into the strategic role of IT is fundamental to the realization of IT benefits. (In this respect, Henderson and Venkatraman's framework is particularly useful.) The failure to think strategically about IT, together with senior management's failure to overcome their resistance to change, are interdependent causes of the so-called IT productivity paradox (i.e., investing more in IT does not improve productivity and often results in less satisfied users and customers). Also, the failure to see IT as a resource similar to time, money, equipment, labour and materials causes senior management to put too much stress on improving current inefficiencies instead of focusing on IT as a catalyst for change.

Reaching consensus about strategic priorities and IT's contribution to strategy is crucial. All too often, executives do not correctly recognize their firm's alignment perspective and the role IT can play in meeting business objectives. Dynamic change in the business environment is often followed by business strategy changes, but IT and senior management perceive these changes differently (Burn and Szeto, 2000). This leads to several misunderstandings concerning the operational role of IT within the company and misunderstandings concerning the role IT can play as an enabler of competitive advantage in the external marketplace. These misunderstandings are exemplified in these typical viewpoints:

- CEOs most often wonder whether IT supports the strategic directions;
- The COO/CFO wonders whether the company's investment in IT is consistent with its business goals and related business operations;
- The Chief Intelligence Officer/IT manager wonders whether IT is aligned with the business, how this alignment can be improved, and whether the IS organization is well prepared to provide business solutions and to deal with accelerating business change.

From perceiving to realizing Strategic alignment helps general management to better *perceive* the potential business value of ICT. Strategic alignment helps in this process of envisioning that value, since it is a necessary cognitive prerequisite for the *realization* of the added value of IT. That is why some people argue for more top management involvement with IT projects (Earl and Feeny, 1994). Daily managerial practices are aimless without a strategic intent for IT. Tallon, Kraemer and Gurbaxani (2000) have gone as far as saying there is no direct effect of managerial practices on realized IT value, only an intermediary effect via the strategic intent for IT.

Tools for creating strategic awareness In the management literature, one finds several tools for increasing senior management's awareness of IT benefits. Three examples of such tools that we find particularly useful are: (1) Broadbent and Weill's typology of IT investments; (2) McFarlan's strategic grid; and (3) the CADIGA rule of thumb.

Peter Weill and Marianne Broadbent (1998) have looked at different types of IT investments and have developed an *investment pyramid*. This investment pyramid distinguishes four types of investment (infrastructural, transactional, informational and strategic) and helps senior management to position the types of IT implementation with their use and importance for the whole organization (see Figure 8.3).

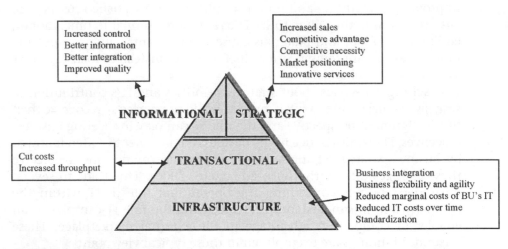

Figure 8.3 Types of IT investment
Source: Weill and Broadbent (1998: 52)

Senior management's awareness of IT can be improved by letting them categorize past and current IT investments to analyse the proportion they take from the central budget (versus the business units' budgets), and to let them question to what extent the related strategic benefits have been or could be obtained.

McFarlan's (1984) *strategic grid* is a good tool for such an analysis. It addresses the following dimensions: (1) strategic impact of existing application systems and (2) strategic impact of applications under development (see Figure 8.4). Companies in the 'support' dimension use IT primarily for support activities, such as payroll processing and administration. Companies in the 'turnaround' dimension are not heavily dependent upon IT at present, but they may look to IT to improve their competitive posture in the market. In the 'factory' dimension, companies may use IT heavily for day-to-day operations, so that IT is viewed as largely strategic (because of the dependency of the organization's operations on mission- or operations-critical IT applications). The 'strategic' dimension companies are now and in the future heavily dependent upon IT for performance and day-to-day operations and for competitive advantage. McFarlan himself, while making this kind of analysis, preferred to talk about the management of the *ICT application portfolio approach*.

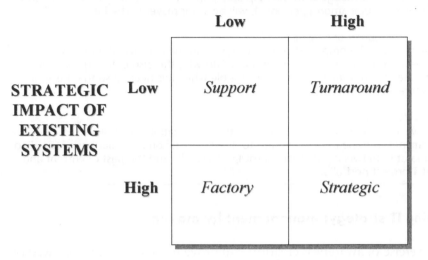

STRATEGIC IMPACT OF APPLICATIONS UNDER DEVELOPMENT

		Low	High
STRATEGIC IMPACT OF EXISTING SYSTEMS	**Low**	*Support*	*Turnaround*
	High	*Factory*	*Strategic*

Figure 8.4 McFarlan's strategic grid
Source: McFarlan (1984: 100)

A third tool for increasing strategic awareness is the CADIGA rule of thumb. This model is an adaptation by Deschoolmeester and colleagues (1995, 2000) of Wiseman's (1985) ideas, and gives business management a list of motives for investing in IT. These motives are summarized in Table 8.1.

Table 8.1 CADIGA – an overview of motives for investing in IT

C   *Cost reduction/Capital control*
Many companies implement an Enterprise Resource Programme (ERP) to obtain more productive procurement and production planning. This way, they can achieve smaller inventories of resources and finished products and also a more optimal use of production resources. Furthermore, through more efficient information processing, smaller teams of purchasers and production planners can do more work.

A   *Alliances (Customers, suppliers, other companies, internal cooperation)*
Integration and cooperation between the functional domains via central databases or coordinated activities in an integrated process are made possible with the aid of ICT. In an extended enterprise, suppliers and customers can cooperate non-stop and in real-time thanks to the new ICT.

D   *Differentiation from competition (quality, speed)*
Via Internet Web browsing, the customer can place his or her order and buy a custom-made product. Also, the cycle time between sales order and delivery can be drastically reduced. Websites where these facilities are available can differentiate one's company from competitors that still follow the traditional way of selling.
I   *Information and knowledge/Innovation*
Having the right information brought to the right decision-maker at the right

Table 8.1 *Cont.*

moment is an essential task of all information management. When wisdom and experience are added to information, one gets knowledge. He who creates and shares the most knowledge with the help if ICT, and has a mentality of learning and of sharing knowledge among personnel, will be a star player in the future.

G *Organizational support of growth*
With the help of ICT, companies can grow in size, in the number of business activities or on a geographic scale. Besides quantitative growth, this also entails qualitative growth, whereby information is more accessible when it is needed so that personnel can be more 'empowered'.

A *Agility and flexibility*
To improve awareness of the role of ICT for the organization, upper-level management has to be flexible enough to question itself on a regular basis regarding the relationship between potential and obtained results and the past or current and future ICT project portfolio.

Formulating IT strategy: management by maxim

The exercise of awareness creation will prove futile if it is not followed by extensive and clear-cut communication towards all organizational internal and external participants about the role and objectives of the IT efforts. Therefore, clear-cut communication concerning the strategic core is required. Earl and Feeny (1994) propose that, before moving to the project management steps of *ex ante* and *ex post* evaluation, strategic orientation through the formulation of strategic '*business maxims*' is needed.

Broadbent and Weill (1997) have shown how these 'maxims' can form a blueprint for the formulation of business strategy. By outlining the strategic context through a SWOT analysis (Strengths, Weaknesses, Opportunities and Threats), management can develop a series of short, sharp strategic statements – called business maxims, which are business guiding principles from which the IT guiding principles can be deduced. By communicating these 'frames' across all management layers, one can keep all the involved parties better informed about the strategic direction. Business maxims, which are very similar to the CADIGA rules of thumb, draw on a firm's mission or strategic statements and aim to articulate an agreed-upon position in a form that executives can readily understand and act on. IT maxims describe how a firm needs to connect, share and structure information and deploy IT across the organization (Table 8.2).

Table 8.2 Five categories of IT maxims

IT maxims	Examples
Expectations for IT investments in the firm	● We use IT to reduce costs through eliminating duplicated efforts. ● Our IT spending must meet defined business needs and show clear cost savings . . .
Data access and use	● The usefulness of data must be recognized beyond the area immediately responsible for its capture. ● Centralized information flow should allow all parts of the firm to spot trends quickly and use them to the firm's advantage . . .
Hardware and software resources	● We will migrate towards hardware and software resources that can process complex transactions globally. ● We will move towards electronic processing of repetitive transactions . . .
Communications capabilities and services	● Our corporate network must provide access to a wide range of applications essential to the delivery of consistent customer service. ● Our corporate network must be capable of carrying high bandwidth applications such as imaging and video-conferencing . . .
Architecture and standards approach	● We have a recommended IT architecture covering hardware, software and connectivity requirements. ● We have agreed on firm-wide IT architecture covering data, hardware, software and communications . . .

Source: Broadbent and Weill (1997: 84)

Ex ante evaluation

The phases of awareness and communication will usually be followed by the budgeting cycle, including the costs and benefits identified in the evaluation stage. In an ideal world, perfect care is given to making the cost–benefit of each IT effort explicit. The potential value of IT investments should be considered both in pre-project selection (*ex ante*) and *post*-investment evaluation. The clear *ex ante* formulation of goals – preferably in the format of a well thought-out business plan – will stimulate the process of, and key persons' involvement in, strategy formulation positively.

IT projects that are either mandatory (like the Euro-conversion projects) or clear-cut substitution projects do not fit easily into this cycle model. Such projects are treated as 'forced projects' because carrying them out is simply unavoidable. Of course, cost-conscious behaviour is appropriate here as well. In addition, IT projects that deal with technological obsolescence have another type of evaluation.

For other IT projects, formulating clear goals *ex ante* will have a positive impact on stakeholder value. In this context, a collection of basic criteria is proposed with which business can assess the feasibility of IT projects and the overall IT application portfolio. Information Economics provides a generalized framework for evaluating and comparing IT investments and projects by ranking – in addition to the financial ROI criterion – several value and risk criteria of specific IT projects. For example, Parker and her colleagues (1989) proposed to combine information value and strategic value for the company and at the same time consider organizational and technological risks when doing (or not doing) an IT project. Table 8.3 summarizes Parker's main recommendations. This has been extended recently with a number of additional criteria that relate to the discussion of sustainable development (e.g., environmental and societal impacts) in Marilyn Parker's (1995) latest work.

Table 8.3 Parker et al.'s (1989) Information Economics

Measures	Explanation
Financial domain	
Return on Investment (ROI)	
Organizational domain	
Strategic match	The degree to which IS fits with the strategic goals of the firm.
Competitive advantage	The degree to which an investment can contribute to a stronger position in the market. Examples are changing the structure of the company or of a company's branch, improving the competitive position, and creating and using all strategic possibilities of IS.
Management information	The degree to which the (to be) implemented IS provides critical information to executive management concerning the core activities of the organization.
Competitive response	The degree to which not investing would be a risk and timely implementation would create an advantage over competitors.
Project or organizational risk	The degree to which the IS to be implemented is dependent on new competences. Some investments in IS can cause large organizational changes.
Technological domain	
Strategic IS architecture	The degree to which the proposed IS matches with the information plan and information architecture.
Definitional uncertainty	The degree to which the users' need for information can be fulfilled adequately.
Technological uncertainty	The degree to which IS demands new technical competences, new hardware, and/or new software.
IS infrastructure risk	The degree to which investments in IS demand more investment in the technical infrastructure, and the degree to which the IS department can support these efforts.

Source: Adapted from Parker and Benson (1989: 22–6)

Ex post evaluation

A *post*-implementation review as a form of impact analysis will help general management to assess the business value of IT. Similar to *ex ante* evaluation, tangible and intangible benefits should be taken into account.

A dual focus is needed on both business level strategies and functional level strategies. For example, on the business unit level, certain applications such as supply chain management software can have a positive potential value for the manufacturing department but a negative potential value for the sales department. Not considering multiple loci of potential value across different company departments leads to the failure of not being able to uncover heterogeneous valuation perspectives (Davern and Kauffman, 2000). This approach is usually rather qualitative, but for management it is quite accessible and understandable.

Next, evaluation at the functional level is possible with Kaplan and Norton's Balanced Scorecard (see also Chapter 3). The Balanced Scorecard can make progress in strategy explicit by assessing the impact of all sorts of organizational projects – in this case, more specifically, the IT project. For recent IT projects, one can evaluate aspects such as innovation and learning, process performance, customer satisfaction and financial results, while taking into account the various stakeholders. By doing so, top management recognizes that IT is only an ingredient – however important in many respects – beside other functional investments for 'improving' the business, such as marketing, R&D, production infrastructure renewal, quality management, etc. Furthermore, the Balanced Scorecard promotes the use of both financial and non-financial measures to monitor the progress of IT (and other) projects, providing a multidimensional approach to *ex post* evaluation.

Distribution of IT efforts

IT efforts and investments should be allocated and distributed in a 'balanced' way across the whole organization. In the IS literature, there is growing consensus that a *federal IS organization* makes it possible to produce a good mix between (1) an internal central IT department and decentralized IT departments, and (2) key-users or IT specialist nodes provided all over the organization, and/or an external IS service provider. Here, a central issue is the appropriate allocation of IT resources and know-how over central parts of the organization and several business units (and their functional departments). Also, the mix between centralization and decentralization of managerial responsibilities and investment decisions regarding IT can enhance the move towards a federal IS organization. The federal organization aims to create higher internal and external stakeholder value, while at the same time creating a more satisfactory situation for management and the collaborators themselves.

When persons responsible for IT are more involved in the business strategy-making process, they will be inspired to offer strategic ideas and they will be more committed to the implementation of the strategic plans. More specifically, the move towards a federal IS organization is easier if the CIO (Chief Intelligence Officer) is a member of the (extended) executive committee. Inclusion of the CIO on the central director's team varies greatly across industries, as we found out in a Belgian survey of 80 companies (banking and insurance: already 43 per cent; manufacturing: only 21 per cent). Such a federal IS organization is characterized by:

- High-level and/or independent position of IT department in the organization chart.
- An IT steering committee (str-ICT-al, overall IT funding level, infrastructure investments, competitive issues solvable by IT);
- IT capable persons 'absorbed' within business lines or departments, and vice versa;
- An appropriate mix of internal (IT dept) versus external IS service provider;
- Appropriate centralization/decentralization of IT/IS competences and know-how.

The pros and cons of decentralization and centralization of the IT department are presented in Table 8.4. It is our firm belief that a balance between a centralized and decentralized position of IT within the organization is not only part of the alignment process, it is also an absolute requirement for the success of IT efforts and investments as observed by the various stakeholders.

Table 8.4 Pros and cons of decentralization and centralization as central governing principle

Decentralization		Centralization	
(IT organization oriented towards contribution to business strategy)		(IT organization being lowest cost service provider for integration of data and communications across (previously) unconnected activities)	
Pros	Cons	Pros	Cons
• Responsiveness to rapidly changing business requirements • Business awareness • Local control of priorities • Appropriateness of solutions • Local cost control	• Architectural diffusion • Redundant cost • No enterprise learning • Isolation of best practice	• Economies of scale • Uniform standards • Architectural control • Asset protection • Enterprise security	• Danger of isolation from users and business • User frustration • Communication costs • Enterprise communications • Integrated data management • Fairness in pricing

Strategic Information Systems alignment and maturity

Reaching strategic IS alignment is not an easy task and requires an organization to have reached a certain level of maturity. Jerry Luftman (2001) has proposed a methodology that enables companies to self-assess the maturity of their Business/IT strategic alignment. Luftman identified six elements of IT/Business alignment and five stages of maturity. This maturity framework is based on the *Capability Maturity Models*® (CMM®) of the Software Engineering Institute (SEI), a research and development centre sponsored by the US Department of Defense and operated by Carnegie Mellon University. By referring to the characteristics of five maturity levels within each of six strategic categories, Luftman contends that companies can generate numeric scores that reflect the maturity of their alignment. Evidently, few companies have already attained the highest maturity level (see Figure 8.5).

	LEVEL 1: Initial/*ad hoc* process	LEVEL 2: Committed process	LEVEL 3: Established focus process	LEVEL 4: Managed process	LEVEL 5: Optimized process
Communications	Business & IT lack understanding	Limited understanding	Good understanding	Bonding, unified	Informal, pervasive
Competency	Some technical measurements	Functional cost efficiency	Some cost effectiveness	Cost effective: some partner value	Extended to external partners
Governance	No formal process	Tactical at functional level; occasionally responsive	Relevant process across organization	Relevant process across organization	Integrated across organization, partners
Partnership	Conflict; IT is a cost of doing business	Process enabler; IT emerges as asset	Process driver; IT seen as asset	IT enables, drives business strategy	IT and business co-adaptive
Scope and architecture	Traditional (e.g., accounting e-mail)	Transaction (e.g., decision-support system)	Integrated across organization	Integrated with partners	Evolve with partners
Skills	IT takes risk, gets little reward; technical training	Differ across functional organizations	Emerging value service provider	Shared risk, rewards	Education/ careers/ rewards across organization

Figure 8.5 Luftman's five levels of IT/Business alignment
Source: Luftman (2001: 12)

Figure 8.5 can be seen as a rephrasing and updating of the classic Gibson and Nolan (1974; Nolan, 1979) view on the technological cycles of innovation and obsolescence. Their scheme laid the foundation for an organization to audit its current situation and to plan and control its IT efforts from initiation to maturity. It helped companies to introduce, implement and develop each wave of IT/IS technology.

COBIT (Control Objectives for Information and related Technology) is a similar framework developed by the Information Systems Audit and Control Foundation and the IT Governance Institute in the USA. The framework provides an answer to the question how to get IT under control such that it delivers the information the organization needs. COBIT has been developed as a generally applicable and accepted standard for good IT security and control practices that provides a reference framework for various types of user (management, IS audit, control and security practitioners). In this framework, IT processes are grouped into four major categories: (1) planning and organization of the IT activities; (2) acquisition and implementation of application software; technology infrastructure and IT procedures and systems; (3) delivery and support; and (4) monitoring of the IT processes (including IT quality assurance and audit). For each of these group of processes, COBIT provides a maturity model for control over IT processes. This gives managers an idea about where they are (eventually in comparison to a best-in-class in the industry), and how they should improve. COBIT also defines critical success factors, key goal indicators and key performance indicators for these different IT processes, and as such is one of the best developed performance management frameworks for the IT function today.

Conclusion

In this chapter, we have explored the concept of strategic IS alignment. The basic question is: What is the optimal fit between an organization's strategy and its IT and IS? We have presented Henderson and Venkatraman's framework, which gives us a very good overview of the various roles IT and IS can play, and what this means from an alignment perspective. Then, we have focused on the question: How to create strategic IS alignment? We have identified five major initiatives for achieving this:

- Augmenting the awareness of the senior management regarding the strategic opportunities made possible by IT;
- Formulating and communicating strategy by higher management – we referred to business maxims as a good tool in this process;
- *Ex ante* evaluation;
- Combining *ex ante* evaluation with *ex post* evaluation;

- Allocating and distributing IT efforts and investments in a 'balanced' way across the whole organization.

Finally, we have also pointed to the concept of maturity, a concept that we will tackle in greater detail in Part III.

Integrated Performance Management
through Effective Management Control

WERNER BRUGGEMAN

Performance measurement and performance management are vivid themes in the literature on management control. So, it is only natural that we investigate how this literature has contributed to the field of Integrated Performance Management. The purpose of this chapter is to describe how management control systems can be used to effectively manage company and business performance. First, we define the scope of management control and describe the link with organizational strategy. Then, we focus on the three elements of the management control system: (1) the management control structure; (2) the control process; and (3) the management control culture (beliefs systems). We will describe these three elements in greater detail and give an overview of the findings in mainstream contingency research studying the effectiveness of control systems in various environmental and organizational contexts.

Management control defined

Management control and the link with strategy

Following Anthony and Govindarajan (1995), *management control* can be defined as a process of motivating managers to perform actions and activities in line with the goals and strategies of the organization. According to this definition, an organization is 'under control' when its members do what the management wants them to do. Management control comprises various tasks, among which are:

- Planning the future activities of the organization;
- Coordinating the activities of the various members of the organization;
- Communicating information;
- Evaluating this information;
- Deciding on the actions to be taken; and
- Influencing people to adapt their behaviour according to the company goals (Anthony and Govindarajan, 1995).

From the definition above, it follows that management control plays a central role in managing the company's performance and the implementation of its strategies. Therefore, it is of vital importance that management behaviour, which is stimulated by the management control system, is consistent with the strategy to be implemented (the so-called 'intended strategy' – see also Chapter 6).

The starting points of the management control process are the mission, the vision and the strategies of the organization. We refer to Chapter 6 for a more thorough discussion of each of these concepts, but recapitulate them very briefly here. The *mission* of an organization is a description in general terms of the role of the company towards its stakeholders. It describes the reasons for the company's existence, its strategic focus and values, as well as how the long-term goals should be realized. The goals are descriptions of the long-term desired future of the company. The mission and goals translate into *strategies*, which specify the way in which the vision aspired to should be reached. The strategy in turn is translated into concrete *performance objectives or targets*. This is usually done through formalized action plans.

Management control and goal congruence

The purpose of management control is to maximize congruence among the goals of the organization, its various entities and its individual managers. This is called *goal congruence*. The way in which managers react to management control information depends to a large extent on their *personal goals*. For effective management control, it is important to be able to measure the impact of these motivators, because they largely determine the behaviour of people in an organization, as well as the desirability of the consequences of their behaviour. The management control system should be designed in such a way that, whenever managers take decisions that fit into their personal goals, these decisions should also be in the interests of the company as a whole. In other words, the management control system must create the conditions to foster a feeling within the members of the organization that they can best realize their personal goals by contributing as much as possible to the realization of the general company goals. It is clear that the way in which managers are evaluated and financially rewarded for their performance plays a significant role in reaching 'goal congruence' (see also Chapter 13).

Goal congruence is an important condition for effective performance management. The problem of goal congruence can be described in more detail in the following way. Corporate goals are translated into departmental goals, and in these departments people are working who also have their personal goals. A first problem that can arise is a lack of congruence between the corporate and departmental goals. For example, a department or division of a company can have a long-term vision that says it is desirable to stay small and be profitable (in other words 'small is beautiful'). On the other hand, top management might be striving for a company goal of strong growth and therefore wants the division to grow. In this case, there is a lack of congruence between the different visions, and a number of meetings will have to be organized to align the goals and strategies.

However, there is also the possibility that the division manager is opposed to the growth of his division because he is personally reluctant to make the required efforts. In this case, there is a conflict between the personal goals of the manager and the goals of the company.

Role of management control in performance management

Verifying whether the company (or the business unit or department) is on track is an important management function. Management control is an important instrument for motivating personnel to act in accordance with the goals and strategies of the organization. This motivation is one of the major driving forces of the performance and the value of the company. The management control system must be adjusted to the goals and the strategies of the company and it must be optimally aligned.

The contribution of control to strategy implementation Robert Simons (1995) has outlined how management control can contribute to effective strategy implementation. In his book, *Levers of Control*, he introduced four key constructs that must be analysed and understood in order to implement strategy successfully: core values, risks to be avoided, critical performance variables and strategic uncertainties. Each construct is controlled by a different system, or lever, the use of which has different implications. These levers are:

- *Beliefs systems*, used to inspire and direct the search for new opportunities.
- *Boundary systems*, used to set limits on opportunity-seeking behaviour. There are three broad categories of boundary systems: business conduct boundaries, internal controls and strategic boundaries.[1]
- *Diagnostic control systems*, used to motivate, monitor and reward achievement of specified goals. Diagnostic control systems attempt to measure output variables that represent important performance dimensions of a given strategy: critical performance variables. These factors must be achieved or implemented successfully for the *intended strategy* of the business to succeed. Diagnostic variables should be measured, monitored and controlled, but reporting on them to higher management is on an exception basis only, when a value falls outside a normal control limit and corrective actions must be taken.
- *Interactive control systems*, used to stimulate search and learning, allowing new strategies to emerge as participants throughout the

organization respond to perceived opportunities and threats. As a fourth lever of control, these systems focus attention on strategic uncertainties and enable strategic renewal (i.e., *emergent strategies*).

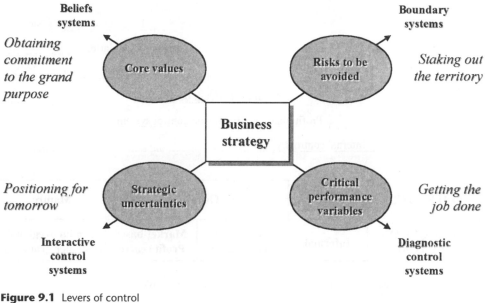

Figure 9.1 Levers of control
Source: Simons (1995: 159)

Control of business strategy is achieved by integrating these four levers of control. The power of these levers in implementing strategy does not lie in how each is used alone, but rather in how they complement each other when used together. Two of the control systems – beliefs systems and interactive control systems – motivate organizational participants to search creatively and expand the opportunity space. These systems create intrinsic motivation by creating a positive informational environment that encourages information sharing and learning. The other two levers of control – boundary systems and diagnostic control systems – are used to constrain search behaviour and allocate scarce attention. These systems rely on extrinsic motivation by providing explicit goals, formula-based rewards and clear limits to opportunity-seeking. These four levers create tension between creative innovation and predictable goal movement. This tension requires managers of effective organizations to know how to achieve both high degrees of learning (innovation) and high degrees of control (efficiency) (Simons, 2000: 304).

Levers of control and the organizational lifecycle

Developing an integrated control system does not happen overnight. Managers of small entrepreneurial firms perform their strategic control rather informally. As the business grows larger, however, informal processes become inadequate. Simons (1995, 2000) illustrates how the levers of control can be successfully implemented as a business grows and matures (see Figure 9.2).

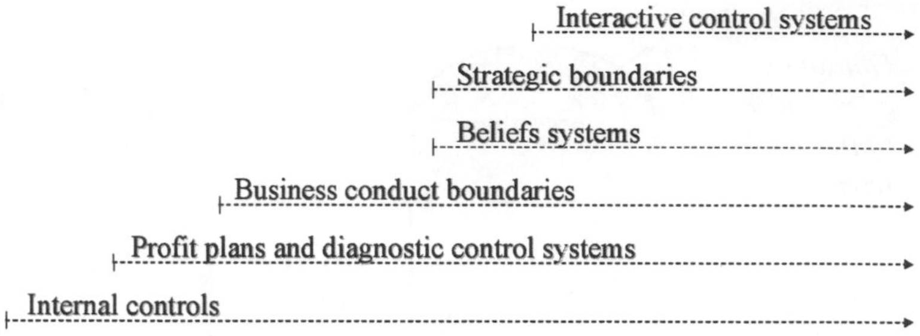

LIFE CYCLE	Small Start-up	Growing		Mature
ORGANIZATION STRUCTURE	Informal	Functional specialization	Market-based Profit centres	Product/regional customer groupings

Figure 9.2 Introduction of control systems over the lifecycle of a business
Source: Simons (1995: 128)

In their most recent book, Kaplan and Norton (2001) point out the importance of using the Balanced Scorecard (see Chapter 3) as an interactive control system. It is clear from Figure 9.2 that an organization must have some experience with other control systems before it can exploit the Balanced Scorecard in this way.

> Diagnostic systems, boundary systems, and internal control systems are all necessary, but they do not create a learning organization aligned to a focused strategy. Some Balanced Scorecard implementation failures occurred because organizations used their scorecard only diagnostically, and failed to get the learning and innovation benefits from an interactive system. The CEOs of successful Balanced Scorecard adopters succeeded because they use the scorecard interactively, for communication and to drive learning and improvement. They set overall strategy and then encouraged people within their organization to identify the local actions and initiatives that would have the highest impact for accomplishing the scorecard objectives. (Kaplan and Norton, 2001: 350)

Management control versus task control

Anthony and Govindarajan (1995) distinguish management control, which ultimately is about implementing strategies, from strategic planning and control and task control:

- *Strategic planning and control* is the process of determining and evaluating the goals of the organization, and formulating or reformulating the broad strategies to be used in attaining these goals. Strategic control refers to the maintenance of the environmental conditions of strategies. Strategic control is used to evaluate the background of existing strategies and the environmental assumptions on which the strategies were formulated. It can also involve the reformulation of strategies.
- *Task control* is the process of ensuring that specific tasks are carried out effectively and efficiently. For example, internal audit and internal control are often associated with task control.

Elements of a management control system

In the previous paragraphs, we have described the importance of management control for strategy implementation and for performance management. In the remainder of this chapter, we go deeper into the details of the management control system and focus on its compounding elements. A *management control system* consists of three basic elements: (1) the management control structure; (2) the management control process; and (3) the management control culture.

The first element, the *management control structure*, deals with the division of the organization into 'responsibility centres'. A distinction needs to be made among the various types of responsibility centre, such as 'revenue centres', 'expense centres', 'profit centres', and 'investment centres'. Determining the optimal structure is part of the task of management control.

The second element in a management control system, the *management control process*, comprises the cycle of: planning for the expected input and output; measuring the results; comparing plan to reality; and, finally, adjusting if necessary.

The third element is the *management control culture* or the *beliefs systems*. This is the combination of communal values and behavioural norms, which determine the behaviour of managers and staff.

Choosing an effective management control structure

To manage an organization according to certain objectives, you must first choose an appropriate management control structure. A *management control structure* is the system of basic principles for the functioning of the organization or the organizational structure in which the management control will take place. Hellriegel, Slocum and Woodman (1992: 5) define the organizational structure as 'the structure and formal system of communication, division of labor, coordination, control, authority and responsibility necessary to achieve the organization's goals'.

Elements of a management control structure

When defining the management control structure, the following questions must be answered:

- What are the various *departments* in the organization?
- What are the *responsibilities* of the various department managers?
- How are the activities of the various departments coordinated, and what are the *coordination mechanisms*?

Defining the departmental structure In organizing for effective performance management, the company may choose a functional organization structure, a multidivisional structure, a matrix organization or a network organization structure.

When choosing the *functional organization structure*, the tasks are grouped based on the functional specialty to which they belong. Traditionally, the following departments are presented in the organizational chart: 'Sales and Marketing', 'Engineering', 'Production', 'Distribution', 'Purchasing' and 'Finance'.

An organization can also be controlled within a *multidivisional structure*, which is a structure based on products or markets instead of functions. If based on *products*, we have a *product-oriented department structure*. The sales, development, production and purchasing activities with regard to a certain product are concentrated in one, individual department. On the other hand, the organization could also be structured around *markets*. In this case, all tasks that deal with a certain geographical market are grouped. The multidivisional structure groups management tasks in *divisions*, each of which focuses on a certain product or geographical area where the products are sold. Division managers are responsible for the daily operational decisions within their division. Top management no longer wants to engage itself in daily problems, but instead focuses on the important strategic decisions (e.g., investment decisions, acquisitions and divestments). When designing a multidivisional structure, the *business unit* concept can be taken as a starting point. In this concept, the organization is structured around *strategic business units* or SBUs. An SBU is an operating unit of a planning focus that groups a distinct set of products or services sold to a uniform set of customers, facing a well-defined set of competitors.

Many companies have a combination of functional and product- or market-oriented structures in their organizational structure. They prefer to work in a *matrix organization*. On the horizontal line, we find an R&D manager, a production manager, a financial manager and a purchasing manager. On the vertical line, we see the various business or product line managers. They are responsible, first of all, for the marketing and sales of their product line, but they must also take care of the coordination between the various functional departments. Staff members in the various functional departments are thus led by two managers.

Defining the responsibility of managers After determining the department structure by which the organization will be controlled, it is important to define the responsibilities of each department. A department or an organizational unit, led by a manager with clearly specified responsibilities, is called a *responsibility centre*. An organizational structure is therefore a hierarchy of responsibility centres.

Delegated *responsibility* demands appropriate *authority*. When assigning the responsibility for a specific output to a certain department, this department should also have control over its output. So, responsibility requires the existence of *'controllability'*. Delegated responsibility also requires an appropriate *'accountability'*. A manager is considered to be 'accountable' when he or she is assessed according to the realization of his or her objectives. In other words, performance is monitored, and if his or her performance turns out to be bad, management will take the necessary actions.

A responsibility centre is not only assessed on its output (which result has been achieved?), but also on its input (how many inputs were used?). In general, a responsibility centre should be assessed on two basic criteria: efficiency and effectiveness. *Efficiency* is the relation between output and input. The more cars that are made in a car manufacturing company with the same production costs, the more efficient the operation is. The cost per unit (i.e., the total production cost divided by the number of units produced) is therefore an efficiency norm. *Effectiveness* expresses the extent to which the realized output is aligned with the goals and strategies to be realized. It could be that the sales department has become more efficient by selling more with the same people, but that the sales efforts were focused on markets in which the company has chosen not to be active for strategic reasons. In this case, the sales efforts were not effective, i.e., they did not contribute to the realization of the corporate strategy. When designing a management control system, one must determine what efficiency and effectiveness mean concretely for each department and how these can be measured. Assigning responsibilities to the departments means determining the right performance measures.

The responsibilities of the manager can be divided into financial, strategic and operational responsibilities. Performance measures must be defined for each of these responsibility areas. We call them financial, strategic and operational performance measures.

With regard to the *financial responsibilities*, we can distinguish among the following types of responsibility centres: expense centres, revenue centres, profit centres and investment centres.

- *Expense centres* are departments that are responsible for the costs they have made (input), but whose output is not measured in financial terms. In a functional organization structure, typical expense centres are the production department, the R&D department, the purchasing department and the financial department. Staff functions are also usually controlled as expense centres.

- *Revenue centres* are departments in which the output, but not the input, is measured in financial terms. Typical revenue centres are the sales departments. Their management task is not concerned with the costs incurred; instead, they strive to reach a turnover objective.
- In a *profit centre*, the manager is responsible for the costs and also for the revenues of the department. Thus, the 'profit centre' manager receives a profit report for his or her department.
- In *investment centres*, the profit as well as the investments ('assets employed') are measured. The department manager has the authority to take investment decisions and is also responsible for the profitability of the investments made. A typical performance measure for investment centres is the return on investment (ROI).

Regarding *strategic responsibilities*, a manager's task not only involves realizing financial goals; the manager and his or her team may also be charged with contributing towards realizing the competitive strategy of their division and the general strategy of the company. For example, the general company strategy may be concerned with growth in all business units and with global operations. Choosing and formulating this strategy may be the work of general management, but translating it into the business unit may be the responsibility of the division manager. The division manager may also be responsible for defining and developing a competitive advantage (in the areas of quality, flexibility and customer service, for example) for his or her business unit. The manager may be responsible for constantly tracking the evolution of customer satisfaction and adapting the competitive strategy in time to this evolution. When strategic responsibilities are also delegated to a lower level in the organization, the manager responsible should be evaluated with regard to the level of success of the chosen strategies. Performance measures must be determined for this as well. The method of the Balanced Scorecard (see Chapter 3) may be of help here.

Finally, regarding *operational responsibilities*, it is obvious that managers of responsibility centres are also responsible for managing daily operations. A number of 'key performance measures' can be defined for this, which are followed up closely by top management. The division manager may be asked to realize objectives with regard to inventory levels, processing times, products out of specification, revision times, etc.

Restriction of responsibilities and freedom of action Each responsibility centre is restricted in its activity by a number of rules and procedures. *Rules* are formal expressions of the behaviours that are permitted and not permitted to the members of a department. *Procedures* are descriptions of steps to be followed in executing a task or in making decisions. Rules and procedures provide a detailed specification of the kinds of responsibility and freedom of action the responsibility centre has or does not have. They indicate how the responsibilities and freedom of action are restricted. The indicated restrictions can be expressed in a positive or negative way. Positive responsibility restrictions describe what the responsibility centre manager may do. Negative restrictions describe what the manager is not allowed to do. Some restrictions relate to responsibilities, others are involved with the manager's freedom of decision.

The freedom of an individual in an organization can also be restricted by general codes of behaviour, which result from existing laws, statutory provisions and ethical values. These are meant to prevent the potential mix of personal and company interests (e.g., they indicate in what way confidential information should be treated). Restriction of responsibilities and freedom of action are all part of the boundary systems of a company. These are 'explicit statements embedded in formal information systems that define and communicate specific risks to be avoided' (Simons, 1995: 112).

Coordination mechanisms When the department structure and the responsibilities of the various departments are defined, rules must be set up with regard to the actions between departments as well. The responsibility for realizing the global company goals and strategies cannot be split up into independent partial responsibilities. Departments and divisions must cooperate in various areas. Therefore, it is important that rules with respect to this cooperation be defined that motivate the managers maximally to target their efforts towards realizing the global company goals. There are two important kinds of rules that coordinate actions between departments: (1) formal coordination mechanisms (task forces, standing committees, integrating managers); and (2) transfer price systems.

Choosing the optimal management control structure

Designing the management control structure involves a number of choices. The decision can be made to manage in a functional structure or in a divisional structure. Within a divisional structure, the divisions can be structured around products, markets, business units, or a combination of these. One can also choose to work in a matrix organization. Then, a choice must be made regarding the degree of delegation of responsibilities. A department can be led as an expense centre, a revenue centre, a profit centre or an investment centre. The responsibilities of these centres can be restricted in various ways, and cooperation between departments can be coordinated by several coordination mechanisms and rules regarding transfer prices.

In some companies, management control is characterized by a detailed set of formal rules, centralized decision power, limited delegated responsibilities and a strict hierarchy of authority. Such a structure is called *mechanistic*. At the other end of the spectrum, we have the *organic* organizations. They are characterized by few rules, decentralized power of decision, group decision-making, broadly defined functional responsibilities and a flexible application of the hierarchic relations.

We can now ask the question: Do optimal choices exist? In order to answer this question, we must first define what makes a management control structure optimal. The answer to this question can be found in the description of the task of management control: *the objective of management control is to motivate managers maximally to realize the corporate goals and to implement the strategies.* So, a management control structure is optimal when it maximally stimulates the desired goal-oriented behaviour and minimally leads to undesired (or dysfunctional) behaviour. To be able to choose a management control structure, one must predict what the effect of the choice will be on the management behaviour and whether the expected effect is desired or not. For example:

- A company that wants to realize a competitive strategy of flexibility (custom-made work) in its business units wonders if it is optimal to manage the departments in a functional organization structure, in which the sales department is responsible for the turnover and the production departments (as expense centres) are responsible for the price of the products made. To be able to answer this question, we need to know to what extent the production managers are inclined to handle specific customer demands in a flexible way when the price of the products is the most important performance measure.

- Universities lead their faculties and departments as discretionary expense centres with respect to educational activities. In the short term, the deans and department heads are responsible for the costs of their faculties and departments, and not directly for the number of students and the revenues. As a consequence, the professors are not motivated to have many students, and they organize very few (if any) activities to influence and increase the number of students in the short term. Faculties and departments could also be managed as profit centres. The question is: What would be the effect on the management behaviour of deans, chairmen and professors? Would they act in a more commercial way? Would they lose their interest in research? Would this lead to overly aggressive competition among universities and, if so, is aggressive competition a corporate strategic choice within educational policy?

To be able to make an optimal choice of management control structure, good insight into the strategy that is to be realized is crucial. The choice of the management control structure must be aligned with the strategic choices of the company. Knowledge of how managers will be influenced by certain structural choices is also important. One can learn from one's own experience or from the experiences of other companies. In most cases, companies learn from their own experience. Setting up a management control structure is a dynamic process. The key is to look for both well-motivated and dysfunctional management behaviours in the existing structure. Ultimately, the process should yield new ideas for improving the structure to promote the desired behaviour and eliminate the dysfunctional behaviour.

Experiences from other companies can also be helpful. A significant part of the literature on management control focuses on research of the general tendencies and patterns in management behaviour in various types of management control structure. A general conclusion is that there is no management control structure that is optimal for all control situations. The optimal management control structure depends on the situation. The research that studies which management control structure best suits which type of environment is called 'contingency research'. This contingency research has focused on two major contingency variables: (1) the environment; and (2) a firm's strategy.

Study of the first contingency variable has helped identify the appropriate structures to fit the levels of *uncertainty in the environment* (Burns and Stalker, 1961; Lawrence and Lorsch, 1967; Galbraith, 1973; Drazin and Van de Ven, 1985). Structure is generally discussed in terms of mechanistic versus organic approaches to organizing, and it is believed that more organic structures are best suited to uncertain environments. These are structures that focus on 'clan control', i.e., social control coordinated by integrative mechanisms such as task forces and meetings.

Contingency research also shows that management control structures should be well suited to the company's chosen *strategy*. Different strategies may require different control structures. A popular typology deals with the strategic mission of business units, which may vary from a 'build' strategy, to a 'hold' strategy, a 'harvest' strategy and, finally, a 'divest' strategy. The objective of a build strategy is to increase market share and production volumes, while a hold strategy tries to protect the existing market share and maintain the current competitive position. A harvest strategy focuses on maximizing cash flow and profit in the short run, even if this is at the expense of market share. Last, the divest strategy concerns the decision to withdraw from a certain business. Other strategy typologies that are often used in the management control literature come from Porter (1985) and Miles and Snow (1978) (see Chapter 6 for more information). Evidence from the strategy/organizational design research suggests that for strategies characterized by a conservative orientation (defenders), harvest and cost leadership are best served by centralized control systems, specialized and formalized work, simple coordination mechanisms, and directing attention to problem areas (Miles and Snow, 1978; Porter, 1985; Miller and Friesen, 1982). For strategies characterized by an entrepreneurial orientation (prospectors), build and product differentiation are linked to a lack of standardized procedures, decentralized and results-oriented evaluation, flexible structures and processes, complex coordination of overlapping project teams, and directing attention at curbing excess innovation.

Designing an effective management control process

Phases in the management control process

The management control process can best be represented by a closed loop control cycle (see Figure 9.3). The process starts from the strategy of the company, from which the action programmes are derived. Once the programmes are set up and approved, their financial implications for the coming year can be expressed in a budget. At the end of the budget period, the actual performance is measured and compared to the budget. The results of this analysis are then reported to top management and used in the evaluation of the efficiency and effectiveness of the responsibility centres concerned and their managers. The management control process thus starts from strategic planning and target setting and consists of the following five phases:

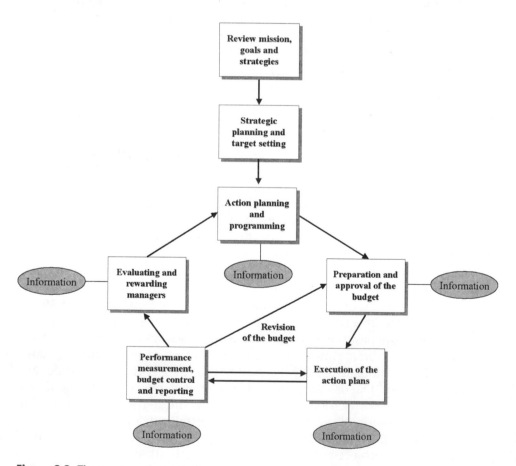

Figure 9.3 The management control process

- Planning action programmes (programming);
- Preparing the budget;
- Executing the plan;
- Measuring performance, following up the budget and reporting; and
- Evaluating and rewarding.

Important design parameters of the control process

When used in an appropriate way, the budgeting process may motivate managers to improve performance. The motivating impact of the budget is influenced by the following parameters.

The level of management commitment to budget targets First of all, companies may use the budget to assess the financial impact of their strategic action plans. In this case, budgeting is primarily used as a feed forward control mechanism and its primary function is to support the planning process ('budgeting for planning'). Budget targets are an indication and show the direction in which the company wants to go, but managers do not feel a strong pressure to realize the targets. Budget targets can also be seen as commitments for the managers. In this case, the budget is used for control.

Top-down versus bottom-up budgeting Budget targets may be imposed *top-down* by executive management (in consultation with the division managers, or not). Besides this, there is also a *bottom-up* process, in which each division sets up its own budget, yet within the general goals and directions of the company. The global company budget is then formed by combining the various sub-budgets.

The level of participation during the budgeting process When setting up a budgeting process, an important parameter is the level of participation managers may have in the target-setting process. We can talk about *participative budgeting* when subordinate managers participate in the budgeting process and in defining the budget objectives. Participative budgeting involves back-and-forth communication between superiors and subordinates – they share information and converge on a mutually acceptable budget. It is generally agreed that involvement in setting up the budget leads to higher acceptance than when the budget is imposed fully from the top. Moreover, it is assumed that participative budgeting has a positive effect on the commitment of the division managers who have to realize the budget later on.

The difficulty of budget targets It is necessary to think about guidelines regarding the *degree of difficulty in realizing the budgets* ('goal difficulty'). Certain companies have a policy of *realistic budgets*, where the budget objective will be accepted if it most probably can be reached. Other companies prefer *challenging budgets*, where top management expects the division managers to work very hard. The basic assumption behind challenging budgets is that managers can always achieve more with their team than they think they can. The task of top management is to stimulate managers to try to excel themselves over and over again. In this situation, managers who submit realistic budgets are evaluated poorly beforehand and a more challenging budget is imposed on them from the top. Whatever the budget philosophy, a budget can be accepted if it holds sufficient task content, i.e., if the team in the department will have to exert a lot of effort to realize the budget. As a general rule, the set targets ought to be realistic but challenging. This means that they may not be set unattainably high, which results in frustration and manipulation of data, but they may also not be too easily achievable, because then most of the performance stimulus disappears.

Tolerance for budget slack It should also be verified whether or not the budget is too pessimistic. Some managers may be inclined to build a certain 'slack' into their budget. The phenomenon of *budget slack* occurs when a manager submits a budget in which a certain 'buffer' is built in so that the budget objectives are relatively easy to reach. Indeed, in a participative budgeting process the tendency might exist to ask more than one strictly needs to cover oneself against unforeseen circumstances or out of fear that top management will reduce the budget by a certain amount. For example, if the purchasing department fears that it will no longer be able to buy raw materials at the prices that were budgeted in the past, it can ask for extra means for this part of the budget. It can also be that managers prefer not to set the budget standards too high in companies where their bonuses are calculated on the degree to which they have reached their budget objectives. In all these cases, the general interests of the company are not respected because, by building in budget slack, the company funds are not optimally allocated.

Fairness in budget target setting When assessing the budget, one should verify whether the task content of the budgets of the various departments are of equal value. The budget negotiation process is not only a vertical negotiation process in the organization, it is also a process of comparing the planned efforts of the various departments. Dynamic managers, who always work with challenging budget objectives, may become demotivated when they discover that other departments are tolerated when they exert less effort (i.e., make less profit or be less productive).

However, equally balancing the task content of the budgets of the various departments presents difficulties because the management problems may differ widely per department (e.g., different management functions, product groups, markets, etc.) and the concept 'task content' is difficult to measure objectively. The task content of a budget depends on the experience of the manager and his or her team. There is also a certain psychological insight involved here. Some managers, along with their teams, feel more quickly swamped with work than others. In any case, clear imbalances in the performances of the various departments need to be eliminated as quickly as possible. For instance, in a profit centre structure, where all divisions are making profits and a certain division is constantly in the red, a thorough restructuring plan must be set up in the short run to make the department profit-making as fast as possible.

Tightness of budget control With regard to following up the budget, a choice can be made between tight and loose control. The tightness of the control is determined by the degree to which restrictions are imposed on the freedom of subordinates and emphasis is placed on reaching the predefined objectives. In most cases, it is assumed that *tight control* provides more certainty that the people in the organization will act as is expected of them. This can be done by determining the activities in detail, by following up very accurately the results of the departments, and by exerting pressure on the responsible managers to adjust quickly potentially unfavourable anomalies. With tight budget control, it is frequently (e.g., monthly) verified whether the real costs and revenues are in accordance with the planned short-term objectives. Undesired anomalies in the budget are not tolerated and must be eliminated quickly. The advantage of tight control is that managers become more aware of the importance of costs and profitability, and they actively seek ways to eliminate inefficiencies.

However, tight control may also have undesired dysfunctional effects. Focusing on short-term results too intently may encourage managers to organize actions that optimize profitability in the short term, but that are disadvantageous in the long term. For example, in order to reach its budget figures, the purchasing department may decide to buy cheaper, but qualitatively inferior, raw materials. However, this may lead to significant quality problems in production and possibly to lower quality end products, which result in losing the goodwill of the customers. When the emphasis is primarily on reaching budget objectives in the short term, managers may also not be motivated to make the strategic investments that are necessary for the long-term survival of the company. Moreover, excessively tight budget control may lead to building in 'slack' when setting up the budget objectives or to playing accounting tricks to artificially boost the short-term results.

On the contrary, with *loose budget control* deviations from the budget that arise in between are overlooked by top management, and there is a trust that potentially unfavourable anomalies will be eliminated by the divisional managers at the end of the budget period. The budget is used more for communication and planning, and there is less pressure to undertake immediate short-term actions to adjust the results.

The use of budget performance in rewarding managers When setting up the budget, for managers of responsibility centres it is required that the proposed objectives be realized (although we know some companies that start paying bonuses when only 80 per cent – and even 60 per cent – of the budget target is realized). At the end of the year, the actual results are compared to the planned objectives and are further analysed by means of variance analysis. In this way, the budget is an ideal basis for evaluating the performances of the responsible managers. Managers who succeed in realizing the proposed objectives must be rewarded for their good performance. This reward may be of a financial nature (e.g., bonus, salary increase or other financial advantages), but the reward may also be more focused on non-financial motivators, such as promotion, extension of responsibilities and recognition. A bonus for performance relative to the budget can be determined subjectively or by formula. To be effective, the reward system must be designed in such a way that it optimally motivates the managers to act in accordance with the corporate goals and strategies.

Optimizing management control process policies

A management control process (and more specifically, the budgeting process) is effective when it motivates managers on the various levels of the organization to perform actions in line with the organizational goals and strategies. From contingency research on management control, evidence suggests links between *strategy* and the characteristics of the management control process.

Defenders, and companies with conservative, cost leadership strategies, find cost control and specific operating goals and budgets more appropriate than entrepreneurs, prospectors and companies with product differentiation strategies (Simons, 1987; Dent, 1990; Chenhall and Morris, 1995). Chenhall and Morris (1995) have found that tight control is suitable for conservative strategies; they also found tight control in entrepreneurial situations but, importantly, operating together with organic decision styles and communications.

Some research has been focused on the relationship between the chosen competitive strategy and the management control process. Differentiation strategies are associated with a de-emphasis on budgetary goals for performance evaluation (Govindarajan, 1988). Govindarajan and Fisher (1990) found that product differentiation with high sharing of resources (between functional departments) and a reliance on behavioural control was associated with enhanced effectiveness. Bruggeman and Van der Stede (1993) found that business units implementing differentiation strategies based on a make-to-order strategy preferred loose control in budgeting, while business units with a cost leader strategy or a differentiation strategy based on standard products found tight budget control more suitable. They also found that bottom-up budgeting and a commitment to budget targets was considered optimal for all competitive strategies. Overall, Van der Stede

(2000) has shown that product differentiation strategies are associated with less rigid budgetary control, but this is also associated with increased budgetary slack.

It has also been suggested that bonus systems must be suited to the strategy. Anthony and Govindarajan (1995) suggest that formula-based bonus determination approaches should be used with a harvest strategy and that subjective bonus determination is optimal for build strategies.

Contingency research has also found relationships between characteristics of the management control process and the level of *uncertainty in the environment*. Companies operating in an environment of unpredictable change require an appropriate set of control process characteristics. Uncertainty has been related to performance evaluation characterized by a more subjective evaluation style (Govindarajan, 1984; Moores and Sharma, 1998), less reliance on incentive-based pay (Bloom, 1998), non-accounting style of performance evaluation (Ross, 1995), and participative budgeting (Govindarajan, 1986). As environmental uncertainty increases, using more participative budgeting increases performance. In contrast, when environmental uncertainty is low, participative budgeting decreases performance. In situations where environments are stable and predictable, there is little informational benefit from participation because superiors have sufficient information to develop budgets.

Companies may also operate in a hostile, difficult environment. This is an environment that is stressful, dominating and restrictive. Environmental hostility has been associated with a strong emphasis on meeting budgets (Otley, 1978). Hostility from intense competition has been related to a reliance on formal control and sophisticated accounting, production and statistical control (Khandwalla, 1972; Imoisili, 1985).

The optimization of target-setting approaches seems to be related to task complexity. Locke and Latham (1990) found that difficult goals lead to higher performance, but this effect is moderated by task complexity. The result leads us to expect that performance will be higher when managers are invited to work towards challenging targets, except when the performance task is too complex.

The appropriateness of bottom-up budgeting has been associated with information asymmetry between superiors and subordinate managers (Shields and Young, 1993). When subordinates have much better information about their business than their superiors do, bottom-up budgeting leads to more accurate budgets, arising from the use of the subordinates' better information. When top-down budgeting is used in the case of high information asymmetry, subordinates may reject the budget because it is not consistent with their information. Top-down budgeting is beneficial in situations where superiors have sufficient knowledge about the subordinate's activities being budgeted.

The role of beliefs systems

The management control culture is the third and final part of the management control system. Managers' behaviours and actions are not only influenced by structural and procedural elements, but also by the formal beliefs systems in the organization. Simons defines beliefs systems as 'the explicit set of organizational definitions that senior managers communicate formally and reinforce systematically to provide basic values, purpose, and direction for the organization' (Simons, 1995: 34). Beliefs systems are an important element of an organization's corporate culture. The *corporate culture* is the set of values, beliefs and norms of behaviour shared by members of a firm that influences individual employee preferences and behaviours (Besanko et al., 2000). Ouchi (1980, 1981; Ouchi and Johnson, 1978) considers culture as an alternative control system in the organization. He introduces the idea of *clan control*, by which he means control through an internal system of organizational norms and values. Culture influences the behaviour of individuals. Individuals who value belonging to the culture will align their individual goals and behaviours to those of the firm and pay more attention to self-control. A culture that is intensively held by most employees is called a strong culture.

Culture can support a company's competitive advantage (Barney, 1986). It is supportive when the values espoused by the culture are very much in line with the chosen direction and the performance objectives of the firm (e.g., a company with a product leadership strategy where all employees love to change things and learn from new experiences). In this case, we talk about a 'high performance culture'. In other words, the culture is clearly aligned with the strategy of the firm. Of course, the opposite also holds. If there is a cultural misfit, culture can also be a source of persistently poor performance. This occurs when the values underlying the firm's culture are in conflict with the chosen strategic direction. For example, a culture stressing efficiency, stability and routine behaviour will not support the implementation of a flexibility strategy. In this case, culture may be a barrier to change and managers will experience a 'low performance culture'.

So, it is important that the majority of the employees believe what top management believes. It is the task of management control to define a set of common beliefs. It frequently happens that top managers have explicitly expressed the vision, the mission, the goals, the key values and the strategies of the firm, but lower-level managers and employees do not share the underlying beliefs. Goal statements about creating shareholder value are experienced as 'grand terminology' when employees do not feel the passion of working on value-creating projects. A strategy of high-quality products will not succeed if all employees are not convinced that they should work to 'zero defect' and do their work 'right the first time'. Many flexibility strategies fail because people do not like 'to change their

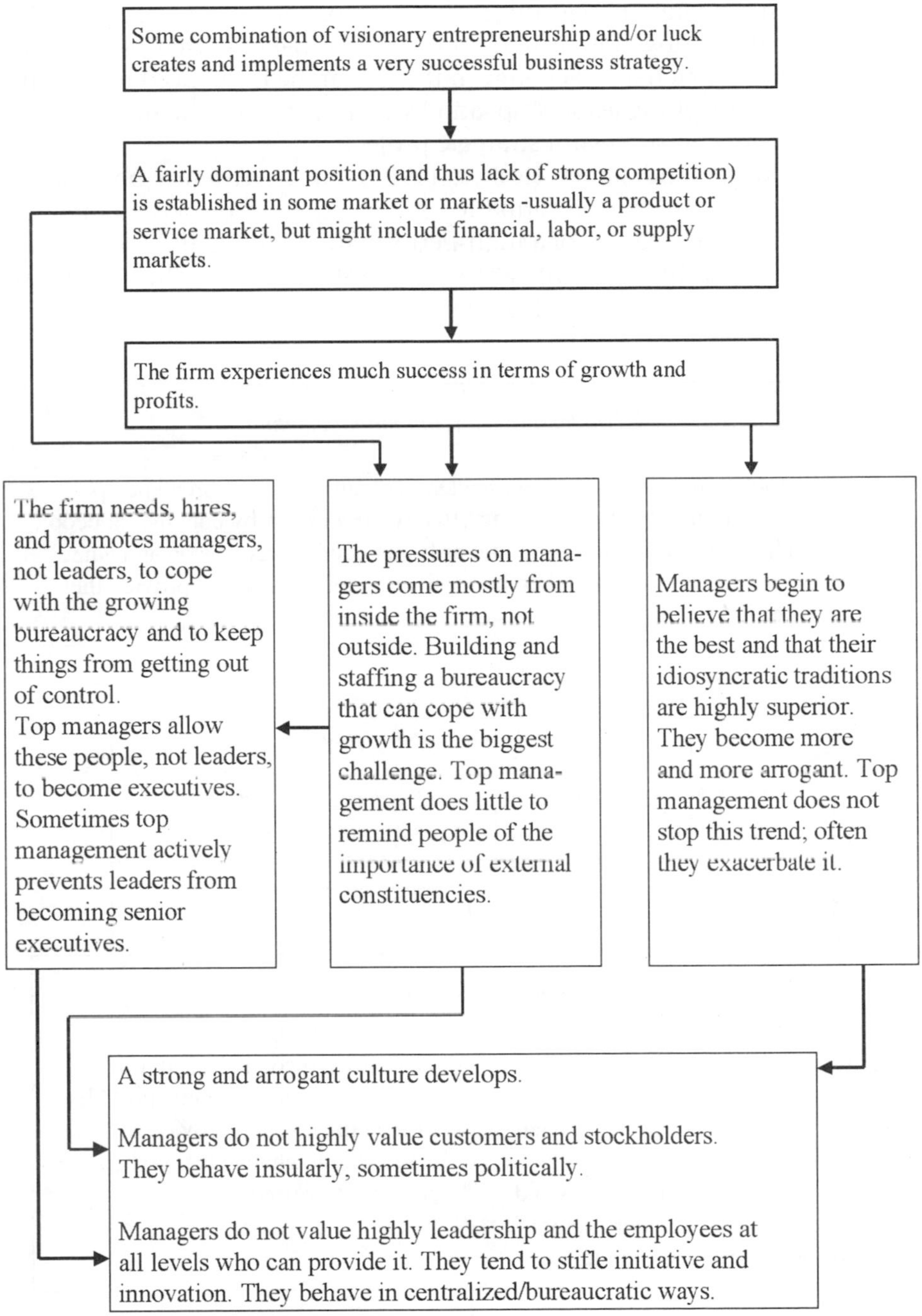

Some combination of visionary entrepreneurship and/or luck creates and implements a very successful business strategy.

A fairly dominant position (and thus lack of strong competition) is established in some market or markets -usually a product or service market, but might include financial, labor, or supply markets.

The firm experiences much success in terms of growth and profits.

The firm needs, hires, and promotes managers, not leaders, to cope with the growing bureaucracy and to keep things from getting out of control.
Top managers allow these people, not leaders, to become executives. Sometimes top management actively prevents leaders from becoming senior executives.

The pressures on managers come mostly from inside the firm, not outside. Building and staffing a bureaucracy that can cope with growth is the biggest challenge. Top management does little to remind people of the importance of external constituencies.

Managers begin to believe that they are the best and that their idiosyncratic traditions are highly superior. They become more and more arrogant. Top management does not stop this trend; often they exacerbate it.

A strong and arrogant culture develops.

Managers do not highly value customers and stockholders. They behave insularly, sometimes politically.

Managers do not value highly leadership and the employees at all levels who can provide it. They tend to stifle initiative and innovation. They behave in centralized/bureaucratic ways.

Figure 9.4 The origins of unhealthy corporate cultures
Source: Kotter and Heskett (1992: 145)

plans.' In general, successful strategy implementation needs beliefs systems supporting the chosen strategy. The beliefs of employees and managers may be hard to change, but they can be influenced by training sessions, by inspiring leadership, and by demonstrating the success of the new strategy and successful strategic projects.

John Kotter and James Heskett (1992) have written a book about corporate culture and performance in which they propose a stepwise approach to the creation of a high-performance culture and focus on the origins of healthy and unhealthy corporate cultures. Their ideas are presented in Figure 9.4 and Figure 9.5.

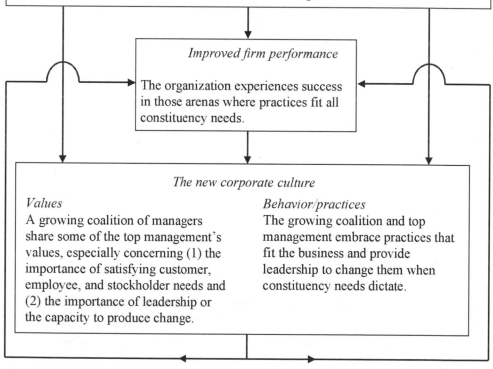

Leadership from top management

One or two top managers are excellent leaders with an outsider's broad perspective yet an insider's credibility. They provide effective leadership by convincing people a crisis is at hand, by communicating in words and deeds a new vision and a new set of strategies for the firm, and then by motivating many others to provide the leadership needed to implement the vision and strategies.

Improved firm performance

The organization experiences success in those arenas where practices fit all constituency needs.

The new corporate culture

Values
A growing coalition of managers share some of the top management's values, especially concerning (1) the importance of satisfying customer, employee, and stockholder needs and (2) the importance of leadership or the capacity to produce change.

Behavior/practices
The growing coalition and top management embrace practices that fit the business and provide leadership to change them when constituency needs dictate.

Figure 9.5 The creation of a performance-enhancing culture
Source: Kotter and Heskett (1992: 147)

Conclusion

Control and evaluation is the fourth component of our Integrated Performance Management Framework. In this chapter, we have shown the important role of management control for strategy implementation and for performance management. Developing an appropriate management control system is a prerequisite for effectively managing an organization.

On a broader level, Simons (1995) has shown that control of business strategy is achieved by integrating four levers of control. These levers create tension between creative innovation (emergent strategies) and predictable goal movement (intended strategies). This proves the crucial role of control in the strategy implementation and performance management process.

We then focused our attention on the three basic elements of the management control system: (1) the management control structure; (2) the management control process; and (3) the beliefs systems. We have analysed optimal management control structures and processes from a goal congruence perspective. That is, we have investigated how to design a management control structure and process that maximally stimulates goal-oriented behaviour and leads to minimal dysfunctional behaviour. Attention is also paid to how strategy affects the choice for a particular management control system. It is clear that management control also interacts with the organizational behaviour component. From Chapter 10 on, we investigate this fifth component in greater detail.

Note

1 *Business conduct boundaries* are those that define and communicate standards of business conduct for all employees. Like the Ten Commandments, they specify actions that are forbidden. *Internal controls* are the policies and procedures designed to ensure reliable accounting information and safeguard company assets. *Strategic boundaries* define what types of business opportunity should be avoided, thereby drawing a box around the opportunities that individuals are encouraged to exploit. Strategic boundaries are installed to ensure that individuals throughout the organization are engaged in activities that support the basic strategy of the business (Simons, 2000: 289).

10 Organizing for Performance

MARC BUELENS[1]

Definitions are very explicit regarding what 'organizing' is all about. For example, Megginson and his colleagues (1989: 4) define it as: '(1) determining what resources and activities are required to achieve the organization's objectives, (2) combining them into workable groups, (3) assigning the individuals the authority necessary to carry out assignments. This function provides the formal structure within which work is defined, subdivided, and coordinated.' But despite clear definitions, managers find organization design decisions very difficult and frustrating. This is also recognized by Michael Goold and Andrew Campbell in their most recent book on organization structures:

> Managers recognize that there are no right answers, and that much depends on complicated tradeoffs between different possible groupings, processes and relationships. They also know that people and behaviors matter as much as strategy and logic. They are aware, too, that organization change can be a highly political process, dominated by personalities and power plays. Managers can sense when the organization is not working well, but they have little confidence in the outcome of most organization redesign processes. (Goold and Campbell, 2002: 1–2)

In this chapter, we start with a discussion of the basic elements of organizational design. Then we ask ourselves the question: How do these different elements fit together? This issue is discussed in the second and third parts of this chapter. We adopt a contingency approach and propose three 'generation' designs. Furthermore, we investigate the implications of these designs for implementing strategy.

Basic elements of organizational design

Organizations are characterized by a certain degree of cohesion or internal logic, mostly described as *consistency*. For example, the way we define our control systems influences the way people will react to them. The way people react to our control systems will influence our leadership styles, and our leadership style will influence the way we design our control systems. Consistency is not only descriptive, it is also prescriptive: consistency points to good organizational design. Organizations 'under norms of rationality' have to show at least some consistency. The more coherent our principles, the fewer internal contradictions, and the better the organizational design.

This starting point is well known in management and organization theory, and is known as *fit*. Theorists, consultants and designers alike, use fit between external and internal environment – and between the different elements of that internal environment – as the dominant criterion for judging organizations. The famous quote by Sumantra Goshal and Christopher Bartlett (1999), 'You cannot manage third generation strategies with second generation organizations and first generation managers', is a typical example of a fit approach. It prescribes fit among strategy, organization and managerial behaviour. Fit approaches are also known as *contingency theories*: the optimal design must take the relevant contingencies into account.

A relevant organization theory has to answer two questions: (1) What are the most relevant elements in our framework? and (2) How do these elements 'fit'? Our approach is summarized in Figure 10.1. We identify three critical domains: challenge, structure (or formal organization) and behaviour. Each domain interacts with the other two, and the relationship between any two elements is dependent on the third.

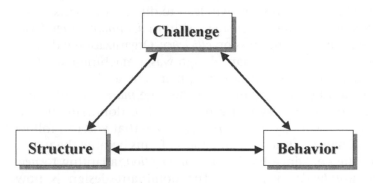

Figure 10.1 Basic elements of organizational design

Challenge

Challenge is a very fruitful starting point in understanding organizations. Challenge is understood as the set of expected outputs or results. The most important organizational challenges are of a strategic or competitive nature: trying to be cheap, operationally excellent, different, innovative, service-oriented, achieving a large reach or a large richness, etc. But not all challenges are of a strategic nature. One has to be organized to produce more efficiently, to serve clients and to meet deadlines. When this challenge is made explicit, concepts such as (strategic) objectives, performance targets and goals are used. A challenge, of course, can remain implicit. Management prescriptions, however, tend to impose clarification of challenges by installing 'management by objectives', 'smart' objectives and budgeting processes. EFQM and Balanced Scorecard models are endeavours to make challenges explicit.

Challenges can be chosen or imposed; they can be very local or all-encompassing ('strategies'); they can be intuitively present in the company culture or the object of an elaborate strategic decision-making process; they can be long-term or short-term.

Challenge is closely related to organizational design, which is largely determined by the expected output of the organization. It is clear that a chemical plant will be organized differently from a psychiatric institution or a university (although many colleagues maintain that the latter two might be rather similar). Challenge is closely related to the 'primary task', the *raison d'être* of the organization. A psychiatric institution is there to cure mentally ill people, a paper mill to produce paper, and a biscuit factory to produce and sell biscuits. When the primary task shifts, becomes ambiguous or when consensus on what it is is difficult to reach, it is almost impossible to get organized. When the main emphasis in the psychiatric institution shifts towards prevention, the institute might become a PR office, a governmental lobby or a publication house. Do armies fight for national glory, to destroy the enemy or is their primary task peacekeeping? Different answers will lead to different designs.

Each dramatic shift in challenge creates a shift in *dominant design logic*. Until 1960, emphasis in challenge was on *efficiency*. Organizational designs reflected this challenge. The dominant design was a machine-like ideal: clear job descriptions, narrow jobs, a strong hierarchy and bureaucratic rules. Over the next 30 years, organizations became *market-oriented* and tried to adapt to continually evolving markets. The dominant design reflected that shift: 'Organize yourself in such a way that you can follow the market.' Divisionalized structures and matrix forms became the norm. Since the 1990s, the challenge has become *innovation*, adapting to *new technologies* and *worldwide competition*. The dominant design is now oriented towards change, flexibility and adaptability.

Challenge is closely related to the *'dominant operational logic'* of the organization. Hospitals, nuclear power stations, theatres, fast-food restaurants and insurance companies all have a dominant operational logic. This could be defined as the 'logical' way processes take place. Outsiders can guess what that dominant operational logic is, insiders know it or at least are disciplined to observe it. Real disasters (and very exceptionally, real breakthroughs) occur when the dominant logic is not respected: patients get sicker, power stations explode, performances are cancelled or the audience leaves in the middle of the play, the hamburger outlet has no fries, and the insurance company has no money to pay its liabilities. Dominant operational logic makes it clear that the freedom to organize is more or less restricted. The dominant operational logic is the result of years of experience, careful observation, early mistakes and collective memory. A radical change in operational logic is very rare and constitutes a real 'paradigm shift'. Typical examples are the shift towards non-inventory production systems (*Kanban*, Just-in-Time, etc.), Internet banking and self-service in the 1950s.

When the challenge becomes very focused and obvious to all parties involved, when room for interpretation has become very narrow (such as in crisis situations), the dominant logic becomes very clear. That is why crisis managers are not supposed to be familiar with the 'classic' dominant logic; instead, they are supposed to organize according to the 'new' (overcoming the crisis) dominant logic.

Structure

Structure is the formal way an organization divides up and coordinates its relevant elements. Designing organizational structures is deciding on differentiation and integration. The first question deals with differentiation: how shall we divide this organization into sub units? This is a very important question because differentiation can lead to specialization and steep learning curves. The differentiation question seems to dominate practice: How shall we divide up our employees? (What kind of organization do we need? Product-based? Matrix? Market-based? Functional?) The coordination question seems to dominate theory.

The problem of grouping We group the tens, hundreds or thousands of employees into work units. Robert Simons defines a *work unit* as a grouping of individuals who use a firm's resources and are accountable for performance. *Accountability* defines the output that a work unit is expected to produce and the performance standards that it is expected to meet (Simons, 2000). This definition implies that the 'grouping problem' will become very cumbersome when individuals are not aware that they are 'using the firm's resources' and when output and performance standards are difficult to define. Knowledge workers, artists, creators of all kinds very often do *not* use many of a firm's resources! That, of course, makes it difficult to 'organize' hospitals, universities, law firms, or R&D departments (unless modern technology overshadows the individual star). In many cases, 'organizing' simply means trying to convince the professional that he or she is using the firm's resources! Although Simons explicitly mentions 'a university history department' as a work unit accountable for performance, we wish him luck in defining the output it is expected to produce and in reaching agreement on the performance standards. Is he going to count the number of students taking history classes and the number of pages professors and research assistants publish? Although this is common practice in many universities, we wonder whether the best historians really care about all this? In the end, is not a great historian the one who defies the practices and standards? Unfortunately, for all people wanting to 'organize for results', modern organizations are more and more inhabited by people who have become aware (or who think) that what the firm is offering them in the way of resources is much smaller than what they offer the firm and who produce output even their superiors have the greatest difficulty judging.

There are very few rules regarding how to divide or group. The most 'natural' rules seem to reflect a principle from experimental design: be sure that the variance within each group is much smaller than the variance between the groups. When you sell similar products to very different markets, organize yourself on a market basis. When you sell very different products to similar markets, be sure that your divisions are product divisions. When the consumers in different countries react very differently, organize yourself by country or operate from one central point.

There are two fundamental ways to form work units: (1) grouping by function (or work-process) or (2) grouping by market (business unit or division) (Simons, 2000).

Units clustered by function The most natural way to streamline a growing organization is to group people by specialized work processes or functions, for specialization can lead to efficiency, steeper learning curves, standardization and the optimal combination of people and tasks. In a functional organization, people specialize in 'sales', 'quality control' or 'accounting and record-keeping'. With the exception of the general manager, each manager is accountable for one functional area. A functional organization is clear, simple and cheap. Coordination between departments, however, is only possible at the highest level, leading to the well-known 'bottleneck' symptoms, where the entire organization waits for 'coordination solutions' provided by the top. More problems stem from a natural tendency towards sub-optimization, where each department specializes in its own priorities and professionalism (including professional hobbies). Loyalty is often to one's own profession, not to the organization.

Functional organizations can be very successful in smaller companies operating in homogeneous markets, where an internal focus is rewarded by strong efficiency gains. Organizations cluster by function when an internal focus and efficiency (which is the major benefit of specialization) are more important than an external focus and effectiveness or market responsiveness. Of course, this is the main reason why universities and general hospitals are organized functionally and why banks are shifting from functional organizations to 'client segment' organizations.

Units clustered by market focus When companies want to reflect their external focus in their organizational design, they will create market-focused divisions, where differences between divisions will be large and differences within divisions will be small. When differences between products are large (compared to differences between regions and customers), units will be clustered by product. *Product divisions* create economies in production, R&D, distribution, and so forth. Market leaders in the 1980s used product divisions. For example, Philips had product divisions for lighting, CD-players, computers, white goods (e.g., dish-washers), and IBM had separate divisions for mainframes, personal computers, typewriters, etc.

When differences between regions are large, units will be clustered by geography. When differences in local cultures, tastes, legislation and economic environment overshadow differences between products or even between clients, *regional business* units create unique solutions to unique contingencies. 'Foreigners' have a tendency to underestimate differences between countries in Asia or within the European Union, or between states in America. 'Locals' tend to overestimate them.

When customers have very distinct needs and attributes, *client divisions* emerge. One can have divisions oriented towards government, industrial customers, type of industry, private clients, small or large companies, professional clients, etc.

Of course, all hybrid forms do co-exist. Sooner or later, companies have to organize on a regional basis. Two salespeople cover separate regions, two plants cannot occupy the same spot, and two entrances must be guarded by two different caretakers (who do exactly the same job, but one at the northern entrance and one at the southern). Still, choosing an organizational design depends on the question: What is our primary criterion for splitting up into groups? A functional organization where the sales are divided into five regions is a functional organization, not a regional one.

From grouping to coordination Once the organization is logically divided, the *coordination* question arises. How shall we integrate the different parts? This will be achieved by influencing the so-called *design parameters*. The most important design parameters are formalization of jobs, formalization of processes, amount of training and indoctrination, and (de)centralization of decision-making. A machine-organization is primarily characterized by elaborate job descriptions, many rules and procedures, limited but highly specialized training, slow and implicit socialization, and centralized decision-making. On the other hand, innovative designs in high-tech start-ups have almost no job descriptions, only a few informal rules, extensive training and visible indoctrination, and decentralized decision-making.

Behaviour

Behaviour is, of course, the 'odd man out' in organizational design. Until recently, we could look at organizational design as though it was a rational process, oriented towards the smooth execution of a challenge. However, the organization chart is not the organization. People must 'carry out' the design. They will or will not understand the challenge, or they will interpret it in very idiosyncratic ways; they will read job descriptions in order to see what is *not* in the description; they will bluntly neglect some rules and might strongly react against socialization processes. People bring in undesirable as well as desirable variation. This occurs when safety or quality measures are not respected, when key people arrive late for important meetings, or when people do not respect the budgeting systems. Desirable variation is introduced when people come up with new solutions for old problems, when creative approaches appear in areas where conservatism has reigned. People are fun. People are the manager's nightmare. And they are both at the same time.

We drew Figure 10.1 in a very classic way: challenge ('strategy') is the most important element, structure follows strategy, and management has to look for goal congruence between the organization and its people in order to put the right person in the right place. This is of course artificial.

One could put 'people first' and create the right job for talented employees and define the 'right' challenge for the existing people. At first glance, this may sound woolly. However, consider all the organizations where professionals dominate and where the kinds of patient one attracts, the kinds of research topic one studies, or the kinds of consultancy project one takes on are determined more by the kinds of available professional than by the 'strategy'. This direction from people to structure is also well known: the more top managers refuse to adjust their structures to their people, the more they simply want it for themselves. Some top structures (such as two CEOs) often reflect a (*lack* of) strong personalities, more than anything else.

Even more unusual might be to put 'structure first'. But the fact that the 'structure follows strategy' paradigm has been heavily challenged proves that this principle is not self-evident. The clearest examples can be found in the fundamental discussions on *Business Process Re-engineering* (BPR). BPR can be seen as a reaction against the trade-off between simple jobs and complex structures. BPR consultants strongly favour complex jobs and simple structures. Even better, of course, is reducing overall complexity, the first step in all good BPR. The basic question then becomes: What drives complexity? Complexity drivers are very often a direct result of strategic choices, the formulation of challenges. In other words, reduction of strategic complexity is a consequence – not a cause – of a change in organizational structure. It is an example of 'strategy follows structure'.

Other elements of organizational design

Organizations can also be understood starting from the links between the three constituent elements (see Figure 10.2). The link between the formal organization and the individual people (in other words, between structure and behaviour) is the *organizational culture*. This is the way the rules of the organizational game are played. People try to make sense of, to understand, what the organization means. Organizational culture describes 'the way we do things around here'. Corporate culture is a strong stabilizing force.

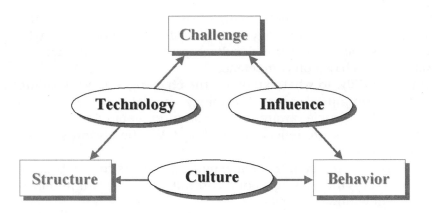

Figure 10.2 Technology, culture and reward systems

The link between challenge and organizational structure is realized through *technology*, or *how* tasks are carried out. Technology encompasses techniques, equipment and know-how. It is a much broader concept than pure technical infrastructure and also includes 'soft technology,' such as interviewing techniques and market approaches.

Finally, the link between challenge and behaviour is realized through *influence processes*, such as charismatic leadership, principal–agent structures, reward systems or governance, as we move in the direction from challenge to behaviour. Moving in the other direction (from behaviour to challenge) is also realized through influence processes, such as attention management, sense-making and market-for-ideas.

A contingency approach towards organizational design

A 'one best way of organizing' approach is relevant when all environments are similar – and this is a very unrealistic assumption. That is why most organization theorists follow an 'it depends on your relevant environment' – or contingency – approach. The problem, however, is to reach agreement on two fundamental questions: (1) What are the most important dimensions in that environment? and (2) How does the organizational design fit with these important dimensions? At a certain level of abstraction, the environment can be captured in the following dimensions (see Figure 10.3):

- *Degree of uncertainty*: to what extent are the challenges stable and predictable? Is technology exception-free? Are people looking for certainty and protection? Is the organizational culture role-oriented? Are the reward systems based on predictability?

- *Degree of complexity*: to what extent are the challenges multiple and even conflicting? Is technology well understood? Are people 'single-minded'? Is the organizational culture problem-oriented? Are the reward systems based on competences?
- *Degree of hostility*: to what extent are the challenges easy? Is failure dramatic? Are mistakes in technology critical and leading to disasters? Are people aware of a 'common enemy'? Does the organizational culture reflect an ideology? Are the reward systems rewarding heroes?
- *Degree of power differences*: to what extent can players counterbalance each other, or is there a single point controlling all relevant resources (money, know-how, experience)?

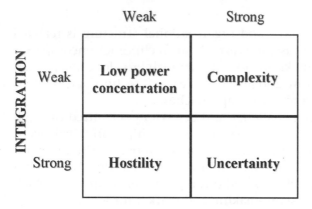

Figure 10.3 Organizational design and contingency factors

The optimal organizational design can be summarized as follows:

- Uncertainty leads to strong differentiation and strong integration. One has to handle two conflicting tendencies at the same time: the organization has to register the uncertainty, and one has to accept diversity, differences, freedom to explore and innovation. Without following 'the law of requisite variety', organizations tend to neglect new signals. At the same time, however, the organization cannot 'act' when differentiation is too strong. That is why the company also needs strong integration (e.g., of all the different signals).
- Complexity leads to strong differentiation and weak integration. The organization allows pronounced decentralization of decision-making and has tailor-made technologies, very often in combination with craftsmanship ('intuition'). It hires many professionals and rewards them for their problem-solving skills, and not for their results.

- Hostility leads to weak differentiation and strong integration. Decision-making is highly centralized and technology is highly predictable. Furthermore, there is a strong pressure to conform to values, goals and procedures on all levels.
- Low power concentration leads to weak differentiation and weak integration. In an eternal power struggle, parties duplicate each other's efforts, do not collaborate, do their 'own thing' and sabotage all attempts to 'rationalize' the organization. This is, naturally, the best road to permanently failing organizations.

Organizing for performance

More and more companies are facing the same kind of environment, which is characterized by:

- Strong international competition;
- Short product, service and process lifecycles;
- Strong premiums for 'application killers';
- Strong influence of 'modern' technology;
- Competitive labour markets (especially for professionals);
- Assertive collaborators;
- Strong pressure on costs, due to marked fluctuations in share price.

This kind of environment pushes an increasing number of companies towards similar challenges such as speed, innovation, flexibility, low cost and high added value. With the exception of 'low cost', which drives towards machine configurations, all the other challenges drive towards 'third generation' designs. In such designs, there is a strong emphasis on decentralization, flat organizations, networks and teamwork (which is more than organizing meetings). But even in such organizations, there will always be sub-systems, such as the accounting department or parts of the production core, where flexibility is to be avoided (or is simply illegal or unethical).

It is clear that most organizations are moving in the direction of these third generation organizations. So, the question arises: What are first generation and second generation organizations? And when are these types of organizational design appropriate? Table 10.1 provides an overview of the three types of organizational design – we call them organization generations – and indicates the relevant design parameters for each generation design. As regards the tables that follow, we offer this caveat to the academic audience: contingency theories often lead to endlessly meticulous descriptions of conditions, associations and interpretations. We will neglect academic prudence in this instance and be very explicitly prescriptive.

Table 10.1 Three generation designs

	First generation	Second generation	Third generation
Basic challenge	Predictability	Serving markets	Innovation
Differentiation	Low	High	High
Integration	High	High	Low
Uncertainty	Low	Medium	High
Complexity	Low	Medium	High
Hostility	High	Low	High
Pyramid	Steep	Steep	Flat
Organizational culture	Role	Task	Informal
Reward	Loyalty	Results	Markets
Job specification	High	High	Low
Training	Intense but narrow	Varied	On-the-job and 'just-in-time'
Socialization	Slow	Systematic	Fast
Procedures	All-present	Numerous	Too little
Supervision	Strict	Situational	Weak
Unit grouping	Functional	Market or product	Process
Decentralization	Low	Medium	High
Teamwork	None	Meetings	Small teams
Technology	Long-linked	Engineering	Intensive

First generation design

A *first generation design* is appropriate when the performance criteria are in the realm of predictability. In practice, this means that first generation designs are difficult to beat when economies of scale are important, when safety is at stake, and when repetition leads to relevant learning curves or when costs are to be kept under control. A first generation design is fundamentally a machine design. Its ideal is reached when all unpredictability is removed. In practice, this leaves no room for 'people'. This is a never-ending process, until a critical minimum is reached, where the complete absence of people would introduce new risks. Technology gradually takes over. In a first generation design, people constitute (almost by definition) the weak link. Table 10.2 gives an overview of all of the characteristics of a first generation design. Furthermore, each of these generation designs has some major weaknesses, as is shown in Table 10.3. A first generation organization can be summarized as follows:

- Challenge – efficient repetition;
- Structure – functional;
- Culture – role culture;
- Systems – procedural.

Machine designs are 'out of fashion' – until Barings Bank or Enron collapses, Tsjernobil explodes, Marc Dutroux escapes, milk is poisoned, and the dot.com companies cannot deliver because their articles are out of stock. This is why it is important to formulate three basic rules for 'machine-design' organizations.

Table 10.2 Characteristics of the three generation designs

	First generation	Second generation	Third generation
Strategy	Strategic planning	Competitive strategy	Core competences
	Economies of scale	Economies of scope	Speed (time to market)
	Mono-product	Diversification	Core business
	Internal focus	Benchmarking	Innovation
	Local markets	International markets	Globalization, hyper-competition
	Market domination	Market research	Flexibility, scenario thinking
Structure	Vertical (hierarchical)	Matrix	Horizontal
	Functional 'boxes'	Business units	Boundary-less organization
		Divisionalized forms	
	Procedural	Report-driven	Learning organization
	Centralized	Headquarters knows best	Decentralized
			Micro profit centres
	One place, one time	A few places, one time	Networking
			Outsourcing
Typical processes	Top-down	Participation	Learning = working
			Direct feedback experimentation
	Instructing	Management by objectives	Virtualization
	Rationality	Goal orientation	Intuition
Management	Planning	Project management	Facilitating
	Unity of authority	Situational leadership	Management by wandering around
	Command & control	Incentives	Coaching
	Paternalism	Human resources management	Emotional intelligence
	Safety stocks	Inventory control	Just in time, one-to-one
	Top-down	Management by objectives	Self-evaluation management
	Control	Participative management	Empowerment
	Simplicity	Mastering complexity	Back to simplicity
	Production management	Marketing management	Knowledge management
	Separation of thinking and doing	Doers can think	Thinkers will do

Principle 1: *The more your challenges lie in the realm of predictability (safety, quality control, efficiency, cost reduction), the more you need a first generation design.*
Principle 2: *The more you need a first generation design, the more you must replace people by technology.*
Principle 3: *The more you need a first generation design, the more you must separate innovation and experimentation from your core processes.*

Second generation design

A *second generation design* is the typical divisionalized design, with its many matrices and elaborate reporting systems. It is the design of the well-known market performers of the 1970–80s: Philips, IBM and Shell. Second generation designs are difficult to beat when an existing (rather slowly evolving) market is to be served.

Table 10.3 Weaknesses of the three generation designs

	First generation	Second generation	Third generation
Strategy	No external focus	No room for opportunities	Fashion-driven
Organization	Managers are bottlenecks	Too many meetings	Unwanted chaos
Typical processes	Lack of flexibility and creativity	Lack of simplicity	Lack of stability
	No learning, not even from mistakes	Cover up	Catastrophic learning processes
Management	Alienating Boredom	'Organization' people 'Peter' principle	Information overload Stress

The emphasis is on market research (to serve the existing markets even better), product improvement, project management, market segmentation and human resource management. Working for a second generation company is the art of applied 'MBA-ology' – ranging from SWOT-analyses to discounted cash-flows, from HRM to 7S and 4P analyses. The dominant design is a matrix design, trying to combine a functional 'first generation design' with a market or project orientation. A second generation organization can be described as follows:

- Challenge – serving an existing market;
- Structure – matrix;
- Culture – management by objectives;
- Systems – elaborate reporting systems.

Principle 4: *The more your challenges lie in serving existing markets, the more you will benefit from a combination of working with objectives, market research, and a full commitment to Total Quality Management.*
Principle 5: *The more you need a second generation design, the closer your ideal organizational design will be to a matrix design. Unfortunately, this is a conflict-loaded, slow, and expensive design. However, the benefits you can reap from the existing markets will keep you driving towards a matrix design.*
Principle 6: *The more you need a second generation design, the price you must pay to keep the jobs rather simple is to accept complex structures and systems.*

Third generation design

First and second generation organizations share a number of characteristics that are challenged in *third generation management*. For example, first and second generation designs:

- Emphasize direction. Management analyses, formulates strategies and knows more than other levels do. Basically, this is a top-town approach.
- Have strong restrictions in time and place: people, machines and buildings.

A *third generation* way of thinking emerges when those basic assumptions are questioned:

- Emphasis on guiding force decreases: 'People at the top will not solve our problems.' Authors in the field of strategy very much dispute the image of the omniscient strategist who passes on his or her ingenious insights to a less well-informed middle management. Emphasis on the self-regulating force increases. There is chaos, radical delegation, decentralization, etc.
- The main driver for an evolving economy is information. Being restricted in time and space becomes a competitive disadvantage.

When we take a closer look at third generation management, we see a strong emphasis on the continuous interaction between the unique company strengths – its core competences, its unique social structure – and an ever-changing environment. Anticipating the market's needs is not sufficient. When your challenge lies in innovation, you must be able to surprise the market with your own, inimitable strengths and specific capabilities. Those capabilities result from continuous developing and learning processes. Those who do not constantly learn about their markets, their technologies, their processes, do not stand a chance.

Knowledge becomes the basic raw material. A central management task becomes: How to attract, retain, develop and integrate knowledge – in its widest sense – into new products and services. Attaining shared knowledge is a priority for setting up third generation organizations. Knowledge management is the name of the game.

Organizations turn into networks. Small, flexible units cooperate in a less rigid, censorious way than in a hierarchy, but in a more 'enriching' way than out on the open market. Typical examples are co-makership, home consultants, preferential suppliers, etc. Those changes are caused by spectacular shifts of technological possibilities in the field of data processing. It is not the technical possibilities but rather the limits of human imagination that determine what is possible and what is not. Individuals are more important than ever: they carry creativity.

A third generation organization can be summarized as follows:

- Challenge – innovation;
- Structure – network;
- Culture – flexibility;
- Systems –company-wide information systems.

Principle 7: *The more your challenges lie in inventing new markets, the more you will benefit from a third generation approach.*

Principle 8: *The more you need a third generation approach, the more you must be ready to rely on individuals.*

Principle 9: *The more you need a third generation approach, the more you come closer to a 'winner takes all' environment. If you succeed, the better for you. If you're the loser, you won't need this text any more.*

Conclusion

In this chapter, we have looked at the first building block of the organizational behaviour component: 'organizational design'. We have started with a discussion of the basic elements of organizational design and how these elements fit together.

Then, we presented three 'generation' designs and discussed the implications of these designs for implementing strategy. In order to characterize these different generation designs, we have borrowed from other management disciplines. The three basic organizational designs are called 'generations' because one can trace a certain evolutionary logic. A well-balanced modern organization can be conceived as a layered structure. The first generation layer is a basic layer guaranteeing control. This is a necessary condition for procurement. A disaster (massive fraud, the collapse of some dot.com companies) can be defined as a collapse of the first generation systems. In practice, optimizing first generation processes means investing in systems, technology and discipline.

The second generation layer is a cultural layer, guaranteeing goal-oriented behaviour. In most cases, this will be a culture of client orientation, quality, budgets. Investments in brands need to make sure that the company culture reaches the client, who must be willing to pay the extra cost. Companies lacking marketing muscle cannot survive in a world of global competition.

The third generation layer is a self-regulating layer, with great emphasis on speed, innovation, small teams and empowerment. Efforts in that direction are useless, however, if not backed up by strong first and second generation processes.

In practice, this means that moving in a single step from first to third generation management is almost impossible. Building a performing organization requires time. It requires a great deal of management attention, energy and devotion of resources. And, as most readers know from daily experience, time is a very scarce resource.

Note

1   The author is glad to acknowledge that this text reflects year-long discussions with his mentor in organization theory, Julien De Clercq.

11 Human Resource Management and Integrated Performance Management: A Mutual Relationship?

DIRK BUYENS, ANS DE VOS AND BART MALFLIET

During the past decade, organizations have come under increasing competitive pressure. This new competitive reality for organizations calls for different capabilities. The human resource management (HRM) function is being increasingly regarded as one of the key functions in the development and implementation of strategic responses to these pressures. Academicians, consultants and practitioners argue that if HRM wants to create added value for the company, it has to become a full strategic partner in achieving the strategic goals. But, to make the shift to strategic partner, HRM faces some new challenges, both internally and externally.

In this chapter, we will outline how HRM can evolve to become a strategic partner. We start this chapter with some major challenges and trends in HRM. Next, we focus on the concept of strategic HRM. We define it, show how it contributes to organizational performance, and then we present a framework (originally developed by Dave Ulrich and his colleagues) that outlines the various functions of HRM. The second section of this chapter presents a management framework that explains how to develop such a strategic HR approach. Finally, we consider how performance measurement and performance management can be used to address the effectiveness of HRM. In this way, we could argue that there is a mutual relationship between HRM and Integrated Performance Management.

Challenges and trends in human resource management

The world is changing – and so are the challenges for HR managers. Performance and profitability will remain important topics in the twenty-first century. According to Charles Handy (1994b), organizations nowadays are tempted to use the 'magic formula': $P = \frac{1}{2} \times 2 \times 3$. This means: 'Give me half of the employees I have today (of course not at random), let them work twice as hard and profit triples.' Cost reduction is one thing; however, increasing revenues is another. Without a focus on growth, an organization often lacks a convincing and inspiring vision for the future. As a result, organizational culture and HR instruments will have to be modified. As Mike Johnson (1995: 44) says: 'The cut, cut, cut manager will be replaced, with someone who can build, change, and develop for the future.' Apart from the general management challenges we described in the first pages of this book, the HR world also faces some more specific challenges.

One of the major new trends in HRM is the development of a *new psychological contract*. The old psychological contract of lifetime employment is being replaced by a new contract in which people have to build up their own certainties. In the future, an individual will have to secure his or her own 'employability', relying on his or her own competences and learning efforts. As a result, employer and employee have other expectations about each other. This new situation presents HR with a number of dilemmas. For example, what about training and education? Should an organization invest in training and education for its employees, even though this increases the probability that they might leave the organization sooner (because of their new or improved skills). And what about selection? An organization now recruits people for a specific job rather than for a lifetime career. However, jobs and functions are becoming less specific and general competences are growing more important.

Another major development in HRM is the focus on *competency management*. The core competences of an organization must be redefined in terms of the retention and integration of individual competences. According to Dave Ulrich (1997a), these core competences and the derived individual competences are the DNA of competitiveness. HRM professionals must frame their activities in accordance with the competences that are needed in the organization. It is no longer sufficient just to hire, train and reward employees.

Developments in *technology* also have consequences for the HRM function. Technology significantly influences how and where work is performed. Managers and HRM professionals, responsible for redefining work in their organization, must determine how technology can be both bearable and productive. In the Information Age, technology can help employees to filter essentials from side issues and thus increase individual performance. In addition, *flexibility* in the organization of labour is becoming common practice. Part-time work, work at home, time credits, and other labour policies support the flexibility of employers and employees. Technology can help organizations to organize themselves in a volatile market, while employees get the opportunity to create their own work–life balance.

In the current changing environment, the search for, and retention of, talent will be the major challenge. Successful companies will be those which are best prepared to attract, develop and retain people who have the competences, the perspective and the experience to lead a global business. The creation of organizations in which intellectual capital is constantly updated will be of enormous importance in HRM practices in the future. Peter Drucker expresses it as follows:

> The knowledge society will inevitably become *far more competitive* than any society we have yet known – for the simple reason that with knowledge being universally accessible, there are no excuses for nonperformance. (Drucker, 1995: 236)

All these trends and developments call for a new approach towards HRM. One can hardly neglect this increasing pressure on HRM to contribute to organizational performance. In the following pages, we will examine how HRM is evolving in search of answers to the new demands.

Strategic human resource management

A definition

Strategic Human Resource Management (SHRM) is defined as linking the HRM function to the strategic goals and objectives of the organization in order to improve business performance and develop organizational cultures that foster innovation and flexibility (Truss and Gratton, 1994; Tyson, 1997). The field of SHRM has grown extensively in the last 15 years. Schuler and Jackson (1999) describe the evolution from personnel management to SHRM as a two-phased transformation: the first transformation being from personnel management to HRM, and the second one being from HRM to Strategic HRM. While the more classic term 'personnel management' referred to 'the optimum utilization of human resources in pursuit of organizational goals' (Legge, 1995: 3), a central feature of the notion of SHRM is 'the creation of linkage or integration between the overall strategic aims of the business and the human resource strategy and implementation' (Gratton et al., 1999a: 7).

The term HRM itself is not new: one can already find examples of its use in the 1950s, especially in North America. But it is only since the 1980s that it has come to denote a radically different philosophy and approach to the management of people at work (Storey, 1989; Hendry and Pettigrew, 1990). Legge (1995) describes how the personnel function used to be seen as an essentially operational responsibility, unconnected with strategic management and unable to demonstrate a unique contribution to the organization's success. According to Legge, this has resulted in a vicious circle for personnel management, causing problems of credibility, marginality, ambiguity and low status in the organization. In response to these criticisms, a more managerial-oriented model emerged in the 1980s, in which personnel specialists integrated their activities more closely with top management and with the long-term strategies of the organization

(Tyson, 1987). The apparent novelty of HRM lay in the claim that by making full use of its human resources a firm would gain competitive advantage (Guest, 1990). So, HRM came to be seen as being too important to be left to personnel managers and, instead, as a key strategic issue demanding the attention of all managers.

Scholars in the field of SHRM have developed various perspectives on how the concept should be interpreted and investigated. As shown in Figure 11.1, Purcell considers two major perspectives, called the 'best fit' and the 'best practices' approaches to HRM (Purcell, 1999). The 'best fit' approach focuses on how the HR function realizes the business strategy and on the relationships existing between HRM (in general or its distinct policies and practices) and business strategy. The accent is on vertical integration of the HR function with the business. HRM needs to fit the strategy. In these 'best fit' models, one of the underlying assumptions is that organizational strategy *precedes* human resource strategy. Elements of the corporate strategy will dominate the HR strategy, although external forces (market, sector, lifecycle or type of organization) are assumed to affect the adoption of specific strategic HR practices. Gratton and her colleagues (1999a, 1999b) have criticized this top-down approach:

> From a conceptual position it could be argued that the concept of a top-down, unitarist planning process is overly simplistic, ignoring the political processes, the fact that organizations do not move sequentially from one predictable stage to another, and that many pursue multiple rather than single strategies. This 'classical' top-down approach to strategy development may fail to take into consideration the realities of organizational decision-making processes. (Gratton et al., 1999a: 7–8)

The second perspective, the 'best practices' approach, is more recent and focuses on the components of HRM, or the 'HR bundle' (Huselid, 1995; MacDuffie, 1995; Purcell, 1999). In this respect, authors have described and examined the interrelatedness of various HR interventions such as selection, training, rewarding and development (also called horizontal integration of HRM).

There is little agreement among researchers as to what practices and policies do lead to better performances. According to Legge (1995), the value of HRM to the business is affected both by the extent to which human resource policies and practices achieve integration with business strategy ('best fit' model) and by the extent to which they are characterized by internal consistency, commitment, flexibility and quality ('best practices' model).

The contribution of HRM to organizational performance

So far, we have presented some fine theories on the concept of SHRM, but the fact remains that the HRM department is seldom seen as a strategic partner in an organization. Despite all the rhetoric about 'the importance

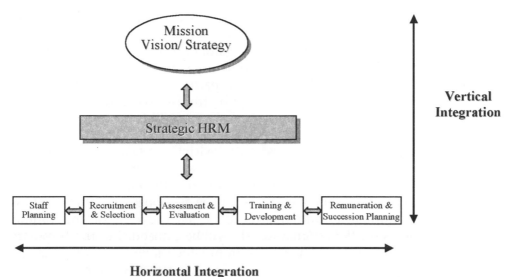

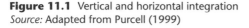

Figure 11.1 Vertical and horizontal integration
Source: Adapted from Purcell (1999)

of human assets as our main source of sustained competitive advantage', in many organizations the HRM function is seen as a costly administrative department, threatened by outsourcing. This bad position of the HRM function (and hence of the HR department) leads to a vicious circle. If the HRM function is seen as a source of fixed cost, it will feel the necessity to prove the efficiency of its policies to avoid cost-cutting and outsourcing. However, if the HRM department does not have any measures for its intangible assets, it will face serious problems measuring and proving its contribution as well. And if it cannot prove this contribution, it will be very difficult to persuade the line managers to use and take advantage of the developed HRM policies and tools. As the line managers will not be convinced, it will be hard to build a case for recognizing HRM as an important strategic department and to obtain strategic investments for valuable HRM practices.

How can HRM professionals get out of this vicious circle and realize a true strategic partnership? Nowadays, many organizations focus on measuring the true contribution of HRM practices in order to prove their added value to both line managers and boards of directors and to make this contribution visible within the organization. However, measuring HRM performance is a tough challenge. Becker, Huselid and Ulrich (2001) turned this problem into an opportunity:

> Simply put, strategic assets keep a firm's competitive edge sharp for the long haul – but by definition they are difficult to copy. Thus HR's problem – that its impact on firm strategy is difficult to see – is the very quality that also makes it a prime source of sustainable competitive potential. (Becker et al., 2001: 2)

We do not agree with this point of view. If HRM is to be a core competence for an organization, it should indeed be difficult to copy by competitors. But at the same time it should be recognizable, analysable and manageable by the organization itself. For the HRM function to achieve the actual upgrade to strategic partner, it is necessary to realize – at least partially – the shift in perception from a fixed-cost department to a *strategic department investing in human capital*. This process needs to be supported by adequate measures of HR performance. If an organization succeeds in realizing this process, HRM's vicious circle may be replaced by a virtuous one. Since HRM will be seen as a strategic department, it will have a good image in the organization and the cost will not be the primary focus. A system of measures will be developed to capture progress in HR performance, and there will be a clear view of the various components of HR performance. HR will be embedded in the corporate strategy map (see also Chapter 3), from which investments in strategic HRM can be deducted and justified. The investments will focus on the added value of the HR department, which reinforces its position as a strategic partner.

Towards a new concept of strategic HRM

So far, we have argued that strategic HRM should include what have been called vertical ('best fit') and horizontal ('best practice') perspectives. Moreover, strategic HRM should strengthen the position of the HRM function by elevating it to strategic partner, realizing the 'virtuous HRM' dynamics in an organization.

An attempt to synthesize these elements can be found in the work of Dave Ulrich and his colleagues (1995; Ulrich, 1997a, 1997b). From a more practical perspective, Ulrich argues that the debate about the value of the HRM function (or its *raison d'être*) should focus on how the function *contributes* to the business (its deliverables) rather than on what it *does* (Ulrich, 1997a). In this respect, Ulrich and his colleagues have developed a framework that describes the added value of the HR function (see Figure 11.2). They consider four key roles that HR professionals must fulfil, and which are conceived as four *result domains*. HRM must deliver results in each of these domains, since these four domains are equally important. The two axes of the model represent HR's focus and types of activity. *Focus* ranges from short-term/operational to long-term/strategic. *Activities* range from managing processes (HR tools and systems) to managing people. The combination of both axes results in four HRM roles: management of strategic human resources ('Strategic Partner'), management of transformation and change ('Change Agent'), management of the employees ('Employee Champion'), and management of the administration of the organization ('Administrative Expert'). Let us look at these four roles in greater detail.

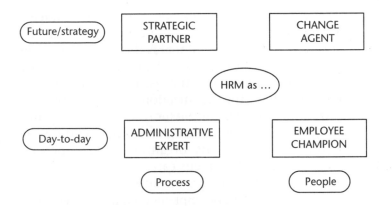

Figure 11.2 HR contribution to the business
Source: Ulrich (1997a: 24)

Management of company infrastructure: administrative expert A traditional HRM responsibility has been to cope with administrative tasks. As the persons responsible for administration/infrastructure, HR professionals must produce and deliver efficient HRM processes for staffing, training, remuneration, succession planning, promotion, and so on. Despite the fact that this role has been undervalued in the recent search for a more strategic focus, successful deliveries on this point still create added value in an organization. HR professionals create structure by continuously exploring and improving the HRM processes.

Management of employee contribution: employee champion This HRM role implies specific involvement in the day-to-day problems, expectations and needs of the employees. In companies in which intellectual capital is a critical resource for the organization, HR professionals should take up an active and more aggressive role in developing this capital. In this way, HR professionals become employee champions by linking the contributions of the employees to the success of the organization. Thanks to active employee champions, who understand the needs of the employees and ensure that they will be dealt with, the overall employee contribution increases.

Management of transformation and change: change agent A third key role in which HR professionals can add value to the organization is the management of transformation and change. Transformation includes a fundamental cultural change within the organization. HR professionals who can manage this transformation become both the guards and the catalysts of organizational culture. Change refers to the ability of an organization to improve the design and implementation of initiatives and to reduce cycle time in all organizational activities (see also Chapter 14). HR professionals can help identify and implement the change processes.

Management of strategic human resources: strategic partner The strategic HRM role focuses on aligning the HR strategies and practices with the business strategy. In this role, the HR professional is the strategic partner who is co-responsible for realizing the success of the business strategy by influencing the capacity for realizing the HR strategy. Translating business strategy into HR practices can help the organization in three important ways. First, the organization can adapt itself more quickly to change because the time span between conceptualizing and implementing the strategy has become shorter. Second, the organization can increase customer satisfaction because the client focus can be made concrete in specific models and actions. Finally, an organization can improve its financial results because the strategy can be implemented more effectively.

According to Ulrich, the management of strategic human resources is only one of the four domains in which the HR function can deliver value for the business. This is clearly a broader scope for HRM than the one incorporated in many theories on strategic HRM, which focus primarily on the HR function as a strategic partner.

How to realize a strategic HRM approach?

Who is responsible for realizing strategic HRM?

Ulrich has identified four key roles for HR professionals to excel in. However, he emphasizes that HR professionals need not fulfil all four roles themselves. To have the responsibility for managing the four result domains is one thing, to design the processes and actions to realize the goals in these domains is yet another. Depending on the processes designed to reach the goal, line managers, consultants, employees, technology or other delivery mechanisms may share the work.

Figure 11.3 is a representation of a possible division of responsibilities within an organization. The exact borders will vary depending on the organization. The difference between involvement in output on the one hand and delivering output on the other hand is often an important point of discussion. HR professionals must guarantee the output and help to define the shared responsibility of each party for delivering the output.

Developing strategic HRM: a process perspective

Defining responsibilities for developing a strategic HRM approach is important but is not sufficient. The *People Capability Maturity Model*[SM] (P-CMM[SM]) addresses *how* to develop and continuously improve the capabilities of the workforce, and achieve a more strategic HRM approach.

The P-CMM[SM] is a maturity framework, originally designed for software development by the Software Engineering Institute (SEI) and Carnegie Mellon University. Nowadays these capability maturity models are

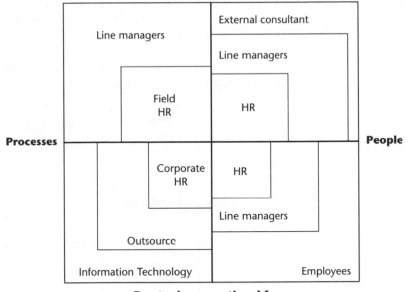

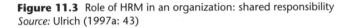

Figure 11.3 Role of HRM in an organization: shared responsibility
Source: Ulrich (1997a: 43)

increasingly used outside the software industry: applications are found in risk management (see also Chapter 5), operations and in HR. The main idea of the P-CMM^SM is to apply Total Quality Management principles to developing the workforce capability. As was already explained in Chapters 5 and 8, the maturity model develops a staged approach towards process improvement and identifies particular improvement steps, depending on the starting position of the organization in the functional domain.

The P-CMM^SM is the translation of such a maturity model to the HR function and pays attention to practices in such areas as work environment, communication, staffing, managing performance, training, compensation, competency development, career development, team-building and culture development. These various practices are grouped in the following major categories:

- Developing competence;
- Building teams and culture;
- Motivating and managing performance;
- Shaping the workforce.

An organization can progress through different levels of maturity. The more mature the organization, the higher the workforce capabilities.

Growth through the maturity levels creates fundamental changes in how people are managed and the culture in which they work (Curtis et al., 1995). Figure 11.4 gives a good overview of how P-CMM[SM] links different HR process categories to various maturity levels.

LEVELS	PROCESS CATEGORIES			
	Developing competence	Building teams and culture	Motivating & managing performance	Shaping the workforce
5 Optimizing	Coaching Personal competency development	Continuous workforce innovation		
4 Managed	Mentoring	Team building	Organization performance alignment Team-based practices	Organizational competency management
3 Defined	Competency development Knowledge and Skills Analysis	Participatory culture	Competency based practices Career development	Workforce planning
2 Repeatable	Training Communication	Communication	Compensation Performance management Work environment	Staffing
1 Initial				

Figure 11.4 Linking process categories to maturity levels
Source: Curtis, Hefley and Miller (1995: 43)

Measuring HRM performance: the HR Scorecard

In the previous section of this chapter, we have outlined the goals and current challenges for the HR profession and how HR could contribute to Integrated Performance Management. Another challenge for the HR department is to measure whether or not it succeeds in realizing its strategic aims. This is the performance measurement story translated to an HR setting.

The Balanced Scorecard, a performance measurement and management framework that was introduced in Chapter 3, has often been used to track the performance of the HR department. As we have already explained in this chapter, the Balanced Scorecard provides a framework for describing, communicating and managing the strategy in a consistent and explicit way, and it can also be implemented on a functional level or for support functions.

One might ask how HRM contributes to setting and realizing the targets in a Balanced Scorecard. When we look at the four traditional perspectives of the Balanced Scorecard, it seems obvious that the added value of HRM will be situated in the 'Learning' and 'Growth' perspective. Because organizational learning and growth stem from the three principle resources – people, systems and procedures – HRM will focus primarily on the people (human) resources. However, in this section we would like to go one step further and investigate the creation of an 'HR Scorecard', starting from the HR goals and incorporating Ulrich's model.

To make an HR Scorecard, an HR manager should not neglect alignment with the business unit or corporate level. Therefore, before designing the HR Scorecard, he or she should be able to formulate answers to the following questions:

1. Does the HRM department know the goals of the business unit or the whole organization?
2. Does the HRM department know the strategy of the business unit/ organization? And what is the place of HRM in the strategy map (see Chapter 3)?
3. Does the HRM department know the content of the Balanced Scorecard of the business unit/organization and the responsibility of HRM to define and realize targets?
4. What is the mission and what are the goals of the HRM department, within Ulrich's framework?
5. How are the HRM goals translated into an HRM strategy and made operational in the various HRM processes (HRM strategy map)?

The answers to these questions will provide the HR manager with the necessary information for creating an HR Scorecard that is aligned with, and tailored to, the goals of the organization. Figure 11.5, visualizes the alignment process (the numbers refer to the five questions above).

An important step for each HR manager is to identify the relevant perspectives of the HR Scorecard. This choice is related to who the stakeholders of the HRM function are and the actions through which HRM is going to reach its goals. Important HR stakeholders are:

- The management of the business unit or the whole organization (for whom HRM is working);
- The line managers who have to be supported;

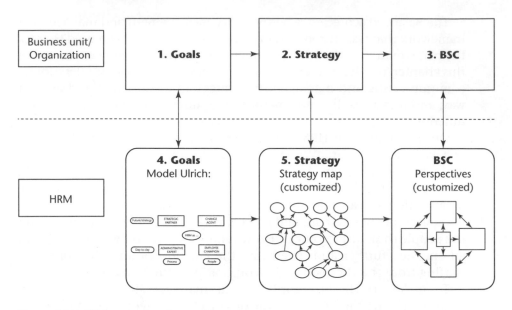

Figure 11.5 HR Scorecard – alignment process

- The employees (who are literally the human resources of the organization);
- The HR professionals.

Many HR Scorecards have been made, taking into account the four major perspectives identified by Kaplan and Norton (1992). Becker, Huselid and Ulrich's (2001) generalized HR Scorecard is one of the most famous ones because they have developed such a scorecard in line with their theoretical framework. We are, however, hesitant to accept the usefulness of this model for each and every organization. Eventually, an HR Scorecard should always be tailored to the unique goals, strategy and culture of an organization. But whatever the form and whatever the content, an HR Scorecard can provide an HR manager with the opportunity to measure the added value of the HR department to organizational performance. The Scorecard can be an instrument for crystallizing the goals of the HRM function and for making sure they are aligned with the organizational goals. As such, an HR Scorecard can help to create a 'virtuous circle of HRM'.

Conclusion

One decade ago, Schuler (1990) stressed the opportunity for the HRM function to shift from 'employee advocate' to 'member of the management team'. To do this, HR professionals need to be concerned with bottom-line profits, organizational effectiveness and survival. This means addressing human resource issues as business issues. To realize this shift, HR managers must adopt a new model of Strategic HRM. In this chapter, we have investigated what Strategic HRM could be, and what are its roles.

Ulrich's model calls for a focus on what the HR function could deliver rather than on what it does. Indirectly, the four domains that are used to describe the added value of the HRM function relate to the discussion about the linkages between HR strategy and HR activities. Reality teaches us that 'planned HR strategy' is not always equal to 'implemented HR strategy', as was presented in the 'vicious circle of HRM'. As discussed in the 'virtuous circle of HRM', a key issue will be to turn HR rhetoric into HR deliverables, thus proving the added value of HR. One valuable tool for combining both the theoretic opportunities and the day-to-day implementation and management is the HR Scorecard. All in all, the challenge remains to investigate further the added value and the contribution of HRM practices to organizational performance.

12 The Informal Organization: Leading for Performance

MARC BUELENS

Leadership and management

Managing an organization is balancing between the long and the short term, between stability and change, and between exploration and exploitation. Deciding between these conflicting alternatives requires (strategic) leadership. The purpose of this chapter is to explore how leadership can contribute to the development of superior strategies and their fast and skilful execution.

Leadership is generally considered to be an extremely important facet of good management. Everybody knows some famous examples, both in the business world and outside it, where leadership has really made the difference. But these examples often convey a somewhat more glamorous image than that of the mundane world of work (Fincham and Rhodes, 1999). In this chapter, we present both a very personal view of what leadership is and a description of some leading theories.

Do we need more leaders and fewer managers?

It is quite common to distinguish between managers and leaders in the way represented in Table 12.1. If we look at this table, the answer to our question above is an unqualified 'yes'. Who could object to 'real leaders'? However, Table 12.1 paints a picture that is a little biased. It becomes clear that the differences that are described refer more to 'good' versus 'bad' than to 'managers' versus 'leaders'. Of course, we need managerial *and* leadership skills in organizations. Just as in politics, the best politicians need leadership *and* political skills, and the best captains on sports teams need leadership *and* athletic skills.

Table 12.1 The difference between managers and leaders

Weak managers . . .	Real leaders . . .
Wait until it happens	Prepare the future
Are happy with the *status quo*	Want change
Are pursuing objectives	Have a vision

Table 12.1 *Continued*

Weak managers . . .	Real leaders . . .
Are experts of the past	Are experts of the future
Do the things right	Do the right things
Follow their job description	Change their job description
Respect budgets	Create value
Avoid mistakes	Seek learning opportunities
See information as power	Share information
Are myopic	Take the broad view
Are difficult to reach	Are approachable
Adore status symbols	Want the best for all
Use reward and punishment	Inspire and motivate

The distinction between management and leadership is more or less ideological, where leadership often stands for the 'good', dynamic, future-oriented, inspiring processes and management for the 'bad', cold, static, bureaucratic, non-inspiring processes. This distinction, however, is purely artificial: there is nothing inherently good or bad about management or leadership as such. To illustrate our point of view, take a look at Table 12.2.

Table 12.2 The difference between managers and leaders (part 2)

Dedicated managers . . .	Sick leaders . . .
Remain humble	Are megalomaniacs
Behave like a good citizen	Spend too much money on pet projects
Listen to collaborators	Listen to themselves
Stay balanced	Become psychopaths
Think before they act	Have big hairy audacious goals
End up with a golden watch	End up in prison or a mental hospital
Remain in the background	Are on the front cover
Follow realistic strategies	Follow wish-driven strategies

Is leadership a 'good' thing by definition?

Very surprisingly, the leadership literature itself has long questioned the real added value of leaders. There is still no real consensus over the assertion that 'leaders make a difference'. Anecdotal and scientific observations point to some disturbing facts: maybe we attribute leadership 'after the fact'. Imagine that Prince Andrew had been killed by an exocet missile in the Falklands War; and imagine that Mrs Thatcher, who was doing very poorly in the opinion polls at that time, had been forced by moral outcry to retreat from the Falklands – she would have been described as the greatest disaster the UK had ever known. All kinds of theories about female leaders would probably have become popular.

It is almost legally forbidden to run the next thought experiment, and that just might make it all the more thought-provoking: what would we have said (and thought!) about people like Patton, Mussolini, Eisenhower, Rommel – and, above all, Churchill – if the Nazis would have won the war? To put it less extremely, when the dot.com hype was at its peak, were the CEOs leading those companies 'brilliant leaders' because their companies were successful on the stock market? If you were reading *Business Week*, *Fortune*, and even the *Financial Times* in 1999 and early 2000, you were inclined to believe that those garage founders had 'a vision' (excuse me: *the* vision), were inspirational, etc. When the bubble finally burst, did those same people suddenly become short-sighted, stupid and less inspirational?

The essence of leadership

Leadership in organizations can be defined as a social influence process in which the leader seeks the voluntary participation of subordinates in an effort to reach organizational goals. Leadership is based on *voluntary participation*. This aspect seems rather obvious and describes the difference between leadership and other types of influence such as threats, manipulation, intimidation, or even the use of very enticing rewards (most people are not 'free' to refuse those rewards). A leader *exercises influence*, while dictators, tyrants and rulers wield coercive power. This means, of course, that a leader's followers enjoy a certain degree of freedom – they allow the leader to exercise that influence. One could say that a leader builds the right to influence, the right to speak. The first step in all persuasion processes is to establish credibility. (Readers more interested in power than in leadership will know that the first step in the power game is to make other people dependent on you.)

In the *long term*, this right to speak is based on well-known elements such as competence, integrity, results, predictability and trust. We cannot overemphasize the fact that leadership is extremely simple: be competent, be consistent, obtain results, be trustworthy (say what you are going to do and just do it). Then why do so many people complain about leadership? There are three basic reasons for that. First, most managers are quite busy 'managing' and simply lack the time and energy to 'lead'. And who said that management is easy? The second reason is overconfidence: most managers (and leaders) promise too much, cannot keep their promises and become failures in the leadership game. The third reason is that very often the long term is impossible: most managers, at all levels, have to obtain results in the short term.

In the *short term*, the leader uses other influencing principles that become apparent at so-called 'moments of truth' ('Ich bin ein Berliner', 'I have a dream'). There seems to be a rather limited set of behaviours defining a (short-term) leadership act. This is the kind of leadership one can observe in meetings, in speeches, in interviews. This kind of leadership is often called '*charismatic*', which seems to imply that it is difficult to describe or understand. The opposite is true. One can (at least for our Western culture) make rich and precise descriptions of what it takes to be a 'charismatic' leader. It takes you only a few moments to judge whether or not a speaker, a chairman of the meeting or a new president is 'charismatic' (in the short term!) This can be summarized by the following statements:

- Identification – effective persuaders build on common ground:

We-feeling	'Je vous ai compris'
I represent you all	Use language at the level of the followers
Feels for the public	Personal appeal
Empathy	Sense of belonging
I understand your situation	Building rapport
Together we can do it	No real distance
I am human	Interaction with public
I really care	I personalize my message

- Positive attitude – powerful:

Strong body language	Enthusiastic
Power speak	Story: the narrator is present
High energy, dynamic, drive, passion	'Open' (ready to be challenged)
Direct	Determined
Lighthouse	Committed

- Positive attitude – encouraging messages to followers:

You are important	You are part of the project
You are respected by me	You are given confidence
You are unique	Sense of self-worth is enhanced
I do it for you	It will depend on you
We serve a greater purpose	We are winners

- Positive tone:

Use of humour	Positive words
Optimism	Hope
Emo-talk	

- The challenge (vision):

Future-oriented	No 'explanation'
Great expectations	Values more than goals
Noble cause	Basic values
Victory will be ours	Success is around the corner
Holy mission	

- 'The great communicator':

Slow (use of silence)	Brief (with some exceptions in Latin countries)
Extremely clear, simple ideas	Emotional
Use of strong metaphors and images	Strong one-liners
Extremely well-prepared	Sticks to the message
Mainly repetitions	Expressive
Staging	Unity of vision and message
Establishes eye contact	Black-and-white images, strong contrasts, polarizes, sometimes even shocks
Creates an illusion	Matches the environment: clothes, stage
Rhetoric	

Charismatic leaders' behaviours establish a common vision of the future. The 'right' vision unleashes human potential because it serves as a beacon of hope and common purpose. It does this by attracting commitment, energizing workers, creating meaning in employees' lives, establishing a standard of excellence, promoting high ideals and bridging the gap between an organization's present problems and its future goals and aspirations. In contrast, the 'wrong' vision can be very damaging to an organization. This is the dark side of charismatic leadership and the basic reason why leadership that is purely based on charisma is extremely dangerous. The biggest company failures, the most stupid wars and almost all crimes against humanity are based on 'charismatic' leadership.

Charismatic leaders set high performance expectations and standards and express confidence in the followers' ability to meet them. This is essential, because employees are more likely to pursue difficult goals when they believe they can accomplish what is being asked of them. Charismatic leaders also serve as role models. Through their actions, they demonstrate the desired values, traits, beliefs and behaviours needed to realize the vision. The more collaborators meet the leader, the clearer it becomes that most leaders do not act as role models, that many behaviours are only 'setting the scene', impression management, professional staging. People listen to what leaders say, but they believe what leaders *do*. On the other hand, when collaborators observe consistency between the long-term influence factors (such as competence and honesty) and the short-term 'espoused theory', leadership is firmly established.

Situational Leadership

Not all situations are similar and not all behaviours are successful in all circumstances. All leaders know this, and most leaders adapt their behaviour to the situation. Research has shown that style-flexibility is applied by almost all leaders. Although many popular models have tried to describe different 'leadership styles', those models tend to overlook the basic reason why they are eventually successful. Let us start with the basic danger of a situational model. Leadership is based on accepted influence. Influence is based on consistency. Basically, a leader is highly predictable to his or her followers. The more the leader changes his or her style, the less predictable he or she becomes. So, how can situational leadership be successful? The major reason is that a good leader is able to 'read' the situation and identify the need for style-flexibility. When the need is clearly identified, the flexibility becomes natural and will be perceived as natural by the collaborators. No one behaves the same way on a company picnic as in the middle of an emergency meeting. Instead of helping to change their behaviour, good models help leaders to read the situation.

With this reservation, we can look at two different models of situational leadership. The first one is by far the market leader; the second one is the most recent approach, based on the rapidly growing discipline of the social psychology of influencing.

Situational Leadership: what do the models tell us?

Hersey and Blanchard's Situational Leadership model Probably the most famous model of Situational Leadership was developed in 1977 by Paul Hersey and Ken Blanchard (who is best known for his 'one-minute manager' bestseller) (Hersey and Blanchard, 1988). Their *Situational Leadership model* is still considered to be 'state of the art' in popular leadership courses.

In order to describe this model, we must clarify several concepts. Leadership behaviour is characterized along two dimensions, called *task-oriented leadership* and *relationship-oriented leadership*. Task orientation is about how well the leader 'maintains standards', 'meets deadlines',

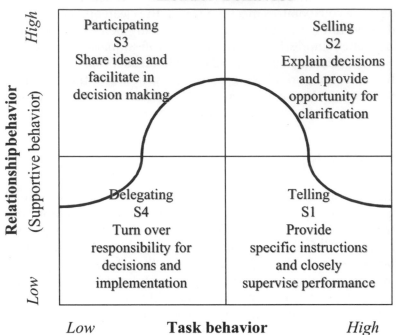

Figure 12.1 Situational Leadership
Source: Hersey (1984: 85)
Reprinted with permission from Dr Paul Hersey (1984). All rights reserved.

'defines objectives in detail', and so forth. Relationship orientation indicates how much the leader cares about good relations with his or her employees. By combining high and low relationship and task behaviours, Hersey and Blanchard created four leadership styles: delegating, participating, selling and telling. Then, using data from various sources, they plotted a curve representing what they called the high probability style. This curve indicates where the highest style-effectiveness correlations appear (see Figure 12.1).

They then captured and measured the key characteristics of situations by looking at the 'readiness' or 'maturity' of the employees ('the followers') (Fincham and Rhodes, 1999). The 'willingness' of the followers relates to their attitude. If a group is willing, then it has the confidence, commitment and motivation to accomplish a specific job or activity. 'Being able' means that the group has the knowledge, skill and experience to accomplish a particular task.

According to Situational Leadership, the appropriate style depends on the combinations of willingness and ability (i.e., the readiness) in a group. The four leadership styles are now related to the situational aspects, as shown in Figure 12.1. Kreitner, Kinicki and Buelens (2002) describe this as follows:

The appropriate leadership style is found by cross-referencing follower readiness (which varies from low to high) with one of four leadership styles. The four leadership styles represent combinations of task and relationship-oriented behaviors (S1 to S4). Leaders are encouraged to use a 'telling style' (directive) for followers with low readiness. This style combines high task-oriented leader behavior, such as providing instructions, with low relationship-oriented behaviors, such as close supervision. As follower readiness increases, leaders are advised to gradually move from a telling to a selling style, then on to a participating and, ultimately, a delegating style. In the most recent description of this model, the four leadership styles are referred to as telling or directing (S_1), persuading or coaching (S_2), participating or supporting (S_3), and delegating (S_4). (Kreitner et al., 2002: 462)

Influencing decision-makers Most business leaders are influencing executives. The key to success here is not the executives' motivation but the way they decide. Their decision-making style is the key to their success and for these leaders the lever to influence. In a recent article, Williams and Miller (2002) present a pragmatic overview of decision styles and different ways of influencing them. Their article is summarized in Table 12.3.

Table 12.3 Influencing decision-makers

	Charismatics	Thinkers	Sceptics	Followers	Controllers
Characteristics	Enthusiastic	Logical	Demanding	Cautious	Accurate
Use words such as	Results, focus, easy	Numbers, proofs, plan	Trust, power	Expertise, previous	Details, facts
Focus on	Results	Models	Credibility	References	Structure

Source: Williams and Miller (2002)

Situational Leadership: a hype?

The importance of models such as those developed by Hersey and Blanchard or Williams and Miller does not lie in their academic rigour. The real importance lies in the open invitation to the leader to pay more attention to his or her leadership environment. That is why a typology, although poorly developed, can be successful. It forces the leader to scan the situation and to decide where the situation fits. It is no accident that all sales courses emphasize a client typology: it forces the seller to study the client. And if one reads the Williams and Miller article carefully, one can readily see that the leadership theory is in fact a sales theory.

Why, then, is so much being written and debated about Situational Leadership? There are at least three reasons. The first reason has to do with the 'share of mind'. Situational leadership is an intriguing and appealing notion. Every textbook devotes many pages to the cubes, bell-shaped curves, and 3D-grids, all representing different models of leadership. Training in Situational Leadership is big business (in fact, most of these training sessions are actually about problem-solving – how to behave in certain situations). However, managers in these sessions are not being *'trained'* in leadership; they listen to funny stories, fill in some questionnaires, do a few role-plays and receive feedback. This is not 'training', this is warming-up. And even if they are being trained, they are certainly not being trained in some important styles (sometimes for ethical reasons, but usually for image reasons) such as being autocratic, or being highly dominant or exploitative, which are very successful styles under some circumstances.

Second, leadership – much more than management – is closely related to our personality. We all have limits to the flexibility in our personality. We can stretch ourselves a little, but we cannot over-stretch. Nevertheless, those training programmes create the 'illusion of control': even I can become a better leader . . .

Third, style flexibility is the hallmark of the healthy leader. We all know sick leaders who do not show any style flexibility at all. Those people are sometimes very visible, harmful and influential – and they serve as terrifying examples. This third reason points to the important fact that a situational view can be very important when we look at the *selection*, not training, of leaders. If one really accepts a situational view of leadership, it is clear that in a dynamic environment leaders cannot be excellent for a very long time. There is a Waterloo for all Napoleons.

Another way to match leaders and situations

There seems to be a rather broad consensus in the literature, and among observers, about which situations match which 'leaders'. Of course, different authors differ in the details (after all, their models are sold via expensive training programmes and leadership questionnaires or via their personal consulting with CEOs), but in essence one could formulate a simple 'fit.' That is: you need *strong* leaders in *unfavourable* situations, and you need *people-oriented* leaders in *favourable* situations.

Strong leaders listen first (because they are not stupid!), but impatiently and they interrupt easily. They are convincing and have a sharp mind (depending on the case at hand, of course: you need different kinds of sharpness when you are leading a gang in the Bronx, a French biscuit factory, or a group of anti-globalization protestors). They see the essence quickly, have a special gift for simplifying things, are not very sensitive to short-term negative feedback (unless this feedback concerns their own ego), are energetic, dominant, selfish (have a very large ego), and want to be 'in control' (e.g., they are 'difficult', or at least demanding patients in hospitals).

People-oriented leaders listen actively, develop empathy, sometimes even sympathy, involve others, take their time for decisions, and then check for their acceptability. They also prefer a compromise to an open conflict, are sensitive to rejection and build trust.

Unfavourable situations can be described as those situations where the leader has no strong power base. These are also the situations where the followers lack the skill, and especially the will, to collaborate. In these situations, there is also strong resistance, and people will take advantage of ambiguous situations.

Favourable situations can be described as those situations where the leader is formally recognized by all parties and where the followers have the skill, and especially the will, to collaborate. In these situations, goals are clear and widely accepted, and rewards for working towards and attaining goals are obvious and shared by all influential parties.

What could be called the *'totally unexpected leadership paradox'* is that leaders move their organizations away from domains where they fit into domains where their own personalities do not fit:

- Strong leaders will quickly establish a strong power distance and fire people who lack the skill and especially the will to collaborate. They will break resistance and make it disappear, set clear goals and develop reward systems, etc. If they succeed, they will find themselves in a 'favourable' situation, where their personality no longer matches the situation. The 'Margaret Thatcher' story is perhaps one of the best examples in this respect.
- On the other hand, people-oriented leaders will install participation and consult people. They will lower power distance and build on talented people who will get promoted (and become incompetent). And they will tolerate long discussions about goals (which become unclear). Through lower power distances, many conflicts will arise and new coalitions will be formed. If people-oriented leaders succeed, they will find themselves in an 'unfavourable' situation, where their personality no longer matches the situation. In this case, we refer to the 'Mikhail Gorbachev' story.

Other aspects of leadership

Does social intelligence make a difference?

Although experts do not agree on the major paradoxes surrounding leadership, one cannot neglect the basic fact that leading is about leading people. One can manage systems, budgets or time. People, however, are managed and led. Since the mid-1990s, the ability to cope with people has often been called *emotional intelligence* (EQ). Technically speaking, EQ comprises two major dimensions: (1) handling one's own emotions; and (2) handling other people's emotions. The first dimension is closely related to concepts such as achievement, motivation, optimism, emotional control, etc. Leaders, entrepreneurs, managers, but also doctors, teachers, negotiators, and even accountants, need this talent. As long as you must 'perform', the motivation to achieve – although not very distinguishing – is very important.

On the other hand, the second dimension plays a key role in all interpersonal behaviour, ranging from sales to therapy, from leadership to teaching. To avoid miscommunication, we will refer to that second dimension not as EQ, but as *social intelligence*. Social intelligence can be considered as the interpersonal dimension of EQ.

Leaders score high on three aspects of social intelligence. First, they are able to start from 'empathic design'. Without empathy, they become cold bloodless psychopaths, the subjects of horror stories, television series and cartoons. Because pure empathy can come very close to sympathy, being too empathic can hinder leaders in their task-oriented behaviour. That is why we have borrowed 'empathic design' from the field of product development. It means that a leader designs new work processes, organizes the division of labour and sets up new services spontaneously with the collaborator in mind. There is a well-known saying in management (formulated most clearly in Stephen Covey's *7 habits of highly effective people*): 'always start with the end in mind'. Leaders start with their followers in mind. They look at the end product through their eyes.

The second dimension of social intelligence in leadership is the ability to influence: leaders persuade easily, they are trusted. The basic skills in this area are better understood as a result of the work on emotional intelligence (Goleman, 1998, 2000). We can summarize these insights in three basic principles:

- Reciprocity: when we give, we will receive; when we allow ourselves to be influenced, we will influence.
- Being positive: our brain cannot cope well with negation, absence and negativity. Leaders are masters in positive re-framing (a crisis is a challenge), are fully aware that emotions are contagious, and exhibit many positive emotions such as praise, optimism and encouragement.
- We are most often influenced by our peers: the more the other resembles our self (to be more precise, our idealized self), the more he or she can influence us. Better leaders are able to join and to establish good relationships; they are part of 'our' group.

It is easy to see that charismatic leaders do intensively apply these three aspects of social intelligence.

Some less expected qualities

Goffee and Jones (2000) have identified a couple of unexpected leadership qualities. First, leaders selectively show their weaknesses. Just as charisma became popular after John Kennedy's presidency, and communication became the name of the game after Ronald Reagan, Bill Clinton has had his legacy too: humble leadership. The real reason, of course, why showing weaknesses might be important is that by showing weaknesses a leader can establish rapport, can show that he or she is one of us. This makes the leader approachable, a basic condition for receiving timely and sensitive information.

Second, leaders rely heavily on their intuition to gauge appropriate timing and course of action. This quality is a very tricky one. Kings wear crowns, but one does not become king by wearing a crown. Intuition and timing are part of all behaviour. Some people are consistently poor in timing, others seem to be masters. Good timing, however, is the result of other qualities such as observing, listening and keeping an open mind. Successful leaders have the greatest difficulties explaining their successes. A great part of those successes are due to good luck. Explaining them by intuition, timing or 'personality' does not really explain them any more than does attributing the successes of a top athlete to 'a winner's instinct'.

Beyond the leadership hype

Peter Drucker (1974), perhaps the greatest of all management writers, has emphasized time and again that real leadership consists in serving the organization and not oneself, as most charismatic leaders tend to do. Leadership that is not grounded in a constitution – in formal acceptance by the followers – is dangerous. It is hard to believe how far the theory and practice of leadership have evolved in the other direction under the influence of the mass media. Entrepreneur, manager, business leader of the year, winning in the corporate Olympics. Modern business leaders often remind us of show horses, more than of humble servants.

Therefore, it is a relief that Jim Collins' (2001) landmark study on lasting success in companies reveals a type of leadership, called 'Level 5 leadership', that is radically different from the charisma hype.[1] Level 5 leaders combine great personal humility with strong professional ambition; they display a compelling modesty, self-effacement and balanced personality (with the exception of their drive for results). Level 5 leaders attribute success to others, not to themselves. Level 5 leaders can be described as plough-horses, not as show horses.

Conclusion

There are about 30,000 published studies on leadership. Most of them are contradictory in nature. Human beings are capable of producing more complex behaviour than simple (or even complex) models can deal with.

In this chapter, we have explored another important aspect of organizational behaviour: leadership. We all know some famous stories where leadership made the difference, but still there is no consensus that leaders always make the difference. We have looked at the essence of (good) leadership, and we listed some characteristics of good leadership, both for the long and the short term. We then focused on the question: What leadership is most appropriate under which circumstances? Hersey and Blanchard's Situational Leadership model has been discussed, but we have outlined that there are other contingency models available as well. Finally, we also described some other – sometimes less expected – qualities of good leadership.

13 Strategic Rewards and Reward Strategies

XAVIER BAETEN

Reward systems become an important means of communicating and reinforcing business goals (Brown, 2001: 2)

Managers and firms talked rewards, but they paid salaries. (Tropman, 2001: xvi)

Are rewards just another big management hype thrown into the strategy bucket, or do strategic rewards really make sense? A lot has been written about strategic rewards, but unfortunately much of it is nothing more than rhetoric. The aim of this chapter is to make the case for strategic rewards, as we are convinced that reward management is a new management discipline that deserves and needs to be further developed. The big challenge is to develop reward strategies and systems that continuously motivate employees to realize (strategic) business objectives. In this respect, rewards are a very important strategy implementation tool. But the reality is far from that. All too often, rewarding is seen as a purely administrative HR activity. The link with strategy is made only for executive managers.

This chapter provides the reader with some new ideas, concepts, research findings, and practical examples in the field of reward management. This will lead to the growing recognition that reward should transcend its traditional back-office role and evolve from its traditional administrative orientation towards a more strategic role. As a consequence, the reward manager's role will also change. While top management plays the role of strategy formulator, the reward manager is the strategy implementer.

This chapter seeks to provide some concrete frameworks and decision-making tools that will help in understanding the power of reward management for tomorrow's organizations. First, we will focus on what rewarding is all about by defining rewards, describing the goals of rewarding and making an inventory of reward instruments. Next, we will try to make the concept of strategic rewards more concrete by providing some clear examples of how to link corporate and business unit strategies to reward systems. Last but not least, we will develop a model for reward management, focusing on the reward drivers, strategies and systems, and also on the effectiveness of reward systems.

Rewarding: what's it all about?

Terminology

Rewarding should be considered an important aspect of the process of strategy implementation. However, there is a lot of misunderstanding about this concept and its content, which is also evidenced by the use of a lot of terms like 'compensation', 'remuneration', 'pay', 'incentives', 'rewards', etc. Therefore, we would first like to focus on terminology and provide the reader with a workable definition of 'reward'.

While many authors limit the discussion to 'pay', we would like to broaden the scope and take the 'total reward' approach, which is much more oriented towards the employee's perspective – the employee as a customer of rewards. This means that we not only take the purely financial elements into consideration, but non-financial rewards as well, like recognition, involvement, information sharing, work–life balance, etc.

We would like to propose the following definition of reward: it refers to all forms of returns – direct and/or indirect, short-term and long-term, financial as well as non-financial – that employees receive as part of their employment relationship.

Rewarding: what is going wrong?

We have found that there are quite a few misunderstandings, and even myths, about rewards, their role and their effects. In this respect, we agree with Pfeffer who states that 'much of the conventional wisdom and public discussion about pay today is misleading, incorrect, or sometimes both at the same time' (Pfeffer, 2002: 141). In order to be completely realistic, we thought it might be interesting to pay attention to some of the arguments that are frequently used by people who do not believe in the strategic importance of reward management.

A debate has been going on in the (academic) literature for some 30 years now about whether or not rewards motivate, which is really going back to the fundamentals of rewarding. We have to admit that there are a number of studies that have found only a slight (and even negative) correlation between pay and performance. Based on these observations, Kohn (2002) wrote a famous *Harvard Business Review* article, where he concluded that rewards ultimately fail because they succeed only in securing temporary compliance. Some more of his arguments:

- Pay is not a motivator. While it is true that earning too little money, especially when compared to colleagues and friends, can de-motivate, this does not necessarily mean that more money will increase motivation. In this respect, pay can be categorized as a 'hygiene' factor rather than as a motivator.

- Rewards punish. They are manipulative and lead to people feeling controlled.
- Rewards rupture relationships. They reduce the possibilities for cooperation. People are pressuring the system for their individual gain.
- Rewards are an easy substitute for what managers really need to do a good job. Developing a bonus system is much easier than providing feedback and participation possibilities, supporting people, making job content attractive, etc.
- Rewards discourage risk-taking because people will only be focused on getting their performance or productivity ratings. In this respect, incentives discourage innovation.

Although some of these arguments certainly make sense, the main comment we have on them is that reward has been quite narrowly defined – in the arguments above, the rewards are rather incentives that are linked to individual performance. As we will see, rewarding entails much more. However, this focus is quite common because individual incentives are extremely popular in the Anglo-Saxon culture, where most of the research on rewarding has taken place. Although incentive systems can be quite efficient – and have proven their efficiency in very specific cases (e.g., rewarding sales people) – we should take a broader view by also paying attention to other techniques, like profit-sharing and team-based pay, which could be used instead of, or in addition to, individual performance-related pay.

The goals of rewarding

There is broad-based acceptance that the core goals of reward systems are motivation, recruitment and retention (Kessler and Purcell, 1992). This agrees well with the introduction to Part II of this book, where it was stated that reward systems help create motivation and commitment on the part of management and the workforce. We would like to concentrate for the moment on what is considered to be one of the most critical questions with regard to the relationship between reward and performance management: Do rewards motivate?

Honestly speaking, we have to admit that pay systems themselves cannot be the single solution that leads to the best performance. There is a broad spectrum of motivators beyond money. Whereas money and employee benefits can be classified as *extrinsic motivators*, there are also a number of *intrinsic motivators*, such as praise, participation and autonomy (Frey, 2002).

Until now, our discussion has mainly focused on the importance of short-term monetary rewards. Here, the broader reward concept, which also takes non-financial reward elements into account, comes into the picture. Alignment of these various motivators is important. Furthermore, alignment also means taking the employees' preferences into account.

Indeed, employees respond differently to the different types of motivator. Some employees are mainly motivated by extrinsic motivators, for others intrinsic motivators have the greatest effect.

It is clear that motivation is about more than only money or pay. The same holds for the relationship between reward and pay. Therefore, it is extremely important that these various motivators be integrated and deliver the same message. For instance, when participation is an important intrinsic motivator for the workforce, it seems logical to also translate this into the financial reward package by providing for financial participation (by means of profit-sharing, employee stock ownership, stock options, etc.). It is also clear that the employees' preferences should be taken into account to fully exploit the motivational power of rewarding. Therefore, a lot of customization will be required.

Reward systems also communicate a lot about the organization's philosophy and thus play an essential role in attracting the right people. For instance, an organization with a high variable wage in relation to the fixed wage, will attract more risk-taking people. This should also be aligned to the organization's philosophy and culture. As such, reward systems play an important role in achieving a good person–organization fit (Cable and Judge, 1994).

Besides motivation, rewarding is also about recruitment and retention. According to Tropman (2001), a reward system should serve different goals depending on the performance of the personnel:

> Encourage retention of the best (top 20 percent). These are the real stars of the firm who should absolutely be retained. They should be paid 20 percent and even more above the market.
> Balance in- and outflow of the middle mass (middle 60 percent). These are regular do-the-job employees who might be broken up into top 30 percent and bottom 20 percent. They should be paid at market or slightly above the market.
> Encourage departure of the rest (bottom 20 percent). They should be paid 10 to 20 percent below the market. (Tropman, 2001: 115)

In practice, the situation might be just the opposite. By this we mean that some reward systems encourage retention of lower performers, while higher performers cannot share in the fruits of their efforts.

Reward instruments

We have already said that reward is about (much) more than just money. To make this more concrete, Tables 13.1 and 13.2 provide a detailed overview of the various financial and non-financial reward 'tools' that are available. Table 13.1 clearly reveals that, even within purely financial rewards, there are a lot of reward tools. Financial rewards can be short- or long-term, related to active or non-active periods, tied to the job the individual is performing, or they can be conditional (e.g., linked to the achievement of specific results). Furthermore, they can be granted in direct monetary form and also in kind (e.g., company car). Table 13.2 provides an overview of non-financial rewards.

Of course, not every organization uses all these tools or uses them to the same degree. Furthermore, cost elements, culture and strategy should be taken into account when choosing which reward vehicles to use. Fit is very important in this respect. Therefore, answering the following questions for each of these reward dimensions will be a very interesting exercise:

Table 13.1 An overview of financial reward instruments

	Direct income	• Fixed wage (paid monthly, weekly, daily) • Bonus, variable pay (recurring and non-recurring – based on individual, team, and/or company performance) • Commission (sales)
	Deferred income	• Stock (employees share ownership) • Stock options
	Employee benefits: Income security	• Retirement and savings plan • Life insurance and death coverage • Medical and medical-related benefit payments (hospital, disability, accident)
Financial rewards	Employee benefits: Income-adding	• Company car • Meal vouchers • Company restaurant • Payment for time not worked in addition to social security (e.g., palliative care) • Discounts • Gifts • Reimbursement of travel costs from home to work
	Employee benefits: Services	• On-site services, like laundry, ironing, shopping service • Sports facilities • (Emergency) child care • Financial planning • Career advice • Medical check-up

- *Where are we now?* Which rewards does the organization currently provide and to what degree?
- *What are the employees' preferences?* Although this is a very important question from a motivational point of view, it is our experience that most organizations do not know enough about this topic. Apparently, they do not take the stakeholder approach and do not see the employee as a 'customer of compensation'. Our own research also addresses this element, and we have seen that there are some general preferences as well as preferences that are related to gender, age, function, etc.
- *Where do we want to be within five years?* This is also related to the analysis of the outcomes of the questions above.

Table 13.2 An overview of non-financial reward instruments

	Psychic income	• Accomplishment in the job, interesting work • Recognition • Trust • Job title • Image of the employer • Working atmosphere (colleagues, line management, accessibility of top management)
	Learning opportunities	• Training budget • Breadth of training entitlement • Learning on the job • Possibilities for job rotation/promotion
Non-financial rewards	Organizational participation	• Being informed about the organization • Autonomy, responsibilities • Being able to give input, suggestions, etc. • Participation in decision-making
	Time	• Flexible working hours • Compressed working week (year) • Additional time-off • Flexibility in granting time-off • Possibilities for part-time work
	Place	• Distance between home and workplace • Tele-work • Desk: ergonomics, space, comfort
	Employment security	• Job security • Employment guarantees offered by the employer

There is a lack of knowledge about employees' preferences regarding reward. The sparse research that is available has proven that there are a number of employee preferences that are quite universal:

- High pay levels;
- Individually oriented pay systems (instead of group-based pay);
- Fixed rather than variable pay;
- Job-based pay;
- Flexible benefits (Barber and Bretz, 2000);
- Base pay increases based on merit (i.e., individual performance) (LeBlanc and Mulvey, 1998).

This makes clear that employees are relatively risk-averse (because they prefer fixed pay) and want their financial rewards to be linked to variables under their control (like their job and their own performance). Also, this demonstrates the individualistic nature of humankind.

However, research has focused primarily on financial rewards. Recent research by the Vlerick Leuven Gent Management School's Strategic

Rewards Research Centre has investigated which elements of the total rewards approach employees find most interesting. Results were obtained from a sample of more than 400 white-collar workers of a company in the metal industry (see Figure 13.1). The employees' message is unambiguous: cash is clearly the most important reward element compared to job security, learning and development, and employee benefits. We do not want to return to the discussion of whether cash motivates or not, but here we clearly see that cash is extremely important and thus is a powerful tool to be used and managed in the strategy implementation process.

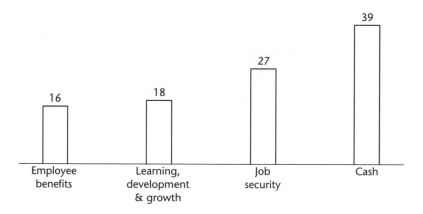

Figure 13.1 Employee preferences – some evidence *(relative importance)*

On the other hand, there is not always a clear distinction between financial and non-financial rewards. For instance, promotion is a non-financial reward element. However, if it is not accompanied by financial rewards (i.e., a higher wage), we fear it might lose its motivational power. Learning and development is another example. Some employees find this element important because it will lead, sooner or later, to promotion or because it will increase their market value. What we mean is that, in many cases, non-financial rewards can or will also have consequences in the area of financial rewards. Furthermore, reward preferences are also linked to socio-demographic variables, such as age, gender and family situation.

In summary, we are convinced that tailoring reward packages to the employees' needs and preferences will improve reward satisfaction and boost employee commitment and motivation. This does not necessarily mean that each individual's package should be tailor-made (this is more the case at the higher levels), because we fully agree that the administrative burden could be quite significant. But there can certainly be a middle ground – for instance, by taking socio-demographic elements into account when designing the benefits package, or by giving employees alternatives to choose from.

Strategic rewards

Definition

Milkovich has put forward a good definition of strategic rewards: 'A strategic perspective on rewards focuses on the patterns of reward decisions that are critical to the performance of the organization. Being strategic about rewards implies support of the business strategy and sensitivity to anticipated environmental pressures' (Milkovich, 1999: 27). To have an influence on organizational performance, reward systems should be in line with the corporate and business unit strategies. Here lies the origin of the name 'strategic rewards'. Unfortunately, we have found no more than ten articles or book chapters that pay explicit attention to the link between corporate or business unit strategy on the one hand, and reward strategies and systems on the other hand. What is more, these studies only take compensation into account (i.e., fixed and variable pay). They do not consider employee benefits or non-financial rewards. It is clear that there is a lot to be done in this field.

Reward systems and organizational implications

The opponents of reward management often cite some examples that have proven that rewarding can affect organizational performance negatively:

Heinz Company paid a bonus to managers if they managed to improve profit compared to the previous year. As a consequence, the managers started to manipulate profits by delaying or accelerating deliveries to customers. By doing this, the managers (and the reward system) compromised long-term growth as well as the value of the company.

At Sears, mechanics working for a car repair operation were rewarded according to the profits earned on repairs requested by customers. As a consequence, mechanics started making unnecessary repairs, which led to closing all the Sears car repair shops in the state.

These examples illustrate that, all too often, organizations see rewarding as a 'quick fix', without analysing the possible counterproductive or suboptimal effects some reward systems might have. However, we are convinced that good reward management – taking into account the organizational goals as well as the employees' preferences – leads to better performance. In this respect, we also found some 'good' examples: Tyco Laboratories' incentive compensation programme is oriented towards maintaining and improving the entrepreneurial spirit, drive, and resourcefulness of managers who think and act like owners. In order to achieve this, the business units' management teams share the team's profits. To make this concrete, incentive compensation is directly tied to each business unit's performance, a factor that is under the control of the business unit's managers. The experience with this system made the CEO of Tyco say he believes the compensation system is at the heart of the company's success (Kohn, 1993).

In mid-1990 at the Safelite Company (the largest car windshield fitting company in the US), fixed hourly wages were replaced by piece rates, with a minimum wage. Piece rates reward workers according to the number of goods they produce. As a result, productivity improved by 44 per cent (Frey, 2002).

These examples make clear that incentive compensation systems can be a key mechanism for motivating executives and other employees, and for facilitating communication of strategic intentions (Gupta and Govindarajan, 1984). If rewarding is not used in this way, the whole strategy implementation process might be seriously weakened (Thompson and Strickland, 1992). Some studies have demonstrated that pay policies are an important driver of success (Montemayor, 1996). Gupta and Govindarajan (1984) have shown that successful organizations have more differentiated incentive schemes than less successful organizations.

Strategy and reward systems: some academic recommendations

Several management publications have tried to link reward strategies and systems to organizational strategy. However, they do not clearly distinguish between reward strategies and reward systems. Even worse, some books continuously refer to reward strategies, but they do not make this concrete at all. As a consequence, the various operationalizations of the reward strategy concept used in the different studies significantly impede interpretation of the research findings. We will try to solve this problem by providing the reader with the reward management model. In this particular section, we would like to focus on the link between reward strategies/systems on the one hand, and corporate or business unit strategies on the other hand. (The various strategy typologies that we refer to are described in greater detail in Chapter 6.)

Boyd and Salamin (2001) have investigated the types of reward system that can be linked to Miles and Snow's (1978) strategy typology. Table 13.3 gives an overview of how the reward systems' characteristics can be linked to this particular strategy typology. Analysers' reward systems contain elements of both systems (Carroll, 1987).

Rewards have also been linked to strategy typology of Treacy and Wiersema (1995) (Table 13.4). Here again, the design of the reward systems should be tied to the business unit's strategic choice (Thompson and Strickland, 1992; Montemayor, 1996).

Table 13.3 Reward systems for Miles and Snow strategy typology

Defenders	Prospectors
• Pay levels meet the market • Moderate differentiation in base pay level, based on individual performance • Moderate level of variable pay, mainly based on individual performance	• Pay levels are above the market • High differentiation in base pay level, based on individual performance • High level of variable pay, namely group or organizational bonus plans. No individual bonus because of work interdependency. High use of deferred compensation
• Performance variables are short-term-oriented and quantitative	• Performance variables are long-term-oriented and qualitative

Table 13.4 Reward systems for Treacy and Wiersema strategy typology

Cost leadership/ Operational excellence	Differentiation/ Customer intimacy	Innovation/ Product leadership
• Centralized reward systems	• Both centralized and decentralized reward systems	• Decentralized reward systems
• Internal equity • Focus: control. Reward policies and procedures are carefully spelled out No exceptions to the rule • Non-participative design • Base pay: below market, narrow grades, seniority-based • Variable pay: lowest level	• External equity • Focus: behaviours and results • Participative design • Base pay: at market, broadbanding, skill- and competency-based • Variable pay: more significant	• External equity • Focus: behaviours and long-term results Flexible policies that enable dealing with unique situations • Participative design • Base pay: above market, broadbanding, significant merit increases • Variable pay: highest level
• Useful performance measures: operational expenses, ROE, profit margins	• Useful performance measures: customer satisfaction, order processing and delivery	• Useful performance measures: revenues and profits coming from new products

Source: adapted from Treacy and Wiersema (1985)

However, not all research findings point in the same direction. We have found results proving that cost leaders and innovators require similar reward strategies, but are clearly different from differentiators. This might mean that the focus (external or internal) of the business strategy should be a main determinant of the reward system.

Some researchers have also examined whether corporate strategy affects reward systems. Managers at the corporate level are concerned with the strategic scope of the organization, and corporate strategy addresses the main concerns of the multidivisional firm. Researchers have focused primarily on diversification (which is about how closely the different businesses of the corporation are related). Gomez-Mejia (1992) has linked the diversification strategy to compensation strategies and has investigated whether performance is driven by the fit between these two strategies. Gomez-Mejia has identified two different reward strategies that integrate different compensation dimensions (Table 13.5). These should be seen as two extremes on a continuum of reward systems and practices.

Table 13.5 Algorithmic versus experiential compensation strategies

Algorithmic compensation strategies	Experiential compensation strategies
• Centralized administrative framework • Mechanistic, predetermined, standardized, repetitive procedures with minimal attention to mitigating circumstances, exceptions to the rule, or external contingency factors; more bureaucratized, formalized pay policies • Above market pay with high job security • Little risk-sharing between employees and the firm • Emphasis on internal equity and hierarchical position as basis for reward distribution • Monitoring of behaviours rather than outcomes • Heavy reliance on job evaluation procedures; narrowly defined grade structure • Seniority is an important criterion in pay allocations • Pay secrecy • Little employee participation • Compensation policies and procedures are carefully spelled out	• Decentralized administrative framework • Flexible and adaptive in order to be moulded to respond to changing circumstances, environmental shifts, fluid organizational structures • Sensitivity to market concerns in setting pay level • Greater employee input • Use of personal skills and attributes as a basis for pay determination • Performance rather than tenure as a criterion for pay allocation • Extensive risk-sharing between employees and the firm • Less emphasis on hierarchical position • Less dependence on superiors • Multiple rewards at individual and aggregate levels given at frequent intervals

Source: adapted from Gomez-Mejia (1992)

Gomez-Mejia (1992) linked the two compensation strategies to various corporate strategies and found that a more experiential compensation strategy is beneficial for single-product firms, while a more algorithmic compensation strategy is beneficial for firms with a more diversified (dominant and related) product range.

In summary, we have found a couple of studies that have linked reward strategies to business strategies and that have proven that a strategic fit affects organizational performance significantly. However, the fit between business strategy and reward strategy is not static. Linking reward strategies to business strategies might be 'tricky' because strategies in today's competitive environment change frequently (e.g., due to mergers and acquisitions). But the strategic management process itself is dynamic as well. There are intended strategies, which have been consciously developed and explicitly formulated. But there are also strategies that become apparent during the course of the trajectory and that are not the result of a thorough, systematic process of environmental scanning.

Therefore, matching compensation and business strategies might be like shooting at a moving target. This means that not only is the degree of fit important, but timing – in order to gain a competitive advantage – is crucial too (Balkin and Gomez-Mejia, 1987a; Milkovich, 1988). Furthermore, we should also be aware that assessment must be continuous. This is made very clear by the words of a senior manager: 'The most important lesson to keep in mind is that strategic alignment is a journey and not an event' (Henderson and Venkatraman, 1993: 482).

Being able to fit reward management to the organization's goals and strategy also implies that reward managers should have information about the future plans of the organization. This means that they should be participating in the long-term planning process because their potential for influencing change might be great (Henderson and Risher, 1987).

Reward management and reward strategies

In the previous paragraphs, we have discussed the importance and the goals of rewarding. We have also provided concrete evidence of how to link reward systems to organizational and business unit strategies. In this section, we will develop a model that helps to manage reward from concept (reward strategy and its drivers) to implementation.

Reward management is not easy. Therefore, organizations should look at reward very carefully and develop a clear *reward strategy* before moving to implementation. This approach can be helpful in addressing many of the difficulties that organizations have with their reward management. These difficulties are:

- Ineffective communications;
- Lack of support systems (market data);
- Poor performance management and/or pay fails to motivate because there is no link to performance, productivity or the contribution the employees make to the organizational goals;
- Weak performance assessment capabilities of line managers who decide on merit increases. More generally, there is also a lack of trust;
- Lack of reward management skills/support;
- Grade drift: because salary bands are narrow, employees must be promoted to receive a higher wage;
- Merit-based pay systems (which are quite popular) annuitize pay rises because each rise goes into the base. This means that the employer has to pay year in and year out for last year's performance Tropman, 2001).

Reward management: the model

In Figure 13.2, we present our reward management model. For the moment, there is a lack of good reward management frameworks that can help managers with critical reward decisions.

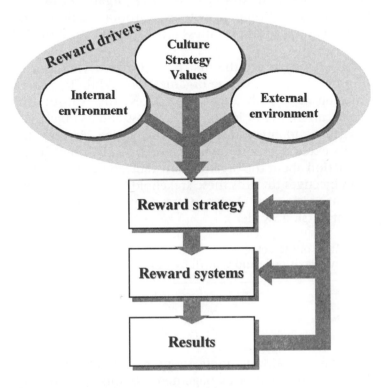

Figure 13.2 Reward management model

This integrated strategic model is applicable to all kinds of organization and is time-independent. Furthermore, it can be applied to the whole workforce, ranging from executives and directors, through managers, to clerical and even blue-collar workers. It is possible, and perhaps even advisable, to start with the most critical jobs or job families. However, reward systems are deeply rooted in the organization and cannot be changed overnight.

The various building blocks of this model of reward management will be discussed in the rest of this chapter.

Reward drivers

Developing a reward system should start with an analysis of reward drivers, which, in their turn, will determine the reward strategy. The most important reward drivers are the organization's culture, values and strategy.

However, the internal and external environments also play a significant role in determining the reward strategy. In this section, our aim is to discuss the most important reward drivers in general and not in detail.

Culture, values and strategies The most important reward drivers come from the culture, values and strategies of the organization. We distinguish among: organizational objectives, corporate culture and management values, corporate and business unit strategies, and the HR strategy.

The organization's *objectives* are the first reward driver. They can be found in the vision and mission of the organization. While the vision informs the future business path and is not necessarily realistic, the mission is about the current definition of the business and its objectives. In this respect, vision and mission also are the bridge between the organization and its external environment. Consequently, they should also provide information about the organization's stakeholders as well as the organization's objectives towards these stakeholders. As an example, let us consider the vision of Volvo Cars Gent (Volvo's largest manufacturing plant outside Sweden):

> What are we ultimately out to achieve?
> Securing our continued existence and growth by providing satisfaction to:
>
> - our employees,
> - our customers,
> - our shareholders,
> - society.

This vision will have important implications for the organization's reward strategy. For instance, senior management's bonus at Volvo Cars Gent should not be determined by short-term financial measures alone. It should also take into account the managers' performance towards employees (e.g., people management skills, retention rates, results of employee satisfaction surveys) and customers (e.g., customer satisfaction). It is our experience that this is forgotten in many cases and consequently the reward system does not send out the right signals. This clearly shows that reward management does not take the reward drivers sufficiently into account.

We have already explained how and to what degree reward systems could be linked to *organizational strategies*. Reward systems should also be aligned with the *organizational culture*. To do so, we must make a distinction between a clan culture and a market culture. A *clan culture* is characterized by fraternal relationships, long-term commitment, a sense of tradition and style, the existence of a collegial network, interdependence, loyalty and collective initiative. A *hierarchy-based reward system* best fits this kind of culture. In such a system:

- Bonuses are relatively small and based on corporate performance;
- Bonus pay-outs increase by level in order to emphasize the importance of long-term commitment;
- Granting a bonus is dependent on a superior's judgement;
- The major factors in a salary increase are tenure and performance;
- Promotion practices express concern for the long-term career of the employees;
- Promotion from within is the standard policy.

A *market culture* is characterized by encouraging a strong sense of independence and individuality, a purely contractual relationship between individual and organization, an absence of job security and loyalty as well as the absence of a common set of expectations regarding management style or philosophy, limited interaction and individual initiative. The reward system that best fits this culture is called the *performance-based reward system*, which is characterized by:

- Bonuses are a very significant part of compensation, and they communicate that the organization places more value on the star performer rather than on the team player;
- Management bonuses are based on the performance of their division;
- Base salary increases are affected by performance and external labour market circumstances (Kerr and Slocum, 1987).

Finally, the reward system should also be linked to the global *human resources strategy* and its actualization in the level of training and development, labour relations, teams, employee involvement, etc.

Internal environment We consider the internal (and external) environment as a constraint on the relationship between organizational strategy and culture and reward systems. For instance, it might be the case that an innovative organization with a results-oriented culture (which is a cultural reward driver) will not pay out a bonus (even if this would be best) just because of its poor performance over the past year (which is an internal reward driver).

The *organizational structure* is an important reward driver related to the internal environment. Although there might be differences among sectors, organizations in general are becoming flatter and have fewer layers. This goes hand in hand with a looser, more flexible definition of the job, more task flexibility, and crumbling barriers between jobs (Kessler, 2000). This means that many job evaluation systems must be adjusted (sometimes even abandoned): pay bands should be broader, and competences should be included as variables determining base pay levels. Therefore, modern job evaluation schemes might become role evaluation schemes that not only pay attention to duties, responsibilities, scope and tasks, but possibly also to knowledge, skills, abilities, attitudes and beliefs needed to perform job duties successfully (Heneman, 2001). Although organizations might have fewer hierarchical levels, there are still various ways in which the work can be organized (see also Chapters 9 and 10). In this respect, a mechanistic organizational structure is characterized by a high degree of formalization, centralization, standardization, and a narrow span of control. An organic organizational structure is just the opposite (Heneman et al., 2001). This will have important implications for the reward strategy.

A second major internal reward driver is the *lifecycle* of the organization or its business unit. Different stages in the lifecycle might require quite different rewarding techniques. During the *start-up* phase, the general HR focus is on maximization of productivity. Base pay will be below market and the emphasis will be on variable pay because of the need to invest money. Therefore, stock options are a very popular reward vehicle in this stage. Furthermore, the emphasis is on the use of long-term incentives that reward market performance. *Growing* organizations or business units are focused towards recruitment and can afford to pay market wages; variable pay is still important. Because *mature* organizations focus on retention, base pay levels compared to the market even increase during maturity phases, while incentives are more focused on cost containment (Balkin and Gomez-Mejia, 1987b, 1987c; Bergmann and Scarpello, 2001).

Larry Greiner (1998) developed another lifecycle perspective in which he identified five growth stages, each with a dominant management style. He also linked different reward systems to these different lifecycle stages, as shown in Table 13.6.

The last internal reward driver we would like to discuss is the *reward history* itself. For instance, organizations might be reluctant to introduce new pay schemes because they have previously had bad experiences with this. Also, it might be extremely difficult to shift to performance-related pay in an organization that has always been paying its employees on a fixed basis. Therefore, we would advise reward managers to also construct a clear picture of the history of the reward system: changes that have been made in the past, experiences with the system, etc. In this respect, we should never forget that rewards in general – and pay in particular – immediately capture everyone's attention, so they cannot be changed every month.

Indeed, there are a number of other factors that are related to the internal environment and that might have an influence on the reward strategy. Without going into detail, we would like to name a few of them:

- A workforce comprising mainly women might pay more attention to work-life related benefits;
- Internal relations with the unions might have an influence on collective bargaining, which has always been an important element in reward management;
- Labour-intensive organizations will have fewer possibilities for paying relatively high wages because this would have a strong influence on their profit;

Table 13.6 Greiner's growth stages and the link with reward systems

Growth stage	Description	Management reward emphasis
Creativity	Emphasis is on creating a product and a market; founders of the company are entrepreneurs and lack management skills	Ownership (stock, stock options)
Direction	Sustainable growth under directive leadership; introduction of organizational structure and accounting systems	Salary and merit increases
Delegation	Decentralized organizational structure; more responsibility for managers of plants and market territories	Individual bonus
Coordination	Formal systems to achieve greater coordination; recruitment of numerous staff members at headquarters with the aim of initiating programmes of control and review; development and use of formal systems and procedures	Profit-sharing and stock options
Collaboration	Spontaneity in management action is emphasized through teams and skilful confrontation of interpersonal differences	Team bonus

Source: adapted from Greiner (1998)

- The ability to pay bonuses might be strongly linked to the profits of the organization.

External environment In many organizations, the reward system is driven by the external environment. For example, base pay systems are based on multi-sector collective bargaining and market data, and employee benefits are directly linked to tax and social security legislation. Apparently, these organizations do not consider reward systems to be a tool for strategy implementation.

A very specific element that we would like to discuss in this context is the geographic environment. In North America, the prevalence of the shareholder model is quite pronounced. This implies a larger proportion of variable pay in the pay package and the predominance of merit-based pay increases. New pay practices (like cafeteria-style benefits and competency-related pay) remain marginal. On the other hand, the European model is characterized by a predominance of job evaluation models, comprehensive benefits packages, and the use of profit-sharing instead of purely linking pay to individual performance. As we can see, both models are quite different and have their own characteristics, advantages and disadvantages. But where are we heading in the future (or where should we be heading)?

Brown (2000) suggests combining the dynamic markets of the USA with the social cohesion of Europe and calls for a 'third way' of reward management, which is about achieving economic efficiency and social justice at the same time. In his view, we should abandon universal approaches and replace them by specific, tailored reward systems. This evolution is also made clear by current emerging practices:

- The use of team and collective bonus schemes in addition to individual performance-related pay;
- Broader pay bands, without going to extremes like 200 per cent. Much more common will be widths of less than 60 per cent;
- Integration of newer considerations (like competences) into job evaluation systems, and a decline in the use of standardized systems.

Developing a reward strategy

Many articles and textbooks talk about reward strategies but do not make this concrete. Indeed, the word 'strategic' is a very popular adjective that is most often used to stress the importance of the noun – all too often without operationalizing this concept. We would like to change this by providing the reader with a hands-on instrument that will be helpful in developing reward strategies.

First of all, we would like to make clear that a reward strategy is a functional strategy, based on, and closely related to, the corporate and business strategies. The reward strategy explains how reward contributes to the (realization of the) strategic objectives of the business. It also translates business and corporate objectives into functional ones. Also, we should take the dynamic nature of the process of strategic alignment into account. Indeed, the challenge is to assess continuously the reward drivers and to position the reward system within the external and internal environment and to fine-tune the internal infrastructure.

Up to now, rewarding has usually been internally oriented: often without even bringing the reward drivers into the picture, let alone developing a reward strategy. In our concept, once the reward drivers have been analysed and inventoried, a number of strategic choices need to be made before they can be translated into a reward system. This is what reward strategies are all about. But there's more. We should not forget that a reward system is also a communication tool. It makes the values of the organization clear to the external environment, and it also sends a message to potential employees. For all these reasons, organizations should think carefully about their reward strategies. To make the concept of reward strategy more concrete, we have identified the strategic dimensions and decisions that should be made in order to develop a reward system that truly contributes to the strategic business objectives (see Table 13.7).

Table 13.7 Dimensions of the reward strategy

Reward process

	□ □ □ □ □	
Collective bargaining	□ □ □ □ □	Management discretion
Reward issues are determined by HR – no line management input	□ □ □ □ □	Reward issues are determined by line managers
Limited employee participation in developing and/or adapting reward systems	□ □ □ □ □	Employee input is important

Reward structure

Centralization (global)	□ □ □ □ □	Local degrees of freedom
Reward management is an administrative and functional HR domain	□ □ □ □ □	Reward management is a strategic department, linked to strategic decision-making
Reward is driven by internal hierarchy	□ □ □ □ □	Reward is driven by the market
Reward arrangements are highly structured and controlled	□ □ □ □ □	Reward arrangements are flexible and loosely managed
Harmonized reward systems for all staff	□ □ □ □ □	Different reward systems for different groups of employees
Job-based	□ □ □ □ □	Person- and/or role-based (flexibility and performance)
Pay is determined by employee qualifications	□ □ □ □ □	Pay is determined by duties and responsibilities linked to job-role
High levels of secrecy	□ □ □ □ □	Open communication
Follow implementation of organizational systems/changes	□ □ □ □ □	Lead implementation of organizational systems/changes

Competitive positioning of reward strategy

No explicit positioning	□ □ □ □ □	Clearly defined positioning
Positioning is determined by base pay	□ □ □ □ □	Positioning is determined by total compensation
Positioning determined by (short- and long-term) financial rewards	□ □ □ □ □	Positioning determined by total rewards
Lag behind market	□ □ □ □ □	Lead market

Table 13.7 *Cont.*

	Reward mix	
Focus on financial rewards	❑❑❑❑❑	Focus on non-financial rewards
Limited risk-sharing between employer and employee (fixed)	❑❑❑❑❑	High levels of risk-sharing between employer and employee (variable)
Limited level of employee benefits focused on income protection	❑❑❑❑❑	High level of employee benefits focused on income protection (caring employer)
No employee choice in composing the reward package	❑❑❑❑❑	Employee choice in composing the reward package (cafeteria plans)
	Performance links	
Reward is not linked to performance	❑❑❑❑❑	Reward is strongly linked to performance
Individual performance	❑❑❑❑❑	Team, business unit, department, company performance
Input-related (competences)	❑❑❑❑❑	Output-related (results)
Financial performance criteria	❑❑❑❑❑	Non-financial performance indicators

The decisions regarding these various dimensions should be taken at the strategic level and should be tied to the analysis of the reward drivers. Therefore, the CEO, the Executive Committee and even the Board of Directors should be (much more) involved in the process.

To develop a reward strategy, each organization should position itself on these different dimensions, which should be seen as continuums. We should mention that there is no absolute 'right' or 'wrong' answer (although some dimensions or wordings might give that impression). It is far more important to make internal and external environments consistent.

Developing reward systems

Once the reward strategy has been developed, the reward manager can start to translate this strategy into the reward system and its various building blocks. This is the process of implementing the reward strategy.

Although reward managers should adopt a total reward approach, there is little known about how the non-financial reward instruments can be used to implement a reward strategy. This should be further developed in future research.[1] It is not our aim to provide the reader with a complete framework on how to develop reward systems. We will limit ourselves to some more general thoughts on developing financial reward systems. Remember that the questions or aspects that are mentioned below can only be further worked out on the condition that the reward strategy has been defined.

Base pay is one of the most important elements of the reward system. Consequently, it is crucial that a good structure for determining base pay be developed. This starts with developing an internal hierarchy of jobs – or, more broadly, roles – as well as determining compensative factors. The degree to which this hierarchy is important and should be worked out in detail has been decided in the reward strategy. However, there should always be some kind of work hierarchy.

The next step is to link this internal hierarchy to salaries, which is also referred to as *grading*. Depending on the reward strategy, organizations might choose either narrow or broader and more flexible ranges. A very important element in this respect is to slot grades and their salaries into the market. Once this has been done, persons should be linked to grades. This can be done very formally, but it is also possible to leave some (or more) space for negotiation (e.g., in case there is a market shortage).

Once the base pay system has been worked out, the reward manager should also decide on *salary increases*. He or she should work out the determining variables (e.g., seniority, cost of living, performance, competences) concretely – their importance as well as the concrete percentages of increase – and who decides upon these salary increases. Indeed, promotion to another grade and its determining factors must be worked out.

In the case of *variable pay*, the first important decision is which employees are eligible for a bonus, as well as the relative importance of variable pay compared to base pay and/or total rewards. In addition, the organization should decide how the bonus/variable pay system will be funded. In some organizations, granting a bonus is dependent on the profitability of the organization or the business unit. It might also be the case that a formula is used to determine the height of the bonus pool. Other critical decisions that have to do with variable pay are the criteria that will be used to determine the bonus (e.g., return on equity, people management skills, customer satisfaction, operational measures, etc.), who decides upon the bonus, and the pay-out frequency. But perhaps the most important element is the link with the performance management process itself: goal-setting, feedback and performance review.

The last element we would like to address is *employee benefits*. Bergmann and Scarpello (2001: 506) define these as 'all the indirect economic compensation the employee receives for continued company membership'. Evidently, employee benefits, as well as pay level and type of work, play an important role in determining the relative attractiveness of the organization to potential employees. Employee benefits are quite specific in the sense that most benefits are normally provided in non-cash or non-direct-cash form. 'Fringe benefits', 'perquisites', 'allowances', 'coverages' and 'subsidies' are frequently used terms, indicating that employee benefits cover a wide range of categories that can be regarded as extras to base pay. The term 'fringe benefit' goes back to the 1920s, when benefits made up only about 3 per cent of payroll expenses (Smith, 2000). Nowadays, employee benefits can make up easily more than 20 per cent of wage costs, depending on the employee category.

The use of employee benefits is sometimes linked to cultural issues: a well-developed employee benefits package on the level of insurance can communicate a caring employer culture. The use of employee benefits is also driven by the external environment, and more specifically by the labour market situation. Indeed, some organizations have been very creative in offering exotic employee benefits to job groups that are extremely rare. We call these benefits 'new age benefits'. Some examples are limousine service for late workers, shopping service, pet care, gardener, granny crèche, company cars for secretaries, etc. Because these benefits are very much related to temporary labour market shortages, they have not become part of the package of 'core benefits' like pensions, medical insurance, or job- or status-related company cars.

It might well be the case that the most important driver for employee benefits is another external one: tax and social security legislation. In many cases and in many countries, specific types of employee benefit (like pension plans, medical insurance, etc.) undergo a fiscal treatment, which is much more interesting than the high social security and tax contributions that have to be paid on salaries. In this respect, many employee benefits actually are no more than tax optimization of the reward package. We think that this situation should be changed and that reward managers should ask themselves whether and how to use these benefits more strategically.

Reward systems: the results

The reward manager's work is not over once the reward systems have been put into practice. It is also extremely important to keep sight of what the results of the reward systems are. We are convinced that employee behaviours are the most important element in this respect. By this we mean that the reward system will lead to behaviours which should be in line with the organization's objectives and goals. However, this is not the only element. A good reward strategy and system should also motivate employees because of goal congruence as well as the feeling that the reward system takes their specific needs into account, i.e., delivering employee value. This will then provide added value in recruitment and retention.

To address the issue of employee valuation of the reward system, organizations should solicit employee input much more than they currently do when developing reward systems and have a good idea of the employees' satisfaction with regard to their reward system, etc. This is not yet common business practice. In this respect, we would like to cite a study where it was found that only 6 per cent of organizations ask for employee input in the process of designing a reward system (Dolmat-Connell, 1999). We still have much to do to realize the concept of stakeholder management that has been worked out in Chapter 2.

Conclusion

Rewarding is the fourth element of the organizational behaviour component. Although it is generally considered to be an important strategy implementation tool, the concept of strategic rewards is not well developed. This chapter presents some models, frameworks, and research findings that will help in understanding the power of reward management for tomorrow's organizations.

We started by defining what rewarding is all about, and what is its major function. Clearly, the goal of rewarding is to motivate, recruit and retain the 'good' people within the organization. All too often, rewarding is about money. Here, we have shown that rewarding is more than money, although money remains an important reward instrument.

We then analysed how rewarding can be used as a strategic tool, i.e., to realize organizational objectives. We have reviewed some of the academic literature that has investigated the link between various reward systems and various strategy typologies.

In the final section, we have provided a first draft of a new reward management model. We have identified the most significant reward drivers, have presented some major elements of the reward strategy, made the link with reward systems and, ultimately, identified the results of these reward systems.

Note

1 It is worth mentioning that there is not always a clear line between financial and non-financial reward. The concept of employee participation is a clear example of this. Employee participation consists of financial participation (e.g., by means of profit-sharing, granting stock (options), etc.) as well as organizational participation (e.g., providing information on the organization, consultation, participation in decision-making). To be effective, both forms of participation should be linked: the return on equity for organizations providing financial as well as non-financial participation is significantly higher than it is for organizations that do not provide these two forms of participation simultaneously (Baeten and Van den Berghe, 2002: 880).

14 Change, Learning and Performance: Three of a Kind?

HERMAN VAN DEN BROECK AND STEVEN MESTDAGH

When managers talk about performance, the topic of organizational change is predominant in the discussion. A central question arises: How can we retain (or develop) a competitive edge in a world full of surprises? Most analyses lead to the same conclusion: some hasty doctoring will be quite insufficient in the current business environment, and a more thorough change approach is needed. However, instead of turning the wheel, many performance management initiatives still entail a 'more of the same' approach: 'Plus ça change, plus c'est la même chose.' Practices that were successful in the past are used again. However, these practices might suppress any chance of adaptability.

Therefore, in this chapter we will outline how the performance concept can be translated into a change management approach and how change, learning and performance are inextricably intertwined. We will present some new ideas on the context in which change takes place and learn how 'change-friendly' organizations can boost themselves to maximum performance, thereby illustrating how two eternal enemies – chaos and order – can be structurally reconciled. We will introduce some basic building blocks for creating change-friendly organizations and demonstrate how behaviour in learning organizations creates a dynamic platform in which organizational change and performance are created or, otherwise, stifled.

Setting the stage: organizations and their change potential

Change has become the daily bread of many managers and is often considered to be their biggest challenge. Still, the question concerning how to cope with change remains largely unanswered. This has much to do with our traditional view of management, which we call 'narrowing management'.

The traditional view of management: 'narrowing management'

Many managers are – almost by definition – genuine control freaks. They like to work towards exactly defined targets and clear-cut strategies. They need precise priorities, rules and procedures, and once they have them, they stick to them in a very rigorous manner. In fact, what managers are striving for is complete mastery over their environment. Many popular management techniques such as Total Quality Management (TQM) and the whole repertoire of statistical measures are designed with only one purpose in mind: getting a better grip on the situation and controlling every single parameter. In this light, managers carry the heritage of Henri Fayol, the pioneer of rational management, who made us believe that control, predictability, coordination and direct guidance are the one and only essence of good managerial practice. As a result, in the classical paradigm, the concept of a 'strong organization' primarily signifies order and firmness, structure and leadership, safety and common goals.

Now, control is beautiful when it works, but too often it degenerates into a compelling addiction. We refer to this tendency as *narrowing management*. For example, the CEO of a large transporting company once said: 'I need a list with all the specific unknown problems we will encounter.' As a withdrawal symptom, this takes the cake. In this approach, management tries to gain a better understanding of the world by classifying it into neat little categories. We want to be able to completely control this world, so lead us to the Promised Land: a perfectly operating society. Narrowing management is characterized by the belief that complex systems can be controlled through understanding and controlling their smaller constituent elements. In this view, one tries to analyse and measure each of these elements separately, severely limiting the interaction of a constituent element with its environment because this facilitates measuring. This brings about simplistic (if not context-banned, at least very context-limited and sterile) cause–effect thinking. Moreover, this thinking is strictly linear: it presumes that one fact has one cause. By knowing the constituent elements, one can then make predictions about the larger system.

In the exact sciences, this mode of thinking is called 'reductionism'. The reductionist scientist who only pays attention to the molecular composition of the hydrogen atom loses sight of the reality of a swirling vortex of water and forgets how the weather moulds it into an overwhelming natural phenomenon. Science – including management – has burdened us with numerous laws that explain exactly how things would happen . . . if there were not any environment.

For years now, management has constrained itself through a similar, narrowing emphasis on constituent elements. Narrowing management accords rigorously separated responsibilities to individuals or individual departments. Narrowing management divides management tasks into all kinds of functional areas and hopes, by taking the clock apart in order to be able to tell the time better. Distinct departments then behave as fortified bastions where trespassers are not tolerated: this task is for marketing, this one's for sales. Meanwhile, the strict boundaries that are drawn around 'cells' limit necessary interaction with the environment, which largely explains why spontaneous tendencies towards adaptation are brought to a standstill. We call this kind of approach the *'control the element' strategy*. Each problem is divided into small, controllable elements. However, by doing so, the function of the whole is lost. We have been brought up with this dominant view for years and it gives us an artificial sense of security. We feel secure about things that are tangible today, here and now. But this means that we are deluding ourselves because these things will only show their real value 'in relation to'. Jeanie Daniel Duck of the Boston Consulting Group has expressed this in a superb way:

> It is like the company is undergoing five medical procedures at the same time. One person's in charge of the root canal job, someone else is setting the broken foot, another person is working on the displaced shoulder, and still another one is getting rid of the gallstone. Each operation is a success, but the patient dies of shock. (Duck, 1993: 109)

Effective change and performance management are illusions in such an environment. Still, we often observe organizations opening up their entire tool box and – in some sort of 'buffet approach' – simultaneously working on TQM, re-engineering and empowerment. However, the key to success does not lie in the meticulous application of each technique in isolation, but in connecting and balancing every aspect, in understanding how each step affects the others and how changing one aspect influences all the rest and, ultimately, affects the whole structure. Another characteristic of narrowing management is that it greatly widens the distance between decision, execution and results. Elements are separated in space and time, since they are easier to control that way.

Narrowing management reduces the total system to wreckage in no time. Managers in a narrowing climate are constantly afraid of entropy, but they combat their fear with partial solutions. Narrowing management combines mechanical element-thinking with the syndrome of the control freak and thus forms a dangerous dark force that paralyses organizations from within.

Accordingly, organizations increasingly look for ways to free themselves from this 'narrowing management' towards a more entrepreneurial mindset. But during this journey, some organizations inevitably end up in an opposite, perhaps even more devastating, dark side. In their enthusiasm, organizations often make the mistake of becoming reckless. The stories of the numerous young, ambitious companies in high-tech industries, which are so busy speeding up and innovating that they crash before they even enter the market, are still fresh in our minds.

Towards a holistic approach: 'broadening management'

Organizations that have followed the narrowing trail for too long are at a dead-end today. In many cases, the traditional arsenal of management tools and techniques has run out, so organizations are compelled to seek their fortune in other directions. According to Margaret Wheatley (1992), the underlying currents in the new thinking are a movement towards holism, towards understanding the system as a system and giving primary value to the relationships that exist among seemingly discrete parts. For years we have done our utmost to tear systems apart; in the new holistic vision, the blocks are put back in place and glued together again. In this paradigm, the most important question is: How might the separate parts contribute to the whole?

Within this new thinking, which we refer to as *broadening management* – one is convinced that complex systems are characterized by a few simple basic rules. Eisenhardt and Sull recently put it into words like this:

> When the business landscape was simple, companies could afford to have complex strategies. But now that business is so complex, they need to simplify. Smart companies have just done that with a new approach: a few straightforward, hard-and-fast rules that define direction without confining it. (Eisenhardt and Sull, 2001: 107)

Managers in the most turbulent environments jump from one opportunity to another, and even improvise when necessary, but they recognize the need for some strategic key processes and simple rules of thumb that lead them through chaos. Some of them encounter dozens of possible innovations daily – a simple rule then acts as a compass to quickly determine which five possibilities receive green lights. Organizations in such environments try to position themselves where the stream of new chances is most intense, hence their *'ad hoc' strategy*. Managers in a narrowing climate fail to notice 'strategy as simple rules' and tie every process to detailed routines. From a broadening perspective, however, simple rules are essential to provide just enough structure to be able to grasp the best opportunities. Or, in the words of Brown and Eisenhardt (1998): simple rules place a company 'on the edge of chaos' – namely, at that point where they can maintain a grip that is just firm enough not to crash into the ravine.

To ensure themselves of continuous performance, these organizations are eagerly searching for more organic structures in order to find a sustainable balance between control and lawlessness. Modern organizational forms adopt a fluid way of approaching the new reality and try to capture both structure and freedom, using metaphors like jazz bands, molecules, schools of sharks, symphonic orchestras, or even white-water canoes, as put forward by Rosabeth Moss Kanter (1997). For narrowing management, being organized and remaining organized are the be-all and end-all. The flip side of the coin, *disorganization*, has never been recognized as a partner. This has led to a schizophrenic blindness that is now exacting a heavy toll. For years we have learned to regard uncertainty, deviant ideas, tolerance for initial failure and intuitive behaviour as perils to be avoided at all costs. For years we have looked the other way, pretended as if these things were non-existent. But they are slumbering in every organization. By ignoring them, we make the mistake of having only incomplete information, causing our decision-making process to be sometimes ridiculously narrow-minded.

Managers should learn to accept chaos and all its accompanying characteristics as a positive force. This acceptance will remove much unhealthy stress from firms. The great challenge for management is to find a balance between self-organization (trusting that chaos is a necessary condition for realizing order) and controlling behaviour (fine-tuning of order). Narrowing management and broadening management are mutual partners. Modern managers are holistic and connect order and chaos.

Entering an age of flexistentialism

In the twenty-first century, management can be raised to a veritable art only when we make abstraction of the two conflicting ambitions in every organization. On the one hand, we must create a closed reality through procedures, rules, blueprints, etc. On the other hand, we must guarantee growth and innovation through freedom, creativity and informality. These apparent contradictions are two dimensions on the same continuum. Therefore, we would like to define management as a perpetual process of choosing between two poles of the same force field, i.e., between *structured simplicity* and *complex diversity* (see Figure 14.1).

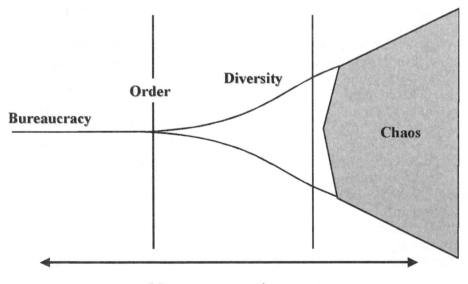

Figure 14.1 Balancing between structured simplicity and complex diversity

The most successful organizations in the modern environment are capable of preserving their own positions within this force field by shifting gracefully between the two poles in order to find a strategic momentum between chaos and order. Circumstantial changes will make them modify their course and head in the direction of the force that is pulling the hardest. Of course, obstinate resistance is an option but, as in judo, it is not worth the risk. The fine art of proper management will be to float along with the environment, instead of stubbornly trying to move to the left side to control more and more parameters, or unconditionally striving for more diversity on the right. In our view, the greatest problems in achieving organizational performance are primarily instigated by a poor awareness of the position one occupies in the managerial environment, rather than by this position as such.

For most organizations, clever anticipation of this seeming dilemma will constitute the main existential challenge in the twenty-first century. In this context, we introduce the term *flexistentialism*, indicating a survival attitude, a state of mind that holds the centre between the call for innovation and the search for consolidation.[1] Within flexistentialism, organizations will no longer define themselves unequivocally on the force field, but they will easily transform their shape when necessary, and lie low when possible, targeting new performance heights along their path.

Flexistentialism and the Learning Organization

So, what do these flexistentialist organizations look like? Do they share some common characteristics that make walking the tightrope between chaos and order a little more comfortable? How can they structurally impart order and control while at the same time guaranteeing the suppleness to innovate and to learn?

Structuring for continuous change

It seems that adaptation to change is almost exclusively tackled in one of the following ways: organizations either (1) desperately try to plug the environmental changes into their existing – perhaps bureaucratic or hierarchical – structures, or (2) throw everything overboard, discarding the traditional structures as obsolete (Miller, 1993; Neumann, 1997). No matter which alternative one chooses, the naked truth is that this kind of black/white reasoning is all too simplistic to be applicable in our modern business environment. Yet it goes on every day.

The first alternative is typical for giant corporations and multinationals: 'If we cannot nicely fit the changing environment into our organizational model, we will bash it into it anyway'. These organizations see that they are not as fast as the others, but they make sure everybody believes they are. An astonishing marketing approach is used to convince others that they are actually innovative. Very often these companies buy small entrepreneurial companies (in fact, buying the illusion that they are flexible). These larger companies believe that the whole world is for sale, but after a while the little mice have died a silent death, crushed by the big elephant . . . So, being 'big and strong' leads to a kind of *megalomania*: organizations think they can cope with anything. These giants have become window dressers, searching for relief in cosmetic solutions. What is announced as a radical change is usually no more than a slight adjustment, a beauty fix, or simply more of the same.

The second alternative is more popular these days, especially in the so-called 'sexy sectors'. From all sides, organizations are forced to put their traditional structures completely aside and heartily embrace the new forms. The word 'structure' becomes almost an insult to them, for it brings back memories of failing bureaucracy and ineffectiveness. The trend to make organizations more horizontal sometimes looks like a complete dismantlement, and what started as a healthy aim towards a flatter organization often ends up in *corporate anorexia*. Of course, organizations need to become flatter, but most of them have just worked themselves into a lather by shredding their middle layers, thinking that that is a ready solution. In our opinion, liposuction alone has never been sufficient to get in shape! Furthermore, organizations are putting up network-like designs where no one can distinguish the beginning or the end. Then, all of a sudden, the managers realize that the actual application of these modern terms is a bit more complex than the books have led them to believe. And after a while, the whole shebang slips into total out-of-controlness – maybe even anarchy – because hardly any control mechanisms are left to glue the various parts back together.

In other words, both alternatives take only one side of the coin into account and therefore miss their intended effect. Traditional structures have become synonymous with 'bureau-*crazy*'. Gradually it becomes clear that their trendy interventions might work as temporary antidotes to chaos. However, after a while they inadvertently get bogged down in 'adho-*crazy*'.

In the twenty-first century, organizations will have to flirt with structure to stand a chance. The organizations of the future will need to be both horizontal and vertical; they will need to be contingent and include both bureaucratic and organic features. Accordingly, they will contain a winning mix of linear, hierarchical aspects and non-linear characteristics, establishing a flexistentialist organization in the purest sense of the word. Therefore, a viable corporation has to shift between 'planned' and 'flexible' forms, a blend of randomness and determinism (Volberda, 1997). Organizations will have to reinforce and build themselves up continually, by ensuring a strong vertical spine to absorb the shocks and by growing a forceful lateral musculature.

Flexistentialist organizations will not ban their existing hierarchical structures to the dustbin, but strive towards a workable balance with the newer horizontal structures. Organizations that have understood this new mindset put this into practice in a number of ways:

- They develop mechanisms to blend cross-divisional thought processes;
- They enhance the channels both for the flow of external information into the organization at all levels and for the lateral flow of internal information within the organization (Neumann, 1997);
- They grant far-reaching authority and autonomy to project teams and, besides some necessary basic agreements and targets, eliminate any formality and interference from above;
- They create 'smallness within bigness' by working with small, surveyable units, teams and workgroups within the larger organizational community;
- They indeed flatten their organizations, yet turn up their nose at the notorious 'managerial sandwich': instead of tearing out the middle, they 'take a sledgehammer and hit the organization at the top, while simultaneously raising the lower levels by means of training and development' (Ridderstrale and Nordström, 2000: 172). Stated differently, flattening organizations is a matter of trimming at the top and blooming at the base, instead of randomly cutting in the middle.

Either way, performance in the twenty-first century will be a matter of versatility, of being *heterarchical* and combining the best of both worlds (Hedlund, 1986). Organizations in peak condition will alternately strike with full force and cool down, while continually listening to the signals the organization, the employees and the environment send. In this context, the well-known concept of the learning organization finds new meaning.

Learning is not compulsory (nor is survival)

Change implies learning. If we adhere to the premise that continuous change is achieved by grafting randomism and organic features on to a strong structural foundation, then it becomes clear that the building is eternally 'under construction'. Moreover, when one strives to maintain a healthy balance between chaos and order, then every cure on the one side often creates a wound on the other side. No wonder organizations continually need to brush up! Nowadays, control freaks and innovators undergo a relentless 'give and take' process. They realize that planning is a learning process, that innovation requires a systematic approach and, above all, that both must go hand in hand.

Not surprisingly, the concept of the *learning organization* is still fresh in our minds, even ten years after the publication of Peter Senge's bestseller-turned-cult-classic *The Fifth Discipline* (1990). Another expensive buzzword? No doubt. Well then, is it useful? Sure it is! After all, without learning, organizations keep repeating those same old practices, turning every change process into something like plastic surgery on a terminal patient. Then improvements are superficial, haphazard and short-lived.

Attentive readers have already noticed that the notion of the learning organization inherently corresponds with what we have called 'broadening management'. Still, it is a tough job to clarify this concept in one single definition. In fact, there are as many definitions as there are adherents to the faith. Peter Senge broke the ice with the following attempt:

> Learning organizations are places where people continually expand their capacity to create the results they truly desire, where new and expansive patterns of thinking are nurtured, where collective aspiration is free, and where people are continually learning how to learn together. (Senge, 1990: 1)

To attain this ideal, Senge proposed a vigorous training in five mysterious disciplines, also called 'component technologies of learning organizations'. According to Senge, holistic thinking, striving for personal mastery (doing what you really want to do with heart and soul), breaking through rooted mental models, building a shared vision, and team learning are the vital ingredients that pave the way towards the learning organization. At the same time, Ikujiro Nonaka (1991) launched a new concept, namely the *'knowledge-creating company'*. He characterized it as places where the creation of knowledge is not a specialized activity, but an everyday form of behaviour, a way of being, where everybody, from the cleaning lady up to the chief executive, is seen as a 'knowledge worker'. The keyword here is the externalization of hidden or 'tacit knowledge'.

This is quite a lot to think about. However, no matter how one defines it, what it all boils down to is the following simple truth: when learning is the goal, new ideas and knowledge are of the essence. However, ideas as such do not carry us forward. Without the accompanying changes in behaviour and in the way the work is organized or executed, the 'learning organization' remains inchoate; only the potential for improvement persists. More than ten years after the theory, companies still have a hard time establishing structures that ensure the necessary flow of (new) ideas through the organization. No wonder there are so many examples of organizations that are masters at creating new knowledge, but that screw things up in the implementation phase.

> Hospitals are supposed to demonstrate a certain medical expertise, but which heart patient who is advised to assume a healthier lifestyle takes this advice seriously when it is prescribed by a corpulent doctor, who himself started drinking and smoking excessively as a result of his relentless workload?

Creating new ideas and translating them into concrete behaviour are the core of any learning process. The problem with most of the idyllic descriptions we heard over the last few years is that a powerful framework for day-to-day practice is very often disregarded. Although brilliantly written, the ideas of Senge, Nonaka and all the others remain rather philosophical and leave many questions unanswered. Therefore, our aim is to provide a breath of fresh air to all those who have a rather pragmatic mindset. . . .

Building blocks of flexistentialism

What secret arsenal of techniques can organizations apply to skilfully knit chaos and order together? How do they find their way in the web of knowledge and ideas that is hung up in and around their organizations? We have devised a number of building blocks, outlining how our notion of flexistentialism can be reflected in practice. Some might sound familiar, others might evoke a slightly surprised reaction – but remember that it is the combination of them all that makes the difference. We have identified the following building blocks:

- Head for sharply defined, but valuable, targets;
- Ensure built-in 'flow';
- Create genuine autonomy;
- Learn with reason and understanding;
- Fine-tune instead of direct;
- Create knowledge through measurement;
- Innovate with fantasy;
- Orchestrate and direct;
- Declare war on sameness.

Heading for sharply defined, but valuable, targets

The 'real' managers among us will love to hear it: well-focused, precise targets remain a prominent requirement. However, within flexistentialism, fewer sub-targets are formulated. Management's only task is to sketch the broad outlines and features, to determine the ultimate aim, but the road towards the goal is left entirely to the autonomy of the responsible team or operator. Call it artistic freedom, if you like.

First of all, every goal is placed in a much wider (value) context. The reason for this is twofold. First, in a changing environment, some extra steering is regularly needed to stay on target. How can somebody make decent adjustments if he or she is unaware of the wider value frame beyond the concrete goal? How can he or she grasp a sudden opportunity, make operational decisions or close a deal when constant nitpicking blocks his or her sight? Problems often arise when people are bombarded from all sides with targets, while the location of the Mecca itself is hardly communicated. Following operational targets, but at the same time remaining vague about the meta-level, is like keeping track in the dark. Second, effort and perseverance are directly proportional to the degree to which people identify themselves with a valuable purpose. When these conditions are fulfilled, management can cut back on its means of control. In each case, the added value in terms of speed and agility is more than obvious. The broad goals of the organization – its overall mission and values – should therefore be known by heart. When things on this level are left unclear, motivation really drops below zero in no time.

Our plea for the authenticity of ultimate goals reaches to the very heart and soul of the learning organization. In fact, we are learning to boost the effectiveness of the larger whole. I as an employee learn and share my knowledge and ideas in the interests of my department. The department follows the same logic in the interests of the business unit. The business unit does the same for the subsidiary, and the subsidiary for the other subsidiaries and eventually for the whole concern. Driven by valuable purpose, the work of every individual employee derives its full meaning. When people have a target they believe in and find worthy of striving for, a great deal of supervision becomes superfluous – for people will organize themselves and find their own autonomous way. Striving for authenticity and integrity is far from the easiest way, but the resulting satisfaction is worth considering – for both the bottom line and the mentality of the employees. Organizations that are clear about who they are and what they want, and who stick to that even when things get rough, prove that this is the road to follow. A manager in the ICT department of a large bank agrees with us:

> You cannot compare in-house personnel with people who are obtained through outsourcing. Externals need to be controlled. And many among them have already been thanked for 'services not rendered'. In a dynamic environment, where a lot of freedom is left to the employee, it is very easy to vegetate behind one's desk and do nothing. That is why I keep an eye on the computers of these external people. Our own staff, that's a different story. Controlling them would be idiotic; throughout the years, we have established a trusting relationship, as a result of which everyone knows exactly what is expected of him. They are permeated by our vision and know exactly how to live by it. I do not need to constantly look over their shoulder to put things straight. As a matter of fact, I do not even care if they are looking at dirty pictures on the Internet the moment I walk in, because I know that when I need them for an emergency on Saturday or Sunday, they are here in just one hour flat!

Ensuring built-in 'flow'

In Chapter 11, we discussed the importance of hiring optimal employees and optimal teams. During recent years, one has defined 'optimal' as 'possessing the right competences'. Indeed, we no longer need to demonstrate the time-saving effect of valuable human resources. However, there is more to organizational performance than meets the eye. According to the ultra-popular psychologist Csikszentmihalyi, the most crucial query should become: How much '*flow*' do my employees create? Therefore, having the right competences is only the alpha – the omega emanates from deeper within.

Flow is not some kind of mysterious oriental concept, but is defined as the psychological state you experience when doing something that is just right for you, something that appears to have been made for you. Essentially, flow is a state of 'being fully absorbed by things,' a state in which people become 'natural performers'. When writing articles or book chapters, we often do not hear people entering our office (we probably would not even hear the bomb drop either!) In a state of flow, hours become minutes and minutes become seconds. Say, Nirvana in management land! Research has demonstrated that people who work in flow experience less negative stress. However, many corporations are undefeated champions in devising policies that eradicate flow in no time, thereby stifling organizational performance on a wider scale and rooting out readiness to change. In the long run, people who are initially 'natural performers' hear every bomb drop! The following example is typical, yet pretty sad:

> A chemical engineering company always wanted to guarantee lifelong employment. People were pampered financially and continually rotated to make sure they did not get bored. Lucas, retired financial director, explains: 'Looking back on my career, I have noticed something strange. Because I was so good as a financial expert, they put me in engineering after only three years. After all, I did have a degree in engineering. A few years later, I could move to operations, then logistics, then a few years abroad, later to sales, and a short pit-stop at HRM to make things complete. I was praised everywhere – they promised I could move into the executive board. Anyway, they promised that to everybody. Each one of us was on a carrousel, we were more concerned with where we would go to than with the job itself. The only thing I ever wanted was the financial department, this is where I had my fun. Fortunately, I was able to move back to finance during the last years of my career.'

One of the best ways to bash the flow out of an organization is by such blind mutant policies. People perform at their best when they can do those things that they are made for. Training is particularly effective when people train themselves in their strengths. Of course, people have to know their weaknesses to know where and when they should appeal to others! Thanks to our intellect, most of us can understand almost any job – but intellect is far from sufficient for filling a job with inspiration and craftsmanship. Let people do those things they are good at. Moreover, by acknowledging flow as a driving force for performance, the supervisor, who usually has to correct what other people mess up, can apply his or her efforts to other, more constructive activities as well.

There are plenty of organizations that complain about people lacking effort, about people cutting corners, arriving late for work and going home early, who chat more than normal – in other words, where action slips into apathy. However, the standard reaction to such situations is often slightly hypocritical. For example, some organizations then reintroduce time clocks or impose detailed performance norms, only to be confronted with the fact that these measures do not solve the problem at all: a lack of action is often tackled with reinforced rules and procedures, while the core of the problem is in fact a problem of values. Time clocks never instill flow, to be sure . . .

The quest for flow in modern organizations also operates at the team level. Effective teams need to embrace a wide spectrum of competences. Diversity is the keyword here, but this has nothing to do with skin colour, religious conviction or sexual preference. Real diversity aims for complementarity of competences, and those competences can be found both at the job level (technical aspects) and at the process level (e.g., leading, coaching, etc.). In their pursuit of flow, organizations almost need to adopt an N=1 model: a unique profile in a unique function. Team sports can provide modern management with models for this. A professional trainer won't merely ask the board of directors to buy a player; he presents a detailed description of the competences of that player, and relates them to the team that is already at hand. In sports, one looks for a specific profile, one that rounds out the whole and thereby lifts 'collective flow' to a higher level. One hand washes the other . . . In this respect, the remarkable absence of assessment data when organizational teams are being put together is no less than appalling. On the other hand, HR departments exert huge efforts in designing evaluation systems to check out how things went and to uncover which weaknesses need 'some catching up'. If one compares these efforts with the total lack of support for composing teams professionally, this is rather hilarious. Unfortunately, many teams consist of ten short-distance runners! If one would use the same logic in soccer or cycling as we do in management, the performance level we see in contemporary sports would drop back to the level of, let us say, 1930.

One of the more delicate consequences of ensuring built-in flow is that organizations should allow people to leave more easily when they do not fit. But these organizations take full responsibility for this event by jointly looking for a job where the employee can find flow again.

In summary, management should be aware of those blind politics that, albeit unintentionally, abolish the flow process and therefore fail to use the full potential of every employee. As a manager, ask yourself: Is my organization really living, or is it just being kept alive?

Creating genuine autonomy

Many managers are like hay wagons, relentlessly overloaded. Perhaps the hay is packed in plastic coverings nowadays, but still the freight is getting more ponderous every day, as more and more weight is piled on each wagon. Some middle managers complain that they are more busy trying to find excuses for why they have not yet fulfilled their task than they are busy with the task itself! In this context, the concept of 'autonomy' urgently needs some re-evaluation.

Less means more. This is not just a witticism, it is a plain fact. If you want your employees to perform optimally, the first step is to reduce their number of priorities. People are only capable of driving foot down when they can still distinguish the wood through the trees. Specialists in both time management and motivation agree that it is preferable to grasp one or two projects fully than seven only half-heartedly.

> What is the difference between the most effective CEOs and their less effective counterparts? When they arrive in the morning, the first group formulates two or three points of action, which they will devote themselves to during that day. The second group is constantly running from pillar to post, doing just about everything all over the place, but at the end of the day they still have the feeling they haven't accomplished anything substantial. The first group arrives at home feeling satisfied, perhaps even summoning the energy to think of another idea. The second group wearily plumps down into their sofas, totally worn out and desperately craving a drink.

Autonomy, in the sense of 'taking up responsibility' and 'deciding independently', is only possible if employees can retain enough perspective. When the hay wagon is vastly overloaded, management has to reinstall control mechanisms to keep things running. This eventually comes down to wasting resources that could be diverted into other, more suitable activities.

Further on, autonomy needs to be re-examined at the team level. Very often, a project team consists of people who take part in several teams, and of course they still have their own department on top of that. Very soon everything gets into a competitive battle, until – in the long run – these people become competitors of themselves. Time, already a scarce resource, is then chopped into little pieces until there is nothing left that is tangible. Indeed, the attentive reader must have remarked: another evaporation of reductionist element-thinking . . . As an example, the following CEO devised a proper antidote.

> The CEO of a small enterprise was pretty much fed up with it. His board of directors only acted like a bunch of parrots who kept on telling him the same old story. They were short of time, were therefore under pressure, and each of them needed extra resources. He introduced two 'rules of play'. Rule number one: during each meeting, people were to talk as if they were in the shoes of the CEO and not as a defendant of their own department. Those topics had to be discussed elsewhere. Rule number two: each member of the board of directors could be responsible for no more than one extra project outside their own department. Those projects were written down on a notice board. 'This gave us an enormous sense of relief, and all the time we used to spend in conflict with each other could now be allocated to our problems. We are actually doing much more now.'

Genuine autonomy not only denotes limiting priorities, it also means leaving competent people alone. Once the targets are specified, it is beneficial to get off people's backs and let them do their thing. As we write this text, no one is checking to see what we are up to – as long as we deliver as promised. If one claims to grant autonomy, mixed signals are sent when one asks for daily or weekly reports. Moreover, this only leads to negative side-effects. For example, the number of subsidiaries that practise the noble art of 'creative accounting' to please headquarters is yet impossible to estimate. Every month, countless employees are making a full-time job of giving the top what they desire. People learn how to adorn facts and figures because a plane full of 'headquarters guys' would descend very soon if they did not (and no one is really eager for that). Moreover, it is equally important to the career of the subsidiary's CEO to come up with good results. The question remains: How long can they continue these games?

Instead of sucking up facts and figures or imposing formalities for control purposes, top management would do better to figure out how they can support people. Managers in a German multinational described this as follows: 'They (the top) continually try to tuck us under a thick blanket of control mechanisms, instead of providing us with the means to fulfil our job more valuably.'

Finally, the '*smallness within bigness*' that we have mentioned is, in fact, synonymous with autonomy in square. Employees in self-organizing teams and workgroups within the wider organization become entrepreneurs in their own right. They each run their own little factory, with all the resulting passion and combined brain power alike. Of course, this works only on the condition that the goals and values of the company are kept in the spotlight. ABB, in particular, is a true master of this discipline:

> ABB has tried more than anybody else to turn 'bigness' into 'smallness.' This is not an easy job, since ABB employs about 215,000 people. It is achieved by organizing the company around a number of levels. Everyone is part of a 'dynamic work group,' consisting of 2 to 5 persons. Next, 2 to 10 of these groups are brought together in a 'dynamic business unit.' There are about 5000 of these units worldwide, each of which forms a microclimate where everyone searches along for ways to become more effective as a group. This way, CEO Percy Barnevik tries to recreate the little print shop his father once started. (Ridderstrale and Nordström, 2000: 199)

Learning with reason and understanding

Only when there is an abundance of information can one make the right decision. By this abundance, we mean information should be made available to anybody, at any place and at any time. Strikingly, many organizations still live with the idea that an employee needs only the information that pertains to his or her specific job. The rest is 'confidential', not to say 'top secret'. For example, many organizations implement all kinds of questionnaire and job-satisfaction survey, but only top management receives full access to the results. The rest of the company is kept in the dark. This is, of course, a perfect way to make the suspicion that already exists regarding these surveys even stronger. Even more strikingly, there are people who think that they need to read all the information that exists. Good luck! Especially today, where people can consult just about any library in the world via the Internet. All in all, it is not about reading it, but about being able to find it when you need it.

People who are given autonomy to do an important job must be able to access any information and knowledge that might be meaningful. After all, in these times of hyper-competition, decisions ought to be taken swiftly, but with reason and understanding. Managers in change-friendly organizations need to enhance the flow of external information into the organization at all levels, and at the same time fine-tune the lateral flow of information among all levels within the organization. As a case in point, Belgacom – a major telecom company in Belgium – gave us this remarkable example:

> At Belgacom, about seven employees 'read for the company.' These people sift through all kinds of sources – management books, lectures, and so on – and put them in a nutshell at the disposal of the other people in the organization. The nice touch, however, is that they do this on the budget of the department of 'training and development'!

In this light, we have named the rules of play that have emerged in this age of flexistentialism as 'Just-in-Time-learning' and 'concurrent learning'. *Just-in-Time learning* means that we wish to learn at the very moment we need the information. At that moment, we must be able to access significant information and process it:

> Many teachers express their discontent with the fact that their students pick information from the Internet and pass it on to each other. However, by forbidding this, these teachers neglect an important aspect of our modern society, and thereby block the development of a skill of ever-growing importance. In fact, more tasks should address this skill!

Concurrent learning means that when knowledge is created it must be on hand as soon as possible – almost simultaneously with the creation of it. Again, the following example is enlightening:

> Juan Moran, founder of Meta4, a Spanish software company, recently banned all paper communication in his company and mandated that it be replaced by e-mail. Of course, this decision partially originates from considerations of speed, because in his sector speed is prerequisite to success. However, this paper ban has a more profound background: letters are most often addressed to only one person and, according to Moran, this is not very conducive to information flow. Therefore, employees are urged to use the 'CC' function lavishly, so that people all over the company remain informed about what's happening in the place. Moreover, all messages are stored in a central database, to which every employee has free access. However, whoever suspects that this measure comes from a tiny, unstructured office is in for a surprise: Meta4 counts about 600 employees and has a strict division of labour (Edmondson et al., 1998).

Fine-tuning instead of directing

Contemporary organizations do not bother investing in lengthy discussions about how to assign responsibilities in organization charts. Instead, they actively reflect on how they can energize the transfer of knowledge (ideas, knowledge, products) through the various departments. For as we all know, in athletics the relay race (4 × 400 metres) is won by passing the baton and not by simply being faster than the others!

Therefore, functions and roles should be described in terms of their service to others and be evaluated accordingly. In veritable learning organizations, executives think proactively about how they can foster cross-functional information and thinking processes. Organizations will have to reinforce and build themselves up continually, but even more importantly they must ensure that the cooperation among the constituent building-blocks runs smoother than ever. The more competent employees are in this matter, the more confident supervisors can be that the output they receive will be first-class, and the more they can put their time and effort into fine-tuning. The contemporary manager conveys, guides and tailors. He hardly directs. His major concern is to gear activities towards his people, instead of making sure they walk in line.

We can indeed make a comparison with the human body. The basic viability of our organism lies in the fluid transmission between cells and organs, not in the functioning of these parts as such. Our spinal column, comparable to the hierarchy of an organization, protects one of the most essential information transfer systems of our body: the central nervous system. Managers should do the same and act as a backbone from which the 'organizational nervous system' emanates. And just as neuroscience has convincingly demonstrated that even the slightest damage to our spinal column can result in severe mental or physical breakdown, tearing out the hierarchical backbone of an organization is equally detrimental to the flow of information. In fact, managers ought to learn how to be neurotransmitters!

Accordingly, the main issue is not to renounce hierarchy, although this is advocated time and again nowadays, but rather to attribute a totally different function to it. The 'new chief' is a kind of mentor, someone who facilitates processes instead of taking them into his own hands or banging on the table. The 'new chief' is a systems thinker at heart, a broadening manager by nature:

> At Libertel, a Dutch telecom company, we recently got acquainted with top executive John de Wit. In spite of this CEO's busy life, he reserved two days each month to withdraw with about 10 to 15 employees. These employees represented a cross-section of people from various departments and levels within the fast-growing company, providing a snapshot of the organization from workers up to senior managers. What particularly attracted our attention was the fact that during this two-day meeting he mostly listened instead of judging; he asked questions instead of making suggestions; he encouraged

people to formulate ideas instead of imposing his viewpoint. He used the tremendous amount of information he gathered that way to foster cooperation among the departments. He succeeded in guiding Libertel through a period of sound and fast growth during the first years. And for the obstinate among us: he did not have to preach very much!

Aristotle revisited: creating knowledge through measurement

Turbulence will never wipe out rational filtering, since – in organizations too – all wisdom is rooted in a sound knowledge of self. Accordingly, control freaks should not despair because rigorous measurement and reliable data-gathering still prevail as preconditions for success: without a systematic problem-solving approach, organizations might have the drive to change and to learn but they lack the necessary fuel.

We partly inherit this viewpoint from the Deming (1986) legacy, guru of the Total Quality Movement (see also Chapter 4), although with some modification. As we have said, planning is a learning process these days, and mastering all parameters is simply an illusion. But learning still requires precision and well-founded thinking, otherwise management just keeps muddling on and change agents end up building castles in the air. Genuine problem-solving, then, even of the most creative kind, always starts from accurate and disciplined measurement and is based on objectivity instead of guesswork. Therefore, Harvard professor David Garvin (1993) argues for a nearly scientific method and a systematic approach in order to diagnose a problem. In this light, Deming fans will certainly remember his 'plan-do-check-act' cycle, others abide by the term *'hypotheses-testing techniques'*.

The passion of the modern entrepreneur arises from a combination of enthusiasm and speed, but in this rush the so-called 'basic-ratios' are often put aside. In other words, in case of a sudden decrease in production, do not panic and immediately change tracks, but try to reveal the hidden patterns that cause the evil. Do not become blinded by the symptoms of the problem, but instead indulge in statistical tools, cause–effect diagrams, and so on. In fact, employees should continually ask themselves: How do we know that this is true? This requires a heightened attention and the awareness that 'approximately' is not good enough when true learning ought to take place.

At Xerox, everybody is rigorously trained to make sure every problem is tackled in a most objective way. Nothing is left to chance: employees learn how to stimulate the generation of ideas and the gathering of information through brainstorming, interviewing and surveying techniques; they are taught basic data analysis techniques, flow charts and the like; they learn how to reach a consensus and at the same time avoid group-think; they are trained in scientific planning methods. Finally, every employee is taught to apply a six-step process in every decision, starting with an accurate analysis of the problem, through generating and evaluating all alternatives, making a well-founded choice, implementing the solution, and finally evaluating it.

Max Bazerman, one of the godfathers of modern decision theory, would probably state: 'Know your basic ratios!' Gather any information there is before making a decision – instead of shooting in the dark. Keep on searching for evidence, even where conventional wisdom says it is no longer necessary – *'fact-based management'*, in other words. Of course, many managers think that they have never done anything else, but as Bob Marley used to sing: in the abundance of water, the fool remains thirsty. It is indeed a well-known fact that most human decisions – in organizations too – are biased by irrelevant factors, as a result of which the abundantly present rational arguments are left out in the cold. Just write down the arguments that are submitted during your next meeting. It might turn out that our 'sensitive filter' is just as asleep as the 'rational filter'.

To conclude, in learning organizations as well, the ancient Aristotelian rule – *Know thyself* as the first step towards wisdom – still persists. Organizational learning can only take off when one has gathered all objective information. But this process must act as a *supply mechanism* to foster entrepreneurship and innovation. All too often we observe the contrary: some organizations are so busy installing SAP systems – wanting to know exactly how many minutes and seconds each employee spent on which operational task – that any initiative and chance for renewal is washed away in trifle and overkill. Healthy eagerness to learn yet again turns into excessive control. The crux then lies in the difference between knowledge an employee can apply to strengthen the organization and knowledge that restricts his or her freedom. According to Robert Simons, control should therefore act as 'a lever for experimenting and learning' (Simons, 2000: 218). In environments where strategic uncertainty is daily reality, control systems need only be devised to 'signal' where employees should pay attention. Control in this context means making sure employees pick up the right information and focus on strategic uncertainties or, as Simons puts it, 'control is there to make sure everybody watches what the boss is watching' (Simons, 2000: 216). Since these employees also keep their own eyes open, management should design 'interactive control systems', which are continuously created and recreated in an ongoing dialogue with the subordinates (see also Chapter 9).

Innovating with fantasy

Companies that want to build in flexistentialism are constantly eager for chances to renew and to reinvent themselves. The main target then becomes spotting new ways to create value. For organizations on the right side of the force field, exploring new horizons has become a primary activity, constantly providing a fresh wind through the organization. Through creative 'probes', try outs and pilot projects – instead of all-encompassing changes – these organizations constantly stay in motion. *'To boldly go where no man has ever gone before'* seems to be their foremost credo. Of all organizations, NASA itself takes this very literally:

> NASA always used to send one enormous satellite to Mars. These capsules where filled to the brim with a gigantic arsenal of high technology, and the best engineers in the world had laboured on it for years. It cost billions, which very often went up in smoke since these capsules regularly incurred heavy damage or crashed against some meteorite. Nowadays, NASA has become smarter by sending dozens of smaller, cheaper satellites into space at once. If one these probes is lost, the others are not jeopardized and, moreover, instead of just targeting Mars, this armada of probes is shot into deep space – seemingly at random – to discover what is still to be discovered in order to solve more scientific enigmas.

In environments where intense experimentation with small innovations is daily bread, one can hardly speak of entrepreneurs. They are *futurepreneurs*, for whom pure enterprising simply does not offer enough kicks (and bucks). These organizations create holes in the future and regard reality from a much broader time perspective than most others do. What most frightens other organizations is exactly what motivates managers 'on the edge'. Accordingly, they eagerly launch experimental products and services, enter into strategic alliances in sectors that have barely seen the light of day and employ the weirdest people.

Of course, there are few organizations that can compare themselves to NASA, and not every company operates in high-technology, dot-com or other sexy sectors. Still, it becomes clear that progress has not got much to do with expansion and growth any more, but rather with innovation, diversity and renewal – even in the more 'established' sectors. Rosabeth Moss Kanter was right when she remarked ten years ago that 'giants are to learn how to dance'. But as some have already noted, a giant is still a giant. Organizations must learn how to be chameleons: as in the popular commercial, the future may be bright, but the future is definitely not only orange. The future can take on every colour, depending on the creativity of the futurepreneurs. Innovation and ambition are the driving engines in this era, fantasy and guts the emerging messages.

Even extremely traditional organizations, such as Sotheby's, the British auctioning firm, realize that further progress will largely depend on renewal. Accordingly, they recently put up a website where you can buy valuable antique objects via the Internet. Prospective buyers can glance through an Einstein manuscript that is for sale, or sniffle through photographs of a dinosaur skeleton. Within the first nine months of launching this website, some 50 million dollars have already gone under the electronic hammer (*Financieel Economische Tijd*, 2000).

In summary, we have to go 'back to the future'. With this in mind, some organizations even 'cannibalize' their own market, taking steps that undermine their own activity at first sight, but which are absolutely vital for further growth. Manufacturers of voluminous encyclopaedias, for example, feared that they would be wiped out of the market by competitors that published these works on CD-ROM. Those who rapidly figured it out cannibalized their own book production by likewise starting to produce CD-ROMs. Encyclopaedia Britannica left things as they were and, with a truck full of books, kept on hawking their hardbound sets from door to door, only to be out-sold by a smiling lady waving an Encarta CD.

Orchestrating and directing

The next question is how to relate innovation and speed to consistent execution, routine and production. The main reason highly innovative organizations go broke is that they do not succeed in keeping the place decently in line. In their rush towards the future, they rack their brains searching for new ways to create value, but at the same time they are too little concerned with those keywords that still compose the essence of good management: efficiency and effectiveness. Innovation is an important weapon, but one that needs to be handled with care. Therefore, organizations ought to establish the pace of change *themselves* and install innovation and renewal structurally, just as a conductor determines the rhythm of an orchestra.

> 3M has issued the explicit rule that 30 per cent of its revenues must be realized through products less than four years on the market. Intel departs from 'Moore's law': pioneer Moore foresaw that the power of a microprocessor would double every 18 months. So, Intel now builds a production facility even when they do not know which chip they will manufacture in it. 'Moore's Law' is obviously not some physical law, but a self-selected agreement that determines the heart-beat of the company. Intel does not change for the sake of a certain event or a threat in the environment, but only because of the passing of time. (Brown and Eisenhardt, 1998: 165–6)

Flexistentialist organizations do not put too much effort in establishing a plan as such, just as a good interviewer does not muzzle his discussion partner by saying, 'well, actually, the next question on my list was in fact . . .'. Trained negotiators also make sure they have a so-called 'BATNA' ('Best Alternative to a Negotiated Agreement'). By doing this, they secure a fall-back position so that they do not have to make excessive concessions when the discussions threaten to come to nothing.

So, orchestrating largely entails establishing targets and rhythm, but building in freedom. Moreover, these targets are set out in a way that renewal is inherently injected into the system. Orchestrating is a key discipline for each organization that senses the pull of the right side of the force field. Just as Nike is able to combine flexibility with rigorous logistics, this way of integrating old and new is the pinnacle of flexistentialism.

Declaring war on sameness

An important step to change-friendliness is to ban all kinds of sameness. Change needs a soul. The best way to bury this soul is to make an organization as homogeneous and consistent as can be. Change thrives on variety and diversity, on people who are willing to step out of line and who can summon the imagination to introduce genuine renewal. For decades organizations have done their utmost to employ people who fit 100 per cent into the organizational culture, and who already share the existing norms and rules. Companies want to hire the 'perfect son-in-law', and in job interviews newcomers are automatically compared with those who are already in. The HR manager thus created the employee in his or her own likeness, and saw that everything was all right. This way, management creates a workforce where employees are clones of themselves and where every form of creativity is severely truncated. In the consulting sector in particular, it is common practice only to employ people who are sure to show up in a three-piece suit every day. By doing this, they create a staff where everybody neatly walks in line. In fact, they systematically drill conservatism, inertia and conformity into the company, instead of assuring a mix of ideas.

The foremost question should be how much 'learning ability' an employee can bring on board and not whether he or she adheres to the dress code. The problem of sameness becomes even more painful when one looks at the 'casual Friday' trend, which is very common in British organizations. On Fridays, everybody is allowed to be him or herself. However, veritable change is only possible if one gives people who think differently a chance. Change-friendly organizations need people with the most diverse backgrounds, education, beliefs and experiences. Otherwise, one makes one of the most tenacious mistakes in change management: more of the same.

Declaring war on sameness also refers to the application of rules and procedures. From the control perspective, sameness is indeed much more elegant. When the principle is 'same rule for everybody', follow-up is much easier. Nevertheless, we still empathize with a software developer who, just like the administrative personnel, was obliged to clock in at 8.00 am sharp. The fact that his creative right-brain operates at peak performance when he is in front of his screen at three o'clock in the morning was simply ignored – but at what cost?

In more standardized production environments, sameness is often required. Naturally, everybody in the morning shift will have to start at the same time, even the supervisor. In more turbulent environments, however, diversity is an asset, both in the people who work there as well as in the way they are treated. What organizations need today is a breeding ground for dissidents: people who question everything around them; who like to think up solutions; who dare to experiment; who *demand* empowerment.

Conclusion: lessons from organizations in peak condition

In Chapter 6, at the start of this second part of the book, we maintained that successful companies are able to exploit and to explore simultaneously. In this chapter, we have focused on the exploration side and wondered how successful companies cope with an ever-changing environment. Flexistentialist organizations continually improve their skill in knitting chaos and order together and thereby reconcile two of the most fierce enemies in management land. Organizations in peak condition gracefully float along with their environment, instead of stubbornly trying to move to the left side to control more and more parameters, or unconditionally striving for more diversity on the right.

Flexistentialist organizations practise 'broadening management'. We have identified several building blocks of flexistentialism. The ideas presented in this chapter are merely a quick snapshot of our upcoming adventure: a comprehensive book on change management in all its shapes and colours. This book is now being published in Dutch under the title *Organisaties op Scherp*. In the book, we describe in further detail how managers can turn change into an exciting event by offering a number of basic ingredients for every change process – a must for every manager who wishes to embrace change without declining into painful amputations.

Note

1   *Flexistentialism*: the best way to gather ideas for a text like this is to wander creatively with a good glass and some fine music. So this term was born of a casual glimpse at the CD of the moment: *Flexistentialism*, a rare compilation CD of the famous jazz and hiphop record label *Ninja Tunes*. Unknowingly, they devised a term that perfectly expresses the antitheses between chaos and order, and that was all we needed . . .

15 Towards a More Integrated Approach to Strategic Alignment

KURT VERWEIRE

In Part II, we have presented our Integrated Performance Management Framework and we identified its five major components. Chapters 6 to 13 provided literature reviews of these components. The underlying theme in each chapter was to identify how each component contributes to an effective strategy implementation. We also added Chapter 14 on organizational change, since many performance initiatives require considerable organizational change. These chapters provided an overview of the main challenges in the various management fields. From these reviews it has become clear that creating alignment with the organization's strategy is a hot topic in many of those management disciplines.

We have defined *strategic alignment* as the process where a link between the organization's strategy and its management and operational system is established. This is the essence of Integrated Performance Management: Integrated Performance Management helps to *focus* the entire organization on the strategy by *aligning* the various elements of the Integrated Performance Management Framework to the organization's strategy. One of the major challenges in this field is to develop a more integrated approach towards Integrated Performance Management. Our Integrated Performance Management Framework is a useful tool to define the scope of the strategic alignment process because it identifies the essential components of the management and operational system. Therefore, one of our central messages is that Integrated Performance Management is only 'integrated' if it considers all five components of the Integrated Performance Management Framework simultaneously!

Why do we need an integrated approach towards strategic alignment?

We believe that this lack of integration is one major reason why many performance management initiatives fail.

We visited a subsidiary of a large European multinational corporation. The subsidiary had always operated independently, but had had for the last four consecutive years some significant performance problems. The profitability was low and revenues stagnated. It turned out that the original business model, which was copied from the largest subsidiary in the group, was not really successful in this particular market. The management team developed a new strategy, focused on delivering better service and more customer orientation, and communicated this strategy to its employees. The company also introduced a Balanced Scorecard to dispose of a performance measurement tool that indicated whether the new strategy yielded good results. Workshops were introduced and the people were able to define performance measures that should monitor their day-to-day activities. Although the management team received a lot of support when the performance measurement system was developed and introduced, the system revealed that only marginal improvements were recorded in profitability and revenue growth. One explanation could be that the strategy was not good. But the problem turned out to be something else. When communicating the new strategy, the management team also stimulated employees to develop new initiatives in line with the new strategic approach. 'Empowerment' was one of the key concepts in their communication. But not much happened. In fact, the employees didn't know what empowerment was all about. For more than 15 years, they had a boss who told them what to do. 'Do what the boss tells you to do', was one of the unwritten rules of the company. Rather than defining performance measures, the management team started to work on the organizational behaviour component. Monthly meetings were planned where, apart from organizational issues, some success stories were presented. The employees got the feeling that taking initiatives was stimulated and rewarded. A new culture was created. Some people had problems with this new culture and left the company, but new people entered. The management team feels that this new organizational culture is supported more by the new employees, but older employees are becoming more supportive as well. Through these monthly meetings, a new group culture has been created, where collaboration is not only allowed, but also stimulated. The management team does not only communicate about empowerment, but also ensures that it occurs in practice. Although it is still too early to judge whether the current approach yields the hoped-for results, the management team feels that the performance starts to improve and that the downward trend is being changed.

This example shows that performance management tools sometimes provide fragmentary or, in our case, inappropriate solutions. The main challenge for this company was not to look for new performance measures, but rather was a behavioural problem. With the coming of a new management team, new rules and a new culture were promoted. But the employees had not adapted to this new way of doing business. The major challenge was situated in the organizational behaviour component and not in the evaluation and control component of our Integrated Performance Management Framework.

As we just said, we believe that an integrated approach towards strategic alignment and performance management can overcome many problems companies face when implementing performance improvement projects. However, we are still a long way from an integrated approach towards strategic alignment. Up to now, the concept of strategic alignment has been tackled in a too fragmentary way: management controllers have investigated how to align control systems with strategy; IT researchers have investigated what strategic information systems (IS) alignment means; operations researchers have identified operations strategies and how to implement them; and in organizational behaviour, researchers from a variety of management disciplines have investigated how to link organizational structures, HR, rewarding and leadership to strategy. All these researchers have focused on their own domains and have only slightly touched upon implications for the other management disciplines.

One of the next major challenges, therefore, is to develop a more integrated approach towards performance management and strategic alignment. It will be necessary to investigate how to link particular strategies with particular operational and support activities, determine the appropriate control mechanisms and tools, and, last but not least, link this to the appropriate organizational behaviour. For example, what is the appropriate organizational structure, what leaders do we need, what people do we need, and how do we reward them? We acknowledge that this is a huge task, but it is necessary to develop a more holistic approach towards management. Only then will we succeed in what we are calling *broadening management* (see Chapter 14).

Towards integrated strategic alignment

Although the topic of Integrated Performance Management is booming, many publications do not spend much time specifying what strategic alignment means for various strategy typologies. These publications mainly present a number of steps that organizations should follow when launching a performance management initiative. We found, however, two interesting books that have elaborated on the concept of strategic alignment and that have tried to build academic foundations for the concept. The first one is Michael Treacy and Fred Wiersema's *The Discipline of Market Leaders* (1995) (see also Chapter 6). The second book is George Labovitz and Victor Rosansky's *The Power of Alignment* (1997).

The Discipline of Market Leaders

The Discipline of Market Leaders is a book that received a lot of attention in the academic press (for several reasons). The main theme of the book is that the very successful players in an industry are the ones that have made clear strategic choices. Market leaders provide the best offering in the marketplace by excelling in one of the following three dimension of value:

- *Best total cost*: achieve the low cost position on product and service support (operational excellence);
- *Best product*: build a better product, for which customers will pay a premium (product leadership);

- *Best total solution*: solve the client's broader problem and share in the benefit (customer intimacy).

These three value disciplines, which were presented in Chapter 6, are well-known concepts in the business world, and they provide useful benchmarks to help companies position themselves in the market. However, *The Discipline of Market Leaders* provides a number of equally important lessons for managers, which received less attention in the business community. One of these lessons is that market leaders build a well-tuned management and operating model dedicated to delivering unmatched value.

> The choice of a value discipline shapes the company's subsequent plans and decisions, coloring the whole organization, from its culture to its public stance. To choose a value discipline – and hence its underlying operating model – is to define the very nature of a company. What sets the inner workings of market leaders apart from their also-ran competitors is the sophistication and coherence of their operating models. (Treacy and Wiersema, 1995: 32)

One of the strengths of Treacy and Wiersema's book is that it clearly specifies the components of the *'operating model'*, and that it also extensively describes the different operating models for the various strategies. These components are:

- Core processes;
- Culture;
- Organization (structure);
- Management systems (including reward and control systems);
- Information technology.

Operationally excellent companies deliver a combination of quality, price and ease of purchase that no one else in their market can match. A lot of attention is therefore paid to processes for end-to-end product supply and basic service that are optimized and streamlined to minimize costs and hassle. Operations are standardized, simplified, tightly controlled and centrally planned, leaving few decisions to the discretion of rank-and-file employees. Management systems focus on integrated, reliable, high-speed transactions and compliance to norms. The culture of operationally excellent companies is one that abhors waste and rewards efficiency.

Product leaders have a totally different operating model. These companies consistently strive to provide their markets with leading-edge products or useful new applications of existing products or services. This value discipline requires a focus on the core processes of invention, product development and market exploitation. Their business structure is loosely knit, *ad hoc* and ever-changing to adjust to the entrepreneurial initiatives and redirections that characterize working in unexplored territory. Management systems are results-driven, and measure and reward new product success, but do not punish the experimentation needed to get there. The culture encourages individual imagination, accomplishment, out-of-the-box thinking and a mindset driven by the desire to create the future.

Finally, *customer intimacy companies* build bonds with customers like those between good neighbours. Customer-intimate companies don't deliver what the market wants, but what a specific customer wants, and this requires a totally different operating model from that of operationally excellent companies and product leaders. Customer intimate companies are obsessed with the core processes of solution development (i.e., helping the customer understand exactly what is needed), results management (i.e., ensuring that the solution gets implemented properly), and relationship management. The business structure delegates decision-making to employees who are close to the customer. Consequently, management systems are geared towards creating results for carefully selected and nurtured clients. Their culture embraces specific rather than general solutions and thrives on deep and lasting client relationships.

The Power of Alignment

The message in *The Power of Alignment* fits with what many performance management publications prescribe: create focus and align your organization. That is, get everyone headed in the same direction with a shared purpose and integrate the resources and systems of the organization to achieve that purpose.

George Labovitz and Victor Rosansky (1997) mainly focus on the alignment challenge. Unlike Treacy and Wiersema, they do not specify various strategies and detect what are the implications for the 'operating model', but they specify clearly how alignment can be achieved. Rather than listing a number of steps, they specify two dimensions of alignment:

- Vertical alignment;
- Horizontal alignment.

As Figure 15.1 indicates, *vertical alignment* links the strategy of the organization with its people, allowing them to take effective action. Recall from our example in the beginning of this chapter that this was one major problem within the organization. A wonderful strategy was developed, but it was never owned by the employees. Labovitz and Rosansky argue that 'when strategy is created with the involvement of employees and customers and deployed rapidly and well, it releases the untapped energy of employees and aligns activities and intentions' (1997: 73). Vertical alignment is about getting strategies down to the employees' daily work.

Horizontal alignment is about the connection between customers and the organization's processes. Successful organizations understand the customers' needs and expectations and align processes accordingly. This message is not new: for example, horizontal alignment has been a key

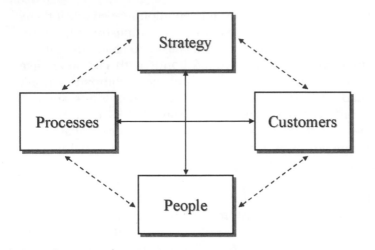

Figure 15.1 Vertical and horizontal alignment
Source: Labovitz and Rosansky (1997: 44)

concern in the Total Quality Management movement. But in many cases, TQM (and re-engineering approaches) failed. According to Labovitz and Rosansky, this is because in many cases the customer voice was left outside the processes of the organization. The only persons who hear customers directly are sales people, customer service people and market researchers. The other employees hear the customer voice either indirectly or not at all. In cases where employees hear the customer voice directly, it is often perceived differently by different functional groups. This results in no shared understanding of what customers really want.

Labovitz and Rosansky show the importance of linking various organizational processes: from strategy formulation and communication, over the operational and marketing processes, to organizational behaviour aspects.

Using the Integrated Performance Management Framework to identify dimensions of strategic alignment

Treacy and Wiersema (1995) and Labovitz and Rosansky (1997) have shown that implementing strategy requires alignment along different dimensions. Treacy and Wiersema started from three different value disciplines, and investigated how the elements of the operating model changed in function as a result of the three value disciplines. Labovitz and Rosansky have merely focused on the alignment process and have identified two major dimensions of strategic alignment: vertical and horizontal alignment. It is our firm belief that our Integrated Performance Management Framework is a useful tool to bring some more structure in the strategic alignment debate.

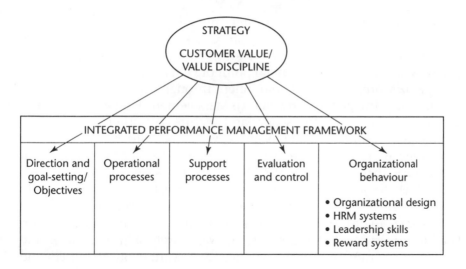

Figure 15.2 Linking strategic alignment to our Integrated Performance Management Framework

Figure 15.2 indicates that alignment can be defined as linking the organizational strategy to the various components of our Integrated Performance Management Framework. Strategy can here be defined as the choice for a particular value discipline, or for a clear and (unique) position in the marketplace. Without any doubt, strategy is the starting point of Treacy and Wiersema's framework. Labovitz and Rosansky do not use the term 'strategy', but they talk about the 'Main Thing', which is the broad vision that the company wants to realize. Labovitz and Rosansky do not specify what the Main Thing is, but they believe that customers help shape it. They explicitly write that 'companies that sustain a position of industry leadership must make an absolute commitment to their customers. That commitment pervades every aspect of their business and the way they meet customer requirements' (Labovitz and Rosansky, 1997: 32). In their model, they incorporate strategic objectives in the customer dimension.

Both publications refer to several components of the Integrated Performance Management Framework. In their scheme, Treacy and Wiersema (1997) explicitly address operational processes. They explain what are core processes for the various strategic directions, and describe the main operational challenges. They also pay explicit attention to the role of IT. But the largest part of the book tackles the organizational behaviour issues and especially organizational design ('organization') and HR issues. Evaluation and control is tackled in the 'management systems' dimension, where they also pay some attention to rewarding issues. Treacy and Wiersema add 'culture', a component that is not explicitly considered in our scheme.

Labovitz and Rosansky's model consists of four elements: customers, strategy, people and processes. As we already said, the organizational strategy encompassed a number of issues that Labovitz and Rosansky classify as customer issues. Their strategy dimension tackles some issues in the direction and the goal-setting process. Like Treacy and Wiersema, Labovitz and Rosansky also pay a lot of attention to the operational processes (but more from a general point of view), and they also consider the organizational behaviour component through the people dimension.

In fact, our Integrated Performance Management Framework can also be used to evaluate the scope and nature of other performance management frameworks. For example, we already described in Chapter 1 how the Balanced Scorecard evolved from a performance measurement to a performance management system. This is also illustrated in Figure 15.3. When Kaplan and Norton introduced the Balanced Scorecard in 1992, they introduced it as a new framework for measuring organizational performance, in order to overcome the limitations of managing only with financial measures. Put differently, it was purely a new control and evaluation instrument. But the Balanced Scorecard evolved. Kaplan and Norton learned that measurement has consequences beyond just reporting on the past. It creates focus for the future because the measures chosen by managers communicate to the organization what is important. The Balanced Scorecard approach helps executive teams to better understand and articulate their strategies. As such, it becomes an interesting and relevant tool in the direction and goal-setting process. Kaplan and Norton formulated it as follows: 'Thus we refined the Balanced Scorecard concept and showed how it could move beyond a performance measurement system to become the organizing framework for a strategic management system' (Kaplan and Norton, 2001: 23).

In their last book, *The Strategy-Focused Organization*, Kaplan and Norton (2001) pay a lot of attention to the behavioural consequences of introducing a Balanced Scorecard. Becoming a strategy-focused organization requires an intense strategic focus leading to instituted comprehensive, transformational change. This implies changes in design, but also in HRM systems and leadership skills. Kaplan and Norton have also investigated how to link incentive compensation to targeted scorecard measures.

The framework can also be used to see which particular dimensions are considered (and which are not addressed) in other performance management frameworks, such as the EFQM Excellence Model or the many Value-Based Management frameworks that are in existence. Ultimately, all these models aim to improve organizational performance, but they differ in how to achieve this goal. The difference is situated in which particular aspects of the Integrated Performance Management Framework are considered important. For example, in Value-Based Management a lot of attention is paid to defining appropriate performance measures for the whole organization ('evaluation and control'), using these measures as performance goals ('direction and goal-setting'), and aligning the managers' and employees' behaviour through appropriate rewarding. In the quality

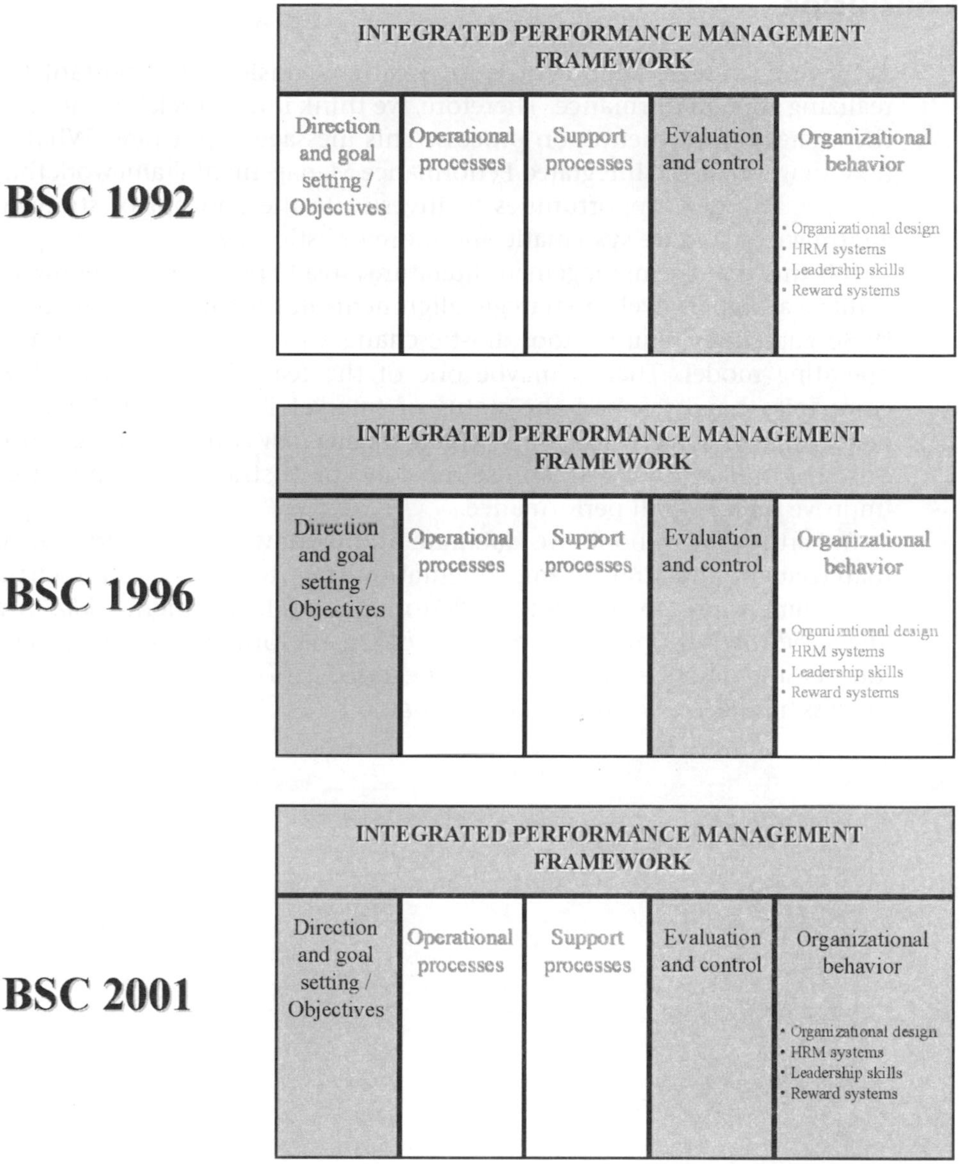

BSC 1992

INTEGRATED PERFORMANCE MANAGEMENT FRAMEWORK				
Direction and goal setting / Objectives	Operational processes	Support processes	Evaluation and control	Organizational behavior
				• Organizational design • HRM systems • Leadership skills • Reward systems

BSC 1996

INTEGRATED PERFORMANCE MANAGEMENT FRAMEWORK				
Direction and goal setting / Objectives	Operational processes	Support processes	Evaluation and control	Organizational behavior
				• Organizational design • HRM systems • Leadership skills • Reward systems

BSC 2001

INTEGRATED PERFORMANCE MANAGEMENT FRAMEWORK				
Direction and goal setting / Objectives	Operational processes	Support processes	Evaluation and control	Organizational behavior
				• Organizational design • HRM systems • Leadership skills • Reward systems

Figure 15.3 Evolution of the Balanced Scorecard according to the Integrated Performance Management Framework

models, such as the EFQM Excellence Model, more attention is paid to operational processes, evaluation and control issues (especially defining appropriate performance measures), and organizational behaviour implications.

The advantage of our Integrated Performance Management Framework is that it offers a systematic and more comprehensive view on performance management and strategy implementation.

Conclusion

Achieving strategic alignment is increasingly considered important for realizing good performance. Therefore, we think it is a crucial element in the strategy implementation process. This message is not new. What is new, however, is the Integrated Performance Management Framework that opens many new opportunities to investigate the concept of strategic alignment in a more systematic and more holistic way.

It is true that the management literature already provides guidelines to achieve a higher level of strategic alignment. But for many companies, these guidelines require (too) drastic changes in the management and operating model. That is maybe one of the reasons why only a few companies have reached the status of 'market leader'. Therefore, we believe that it is necessary to investigate further *how* companies – and not only the market leaders – can use the concept of strategic alignment to improve their overall performance.

In Part III of this book, we elaborate on the 'how' of the performance management and strategy implementation trajectory, and we present a new dimension to Integrated Performance Management. *Maturity alignment* focuses on the process side of the performance management journey and describes how well the Integrated Performance Management process has been and should be developed.

PART III

Adding a New Dimension to Integrated Performance Management: Introducing the Concept of Maturity Alignment

Adding a new dimension to Integrated Performance Management: introducing the concept of maturity alignment

In the second part of this book, we have presented our Integrated Performance Management Framework. This framework defines the scope of Integrated Performance Management by identifying the essential components of the management and operational system. One of our central messages so far has been that Integrated Performance Management is only 'integrated' if it considers all five components of the Integrated Performance Management Framework at the same time.

In the various chapters of Part II, specialists from the different management disciplines have investigated how each component can be aligned with an organization's strategy and can contribute to an effective strategy implementation. Clearly, strategic alignment is one of the priorities on the management research agenda! However, we are still a long way from an *integrated approach* towards *strategic alignment*. This lack of integration has, according to us, been one of the major reasons why many performance management projects have only met with mediocre success. But there is another reason for these disappointing results.

Here, we come to the truly innovative part of the book. The second major message of this book is that the performance management literature needs to look more closely at the performance management *process*. It is nice to develop challenging goals on how to become the most customer-oriented or innovative company in your industry. But if your organization is not prepared and ready, these goals become hollow slogans that ultimately do not make any sense at all for the organization. It is also nice to define operational challenges for your company and to describe monitoring systems that offer management immediate insight into how well the organization is performing. But, unless you specify how you will reach these goals, these challenges are nothing more than a thinking exercise with no added value for the people who need to implement the strategic goals.

The concept of *maturity alignment* helps to overcome these problems and offers us many new insights into the process side of the Integrated Performance Management challenge. Our central proposition is that the five components of our Integrated Performance Management Framework must be aligned, not only from a strategic perspective, but also from a maturity perspective (see Figure III.1).

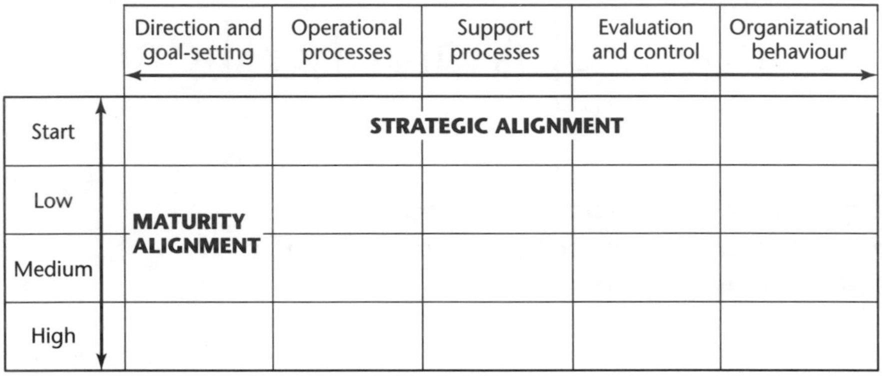

	Direction and goal-setting	Operational processes	Support processes	Evaluation and control	Organizational behaviour
Start		STRATEGIC ALIGNMENT			
Low	MATURITY ALIGNMENT				
Medium					
High					

Figure III.1 Introducing maturity alignment: a new dimension to Integrated Performance Management

Where does the concept of maturity alignment come from?

The concept of maturity alignment comes from the business world and was developed within the largest Belgian utility company, Electrabel. Electrabel is a subsidiary of Tractebel, the energy arm of the Suez Group, a services group providing global solutions in energy, water and waste services for various customer groups.

For many decades, Electrabel operated in a Belgian regulated environment. Performance management was based on the stakeholders' expectations of long-term policy, cost-plus pricing, high degree of integration between production and distribution of electricity, and a focus on technical skills. However, the business environment has changed significantly since the deregulation of the energy market, with:

● New activities added to the product portfolio (such as trading, services);
● Shorter-term contracts and investments;
● More demanding customers;
● Acquisitions and additional markets in Europe.

As a result of competition and developments in the political and socio-economic sphere, the stakeholders have become much more critical and demanding. Risk management and resource management are growing in importance, and the organization has become aware that good performance management contributes significantly to bottom-line performance.[1] In fact, performance management has become an essential prerequisite for a sustainable and flexible organization.

The performance management framework within Electrabel – now called the Integrated Performance Management System – is the result of an intensive study and consolidation of the auditing, quality and risk management literature. The model has been in use since 1995 in a broad range of business domains involving numerous organizational entities. Its practical relevance has always been one of the major concerns of Electrabel's management team.

This performance management framework has been discussed extensively with various professors of the Vlerick Leuven Gent Management School. During this research trajectory, we realized that the model is highly generic and also relevant to organizations operating in business domains other than those of Electrabel.[2] We saw that the framework is useful for managing business units, departments, more functional units, and even projects within an organization. Furthermore, the model is useful both for quality assurance and for carrying out improvements, either by self-assessment or by audit. It is a relevant management tool for helping organizations reach their objectives, and it adds a new perspective to the topic of Integrated Performance Management.

Structure of Part III

In the rest of this book, we present this new dimension of Integrated Performance Management. In Chapter 16, we introduce the concept of maturity alignment and identify what is new about it and how it contributes to an effective strategy implementation. We will show that this concept offers us new insights as to why so many performance initiatives fail. Maturity is a concept that has its roots in the Total Quality Management literature. It is now increasingly being used in various management fields, but it has not yet received the widespread academic attention it deserves. In Chapter 16, we present four different maturity stages: (1) Start; (2) Low; (3) Medium; and (4) High. Organizations that are situated in the Start maturity phase have totally different management and operational systems from firms operating in the Low, Medium or High maturity phases. This implies that the characteristics of the Integrated Performance Management Framework are totally different in these various maturity stages. The central message of Part III is that managers should ensure that all components of the Integrated Performance Management Framework are situated on about the same maturity level. In other words, the five components of the Integrated Performance Management Framework should be aligned from a maturity perspective. In Chapter 16, we investigate what maturity alignment means in practice and what happens when the components of the Integrated Performance Management Framework are not aligned. Finally, we describe how organizations can change their maturity level and present a trajectory on how to improve the management and operational system.

Chapter 17 elaborates on this maturity concept and addresses the question: How do we find the optimal maturity level and how do we link this to performance? Maturity alignment is an interesting concept, but determining the optimal maturity level for the organization is equally important. One of our propositions is that many management books provide stories and recipes that are irrelevant for many companies. In Chapter 17 we also investigate the link between our maturity framework and performance. First, we introduce a new definition of performance and investigate how firms operating in the various maturity stages look at this performance concept. We then conclude the chapter by investigating the financial implications of moving up in the Integrated Performance Management Framework. Although it is still impossible to express in a metric whether organizations should further develop their management and operational systems, it is interesting to examine in a more conceptual way the financial implications of operating in the various maturity stages.

Notes

1   For a long time, Electrabel used the term 'business quality management'. As will be shown in Chapters 16 and 17, their model incorporated many aspects of the Total Quality Management frameworks, which try to address how the quality of the organization as a whole can be guaranteed.

2   Electrabel has adopted a strong process-orientation in their organizational model. A business domain groups all activities that contribute to a series of specific, well-defined objectives. Within the company, there are about 50 business domains. These business domains deal with both primary activities (such as purchasing, operations, marketing and sales, service and distribution) and secondary activities (personnel, finance, MIS and management). Examples of business domains are: health and safety, distribution of electricity to customer segment A, distribution of electricity to customer segment B, marketing directly to customers, logistics and maintenance of buildings, nuclear waste management, management development, etc. Some of the business domains are part of one business unit; other business domains can be found in various business units of the company.

16 Introducing Maturity Alignment: Basic Concepts

PHILIP DE CNUDDE, BERNARD HINDRYCKX,
MARIO BAUWENS, BERNARD CARRETTE
AND KURT VERWEIRE

One of the innovative aspects of *Integrated Performance Management* is the introduction of a new dimension to performance management. Creating strategic alignment is necessary, but not sufficient. In this chapter, we argue that the five components of the Integrated Performance Management Framework must be aligned from a maturity perspective as well. Maturity focuses on the process side of the performance management trajectory. Maturity alignment indicates how well the various elements of the Integrated Performance Management Framework are developed in relation to each other.

We start this chapter with an exploration of the maturity concept and investigate its academic roots. We describe four distinct maturity levels and link them to our Integrated Performance Management Framework. Then, we investigate what maturity alignment means in practice and what happens when the components of the Integrated Performance Management Framework are not aligned. Finally, we describe how organizations can change their maturity level.

Introducing the maturity concept

Maturity is a concept that is used in various contexts and for various purposes. In the strategy literature, maturity is used to denote 'mature markets', i.e., saturated markets. Maturity, as we use it here, has a different background and has its roots in Total Quality Management. Philip Crosby (1979), one of the quality gurus, developed a *maturity grid* that indicates the stages that companies go through in adopting quality practices. Crosby suggested that small, evolutionary steps – rather than revolutionary ones – are the basis for continuous process improvement. As such, he defined five evolutionary stages for adopting quality practices in an organization. This basic idea was refined and new maturity frameworks emerged. The most famous ones are the *Capability Maturity Models® (CMM®)* of the Software Engineering Institute (SEI), a research and development centre sponsored by the US Department of Defense and operated by Carnegie Mellon University. These maturity frameworks were originally developed for software organizations, but they are increasingly being used in other contexts as well, such as risk management, HR management and business process orientation.

The Capability Maturity Models® provide guidance for improving an organization's people, processes and technology assets to improve long-term business performance. How is this done? The Capability Maturity Models® focus on *enterprise-wide process improvement* as a key success factor for an organization's competitive advantage. In this view, successful organizations are mature organizations. Mature organizations have organization-wide abilities for managing processes. They communicate well, and the roles and responsibilities are clearly defined. They are proactive, and their schedules and budgets are realistic and based on historical performance. Continuous improvement is a key element in their management system, and product and process problems are tackled in a systematic way.

However, transforming an organization from immaturity to maturity does not happen overnight. One of the major strengths of the Capability Maturity Models® is their staged approach towards process improvement. The models offer an organization better insights into how to develop towards maturity. The different stages are ordered in such a way that improvements made in one stage provide the foundation for improvements in the next stage. By focusing on a limited set of activities and working aggressively to achieve them, an organization can steadily improve its organizational processes and make lasting gains in performance and competitiveness (Paulk et al., 1993; Curtis et al., 1995). The Capability Maturity Models® identify five stages for moving from *ad hoc*, chaotic processes towards mature, disciplined and well-conceived processes. The original *Capability Maturity Model*SM *for Software* described the five maturity levels as follows:

(1) Initial – The software process is characterized as *ad hoc*, and occasionally even chaotic. Few processes are defined, and success depends on individual effort.

(2) Repeatable – Basic project management processes are established to track cost, schedule and functionality. The necessary process discipline is in place to repeat earlier successes on projects with similar applications.

(3) Defined – The software process for both management and engineering activities is documented, standardized, and integrated into a standard software process for the organization. All projects use an approved, tailored version of the organization's standard software process for developing and maintaining software.

(4) Managed – Detailed measures of the software process and product quality are collected. Both the software process and products are quantitatively understood and controlled.

(5) Optimizing – Continuous process improvement is enabled by quantitative feedback from the process and from piloting innovative ideas and

technologies. (Paulk et al., 1993: 8–9); special permission to reproduce 'Capability Maturity Model for Software, Version 1.1', © 1993 by Carnegie Mellon University, is granted by the Software Engineering Institute)

Four distinct maturity levels for integrated performance management

Because it offers new insights into the performance management process, the concept of maturity is also relevant to Integrated Performance Management. Performance management systems are dynamic and (have to) evolve over time. In a classic *Harvard Business Review* article called 'Evolution and revolution as organizations grow', Larry Greiner (1998), professor of management and organization at the University of Southern California's Marshall School of Business in Los Angeles, identified a series of developmental phases through which companies tend to pass as they grow. Each phase is characterized by a dominant management style and ends with a period of revolution, or substantial organizational turmoil and change, caused by a dominant management problem. In such a period, managers must find a new set of organizational practices that will become the basis for managing the next period of evolutionary growth. Thus, the resolution of each revolutionary period determines whether or not a company will move forward into its next stage of evolutionary growth. The article is interesting because it shows that management practices that work well in one phase may bring on a crisis in another. It is extremely important for the management team to identify the organization's particular stage of growth in order to determine the appropriate way of 'running the business'.

So, a crucial question is: What is the appropriate way of running the business? This question can be answered by adding the maturity dimension to the Integrated Performance Management Framework, introduced in the second part of this book (see Figure 16.1).

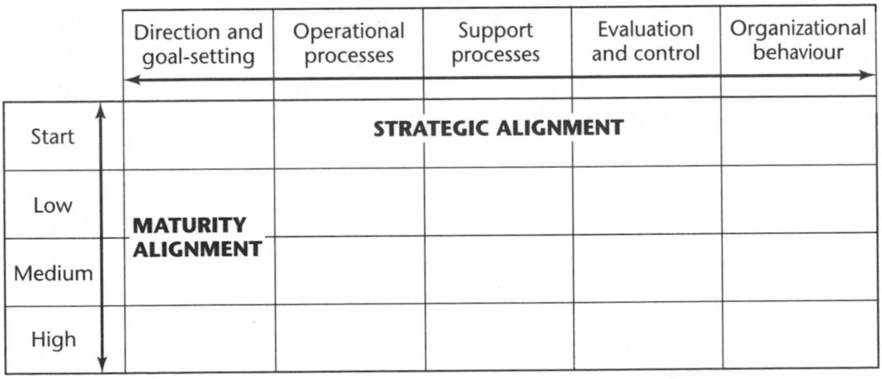

	Direction and goal-setting	Operational processes	Support processes	Evaluation and control	Organizational behaviour
Start		STRATEGIC ALIGNMENT			
Low	MATURITY ALIGNMENT				
Medium					
High					

Figure 16.1 Linking the maturity dimension to the Integrated Performance Management Framework

In the next section of this chapter, we will describe how the different maturity levels correlate with the different components of the Integrated Performance Management Framework. Our starting point is that each component of the Integrated Performance Management Framework has specific characteristics depending upon its maturity level. Change in quality level requirements induces subsequent developments in the management system, and this must be carefully supervised. Deciding how well you develop your management system is an important, but often unconscious, decision, which significantly influences the way you do business and how you compete.

Start maturity level: 'Pioneer environment of launching and trying'

If a company decides to create a new business activity or to explore new territories, it will probably set up a new organizational unit. The management system that is often found in these types of organization is one that supports an attitude of launching and trying, necessary for coping with a high degree of uncertainty. What are the characteristics of the five elements of the Integrated Performance Management Framework in such an environment?

The *direction and objectives* are only partly known. There is no explicit vision and critical success factors in the industry are not systematically identified. There is no explicit strategy that tells organizational members how to reach the overall goals. The action plan is limited to the initial implementation and focus is on immediate outcomes: Have we sold enough of our products? Are customers happy with our product or service? Most often, these outcomes are determined in general terms.

A number of unconnected *operational processes* are set up which should provide an immediate answer to the challenges the organization is facing. For example, when a university develops a new programme, the faculty tries to find participants and good organizational facilities, and develops a nice programme. Nothing more, nothing less. Products and services are produced and generated by trial and error. The organization continues what works, and skips what does not work. It is almost impossible to guarantee a certain quality level for the products or services and to produce repeatable results. Reactions to accidents are highly pragmatic. There is clearly no process-oriented approach (as described in Chapter 7), and there is frequent overlap between different activities. Returning to our example of the business school, another department within the school sets up a similar management programme without knowing that their colleagues have already organized such a programme.

Regarding the *support processes*, contributions and responsibilities are informally engaged and based on interpersonal relationships, habit and individual goodwill. There is a lack of experience, interfaces are fuzzy and there is no clear distinction between operational roles and supporting roles. Material resources, methods, communication and documentation are provided according to need and by simple request, without strict accountability. For example, if you need floppy disks, you buy them from the computer shop next door. The only concern is to get some initial *results*: to see if the product or service works or is in accordance with expectations. The control system itself is very informal.

Overall performance is driven by the enthusiasm of the participants to succeed; they enjoy a high degree of freedom and creativity. A key person within the organization takes the lead: this person directs towards immediate implementation. Control principles are primarily interactive. The organizational chart is simple and vertical, with a certain degree of clannishness (and even nepotism). Belonging to 'the family' is important and successes are celebrated. There are, however, no formal reward systems.

Low maturity level: 'Artisanal habits'

Organizations reach a next step in the maturity continuum when they enter the Low maturity stage. We have called this level the stage of 'artisanal habits' and it is characterized as follows.

The main *direction and objectives* are identified: the organization knows its main customers and suppliers, services and products. Customer requirements are known. If the unit is part of a larger organization, its scope is defined in relation to other units of the organization. Key objectives are formulated, as well as the main characteristics of the deliverables. If problems occur, top management decides which initiatives to take. Company values are mostly implicit.

The *operational approach* is task-oriented and the tasks are grouped or carried out in phases. The activities are planned and there are well-defined expectations for each task. Care is taken to ensure that all tasks do work; hence, the focus on product control. Improvement projects are defined for particular activities, but there are hardly any efforts to make structural improvements to the process. The organization is internally oriented; only in exceptional cases is attention paid to external experiences and preventive measures. Competences are defined in terms of having the necessary technical competences.

Structure is gradually built up in the *supporting activities*. Budgets, IT tools and other elements of infrastructure are made available if you can convince superiors of the added value of your projects. Communication is irregular and provided through several channels, primarily to coordinate activities among different departments. Regulatory requirements and key technical issues are documented. Training and exchange of information occur on the job.

The operating budget is the main *control and evaluation* tool. Large projects are financed on the basis of well-developed case files. Control principles are primarily diagnostic, and quality checks are installed to see whether there are any unacceptable incidents or deficiencies. Efficiency is a major goal. The organization is structured functionally and can be characterized as a *first generation organization* (see Chapter 10).

There is a hierarchical, and sometimes also paternalistic, mentality in the organization: the boss maps out the route to be followed with only limited consultation with the other organizational members. Mental coalitions are formed between leading individuals and units of the organization. A few individuals are considered as guardians of knowledge and these persons have some responsibilities within the organization. There is a great feeling of togetherness, especially when special efforts are required. The working atmosphere is family-like and there is a lot of cooperation among team members. Performance evaluation is determined mainly by good workmanship and 'belonging to the family'. The remuneration system is traditional.

Medium maturity level: 'Structured professional approach'

An organization in the Medium maturity stage has an unambiguous, well-known and broad *vision* taking into account the expectations of its most important and relevant stakeholders. Customers are considered as very important stakeholders; hence the specific focus is on customer expectations. The vision is consistent with the corporate vision and is based on risk considerations and strategic concerns. The company values are explicitly defined, but interpretation problems still occur. Action plans are defined in SMART (Specific, Measurable, Achievable/Acceptable, Realistic/Relevant and Time-bound) terms and the necessary resources are made available. Organizational members are involved in the goal-setting process and they draw up improvement programmes to raise system performance and to attain the imposed targets.

Operationally, the process flow has been defined and implemented, the activities are well coordinated, and in addition to product control there is process control. Undesired incidents are recorded and analysed in order to reduce their frequency and minimize their impact. Where necessary, re-engineering projects are initiated and process activities are upgraded. The need for problem-solving is reduced due to preventive actions. This requires the organization to be more externally focused.

Support processes are formal and powerful. Management accounting, documentation, IT tools and other infrastructure elements are well developed. Communication, both internal and external, is extensive and well structured. Special attention is paid to streamlining the interfaces between the various organizational units. Knowledge management becomes a central theme on the agenda. Significant amounts are spent on competence development and training, which are both technical and value-oriented. Widespread use is made of basic procedures, general rules and quality standards.

Besides managing the budget, the *control system* also includes beliefs systems and a range of diagnostic control tools. It also imposes strategic boundaries (see Chapter 9). Performance measurement is an important activity: key performance indicators, derived from the organization's strategy, are identified and measured. This performance measurement system also provides the input for the targets and objectives of the next period. There is room for flexibility: action plans can be re-oriented. System audits are common and the organization tries to find out about good practice and to obtain professional advice from outside experts.

Teamwork is the key word for the *organizational behaviour* component in the medium maturity phase. Each player is expected to work as part of a team and to observe standards that have been drawn up in common. The organization takes process flows into account (cross-functional or matrix, according to the business model), but is fairly complex with operational divisions and shared staff services. Projects are managed by consulting and decision-making committees. Many initiatives and incentives are installed to promote a high degree of involvement and commitment, and organizational members are motivated to participate in projects and to develop multidisciplinary skills. Performance assessment and remuneration increasingly relate explicitly to the objectives at the unit level (in addition to the team and individual levels). The remuneration consists of a fixed and a variable part.

High **maturity level: 'Competent do environment'**

The High maturity level is called the 'competent do environment'. This is the organization that is described and promoted in today's management books.

In a High maturity organization, all organizational members know the *mission and vision* of the company by heart. The vision takes into account all categories of stakeholders. Company values have been internalized by all members – top management simply has to stress a few 'non-negotiable' rules. The vision and the goals are ambitious and foster innovation in the organization. The action plans are SMART and initiated by the employees. When personal objectives are set, care is taken to obtain a good fit between corporate and individual objectives. The mission, vision and action plans are adjusted proactively, according to changes in the external environment or when performance is unsatisfactory.

The *operational processes* are extended by including all sorts of support tasks. There is a dynamic process of continuous, small changes. Process re-engineering (e.g., of the supply chain) is carried out quickly and efficiently, because the employees adapt easily to a changing work environment. Efficiency is increased through frequent consultation among team members in the course of the day-to-day activities. Wasted effort and variability in results are minimized.

Supporting activities are integrated within the operational process to a very great extent, thanks to the multidisciplinary skills of the players. Team communication is an ongoing concern, which requires an open mind and a participative culture. Routine work is facilitated by the extensive use of IT systems and other automation tools, so employees can spend a lot of time on system improvements. This calls for an HR approach in which competence management is central. Domain experts are available internally to provide advice and assistance in exceptional cases.

Performance is extensively *monitored* and managed by a series of performance indicators. Measurement procedures are applied in a consistent and efficient way, using appropriate IT tools. Trends are carefully analysed and targets are closely monitored. Actions plans are dynamically reviewed. In case of abnormal results, a detailed diagnosis is performed to determine the underlying causes of this variation. Control systems are broad and include beliefs systems, boundary systems, diagnostic and interactive controls (see Chapter 9). The interactive control system implies that attention is paid to peer reviews and benchmarking (best practices, not necessarily from the organization's own industry). All this input is used to review the direction and objectives when change is necessary. This can lead to alterations in the mission, vision or action plans, and process re-engineering or re-orientation of support activities. Costs can be accurately defined and allocated, and are used to determine the budgets for the various activities.

In such an environment, responsibilities and authority are assigned at the lowest hierarchical levels. Interfaces are flexibly defined. All players are very closely involved in monitoring the results and are encouraged to provide suggestions for improving performance. The employees work closely together in teams and 'delegating' is the appropriate leadership style (see Chapter 12). In practice, it is sufficient to refer to a few non-negotiable rules and principles. A no-blame atmosphere rules. The *organizational structure* is complex and not always transparent, but such a structure is necessary to deal with a lot of internal and external developments. Change and flexibility have become intrinsic to the organization. The organization is lean and mean. People are highly empowered and – as a team – are highly committed to the challenge of the organization. The mentality is very much results-driven: striving for excellence is a prerequisite. The remuneration system is based on both the values of the organization and the results achieved, and on the attitude of the team and the individual.

Maturity alignment as a prerequisite for successful Integrated Performance Management

Integrated Performance Management and maturity alignment

In the previous section, we have introduced the concept of maturity and identified four different maturity levels for Integrated Performance Management. All this is summarized in Figure 16.2.

	1. Direction/ objectives	2. Operational processes	3. Support processes	4. Evaluation and control	5. Organizational behavior
Start	Partly known	Activities not linked	Informal according to needs	Informing	Ad hoc
Low	Identified	Structured	Conventional	Coordinated measuring	Cooperation
Medium	Unequivocally known	Streamlined	Formal and powerful	Correcting	Disciplined teamwork
High	Broadly revised	Autonomous and flexible	Integrated and optimized	Learning	Self-directing teamwork

START	Pioneer environment of launching and trying
LOW	Artisanal habits
MEDIUM	Structured professional approach
HIGH	Competent do environment

Figure 16.2 Integrated Performance Management and the four maturity levels

We have used this framework for several years in Electrabel to monitor and manage the performance of several departments, and we have started to use this framework in other organizations. One of our most important observations is that organizations (and departments) face serious problems when the components of the Integrated Performance Management Framework are misaligned from a maturity perspective. There is a lot of tension in such organizations (and departments) because of problems between management and the workforce. Furthermore, such organizations are characterized by a huge waste of effort, many services of bad quality that are not delivered in time, many unrealized plans and bad measurements of key processes.

Maturity misalignment

Figure 16.3 presents three different organizations, with different types of maturity alignment.

Situation A describes an organization where objectives outrun operational processes, supporting activities, evaluation and control processes. For example, a company has defined and communicated a clear vision, captured in a challenging mission statement. However, the organization lacks efficient operational processes and appropriate supporting processes, and there is no discipline to measure and manage

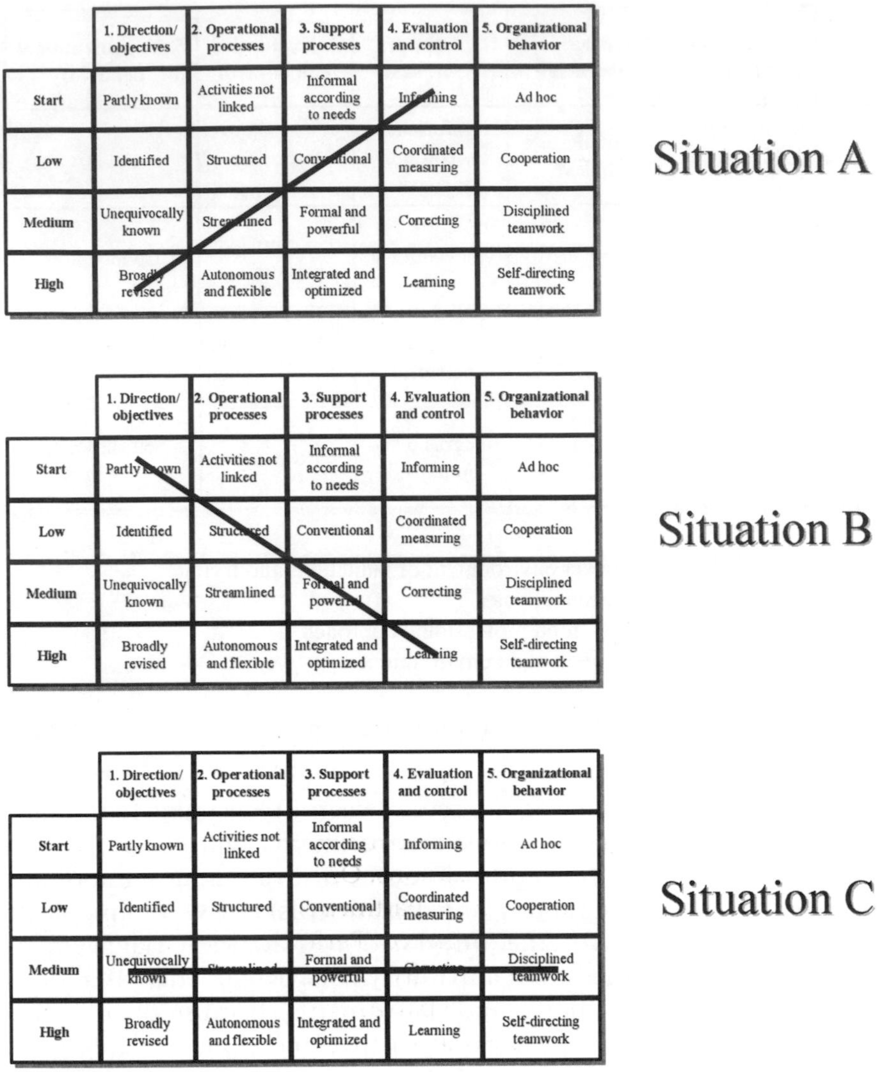

	1. Direction/ objectives	2. Operational processes	3. Support processes	4. Evaluation and control	5. Organizational behavior
Start	Partly known	Activities not linked	Informal according to needs	Informing	Ad hoc
Low	Identified	Structured	Conventional	Coordinated measuring	Cooperation
Medium	Unequivocally known	Streamlined	Formal and powerful	Correcting	Disciplined teamwork
High	Broadly revised	Autonomous and flexible	Integrated and optimized	Learning	Self-directing teamwork

Situation A

	1. Direction/ objectives	2. Operational processes	3. Support processes	4. Evaluation and control	5. Organizational behavior
Start	Partly known	Activities not linked	Informal according to needs	Informing	Ad hoc
Low	Identified	Structured	Conventional	Coordinated measuring	Cooperation
Medium	Unequivocally known	Streamlined	Formal and powerful	Correcting	Disciplined teamwork
High	Broadly revised	Autonomous and flexible	Integrated and optimized	Learning	Self-directing teamwork

Situation B

	1. Direction/ objectives	2. Operational processes	3. Support processes	4. Evaluation and control	5. Organizational behavior
Start	Partly known	Activities not linked	Informal according to needs	Informing	Ad hoc
Low	Identified	Structured	Conventional	Coordinated measuring	Cooperation
Medium	Unequivocally known	Streamlined	Formal and powerful	Correcting	Disciplined teamwork
High	Broadly revised	Autonomous and flexible	Integrated and optimized	Learning	Self-directing teamwork

Situation C

Figure 16.3 Maturity level alignment

performance. It is clear that this is an inappropriate situation which, if the slope of the curve is significant, can create a lot of frustration among decision-makers. Do you recognize some elements of this situation in your organization?

When processes are not organized to work towards objectives, the expected performance will never be attained: 'vision without action is merely a dream'. Imagine a service company that defines its competitive advantage in terms of customer orientation, but lacks adequate and well-structured complaint processes.

If clear objectives are set without adequate measurement, it will be impossible for management to judge if they are on the right track. Managers get confused by biased and conflicting information. This will definitely create frustration. In one company, objectives were set to achieve a Return on Capital Employed (ROCE) of 10 per cent. However, every division used its own definition of how to calculate ROCE.

In some departments, we saw clear, well-defined objectives. However, some managers led their division and team in a very task-oriented way without giving any responsibility to their people. The objectives were never owned by the employees and the objectives quickly became: 'Do as the boss says.' A similar problem exists – on a higher level – with some multinational corporations: local managers often receive the message that they are accountable for their own bottom line, while most decisions on revenue and cost drivers are decided and imposed by the head office.

Situation B is different. In this organization, results are intensively monitored, but operational processes are poor and objectives are not clear, so that teams are not sure about which direction the organization wants to go (e.g., after a merger or acquisition). This is unreasonable and leads to frustration among employees of the operational departments. Similarly, an organization that installs formal and powerful support activities without a clear vision and a process-oriented approach is wasting time and resources. Some examples:

Putting powerful support systems in place without considering the process may lead to high costs without benefits. The failure of numerous ERP projects is due to the fact that operational processes and the support system (ERP) have not been aligned. Hence the formula: OP + NT = ET, which stands for: old processes + new technology = expensive technology.

Putting highly sophisticated performance monitoring on hardly organized processes is dangerous because there is no assurance that the measurements reflect reality. For example, a service company measures and internally benchmarks maintenance interventions after service calls from its customers on the basis of elapsed time between various crucial process steps (client call, planning of the intervention, the intervention, closure of intervention, invoicing of customer). The processes, however, are not at all streamlined around these process steps. In the meetings about these monitoring activities, there is more discussion about the interpretation of the measurement than about actual performance and correction.

Linking incentives to objectives that employees cannot influence is a dangerous thing. One of the common problems is that companies want 'A' but pay for 'B'. For example, the management of a plant wanted to limit the duration of major overhauls by re-engineering the work of the maintenance crews. Nobody seemed to be very enthusiastic about going along with the idea. After a while, the management realized why. An HR procedure defined the bonus for major overhauls in direct proportion to the duration of the overhauls: the longer the overhaul, the bigger the bonus!

Situation C in Figure 16.3 is an example of a maturity-aligned organization. All components of the Integrated Performance Management Framework are situated on the same maturity level. No tensions exist between the different management components. In fact, this is not an optimal situation either, as it could result in an inflexible organization. Therefore, it is advisable to allow some tension between the levels of development of the various performance management components in order to foster system dynamics. It makes an organization vigilant and more flexible to move to the next stage of development. However, if the tension is too high, the organization risks encountering serious problems with the Integrated Performance Management process. Practice has taught us that the distance between the five management components of our framework should not be greater than one grid square. Otherwise, tensions start to build up, either with the management team and/or with the employees. In such cases, we advise attending to the less mature components and not to develop (and even reduce) the maturity of the most developed component.

Too much attention paid to high maturity concepts?

Looking at an organization this way provides us with some good insights as to why many performance management initiatives fail. Many companies try to apply the new management hypes that were developed by business schools and consultants in their organization, often with only mediocre success. For example, Balanced Scorecards (or whatever other balanced performance measurement frameworks), empowered employees, knowledge workers, lean and mean (i.e., flexible and learning) organizations are some of the 'holy grails' for modern companies. However, these all require an organization to be either at the Medium or High maturity stage. Managers often overlook the fact that some elements of their management system (one of the five components of the Integrated Performance Management Framework) are still situated in the Start or Low maturity stage. It is clear that new management initiatives will succeed only if the whole performance management system is adapted and organized according to the appropriate maturity level. This means that you not only educate and empower your employees, but also that you create the appropriate organizational structures and have the appropriate leaders, reward and HR systems. This calls for a real integrated approach, where attention is paid to all components of the Integrated Performance Management Framework.

In the first chapters of this book, we have discussed the fact that performance measurement frameworks have taken the business community by storm. Looking at this development with a maturity framework in mind helps us understand that many of these initiatives are a waste of time and money. Many performance measurement initiatives occur in Start or Low maturity organizations. In these maturity phases, organizations need evaluation and control systems that help them detect whether immediate goals are being realized and whether tasks are being performed as planned. All too often, the measurement systems are too complicated or the intensity of monitoring is too high. In such situations, performance measurement either becomes a management hobby – i.e., the focus is on the graphics and pictures, rather than on the real situation – or opportunism is stimulated, whereby people start to behave according to the performance measures they are supposed to deliver.

Changing your maturity level

Some basic principles

Organizations grow and management systems should evolve accordingly. One of the main advantages of the maturity framework is that it provides a dynamic perspective on the performance management process. When a new organization is set up, the management system will exhibit many characteristics of the Start maturity phase. As the organization evolves over time and gets bigger and older, its management system will probably become more mature. But how to evolve towards a higher maturity phase? And are there any basic principles that managers should keep in mind when they want to change their management system's maturity?

In a stable organization, all the components of the Integrated Performance Management Framework have about the same maturity level. When an organization wants to move to a higher maturity level (Start → Low → Medium → High), it should be aware of a number of basic principles if it wants to reach a well-balanced and aligned new reference point:

- It is necessary to pass through all maturity levels if you want to reach the highest maturity level. You cannot skip a maturity level along your improvement journey.
- Moving from one maturity level to the next best occurs through little steps, keeping the five components of the Integrated Performance Management Framework as aligned as possible (see Figure 16.4). This is in line with Total Quality Management recommendations, which also favour an approach of continuous process improvement, based on small, evolutionary steps rather than revolutionary innovations (Imai, 1986).

An increase in maturity is best triggered by the most developed of the first four IPM components. For example, an organization can decide to move to a higher maturity level because of more clearly formulated objectives (higher expectations), pressure from the employees (people are ready for it), better resources (e.g., as a result of automation), or evaluation

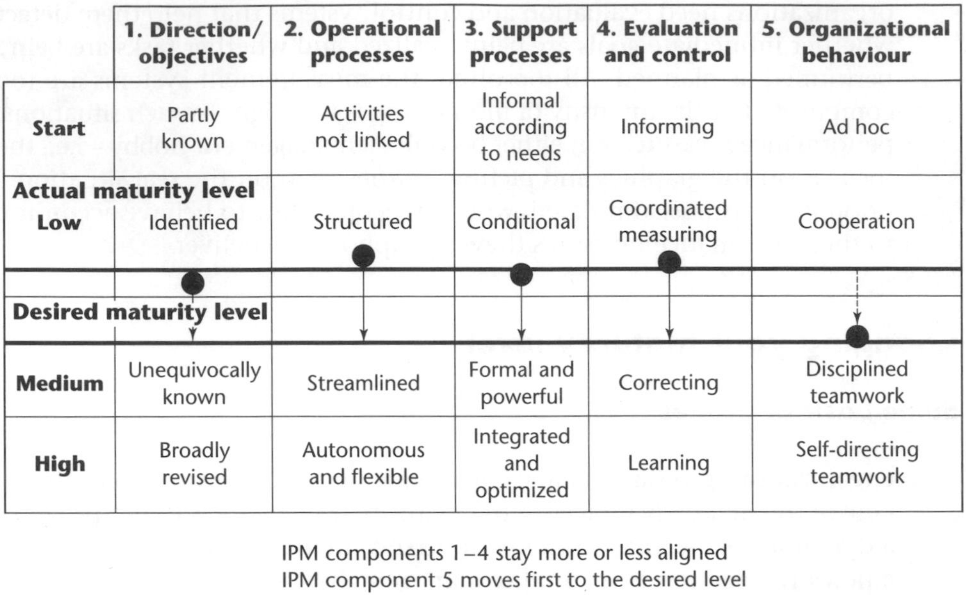

	1. Direction/ objectives	2. Operational processes	3. Support processes	4. Evaluation and control	5. Organizational behaviour
Start	Partly known	Activities not linked	Informal according to needs	Informing	Ad hoc
Actual maturity level					
Low	Identified	Structured	Conditional	Coordinated measuring	Cooperation
Desired maturity level					
Medium	Unequivocally known	Streamlined	Formal and powerful	Correcting	Disciplined teamwork
High	Broadly revised	Autonomous and flexible	Integrated and optimized	Learning	Self-directing teamwork

IPM components 1–4 stay more or less aligned
IPM component 5 moves first to the desired level

Figure 16.4 Maturity level improvement

of performance indicators (showing that the results are unsatisfactory). While a change in maturity level involves well-defined and more or less clear (and rational) actions within the first four IPM components, an organization must also anticipate where to position the organizational behaviour component. Preferably this should be in line with the desired level of maturity. In our example, presented in Figure 16.4, managers must ensure that the different teams and units adopt a style of 'disciplined teamwork' (which is the organizational behaviour characteristic of the Medium maturity level). The position of the fifth IPM component is a measure of the organizational capacity and a measure of the quality potential of change: if the organizational capacity lags behind the other IPM components, the performance management system will actually regress in quality.

Changing organizational behaviour is neither an easy nor a rapid process. Usually, these changes are a global company matter (or at least a business unit matter), and they require lots of time and effort. In particular, they require strong HR support. At the same time, the organizational structure, the leadership style, the remuneration system and especially the corporate culture must be in line with the future direction of the organization. However, managers must be aware that it is dangerous to promote High maturity organizational behaviour in Low maturity environments. Culture is an important aspect of organizational behaviour and managers should be aware of its impact. If managers do not take culture into account, chaos and complete loss of control may result. Here is an example that illustrates this:

In an administrative department of a large company, a department manager retired and was replaced with a manager from outside the organization. The retiree had been very task-oriented, led his department with an iron fist, knew everything that happened, and had a hand in every decision. The new manager was a man with a global vision, who promoted broad delegation and who was very externally oriented. This large leap in leadership profile created complete chaos in the department. Power games were played and performance significantly decreased.

An organized strategy for 'improvement'

Maturity and improvement strategies Moving to a higher maturity level is impossible without an organized strategy for improvement. Organizations that move from Start to Low maturity face change processes different from those that organizations moving from Medium to High maturity face. Without such a strategy, it is more difficult to achieve consensus between management and staff on which improvement activities to undertake first. Recall that this is one of the basic principles of the Capability Maturity Models® of the Software Engineering Institute (SEI) (and of Total Quality Management approaches in general). There, it is important to identify the particular development stage of a particular process. This allows managers to focus on those improvement activities that offer the highest efficiency and effectiveness gains.

Thus, your improvement activities require a well-directed effort and constant management attention. The emphasis of the management system, or the type of effort to be made, depends on the departure level within the maturity grid (see Figure 16.5). At the same time, it is critical that the organizational behaviour component does not impede the move to a higher maturity level.

- Start to Low: develop objectives – pay attention to the visioning process;
- Low to Medium: develop operational process – structure your operations;
- Medium to High: develop and improve supporting activities;
- Consolidation of High level: evaluate global results and review the whole management system – focus on learning.

Maturity and leadership style The difference in management emphasis, depending on the starting position within the maturity framework, also implies different leadership styles to move the organization to a higher maturity level. Here, we can refer to Hersey and Blanchard's (1988) Situational Leadership model that was presented in Chapter 12. Hersey and Blanchard defined four leadership styles (delegating, participating, selling and telling) and indicated under which circumstances these styles were most effective. For each desired level of maturity, there is an appropriate management style and/or management profile for improving the business quality.

- At Start level: mainly directing/telling (providing specific instructions and closely supervising performance);
- At Low level: mainly convincing and encouraging individuals on the spot (selling);
- At Medium level: participating and providing process (team) support;
- At High level: delegating and ensuring maximum (team) performance.

For example, an organization can be brought from Low to Medium maturity by the conscious effort of a multidisciplinary manager with the support of a manager with operational experience. An authoritarian leader can be instrumental in bringing an organization from the Start to the Low maturity level.

	1. Direction/ objectives	2. Operational processes	3. Support processes	4. Evaluation and control	5. Organizational behaviour
Start	Partly known	Activities not linked	Informal according to needs	Informing	Ad hoc
Low	Identified	Structured	Conditional	Coordinated measuring	Cooperation
Medium	Unequivocally known	Streamlined	Formal and powerful	Correcting	Disciplined teamwork
High	Broadly revised	Autonomous and flexible	Integrated and optimized	Learning	Self-directing teamwork

Figure 16.5 Management emphasis for maturity level improvement

Optimal improvement strategies Finally, it is important to determine how much tension is needed to move the organization to the desired maturity level. For this purpose, an organization needs to be aware of the current level of maturity of all its performance management components. If the gap between the current maturity level and the desired maturity level is small, improvement activities are limited and fairly simple to implement. However, no real perceived progress in performance will be made because the improvements are only marginal. If the gap is large, improvement activities are more substantial. But if the reference maturity level is more than one grid square away from the existing level, improvement strategies will be too ambitious and are therefore unrealistic (see Figure 16.6). Thus, it is important to determine the desired maturity level in relation to the actual maturity level. The conclusion is that performance management initiatives should be limited to 'single gap' actions.

Single gap

	1. Direction/ objectives	2. Operational processes	3. Support processes	4. Evaluation and control	5. Organizational behaviour
Start	Partly known	Activities not linked	Informal according to needs	Informing	Ad hoc
Low	Identified	Structured	Conditional	Coordinated measuring	Cooperation
Medium	Unequivocally known	Streamlined	Formal and powerful	Correcting	Disciplined teamwork
High	Broadly revised	Autonomous and flexible	Integrated and optimized	Learning	Self-directing teamwork

(1) ... (2)

OK

Double gap

	1. Direction/ objectives	2. Operational processes	3. Support processes	4. Evaluation and control	5. Organizational behaviour
Start	Partly known	Activities not linked	Informal according to needs	Informing	Ad hoc
Low	Identified	Structured	Conditional	Coordinated measuring	Cooperation
Medium	Unequivocally known	Streamlined	Formal and powerful	Correcting	Disciplined teamwork
High	Broadly revised	Autonomous and flexible	Integrated and optimized	Learning	Self-directing teamwork

(1) ... (2)

Marginal gap

	1. Direction/ objectives	2. Operational processes	3. Support processes	4. Evaluation and control	5. Organizational behaviour
Start	Partly known	Activities not linked	Informal according to needs	Informing	Ad hoc
Low				Coordinated measuring	
Medium	Unequivocally known	Streamlined	Formal and powerful	Correcting	Disciplined teamwork
High	Broadly revised	Autonomous and flexible	Integrated and optimized	Learning	Self-directing teamwork

(1) ... (2)

(1) Actual maturity level
(2) Desired maturity level

Figure 16.6 Integrated Performance Management improvements and added value

Conclusion

In this chapter, we have introduced a new concept called maturity alignment. This concept offers us new insights into the causes of success and failure of performance management initiatives. The maturity concept focuses on the process side (rather than on the content side) of Integrated Performance Management, and its roots come from Total Quality Management practices. The framework we have presented in this chapter identifies four major maturity stages: (1) Start, (2) Low, (3) Medium, and (4) High. The characteristics of the Integrated Performance Management System should be totally different for each of these maturity stages. Managers should ensure that all components of the Integrated Performance Management Framework are situated on about the same maturity level, otherwise there will be tensions with the managers and/or the employees and the performance management initiatives will not be successful. Ensuring alignment (and avoiding misalignment) among all five performance management components is key for successful performance management.

The framework is also interesting because it provides a dynamic perspective on performance management. Like the quality models, it also gives recommendations on how to progress from one maturity level to another. However, some important questions remain. For example, what is the optimal maturity level for an organization? And how can we measure whether or not we are on the right track? These questions will be tackled in the next chapter.

17 Finding the Optimal Maturity Level and Linking it to Performance

BERNARD HINDRYCKX, PHILIP DE CNUDDE, MARIO BAUWENS, BERNARD CARRETTE AND KURT VERWEIRE

In the previous chapter, we introduced the concepts of maturity and maturity alignment. We consider maturity alignment to be the second dimension of Integrated Performance Management, equally important as strategic alignment (which was tackled throughout Part II). That is, managers must ensure that the five major building blocks of the Integrated Performance Management Framework are aligned to the strategy, and also that they are aligned from a maturity perspective.

Of course, one of the major challenges for organizations is to determine the optimal maturity level. Is the Start maturity phase satisfactory, or should organizations strive for alignment around the High maturity level? This is an extremely important question, which has never been addressed in the management literature. In this chapter, we will explain how to tackle this issue.

At the same time, we want to make the link between maturity and performance. In this particular section, we will challenge the current view on performance and how to be successful.

Finding the optimal maturity level

In Chapter 16, we showed how maturity misalignment is a major problem for many performance management initiatives. Organizations can improve the efficiency and effectiveness of their strategy implementation significantly if they create an optimally aligned operational and management system, based on the various components of our Integrated Performance Management Framework. Creating a well-aligned organization is one thing; equally important is to determine the optimal maturity level for the organization. Most management books prescribe Medium and High maturity level solutions for tackling the current management problems. For example, the Flexible Organization, the Strategy-Focused Organization, the Learning Organization, are all typical examples of organizations situated in the higher maturity levels. But is this the solution for every organization? Our answer is: 'Definitely not!'

What is the actual maturity level of an organization?

To find out whether or not you are on the right track, you need to answer two questions: (1) What is the actual maturity level of your organization? and (2) Is this maturity level sufficient?

It is important to define the *actual maturity level* for all five components of the Integrated Performance Management Framework. Only after you have defined the current maturity level of your management and operational system is it possible to decide which particular actions to take in order to improve performance and get on the right track. Analysing the current status of your performance management system not only provides insight into the average maturity level of your organization, but it also reveals any misalignment among the components of the Integrated Performance Management Framework. We have developed an instrument that helps you determine the actual maturity level of the five building blocks of the Integrated Performance Management Framework.

What is the desired maturity level of an organization?

Once you have determined the current maturity level of your management and operational system and you have created maturity alignment, you should ask whether this maturity level is sufficient. In other words: Have you reached the *desired maturity* level? The desired maturity level for an organization indicates how well the operational and management system *should* be developed (and controlled).

The answer to this question mainly depends on the *franchise (or reputation) risk* of the organization. Recall from Chapter 5 that the franchise (or reputation) risk is the risk that the value of the entire business erodes due to a loss of confidence by critical stakeholders. As such, it is a measure of an organization's stakeholder vulnerability. We consider it to be a consequence of excessive risk in one of the sources of organizational risk (see Chapter 5).

Whatever the source of risk (internal or external), an organization must ensure that it manages its most significant risks. Risk control is an important tool in this perspective. It minimizes a firm's exposure to risk so that the objectives of the organization can be achieved.[1] Risk control does not mean that the firm does not face any risks. What it means is that the residual risks, which we have defined as the risks that remain after the risk control process, are *acceptable*. Risks with a high strategic impact should be adequately controlled in order to keep the residual risk acceptable. Risks with a lower strategic impact need less risk control. This is graphically represented in Figure 17.1.

The *acceptable residual risk* is the risk that the management takes when doing business. It is the level of stakeholder vulnerability that the organization accepts. The level of acceptable residual risk differs from

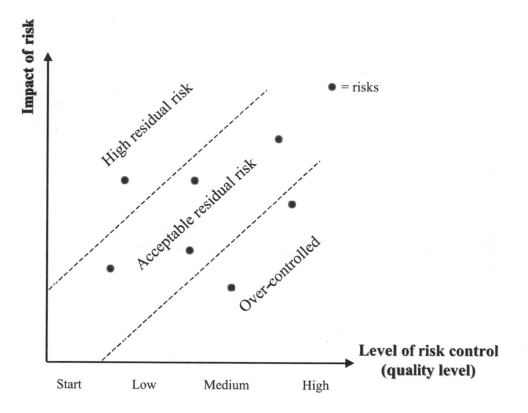

Figure 17.1 Risk control and residual risk

company to company and depends on top management's risk appetite. Some organizations clearly take more risks than others. Credit ratings are a measure for the level of residual risk that an organization takes. Companies with a triple 'A' rating are considered less risky: they have lower acceptable residual risks. Companies with a 'B' rating are considered more risky; they set higher acceptable residual risk limits. (Note that we are not saying how much risk an organization *should* take.)

Given this company-wide acceptable residual risk (read the credit rating the organization wants to achieve), an organization monitors its various business units and departments. If the risk level of a particular department exceeds the acceptable risk level, the organization should take actions to reduce the risk within this department.

Figure 17.1 indicates that high levels of risk control (and quality management) are associated with fewer 'high residual risks'. The alert reader will have noticed that we have depicted the four maturity levels on the X-axis. Typically, High maturity organizations will have almost no 'high residual risks'. On the other hand, Start maturity organizations face more 'high residual risks'.

The concept of acceptable residual risk is very important for explaining the link between stakeholder vulnerability and Integrated Performance Management. In Figure 17.2, we use the same axes as Figure 17.1, with the only difference that we depict the 'failure probability' instead of the 'level of risk control' on the X-axis. Intuitively, it is clear that high levels of risk control are associated with low levels of failure probability. Thus, the failure probability can be considered as the inverse of the level of risk control (and the maturity level).

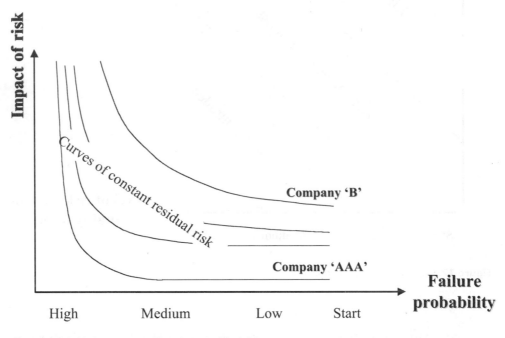

Figure 17.2 Various curves of constant residual risk

Figure 17.2 presents various curves of constant residual risk. These curves are benchmarks for the various risk levels that organizations can take. The closer the curves are situated to the origin, the lower the acceptable residual risks for the organization. For example, Company AAA sets a lower acceptable residual risk level than Company B (hence the name 'AAA').

Once an organization has decided on its acceptable residual risk level, it must apply this 'risk benchmark' to its various departments and business units. Assuming that our organization considers the upper residual risk curve (indicated by the bold line in Figure 17.3) as the benchmark for the whole organization, then it must align all its departments to this particular risk level. This means that it must undertake actions to reduce the risks within the 'under-controlled' departments and bring them to the acceptable residual risk level. These actions should either reduce the impact of the risks or reduce the failure probability of the risks of that department. Figure 17.3 also shows that one department is over-controlled, given the risk benchmark of the company.

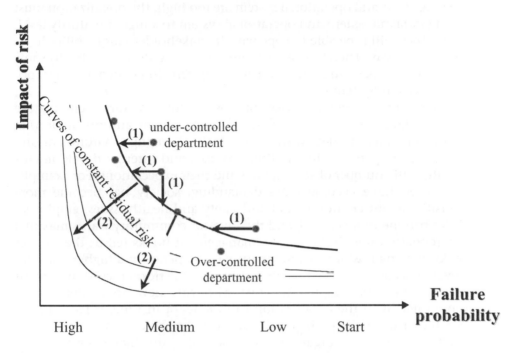

Figure 17.3 Risk management and Integrated Performance Management

Figure 17.3 presents two different types of action. Action (1) indicates that organizations bring the residual risks of under-controlled departments to more acceptable levels. Once the departments have reached a similar risk level, the organization can decide to move to a curve with a lower residual risk. This is action (2). Then the organization takes further actions to reduce the residual risk of all the departments and of the company as a whole. Ultimately, Integrated Performance Management is about determining your acceptable residual risk level (and level of stakeholder vulnerability), and then bringing all your departments or business units to that level.

The various curves of constant residual risk change over time. Various stakeholders get higher expectations. This means that the curves move downwards and that the departments have to increase efforts to decrease the impact of the risks or decrease the failure probabilities. In other words, to keep the residual risk constant within a more challenging environment, organizations have to increase their maturity level. If they are not able to do so, they 'regress' and the residual risk becomes higher. This shows how risk management and performance management are related.

Thus, finding the optimal maturity level for an organization requires that we decide on an acceptable residual risk level and an acceptable level of stakeholder vulnerability. If the residual risks associated with the current management and operational system are too high, the organization must bring its management and operational system to a higher maturity level. Only then will it be able to cope with its stakeholder vulnerability in an acceptable way. Therefore, a company that is highly vulnerable to some of its core stakeholders needs a more mature Integrated Performance Management System.

Many management books propose solutions for high mature organizations. In their introductions, management authors argue that companies have to deal with a constantly changing environment and growing competition. In addition, external and internal developments multiply the number of stakeholders and their expectations. For example, customers have become more demanding, society has become more sensitive about environmental and safety and health issues, employees have become more critical, and the investor community wants maximal shareholder value. In fact, these management books tell us that higher risks of doing business require managers to operate at a higher maturity level. As a consequence, the whole Integrated Performance Management System must be adapted to cope with this new, more demanding environment. If the organization cannot adapt in time, it faces a high strategic risk, as the probability that it cannot achieve its strategic goals increases. Then, an organization must make sure that it improves its Integrated Performance Management System by bringing it to a higher maturity level.

As we have already said, risks do not remain constant – they evolve over time. And so do organizations. As organizations grow and evolve, new risks emerge. And the relative importance of stakeholders also changes as the organization further develops. Consider the following examples:

- Organizations develop because they successfully launch products and/or services on to the market. The more successful they are in selling a product and/or service, the larger the revenues are for this company. If these revenues account for a large part of the overall revenues of the company, managers will be more conscious about potential risks that could lead to a decrease in revenues. Consequently, managers start analysing the competitive environment, developing quality assurance initiatives, and monitoring and controlling whether the organization is still on the right track. In this way, organizations change their operational and management processes and bring them to a higher maturity level.

- Companies that are listed on the stock exchange enter a new phase in their lifecycle. Having a good, transparent management system is a precondition for success in such an environment. If the company is not able to show that it controls and manages its most important risks, the damage to its reputation can be substantial, leading to a drastic share price decrease.

- Companies that become market leaders create additional stakeholders. Of course, increased size often means increased market power. But on the other hand, their visibility makes them more vulnerable to other types of stakeholder: restructuring becomes more difficult (as the unions become important stakeholders), they take on new responsibilities, and the company needs to communicate its strategy (implementation) to a larger group of stakeholders. All this requires a more mature operational and management system.

- One could argue that the current trend towards Corporate Social Responsibility (see Chapter 2) is an example of increased expectations from the society towards business. Business has to manage these increasing expectations by installing stakeholder-driven management (see also Chapter 2). These evolutions will force more and more companies to higher maturity levels, which again proves that a shift in stakeholder vulnerability compels firms to change the maturity of their Integrated Performance Management System.

Although we have explained *conceptually* how to determine the optimal maturity level for an organization, we do not yet have an instrument that helps organizations determine their desired maturity level. Ultimately, it is our aim to develop such a tool or framework to investigate the strategic risk of an organization and its stakeholder vulnerability and link them to our Integrated Performance Management Framework.

Moving from the current to the desired maturity level

Although there are no concrete tools for determining the desired maturity level for an organization, managers will feel whether the actual maturity level of the Integrated Performance Management System is sufficient or not. If the major risks are under control, management needs to focus on aligning the various components of the Integrated Performance Management Framework, as explained in Chapter 16.

If the organization feels that it is losing its grip on its major strategic risks and has significant problems with important stakeholders, it must adapt its management and operational system and bring it to a higher maturity level. How this is done has been explained in the previous chapter. The staged approach that we presented helps organizations focus on a limited set of activities. Working aggressively to achieve the goals set for these activities allows an organization steadily to improve the maturity of its management system and cope with higher risks (Paulk et al., 1993).

Maturity and performance

In the first chapter of this book, we defined Integrated Performance Management as a process that helps an organization formulate, implement and change its strategy in order to satisfy its stakeholders' needs. Our maturity framework has indicated four managerial phases for an organization:

- Start maturity phase: 'pioneer environment of launching and trying';
- Low maturity phase: stage of 'artisanal habits';
- Medium maturity phase: 'structured professional approach';
- High maturity phase: 'competent do environment'.

Organizations can be successful at any maturity stage. Thus, the maturity level of an organization does not say anything about the success of the organization. It is clear that High maturity organizations can better cope with more challenging environments than organizations situated at the Start or Low maturity levels. But managing an organization in a High maturity way in an environment with low (internal and external) risks is a waste of time and resources. So, depending on the nature of the threats (and opportunities), an organization needs to identify what its optimal maturity level is.

In this section, we will also show that organizations look differently at the performance concept according to their maturity stage. It is not our aim to identify performance measures for each particular maturity stage. This is an impossible task anyway because performance measures should be determined by the strategy of the organization. Since strategies differ, performance measures will also differ. Instead, we would like to present a new way of looking at performance, one that has been implicitly present in some of the chapters of Part II.

Performance as a balance between sustainability and flexibility

For our new definition of performance, we go back to Chapter 14, where we tackled the concept of organizational change. In that chapter, we looked at why many companies have difficulties being successful in a changing environment. One of the answers is that today's most successful organizations are capable of choosing between two poles of the same force field: *structured simplicity* versus *complex diversity*. In Chapter 14, Herman Van den Broeck and Steven Mestdagh argued that successful organizations are capable of preserving their own positions within this force field by shifting gracefully between the two poles. Circumstantial changes will make them modify their course and head in the direction of the force that is pulling the hardest. Flexistentialist organizations have a survival attitude, a state of mind that holds the centre between the call for innovation and the search for consolidation. Within flexistentialism, organizations will no longer define themselves unequivocally on the force field, but they will easily transform their shape when necessary, and lie low when possible, targeting new performance heights along their path.

These ideas provide the foundations for what we consider are the prerequisites for great performance. We have identified two major characteristics of successful organizations: they need some strategic key processes and simple rules of thumb that create *sustainability*.[2] At the same time, they need to be *flexible* to jump from one opportunity to the next. Sustainability refers to structured simplicity; flexibility refers to complex diversity.

We define *sustainability* as the degree to which the managerial and operational system is able to deliver the same set of solutions for a particular problem. For example, a manufacturing company that is able to produce the same products over and over again has sustainable operations. Or, a financial institution that is able to show each customer his current investment portfolio without any mistakes has a sustainable operational process. Managers who are able to manage their organization in a consistent way have sustainable management processes. Sustainability refers to the control side of management: if an organization is under control, it will be able to provide sustainable results.

Flexibility refers to the degree of adaptability and the speed with which changes can be implemented. Entrepreneurial organizations are very flexible since they can easily adapt to changing circumstances. If revenues for a particular product decrease, they can easily switch and focus on another business line. Many of today's large organizations lack this flexibility. That is why many current management textbooks stress the need for more flexibility (Volberda, 1998; Nonaka et al., 2000; Senge, 1990; Ridderstrale and Nordström, 2000).

The idea that organizations need to be both sustainable and flexible was present in other chapters of Part II of this book. Recall that we described the strategy formation process in Chapter 6. There we distinguished between intended and emergent strategies and we introduced the concepts of *exploration* and *exploitation*. It was management guru Henry Mintzberg (1994) who recommended a balance between deliberate and emergent strategies. Only in this way are organizations able 'to exercise control while fostering learning. Strategies, in other words, have to form (emergent strategies) as well as be formulated (deliberate strategies)' (Mintzberg et al., 1998: 11). Of course, exploration ('flexibility') and exploitation ('sustainability') require two different mindsets and different management processes. These differences can create tensions within an organization, but successful firms can balance these two approaches.

This was also one of the major findings in *Built to Last*, the management book by James Collins and Jerry Porras (1994), which provided insights into 18 of the most successful and admired companies of the twentieth century (see also Chapter 6). The major recommendation of that book is to build your company so that it preserves a passionately held core ideology and simultaneously stimulates progress in everything but that ideology. Preserve the core and stimulate progress. A truly visionary company embraces both ends of a continuum: continuity and change, conservatism and progressiveness, stability and revolution, predictability and chaos, heritage and renewal, fundamentals and craziness. And, and, and. (Collins, 1995: 86)

Collins and Porras call this approach the *'Genius of the And'*.

This 'Genius of the And' approach was also contained in Chapter 9 on management control. There, we analysed various control systems and presented Robert Simons' (1995) *Levers of Control*, which is based on Mintzberg's view of the strategy formation process. Simons identified four levers of control – key constructs that must be analysed and understood for the successful implementation of the strategy: core values; risks to be avoided; critical performance variables; and strategic uncertainties. Each of these constructs is controlled by a different lever. Simons explicitly stated that 'the power of these levers in implementing strategy does not lie in how each one is used alone, but rather in how they complement each other when used together (Simons, 1995: 152). According to Simons, these four levers create tension between creative innovation and predictable goal movement. This tension implies that managers of effective organizations must know how to achieve both high degrees of learning (innovation) and high degrees of control (efficiency) (Simons, 2000: 304).

In summary, we have introduced a new way of looking at performance. This view has also been adopted by a number of leading academic references. In their view, successful organizations are both sustainable and flexible. Although we acknowledge that performance should be considered in terms of flexibility and sustainability, we do not fully agree with this statement. We will explain this by introducing the concept of maturity.

Linking sustainability and flexibility to maturity

Our hypothesis is that an organization's degree of flexibility and sustainability depends on its maturity level (see Figure 17.4).

Organizations in the *Start* maturity phase are very flexible: they are able to change operational processes within a very short time frame if things go wrong. The lack of formal managerial systems increases their flexibility as well. However, organizations in the Start maturity phase lack sustainability. Since there is no structure in their managerial and operational processes, Start maturity organizations have difficulties in producing (high) quality products or solutions over and over again. In many cases, unexpected problems occur that need to be fixed and solved immediately. Whether or not these problems can be overcome depends on the craftsmanship and the quality of the people.

Organizations move towards the *Low* maturity phase if they increase

Performance

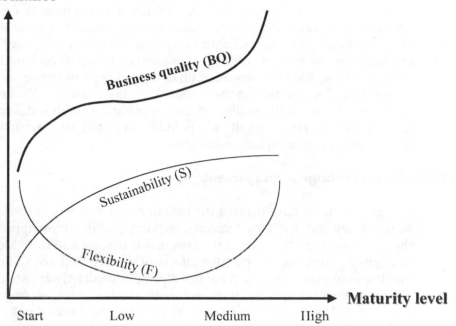

Figure 17.4 Maturity level and overall business quality

the sustainability of their managerial and operational processes. These organizations begin to formulate how they will tackle a particular business opportunity (i.e., they start thinking about a strategy), they structure operational and support processes, and they develop the first control systems. Control principles are mainly diagnostic and quality checks are installed to see whether there are any unacceptable accidents or deficiencies. Often sustainability is built in at the expense of flexibility. Organizations become more structured, but they have difficulties adapting to changing circumstances.

In the *Medium* maturity phase, the focus is on increasing the flexibility of the organization again. Powerful support systems are installed to help organizations streamline the interfaces between the different organizational units. Much attention is paid to performance measurement, the organization starts to look outside for best practices and installs the first knowledge management systems. All this is done to preserve sustainability and create more flexibility. An important aspect is the collaboration between various departments. Teamwork becomes increasingly important in this and the next stage.

High maturity organizations combine high sustainability with high flexibility. This is the real flexistentialist organization, described in Chapter 14, which captures both structure and chaos, or exploitation and exploration. In these situations, the business quality – i.e., the level of development of the operational and managerial processes – is the highest. Clearly, this type of organization is able to cope with the most challenging environments. But reaching this maturity stage requires a great deal of effort, and not every organization is ready to adopt this maturity stage. Furthermore, we have seen many companies that are successful in the Start, Low and Medium maturity phases. So, the maturity level of an organization does not predict the success of the organization. What counts is the stakeholder vulnerability of an organization. If this stakeholder vulnerability is rather small, we predict that Start or Low maturity organizations can be equally successful.

Maturity and change management

In Figure 17.4, we have defined the overall *business quality* as the sum of sustainability and flexibility. Increased business quality is most apparent in the transition from the Start to the Low maturity stage and from Medium to High. By contrast, the positive effects of quality initiatives aimed at moving from Low to Medium are not always immediately apparent, and the usefulness of quality improvements at this stage is frequently questioned. The organization needs to get past the 'turning point', i.e., dealing with a significant 'change wall'. In Figure 17.5, we consider moving from Start to Low and from Medium to High equivalent to 'jumping over hurdles'. The move from Low to Medium is tougher and requires more change management effort. We consider it equivalent to 'pole vaulting'.

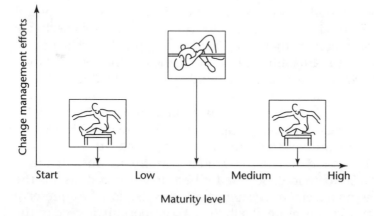

Figure 17.5 Change management and maturity

Table 17.1 presents the major challenges that are associated with a move from the Low to the Medium maturity level. Moving up from Start to High unavoidably requires a passage through the Low and Medium levels: a period of structured approach is necessary in order to progress from 'artisanal habits' to a 'competent do environment'. In such an environment of intelligent creativity, synergies and organizational capabilities can be fully deployed. However, the transition from the Low to the Medium maturity level represents a radical change, as local customs must be abandoned in favour of a more enterprise-wide approach. This change is about 'breaking down the walls' of the different departments to introduce global business practices that capitalize on synergies and scale effects for the whole company. The changes are accompanied by a feeling of loss of identity and accustomed, locally developed good practices.

Table 17.1 Change considerations related to the maturity level

Start/Low	Medium/High
Getting things done by meritorious effort ('external commitment').	Getting things done collectively ('internal commitment'); achieve by successful contributions
Lead hierarchically; order/impose; do what is asked	Lead and coach teams; complete the task with individual emphasis
Operational work is noble; support activities are necessary evil	Success is the result of close coordination and integration of operational and support tasks
Financial returns are the main thing; a satisfying work environment is a bonus	Stakeholders' expectations are becoming more important
Solidarity at each level of the hierarchy; everyone is expected to do their job at their own level	Individuals complement one another as team members; attention is paid to competence and the degree of participation
Bonding by belonging to the organizational entity (organization/department/unit)	Bonding by membership of the team and shared challenge of project
The hierarchy is the owner and benefactor; personnel are the passive mass	Industrial democracy, empowerment, and self-realization

$$\longrightarrow$$

Breakthrough

Although flexibility was one of the major buzzwords of the 1990s, this preoccupation can also be interpreted as a preference for remaining in the Start or very Low maturity levels, which demand relatively few quality efforts. However, sustainability is just as important, as lack of confidence can paralyse creativity and lead to rigidity.

The fundamental difference between the Start and the High maturity levels cannot be emphasized strongly enough: only the High maturity level guarantees maximum business quality, with a chance of survival in an ever more demanding environment. This explains why TQM programmes are so popular within highly competitive companies.

Within the maturity matrix, sustainability and flexibility are not seen as mutually exclusive. An increasing number of researchers see in it the essence of good management: 'Managing the tension between creative innovation and predictable goal achievement is . . . the key to profitable growth' (Simons, 1995: 158). But again, this statement primarily refers to Medium and High mature organizations.

Maturity, business quality and financial performance

Finding the optimal balance between sustainability and flexibility is the ultimate goal of management. It has become clear that High maturity organizations are best suited to manage this balance between sustainability and flexibility. But as we have already indicated, not all companies are able to go for this High maturity stage. Nor is it necessary to do so. Ultimately, this is a function of the strategic risk the organization faces.

There is another argument for why companies should carefully determine what their optimal maturity level is. This relates to the financial aspect of business quality. In many organizations, reporting business quality activities and effectiveness in financial terms is important for proving how continual improvement of the quality system – in our case, the Integrated Performance Management System – is linked to the performance improvement of the organization.

There is a huge debate in the quality literature about the relevance of investigating the *cost (and benefit) of quality*. Many quality gurus believe in the importance of measuring the cost of quality. On the other hand, Deming, another quality guru, is less convinced and has always maintained that measuring the cost of quality is a waste of time and money due to numbers that are 'unknown and unknowable' (Deming, 1986; Angel and Chandra, 2001). The absence of adequate tracking systems and not knowing how to track the costs and benefits of quality initiatives are major reasons why tracking costs of quality seldom occurs (Sower et al., 2002). This is surprising to us because there is general agreement about how crucial quality is for an organization's competitive advantage. What is more, there is also strong academic agreement on the components of the costs of quality.

To obtain a picture of the financial aspects of Integrated Performance Management, we first present the traditional view of the costs of quality. Then, we will translate these costs of quality into a performance management context.

In quality management, a distinction can be made between four types of cost of quality. The cost of quality is defined as 'all costs specifically associated with the achievement or non-achievement of product or service quality as defined by all product or service requirements established by the company and its contracts with customers' (Hagan, 1986: 3). These costs are categorized as either price of conformance or price of non-conformance. The *price of conformance* includes both prevention and appraisal costs. Alternatively, the *price of non-conformance* includes external and internal failure costs (Table 17.2).

Table 17.2 The difference between various types of quality cost: price of conformance and price of non-conformance

Price of conformance	Price of non-conformance
Discretionary and voluntary	Non-discretionary
Acceptable	Involuntary
Control-related	Unacceptable
Controllable	Uncontrolled
Hard and quantifiable	Often soft and qualitative
Visible	Hidden

Source: Angel and Chandra (2001: 112)

Prevention costs Prevention costs are those costs incurred by trying to prevent problems, failures and errors. Prevention costs typically include:

- Costs for quality programme management;
- Training and education;
- Quality promotion;
- Process capability studies;
- Failure mode and effect analysis;
- Quality function deployment (see also Chapter 7);
- (Re)design of experiments and manufacturing;
- Market research;
- Internal and external customer surveys;
- Quality planning and preventive maintenance;
- Supplier certification programmes;
- Cross-functional design teams, etc.

Appraisal costs Appraisal costs are traditionally defined as those costs associated with defect or problem detection activities. These costs include:

- The costs of internal audits;
- Review of completed work;
- The time and effort required to inspect inputs, processes and outputs;
- Obtaining process inspection and test data;
- Investigating quality problems and providing quality reports, etc.

Internal failure costs Internal failure costs are defined as costs associated with errors dealt with inside the operation (Slack et al., 1998). Internal failure costs typically include the costs of unwanted events such as:

- Scrap, rework and retest;
- Equipment downtime;
- Yield losses;
- Final disposition (Angel and Chandra, 2001).

External failure costs Finally, external failure costs develop when an error goes out of the operation to a customer. These costs include:

- Loss of customer goodwill affecting future business;
- Aggrieved customers who may take up time;
- Litigation (or payments to avoid litigation);
- Guarantee and warranty costs;
- Costs of excessive capability (e.g., too much coffee in the pack or too much information to the client) (Slack et al., 1998).

Relationship between quality cost categories There is a huge debate in the cost management literature about the distribution of quality costs as an organization's quality systems mature. In traditional quality management, it has been assumed that failure costs reduce as the money spent on appraisal and prevention increases. This implies that there is an optimal quality level and, after this point, the costs of improving quality are growing larger than the benefits that improved quality brings (see Figure 17.6(a)).

Proponents of the TQM approach have challenged the traditional model. They have argued that failure costs in the traditional model are greatly underestimated. The traditional model does not take into account the management time wasted in organizing rework and rectification. According to the TQM proponents, even more important are the loss of concentration and the erosion of confidence between parts of the operations. All this indicates that failure costs are much larger in reality.

Therefore, TQM advocates reject the optimum-quality level concept and strive to reduce all known and unknown failure costs. They wonder why any operation should accept the inevitability of errors (Slack et al., 1998). This basic assumption is also incorporated in the Six Sigma way of doing business. As we have outlined in Chapter 4, the basic idea behind Six Sigma is to limit the number of defects as much as possible in order to reduce failure costs. Therefore, the TQM proponents propose Figure 17.6(b) when linking quality maturity stage and cost of quality.

Applying the costs of quality to Integrated Performance Management How can we translate these 'cost of quality' principles to Integrated Performance Management? And what are the benefits and costs associated with moving up the maturity levels of the Integrated Performance Management System?

To answer these questions, we have also distinguished between the price of conformance and the price of non-conformance. For the latter category,

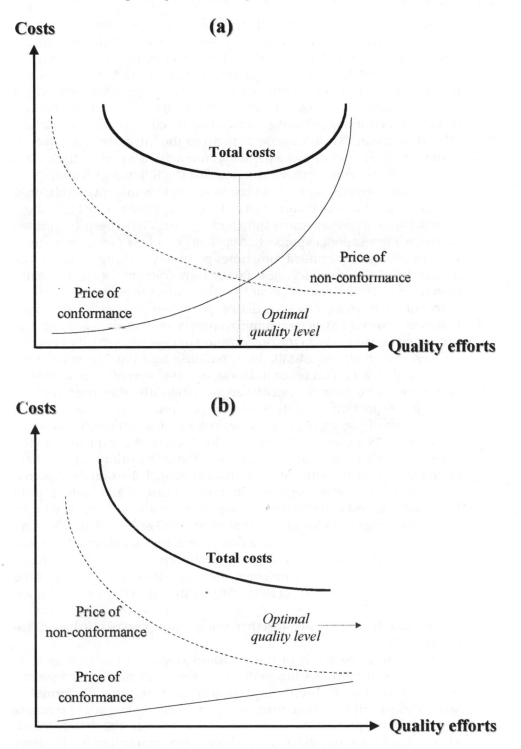

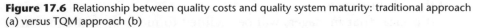

Figure 17.6 Relationship between quality costs and quality system maturity: traditional approach (a) versus TQM approach (b)

we rely on the notion of external and internal failure costs. However, we redefine the concept of conformance costs as the sum of the 'prevention costs' and the 'actual business costs'. The *actual business costs* include all costs to keep the management and operational system going. The actual business costs are a broadening of the concept of appraisal costs, which focus too narrowly on the quality assurance function (rather than on Integrated Performance Management). The actual business costs include all costs made in the various components of the Integrated Performance Management Framework for a particular moment. If we relate these costs to our maturity framework, we can describe the following picture.

The actual business costs rise in the Start and Low maturity levels, until they reach the Medium maturity level. Once they have reached that stage, they begin to decrease because sufficient resources have been committed to assure a professional approach. Managers of a Low maturity business who are not quality-minded sometimes point to the rising costs of more quality as an excuse for not taking any quality or performance management initiatives. It is clear that they miss the point.

In this new framework, we define *prevention costs* as all the costs necessary to make structural improvements in the management and operational system within the organization or department. Examples are: modifying or replacing installations, building additional infrastructure, introducing new IT tools or control tools, etc. The prevention costs are low in the Start to Medium maturity levels, and thereafter they rise rapidly to infinity (100 per cent maturity means that the residual risk is almost zero; and the cost of preventing any further risk becomes infinitely great).

Failure costs are similar to the traditional costs of the quality models and include all costs resulting from 'not doing the things right'. These failure costs can be both internal and external. For example, internal failure costs include: damage to equipment in case of an accident, yield losses, rework, and so on. External failure costs are all costs associated with not doing things right for the stakeholders. Good examples are: cleaning costs after pollution, costs of remakes (when the customer returns the products), costs associated with managing the reputation of the company, loss of motivation of your employees, etc. The failure costs decline as the level of maturity rises (100 per cent maturity means that the risk of failure is zero).

If we add the three curves together, the resulting curve is U-shaped (see Figure 17.7).

Determining the levels of these various costs is a challenging task. Nevertheless, it is interesting to do this exercise to make management conscious of the financial implications of Integrated Performance Management. All too often, managers focus only on the actual business costs and the prevention costs, and they neglect the failure costs. Identifying your stakeholder vulnerability helps you determine the level of these failure costs.

It is clear that managers will be inclined to move up to the maturity

Costs

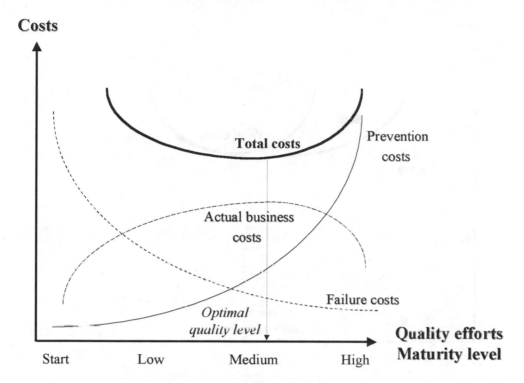

Figure 17.7 Cost of Integrated Performance Management

level where the costs of Integrated Performance Management are the lowest. These minimal total costs can be reached at the Low, Medium or High maturity phases, depending on the shape of the three cost curves. In Figure 17.7, the minimal performance management cost is situated between the Medium and High maturity phase.

An organization or department that wants to raise its maturity level from Low to Medium/High should have sufficient financial resources to cover increasing actual business costs (over a period of months or years, assuming that major failures do not occur in the meantime). If the available resources are limited, then care must be taken not to cannibalize the development of other departments.

Figure 17.8 shows that increased stakeholder vulnerability implies higher failure costs. This increased stakeholder vulnerability can be due to an increasingly competitive environment, or more sensitivity of certain stakeholders to particular business issues. Whatever the reason, the optimum maturity level shifts upwards. This also demonstrates the dynamic nature of this exercise: as companies and organizations evolve, the cost picture might change as well.

Figures 17.7 and 17.8 have focused primarily on the cost implications of the various stages in the Integrated Performance Management trajectory, but Integrated Performance Management affects the *revenue* side

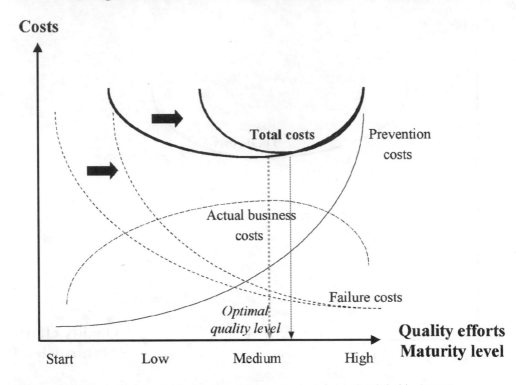

Figure 17.8 Cost of Integrated Performance Management – increased stakeholder impact

as well. For example, a good management system should help identify good opportunities. These revenue implications also favour Medium and High maturity management and operations systems.

Conclusion

In this chapter, we have elaborated on the maturity concept that was introduced in Chapter 16. Creating an aligned organization is one thing; equally important is to determine the optimal maturity level for the organization. We have shown that the optimal maturity level depends on the extent to which the organization is able to monitor and manage the risks created by its most important stakeholders. An organization that is highly vulnerable to some of its core stakeholders needs a more mature performance management system.

In a second part of this chapter, we explored the link between maturity and performance. First, we redefined the performance concept as the ability to be both sustainable and flexible at the same time. We found evidence that our view of performance is shared by some of the leading academicians in management. We believe that an organization's degree of flexibility and sustainability depends on its maturity level: only High maturity organizations are able to combine these two extremes. Organizations in the Start maturity phase are flexible but lack sustainability; organizations in the Low maturity phase have moved to the other end of the continuum and often lack the necessary flexibility. Then, one of the main challenges that organizations face when trying to move to the Medium and High maturity phases is to build in flexibility while maintaining the sustainability they have gained.

Finally, we have also explored the financial implications of our Integrated Performance Management Framework and have made a conceptual exercise to associate various cost (and benefit) elements with each particular stage.

Notes

1   In Chapter 5, we defined risk control as a risk management technique that minimizes a firm's exposure to risk. In the traditional risk management literature, risk control encompasses risk avoidance and risk reduction. If the pay-offs of a strategy or investment are too uncertain, a firm can choose to abstain from that strategy or investment. This is risk avoidance. Risks that cannot be avoided can be reduced in three different ways: (1) loss prevention; (2) loss control; and (3) diversification. We refer you to Chapter 5 for more details on these different risk management techniques.

2   The notion of sustainability has nothing to do with the concept of 'sustainable development', as presented in Chapter 2. A good synonym for sustainability in this context is 'repeatability'. This used to be the term used in the Capability Maturity Models® (CMM®) of the Software Engineering Institute (SEI).

References

Abell, D. (1980) *Defining the business: The starting point of strategic planning*, Prentice-Hall, Englewood Cliffs, NJ.

Ameels, A., Bruggeman, W. & Scheipers, G. (2002) 'Value-based management control processes to create value through integration: A literature review', *Vlerick Leuven Gent Management School*, D/2002/6482/18, Gent.

Angel, L.C. & Chandra, M.J. (2001) 'Performance implications of investments in continuous quality improvement', *International Journal of Operations & Production Management*, 21 (1/2): 108–20.

Anthony, R. & Govindarajan, V. (1995) *Management control systems* (8th edition), Irwin, Homewood, IL.

Antos, J. (1992) 'Activity-based management for service, not-for-profit and governmental organisations', *Journal of Cost Management*, Summer: 13–23.

Armitage, H.M. & Fog, V. (1996) 'Economic value creation: What every management accountant should know', *CMA Magazine*, October: 21–4.

Armstrong, M. & Baron, A. (1998) *Performance management: The new realities*, Chartered Institute of Personnel and Development, London.

Atkinson, A.A., Waterhouse, J.H. & Wells, R.B. (1997) 'A stakeholder approach to strategic performance measurement', *Sloan Management Review*, 38 (3): 25–37.

Bacidore, J.M., Boquiest, J.A., Milbourn, T.T. & Thakor, A.V. (1997) 'The search for the best financial performance measure', *Financial Analysts Journal*, May/June: 11–20.

Baeten, X. & Van den Berghe, L.A.A. (2002) 'Participatie van medewerkers: Houdingen en feiten op het vlak van financiële en organisatorische participatie', in Peeters, L., Matthyssens, P. & Vereeck, L. (eds), *Stakeholder Synergie*, Garant, Leuven.

Baker, J.A. (1991), cited in *Partners in Print*, 3 (6) November–December.

Balkin, D.B. & Gomez-Mejia, L.R. (1987a) *New perspectives on compensation*, Prentice-Hall, Englewood Cliffs, NJ.

Balkin, D.B. & Gomez-Mejia, L.R. (1987b) 'The strategic use of short-term and long-term pay incentives in the high-technology industry', in Balkin, D.B. & Gomez-Mejia, L.R. (eds), *New perspectives on compensation*, Prentice-Hall, Englewood Cliffs, NJ pp. 237–46.

Balkin, D.B. & Gomez-Mejia, L.R. (1987c) 'Toward a contingency theory of compensation strategy', *Strategic Management Journal*, 8: 169–82.

Barber, A.E. & Bretz, R.D. (2000) 'Compensation, attraction and retention', in Rynes, S.L. & Gerhart, B. (eds), *Compensation in organizations: Current research and practice*, Jossey-Bass, San Francisco, pp. 32–60.

Barney, J.B. (1986) 'Organizational culture: Can it be a source of sustained competitive advantage?', *Academy of Management Review*, 11: 656–65.

Barney, J.B. (1997) *Gaining and sustaining competitive advantage*, Addison-Wesley, Reading, MA.

Becker, B., Huselid, M. & Ulrich, D. (2001) *The HR scorecard linking people, strategy and performance*, Harvard Business School Press, Boston, MA.

Benihana case (1972) *Harvard Business School case study*, 9–673–057, Boston, MA.

Bergmann, T.J. & Scarpello, V.G. (2001) *Compensation decision making*, Harcourt, Brace Jovanovich, New York.

Berry, L.L., Parasuraman, A. & Zeithaml, V.A. (1988) 'The service-quality puzzle', *Business Horizons*, September–October, pp. 35–44.

Besanko, D., Dranove, D. & Shanley, M. (2000) *Economics of strategy* (2nd edition), John Wiley & Sons, New York.

Biddle, G.C., Bowen, R.M. & Wallace, J.S. (1997) 'Does EVA® beat earnings? Evidence on associations with stock returns and firm values', *Journal of Accounting and Economics*, 24 (3): 301–36.

Black, A., Wright, P. & Bachman, J.E. with Davies, J. (1998) *In search of shareholder value: Managing the drivers of performance*, Financial Times/Pitman Publishing, London.

Blackburn, J. (1991) *Time-based competition: The next battleground in American Manufacturing*, The Business One Irwin/Apics Series in Production Management, Richard D. Irwin, Homewood, IL.

Bloom, M. (1998) 'Relationship among risk, incentive pay and organizational performance', *Academy of Management Journal*, 41 (3): 283–97.

Bodie, Z., Kane, A. & Marcus, A.J. (1999) *Investments*, Irwin/McGraw-Hill, Boston, MA.

Booth, R. (1997) 'Performance management: Making it happen', *Management Accounting*, 75 (10): 28–30.

Boyd, B.K. and Salamin, K. (2001) 'Strategic reward systems: A contingency model of pay system design', *Strategic Management Journal*, 22: 777–92.

Broadbent, M. & Weill, P. (1997) 'Management by maxim: How business and IT managers can create IT infrastructures', *Sloan Management Review*, 38 (3): 77–92.

Bromiley, P., Miller, K.D. & Rau, D. (2001) 'Risk in strategic management research', in Hitt, M.A., Freeman, R.E. & Harrison, J.S. (eds), *The Blackwell handbook of strategic management*, Blackwell, Oxford.

Brown, D. (2000) 'The third way: The future of pay and rewards strategies in Europe', *WorldatWork Journal*, 9 (7): 15–25.

Brown, D. (2001) *Reward strategies: From intent to impact*, Short Run Press, Exeter.

Brown, D.M. & Laverick, S. (1994) 'Measuring corporate performance', *Long Range Planning*, 27 (4): 89–98.

Brown, J., Macaskill, D. & Owen, H. (2000) 'The Stern Stewart and Marakon Shareholder Value Added metrics: A comparative study with implications for the management accountant', Napier University Business School, Paper presented at the BAA (Scotland) Conference, September.

Brown, M.G. (1996) *Keeping score: Using the right metrics to drive world-class performance*, Quality Resources, New York.

Brown, S.L. & Eisenhardt, K.M. (1998) *Competing on the edge: Strategy as structured chaos*, Harvard Business School Press, Boston, MA.

Bruggeman, W. & Van der Stede, W. (1993) 'Fitting management control systems to competitive advantage', *British Journal of Management*, 4: 205–18.

Bruggeman, W., Decoene, V. & Everaert, P. (2001) 'An empirical study of the impact of BSC-based variable remuneration systems on performance motivation of operating managers', *Working Paper*, Ghent University, Faculty of Economics and Business.

Bruns, W. (1998) 'Profit as a performance measure: Powerful concept, insufficient measure', Paper presented at Performance Measurement: Theory and practice, the first international conference on performance measurement, Cambridge, 14–17 July.

Burn, J.M. & Szeto, C. (2000) 'A comparison of the views of business and IT management on success factors for strategic alignment', *Information & Management*, 37: 197–216.

Burns, T. & Stalker, G. (1961) *The management of innovation*, Tavistock, London.

Buttle, F. (1996) 'Servqual: Review, critique, research agenda', *European Journal of Marketing*, 3 (1).

Byrne, J.A. (1993) 'The horizontal corporation', *Business Week*, 13 December: 76–81.

Cable, D.M. & Judge, T.A. (1994) 'Pay preference and job search decisions: A person–organisation fit perspective', *Personnel Psychology*, 47: 317–48.

Campi, J.P. (1992) 'It's not as easy as ABC', *Journal of Cost Management*, Summer: 5–11.

Canadian Institute of Chartered Accountants (1995) *Guidance on control*, Canadian Institute of Chartered Accountants, Toronto (Ontario).

Carlzon, J. (1987) *Moments of truth*, Ballinger, Cambridge.

Carroll, S.J. (1987) 'Business strategies and compensation systems', in Balkin, D.B. & Gomez-Mejia; L.R. (eds), *New perspectives on compensation*, Prentice-Hall, Englewood Cliffs, NJ, pp. 343–55.

Chakravarthy, B.S. (1986) 'Measuring strategic performance', *Strategic Management Journal*, 7: 437–58.

Chakravarthy, B.S. & White, R.E. (2002) 'Strategy process: Forming, implementing and changing strategies', in Pettigrew, A., Thomas, H. & Whittington, R. (eds), *Handbook of strategy and management*, Sage, London.

Chase, R.B., Aquilana, N.J. & Jacobs, F.R. (1995) *Production and operations management: Manufacturing and services* (7th edition), Irwin, Homewood, IL.

Chenhall, R.H. & Morris, D. (1995) 'Organic decision and communication processes and management accounting systems in entrepreneurial and conservative business organizations', *Omega, International Journal of Management Science*, 23 (5): 485–97.

Clarke, C.J. & Varma, S. (1999) 'Strategic risk management: The new competitive edge', *Long Range Planning*, 32 (4): 414–24.

Cohen, L. (1995) *Quality function deployment: How to make QFD work for you*, Addison-Wesley, Reading, MA.

Collins, J.C. (1995) 'Building companies to last', *Inc*, 17 (7): 16 May, p. 42.

Collins, J. (2001) *Good to great*, Random House, London.

Collins, J.C. & Porras, J.I. (1994) *Built to last: Successful habits of visionary companies*, HarperBusiness, New York.

Collins, J.C. & Porras, J.I. (1995) 'The ultimate vision', *Across the Board*, 32 (1): 21.

Committee of Sponsoring Organizations of the Treadway Commission (COSO) (1992) *Internal control: Integrated framework (executive summary)*, The American Institute of Certified Public Accountants, Jersey City, NJ.

Congram, C. & Epelman, M. (1995) 'How to describe your service: An invitation to the structured analysis and design technique', *International Journal of Service Industry Management*, 6 (2): 6–23.

Co-operative Bank (2001) *The partnership report 2000: Making our mark*, The Co-operative Bank, Manchester. See also website: www.co-operativebank.co.uk

Crosby, P.B. (1979) *Quality is free*, McGraw-Hill, New York.

Cummins, D.J., Phillips, R.D. & Smith, S.D. (1998) 'The rise of risk management', *Economic Review*, Federal Reserve Bank of Atlanta, First Quarter: 30–40.

Curtis, B., Hefley, W.E. & Miller, S. (1995) 'People Capability Maturity Model^{SM}', *Report Software Engineering Institute (Carnegie Mellon University)*, CMU/SEI-95–MM-02, Pittsburgh, PA.

Davenport, T.H. (1993) *Process innovation*, Harvard Business School Press, Boston, MA.

Davern, M.J. & Kauffman, R.J. (2000) 'Discovering potential and realising value from Information Technology investments', *Journal of Management Information Systems*, 16 (4): 121–43.

De Carvalho, F.A. & Leite, V.F. (1999) 'Attribute importance in service quality: An empirical test of the PBZ conjecture in Brazil', *International Journal of Service Industry Management*, 10 (5): 487–507.

DeFeo, J.A. (2001) 'The tip of the iceberg: When accounting for quality, don't forget the often hidden costs of poor quality', *Quality Progress*, May: 29–37.

DeLoach, J. (2000) *Enterprise-wide risk management: Strategies for linking risk and opportunity*, Arthur Andersen, Financial Times/Prentice-Hall, London.

Deming, W.E. (1986) *Out of the crisis*, Massachusetts Institute of Technology, Center for Advanced Engineering Study, Cambridge, MA.

Dent, J.F. (1990) 'Strategy, organization and control: Some possibilities for accounting research', *Accounting, Organizations and Society*, 15: 3–25.

Deschoolmeester, D. & Auwers, T. (1995) 'BPR hands-on, instructing a methodology to senior executives: Experiences in practice', Paper presented to the third European Conference on Information Systems, Athens, Greece.

Deschoolmeester, D. & Braet, O. (2000) 'Evaluation of ERP investments in the Belgian assembly industry', European Conference for Information Technology Evaluation, Brunel University, Uxbridge, UK.

Desmet, S., Van Dierdonck, R. & Van Looy, B. (1998) 'Servitization: The blurring boundaries between manufacturing and services', in Van Looy, B., Van Dierdonck, R. & Gemmel, P. (eds), *Services management: An integrated approach*, Pearson Education, London, pp. 33–44.

Dess, G.G. & Lumpkin, G.T. (2001) 'Emergent issues in strategy process research', in Hitt, M.A., Freeman, R.E. & Harrison, J.S. (eds), *The Blackwell handbook of strategic management*, Blackwell, Oxford.

Dodd, J.L. & Chen, S. (1996) 'EVA: A new panacea?', *Business and Economic Review*, 42 (July–September): 26–8.

Dolmat-Connell, J., (1999) 'Developing a reward strategy that delivers shareholder and employee value', *Compensation & Benefits Review*, 31 (2): 46–53.

Donaldson, T. & Preston, L. (1995) 'The stakeholder theory of the corporation: Concepts, evidence and implications', *Academy of Management Review*, 20 (1): 65–91.

Drazin, R. & Van de Ven, A. (1985) 'Alternative forms of fit in contingency theory', *Administrative Science Quarterly*, 30: 514–39.

Drucker, P.F. (1974) *Management: Tasks, responsibilities, practices*, Harper & Row, New York.

Drucker, P.F. (1988) 'The coming of the new organization', *Harvard Business Review*, January–February: 45–53.

Drucker, P.F. (1995) *Managing in a time of great change*, Truman Talley Books/Dutton, New York.

Dubé, L., Johnson, M.D. & Renaghan, L.M. (1999) 'Adapting the QFD approach to extended service transactions', *Production and Operations Management*, 8 (3): 301–17.

Duck, J.D. (1993) 'Managing change: The art of balancing', *Harvard Business Review*, November–December: 109–19.

Earl, M.J. & Feeny, D.F. (1994) 'Is your CIO adding value?', *Sloan Management Review*, 35 (3): 11–20.

Edmondson, G., Popper, M. & Robinson, A. (1998) 'Spain's success: No longer a Latin laggard, the country's economy is fast becoming one of Europe's healthiest', *Business Week*, 3 August.

Edosomwan, J.A. (1996) *Organizational transformation and process reengineering*, St Lucie Press and the Quality Observer Corporation, Fairfax, VA and Delray Beach FL.

Eisenhardt, K.M. & Sull, D.M. (2001) 'Strategy as simple rules', *Harvard Business Review*, January: 107–16.

Elkington, J. (1997) *Cannibals with forks*, Capstone, Oxford.

European Foundation for Quality Management (1994) *Business improvement through self-assessment*, No. 3, EFQM, Brussels.

European Foundation for Quality Management (1999a) *EFQM: The European quest for excellence*, Tenth anniversary book, EFQM, Brussels.

European Foundation for Quality Management (1999b) *The EFQM Excellence Model*, Pabo Prestige Press, Tilbury.

European Foundation for Quality Management (2001a) *The EFQM in action*, EFQM, Brussels.

European Foundation for Quality Management (2001b) 'ISO 9001:2000: A new stage on the journey to excellence', Excellence Network, *European Foundation for Quality Management*, 1 (2): February–March: 4–7.

Evans, J.R. & Dean, J.W. (2000) *Total quality: Management, organization and strategy*, South-Western College Publishing/Thomson Learning, Cincinnati, OH.

Evans, J.R. & Lindsay, W.M. (1999) *The management and control of quality*, South-Western College Publishing/Thomson Learning, Cincinnati, OH.

Feigenbaum, A.V. (1951) *Quality control: Principles, practice and administration*, McGraw-Hill, New York.

Feigenbaum, A.V. (2001) 'How to manage for quality in today's economy', *Quality Progress*, 27–29 May.

Figge, F. & Schaltegger, S. (2000) *What is stakeholder value? Developing a catchphrase into a benchmarking tool*, Universität of Lüneburg & Pictet & Cie, Report published in association with the United Nations Environment Programme, Lüneburg.

Financieel Economische Tijd (2000) 'Electronische poot wordt belangrijker voor Sotheby's', 28 November.

Fincham, R. & Rhodes, P. (1999) *Principles of organizational behaviour*, Oxford University Press, Oxford.

Fitzgerald, L., Johnson, R., Brignall, J.J., Silvestro, R. and Voss, C. (1991) *Performance measurement in service businesses*, The Chartered Institute of Accountants, London.

Freeman, R.E. & McVea, J. (2001) 'A stakeholder approach to strategic management', in Hitt, M.A., Freeman, R.E. & Harrison, J.S. (eds), *The Blackwell handbook of strategic management*, Blackwell, Oxford, pp. 189–207.

Frey, B.S. (2002) 'How does pay influence motivation', in Frey, B.S. & Osterloh, M. (eds), *Successful management by motivation: Balancing intrinsic and extrinsic incentives*, Springer, Heidelberg.

Galbraith, J. (1973) *Designing complex organizations,* Addison-Wesley Reading, MA.

Garvin, D.A. (1984) 'What does product quality really mean?', *Sloan Management Review*, 26 (1): 25–43.

Garvin, D.A. (1993) 'Building a learning organization', *Harvard Business Review*, July–August: 78–92.

Garvin, D.A. (1998) 'The processes of organization and management', *Sloan Management Review*, 39 (4): 33–50.

Gates, S. (1999) 'Aligning strategic performance measures and results', *Research report – The Conference Board*, 1261–99–RR, New York.

Gemmel, P. (2000) *Beheersen en herdenken van processen: Op zoek naar de patiënt*, Dossier Ziekenhuiswetgeving, Kluwer, Amsterdam.

Ghoshal, S. and Bartlett, A. (1999) *The individual corporation: A fundamentally new approach to management*, Harper Business, New York.

Gibson, C.F. & Nolan, R.L. (1974) 'Managing the four stages of EDP growth', *Harvard Business Review*, January–February pp. 76–84.

Goffee, R., & Jones, G. (2000) 'Why should anyone be led by you?', *Harvard Business Review*, September–October: 62–70.

Goleman, D. (1998) 'What makes a leader', *Harvard Business Review*, November–December: 93–102.

Goleman, D. (2000) 'Leadership that gets results', *Harvard Business Review*, March–April: 78–90.

Gomez-Mejia, L.R. (1992) 'Structure and process of diversification, compensation strategy, and firm performance', *Strategic Management Journal*, 13: 381–97.

Goold, M. & Campbell, A. (1998) 'Desperately seeking synergy', *Harvard Business Review*, September–October: 130–43.

Goold, M. & Campbell, A. (2002) *Designing effective organizations: How to create structured networks*, Jossey-Bass, San Francisco and London.

Goold, M., Campbell, A. & Alexander, M. (1994) *Corporate-level stratégy: Creating value in the multibusiness company*, John Wiley & Sons, New York.

Govindarajan, V. (1984) 'Appropriateness of accounting data in performance evaluation: An empirical examination of environmental uncertainty as an intervening variable', *Accounting, Organizations and Society*, 9: 125–35.

Govindarajan, V. (1986) 'Impact of participation in the budgetary process on managerial attitudes and performance: Universalistic and contingency perspectives', *Decision Sciences*, 17: 496–516.

Govindarajan, V. (1988) 'A contingency approach to strategy implementation at the business unit level: Integrating administrative mechanisms with strategy', *Academy of Management Journal*, 31: 828–53.

Govindarajan, V. & Fisher, J. (1990) 'Strategy, control systems and resource sharing: Effects on business unit performance', *Academy of Management Journal*, 33: 259–85.

Grant, R.M. (1995) *Contemporary strategy analysis: Concepts, techniques, applications* (2nd edition), Blackwell, Oxford.

Gratton, L., Hope-Hailey, V., Stiles, P. & Truss, C. (1999a) *Strategic human resource management*, Oxford University Press, Oxford.

Gratton, L., Hope-Hailey, V., Stiles, P. & Truss, C. (1999b) 'Linking individual performance to business strategy: The people process model', *Human Resource Management*, 38 (1): 17–31.

Greiner, L.E. (1998) 'Evolution and revolution as organizations grow', *Harvard Business Review*, May–June: 55–67 (Reprint of a 1972 *HBR* article).

Guest, D. (1990) 'Human resource management and the American dream', *Journal of Management Studies*, 27 (4): 378–97.

Günther, T., Landrock, B. & Muche, T. (1999) 'Profit versus value-based performance measures', Unpublished working paper, Dresden University, 1–27.

Gupta, K. & Govindarajan, V. (1984) 'Build, hold, harvest: Converting strategic intentions into reality', *The Journal of Business Strategy*, 4: 34–47.

Hagan, J.T. (1986) *Principles of quality costs*, American Society for Quality Control, Milwaukee, WI.

Haller, M. (1999) *Marketing and risk management: Concepts for the optimal fulfilment of the insurance function in a competitive environment*, Syllabus MBA in Financial Services and Insurance (Module 2), Institut für Versicherungswirtschaft, University of St Gallen, Switzerland, p. 21.

Hambrick, D.C. & Fredrickson, J.W. (2001) 'Are you sure you have a strategy?', *Academy of Management Executive*, 15 (4): 48.

Hamel, G. (2000) *Leading the revolution*, Harvard Business School Press, Boston, MA.

Hammer, M. & Champy, J. (1993) *Reengineering the corporation: A manifesto for business revolution*, HarperBusiness, New York.

Handy, C. (1994a) *The age of paradox*, Harvard Business School Press, Boston, MA.

Handy, C. (1994b) *The empty raincoat: Making sense of the future*, Hutchinson, London.

Harrison, J.S. & St John, C.H. (1998) *Strategic management of organizations and stakeholders: Concepts and cases* (2nd edition), South-Western College Publishing (ITP), Cincinanati, OH.

Hart, S.L. (1992) 'An integrative framework for strategy-making processes', *The Academy of Management Review*, 17 (2): 327–51.

Hauser, J.R. & Clausing, D.P. (1988) 'The house of quality', *Harvard Business Review*, May–June: 63–73.

Hayes, R.H. & Wheelwright, S.C. (1984) *Restoring our competitive edge*, Wiley, London and New York.

Hayes, R.H., Clarck, K. & Wheelwright, S. (1988) *Dynamic manufacturing*, The Free Press, New York.

Hedlund, G. (1986) 'The hypermodern MNC – a hetcrarchy?', *Human Resource Management*, Spring: 9–36.

Hellriegel, D., Slocum, W.J. & Woodman, D.W. (1992) *Organizational behavior*, West Publishing Company, St Paul, MN.

Henderson, D. (2001) *Misguided virtue: False notions of corporate social responsibility*, The Institute of Economic Affairs, London.

Henderson, J. & Venkatraman, N. (1993) 'Strategic alignment: Leveraging information technology for transforming organizations', *IBM Systems Journal*, 32 (1): 472–84.

Henderson, R.I. & Risher, H.W. (1987) 'Influencing organizational strategy through compensation leadership', in Balkin, D.B. & Gomez-Mejia, L.R. (eds), *New perspectives on compensation*, Prentice-Hall, Englewood Cliffs, NJ, pp. 331–42.

Hendry, C. & Pettigrew, A. (1990) 'Human resource management: An agenda for the 1990s', *The International Journal of Human Resource Management*, 1 (1): 17–43.

Heneman, R.L. (2001) *Business-driven compensation policies: Integrating compensation systems with corporate business strategies*, AMACOM, New York.

Heneman, R.L., Fisher, M.M. & Dixon, K.E. (2001) 'Reward and organizational systems alignment: An expert system', *Compensation and Benefits Review*, 33 (6): 18–29.

Hennell, A. & Warner, A. (1998) *Financial performance measurement and shareholder value explained*, Financial Times Management, London.

Hersey, P. (1984) *The management of organizational behavior*, The Centre for Leadership Studies, Escondido, CA.

Hersey, P. & Blanchard, K.H. (1988) *Management of organizational behaviour* (5th edition), Prentice-Hall, Englewood Cliffs, NJ.

Huselid, M. (1995) 'The impact of human resource management practices on turnover, productivity, and corporate financial performance', *Academy of Management Journal*, 38: 635–72.

Imai, K. (1986) *Kaizen: The key to Japan's competitive success*, McGraw-Hill, New York.

Imoisili, O.A. (1985) 'Task complexity, budget style of evaluating performance and managerial stress: An empirical investigation', Unpublished dissertation, Graduate School of Business, University of Pittsburgh, PA.

Institute of Management Accountants & Arthur Andersen LLP (1998) *Tools and techniques for implementing integrated performance measurement systems: Statement on Management Accounting 4DD*, Montvale, NJ.

Jackson, S. (1999) 'Achieving a culture of continuous improvement by adopting the principles of self-assessment and business excellence', *International Journal of Health Care Quality Assurance*, 12 (2): 59–64.

Johnson, G. & Scholes, K. (1999) *Exploring corporate strategy* (5th edition), Prentice-Hall, London.

Johnson, H.T. & Kaplan, R.S. (1987) *Relevance lost – The rise and fall of management accounting*, Harvard Business School Press, Boston, MA.

Johnson, M. (1995) *Managing in the next millennium: A unique collection of insight from the world's top management commentators*, Management Centre Europe, London.

Jorion, P. (2001) 'Value, risk and control: A dynamic process in need of integration', in Financial Times, *Mastering risk. Vol. 1: Concepts*, Pearson Education, Harlow.

Jorissen, A. & Bruggeman, W. (1999) *De Balanced Scorecard in de praktijk: Een leidraad voor strategische prestatiemeting*, Maklu, Antwerpen-Apeldoorn.

Kaplan, R.S. & Norton, D.P. (1992) 'The Balanced Scorecard: Measures that drive performance', *Harvard Business Review*, January–February: 71–9.

Kaplan, R.S. & Norton, D.P. (1993) 'Putting the Balanced Scorecard to Work', *Harvard Business Review*, September–October: 134–47.

Kaplan, R.S. & Norton, D.P. (1996a) 'Using the Balanced Scorecard as a strategic management system', *Harvard Business Review*, January–February: 75–85.

Kaplan, R.S. & Norton, D.P. (1996b) 'Linking the Balanced Scorecard to strategy', *California Management Review*, 39 (Fall): 53–79.

Kaplan, R.S. & Norton, D.P. (2000) 'Having trouble with your strategy? Then map it', *Harvard Business Review*, September–October: 167–76.

Kaplan, R.S. & Norton, D.P. (2001) *The strategy-focused organization: How Balanced Scorecard companies thrive in the new business environment*, Harvard Business School Press, Boston, MA.

Keegan, D.P., Eiler, R.G. & Jones, C.R. (1989) 'Are your performance measures obsolete?', *Management Accounting*, 70 (12): 45–50.

Kennerley, M. & Neely, A. (2002) 'Performance measurement frameworks: A review', in Neely, A. (ed.), *Business performance measurement: Theory and practice*, Cambridge University Press, Cambridge, pp. 145–55.

Kerr, J. & Slocum Jr., J.W. (1987) 'Managing corporate culture through reward systems', *Academy of Management Executive*, 1 (2): 99–107.

Kessler, I. (2000) 'Remuneration systems', in Bach, S. & Sisson, K. (eds), *Personnel management: A comprehensive guide to theory and practice*, Blackwell, Oxford, pp. 264–86.

Kessler, I. & Purcell, J. (1992) 'Performance related pay: Objectives and application', *Human Resource Management Journal*, 2 (3): 16–33.

Khandwalla, P. (1972) 'The effects of different types of competition on the use of management controls', *Journal of Accounting Research*, Autumn: 275–85.

Kingman-Brundage, J., George, W. & Bowen, D. (1995) 'Service logic: Achieving service system integration', *International Journal of Service Industry Management*, 6 (4): 20–39.

Knight, J.A. (1998) *Value-based management: Developing a systematic approach to creating shareholder value*, McGraw-Hill, New York.

Kohn, A. (2002a) 'Why incentive plans cannot work', in *Harvard Business Review on Compensation*, Harvard Business School Press, Boston, MA, 29–49.

Kohn, A. (2002b) 'Rethinking rewards', in *Harvard Business Review on Compensation*, Harvard Business School Press, Boston, MA.

Kotter, J.P. & Heskett, J.L. (1992) *Corporate culture and performance*, The Free Press, New York.

Kreitner, R., Kinicki, A. & Buelens, M. (2002) *Organizational behaviour* (2nd European edition), McGraw-Hill Education, Maidenhead.

Labovitz, G. & Rosansky, V. (1997) *The power of alignment: How great companies stay centered and accomplish extraordinary things*, John Wiley & Sons, New York.

Lamotte, G. & Carter, G. (2000) 'Are the Balanced Scorecard and the EFQM Excellence Model mutually exclusive or do they work together to bring added value to a company?', paper prepared for the EFQM common Interest Day, 17 March.

Laster, D. (1999) 'The conventional approach to risk management', in Shimpi, P.A. (ed.), *Integrating corporate risk management*, Swiss Re New Markets, New York.

Lautenschläger, M. (1999) 'The structure and development of the MLP Group', Presentation at the MBA in Financial Services & Insurance (MBA-FSI), Edition 1 – Module 2, 12 March, Ittingen.

Lawrence, P. & Lorsch, J. (1967) *Organization and environment*, Irwin, Homewood, IL.

Leavitt, H.J. (1965) 'Applied organizational change in industry: Structural, technological and humanistic approaches', in March, J.G. (ed.), *Handbook of organizations*, Rand-McNally, Chicago, IL.

LeBlanc, P.V. & Mulvey, P.W. (1998) 'How American workers see the rewards of work', *Compensation and Benefits Review*, 30: 24–8.

Legge, K. (1995) *Human resource management: Rhetorics and realities*, Macmillan, Basingstoke.

Lehn, K. & Makhija, A.K. (1996) 'EVA & MVA as performance measures and signals for strategic change', *Strategy & Leadership*, May/June: 34–8.

Liberators, R.L. (2001) 'Teaching the role of SPC in industrial statistics', *Quality Progress*, July: 89–94.

Liedtka, J.M. (2001) 'Strategy formulation: The roles of conversation and design', in Hitt, M.A., Freeman, R.E. & Harrison, J.S. (eds), *The Blackwell handbook of strategic management*, Blackwell, Oxford.

Locke, E.A. & Latham, G.P. (1990) *A theory of goal setting and task performance*, Prentice-Hall, Englewood Cliffs, NJ.

Luftman, J. (2001) 'Assessing Business-IT alignment maturity', *Communications of the AIS*, 4: Article 14.

Lynch, R. (1997) *Corporate strategy*, Pitman, London.

Lynch, R.L. & Cross, K.D. (1991) *Measure up: The essential guide to measuring business performance*, Mandarin, London.

MacDuffie, J.P. (1995) 'Human resource bundles and manufacturing performance: Organizational logic and flexible production systems in the world auto industry', *Industrial and Labor Relations Review*, 48: 197–221.

Markides, C.C. (1999a) 'A dynamic view of strategy', *Sloan Management Review*, 40 (3): 55–63.

Markides, C.C. (1999b) 'In search of strategy', *Sloan Management Review*, 40 (6): 6.

McCarthy, D.J., Markides, C.C. & Mintzberg, H. (2000) 'View from the top: Henry Mintzberg on strategy and management – Commentary/Response', *The Academy of Management Executive*, 14 (3): 30–42.

McCormack, K.P. & Johnson, W.C. (2001) *Business process orientation: Gaining the E-business competitive advantage*, St Lucie Press, Boca Raton, FL.

McFarlan, F.W. (1984) 'Information technology changes the way you compete', *Harvard Business Review*, May–June, pp. 98–103.

McTaggart, J., Kontes, P.W. & Mankins, M.C. (1994) *The value imperative*, The Free Press, New York.

Megginson, L.C., Mosley, D.C. & Pietri, P.H. Jr. (1989) *Management: Concepts and applications*, Harper & Row, New York.

Miles, R.E. & Snow, C. (1978) *Organizational strategy, structure, and processes*, McGraw-Hill, New York.

Milkovich, G.T. (1988) 'A strategic perspective on compensation management', *Research in Personnel and Human Resources Management*, JAI Press, Greenwich, CT, 6: 263–88.

Miller, D. (1993) 'The architecture of simplicity', *Academy of Management Review*, January: 116–34.

Miller, D. & Friesen, P.H. (1982) 'Innovation in conservative and entrepreneurial firms: Two models of strategic momentum', *Strategic Management Journal*, 3 (1): 1–25.

Min, H. & Galle, W.P. (1999) 'Electronic commerce usage in business-to-business purchasing', *International Journal of Operations and Production Management*, 19 (9): 909–21.

Mintzberg, H. (1987) 'Crafting strategy', *Harvard Business Review*, 65, July–August: 66–75.

Mintzberg, H. (1994) *The rise and fall of strategic planning*, Prentice-Hall, New York.

Mintzberg, H., Ahlstrand, B. & Lampel, J. (1998) *Strategy safari: A guided tour through the wilds of strategic management*, Prentice-Hall, New York.

Mitchell, R., Agle, B. & Wood, D. (1997) 'Toward a theory of stakeholder identification and salience: Defining the principle of who and what really counts', *Academy of Management Review*, 22 (4): 853–86.

Montemayor, E.F. (1996) 'Congruence between pay policy and competitive strategy in high-performing firms', *Journal of Management*, 22 (6): 889–908.

Moores, K. & Sharma, D. (1998) 'The influence of environmental uncertainty on performance evaluation style and managerial performance', *Accountability and Performance*, 4 (2): 1–16.

Morin, R.A. & Jarell, S.L. (2001) *Driving shareholder value: Value-building techniques for creating shareholder wealth*, McGraw-Hill, New York.

Moss Kanter, R. (1997) *On the frontiers of management*, Harvard University Press, Cambridge, MA.

Neely, A. & Adams, C. (2000) 'Perspectives on performance: The performance prism', *Focus Magazine for the Performance Management Professional*, 4 (August).

Neely, A., Adams, C. & Kennerley, M. (2002) *The performance prism: The scorecard for measuring and managing business success*, Financial Times/Prentice-Hall, London.

Neely, A. & Austin, R. (2002) 'Measuring performance: The operations perspective', in Neely, A. (ed.), *Business performance measurement: Theory and practice*, Cambridge University Press, Cambridge, pp. 41–50.

Neumann, F.X. (1997) 'Organizational structures to match the new information-rich environments: Lessons from the study of chaos', *Public Productivity & Management Review*, September: 86–100.

Nilsson, L.-E. & Samuelsson, P. (2000) 'Self-assessment for business excellence in large organizations: The EFQM Excellence Model as a tool for continuous improvement', Masters Thesis, Chalmers University of Technology, Sweden.

Nolan, R.L. (1979) 'Managing the crises in data processing', *Harvard Business Review*, March–April, 115–23.

Nonaka, I. (1991) 'The knowledge-creating company', *Harvard Business Review*, November–December: 96–105.

Nonaka, I., Toyoma, R. & Nagata A. (2000) 'A firm as a knowledge-creating entity: A new perspective on the theory of the firm', *Industrial & Corporate Change*, 9 (1): 1–20.

O'Brien, J.A. (1997) *Introduction to information systems* (8th edition), Irwin McGraw-Hill, New York.

O'Byrne, S.F. (1996) 'EVA® and market value', *Journal of Applied Corporate Finance*, 9 (1): 116–25.

Otley, D.T. (1978) 'Budget use and managerial performance', *Journal of Accounting Research*, 16 (1): 122–49.

Otley, D.T. (1999) 'Performance management: A framework for management control systems research', *Management Accounting Research*, 10 (December): 363–82.

Ouchi, W.G. (1980) 'Markets, bureaucracies and clans', *Administrative Science Quarterly*, 25: 129–140.

Ouchi, W.G. (1981) *Theory Z*, Addison-Wesley, Reading, MA.

Ouchi, W.G. & Johnson, B. (1978) 'Types of organizational control and their relationship to emotional well-being', *Administrative Science Quarterly*, 23: 293–317.

Parasuraman, A., Zeithaml, V.A. & Berry, L.L. (1985) 'A conceptual model of service quality and implications for further research', *Journal of Marketing*, 49 (Fall): 45–50.

Parker, M.M. (1995) *Strategic transformation and information technology: Paradigms for performing while transforming*, Prentice-Hall, Englewood Cliffs, NJ.

Parker, M.M., Trainor, H.E. & Benson, R.J. (1989) *Information strategy and economics*, Prentice-Hall, Englewood Cliffs, NJ.

Paulk, M.C., Curtis, B., Chrissis, M.B. & Weber, C.V. (1993) 'Capability Maturity Model[SM] for Software, Version 1.1', *Technical Report Software Engineering Institute (Carnegie Mellon University)*, CMU/SEI–93–TR–024, Pittsburgh, PA.

Pearson, T.A. (2001) 'Measure for six sigma success', *Quality Progress*, February: 35–40.

Pfeffer, J. (2002) 'Six dangerous myths about pay', in *Harvard Business Review on Compensation*, Harvard Business School Press, Boston, MA, pp. 141–66.

Porter, L.J. & Tanner, S.J. (1996) *Assessing business excellence: A guide to self-assessment*, Butterworth-Heinemann, Oxford.

Porter, M.E. (1985) *Competitive advantage: Creating and sustaining superior performance*, The Free Press, New York.

Post, J.E., Preston, L.E. & Sachs, S. (2002) *Redefining the corporation: Stakeholder management and organizational wealth*, Stanford Business Books, Stanford, CA.

Prahalad, C.K. & Hamel, G. (1989) 'Strategic intent', *Harvard Business Review*, May–June, 63–76.

Purcell, J. (1999) 'Best practice and best fit: chimera or cul-de-sac?', *Human Resource Management Journal*, 9: 26–41.

Quinn, J.B., Doorley, T.L. & Paquette, P.C. (1998) 'Beyond products: Service-based strategy', *Harvard Business Review*, March–April: 58–68.

Ramaswamy, R. (1996) *Design and management of service processes: Keeping customers for life*, Addison-Wesley, Reading, MA.

Rappaport, A. (1986) *Creating shareholder value*, The Free Press, New York.

Reeves, C.A. & Bednar, D.A. (1994) 'Defining quality: Alternatives and implications', *Academy of Management Review*, 19 (3): 419–45.

Reilly, B., Hope-Ross, D., Luebbers, J. & Purchase, E. (2000) 'E-procurement: A blueprint for revolution or hype?', *Strategic analysis report*, Stamford, CT: Gartner Group, 9 February.

Ridderstrale, J. & Nordström, K. (2000) *Funky business*, Bookhouse Publishing, Harlow.

Roberts, M.W. & Silvester, K.J. (1996) 'Why ABC failed and how it may yet succeed', *Journal of Cost Management*, Winter: 23–35.

Ross, A. (1995) 'Job-related tension, budget emphasis and uncertainty', *Management Accounting Research*, 6: 1–11.

Rotch, W. (1990) 'Activity-based costing in service industries', *Journal of Cost Management*, Summer: 4–13.

Roth, A. & Griffith, C. (1990) 'Operating strategies for the 1990s: Elements comprising world-class manufacturing', in Voss, C.A. (ed.), *Manufacturing strategy, process and content*, Chapman Hall/Van Nostrand, New York.

Schendel, D. & Hofer, C. (1979) 'Introduction', in Schendel, D. & Hofer, C. (eds), *Strategic management*, Little Brown, Boston, MA.

Schuler, R.S. (1990) 'Repositioning the human resource function: Transformation or demise?' Academy of Management Executive, 4 (3): 49–60.

Schuler, R.S. & Jackson, S.E. (eds), (1999) *Strategic human resource management*, Blackwell, Oxford.

Senge, P. (1990) *The fifth discipline: The art & practice of the learning organization*, Doubleday, New York.

Shewhart, W.A. (1931) *Economic control of quality of manufactured product*, Van Nostrand, New York, pp. 53–4.

Shields, M. & Young, M. (1993) 'Antecedents and consequences of participative budgeting: Evidence on the effects of asymmetric information', *Journal of Management Accounting Research*, 5: 265–80.

Shimpi, P.A. (ed.), (1999) *Integrating corporate risk management*, Swiss Re New Markets, New York.

Shostack, G.L. (1984) 'Designing services that deliver', *Harvard Business Review*, January–February, 133–9.

Shostack, G.L. (1985) 'Planning the service encounter', in Czepiel, J.A., Solomon, M.A. & Surprenant, C.F. (eds), *The service encounter: Managing employee–customer interactions in service businesses*, Lexington Books, New York.

Shostack, G.L. (1987) 'Service positioning through structural change', *Journal of Marketing*, 51 (1): 34–43.

Simons, R. (1987) 'Accounting control systems and business strategy: An empirical analysis', *Accounting, Organizations and Society*, 12: 357–74.

Simons, R. (1995) *Levers of control: How managers use innovative control systems to drive strategic renewal*, Harvard Business School Press, Boston, MA.

Simons, R. (2000) *Performance measurement and control systems for implementing strategy: Text and cases*, Prentice-Hall, Upper Saddle River, NJ.

Skipper, H.D. Jr. (1998) *International risk and insurance: An environmental-managerial approach*, Irwin McGraw-Hill, Boston, MA.

Slack, N., Chambers, S., Harland, C., Harrison, A. & Johnston, R. (1995) *Operations management*, Pitman Publishing, London.

Slack, N., Chambers, S., Harland, C., Harrison, A. & Johnston, R. (1998) *Operations management* (2nd edition), Pitman, London.

Smith, I. (2000) 'Benefits', in Rynes, S.L. & Gerhart, B. (eds), *Compensation in organizations: Current research and practice*, Jossey-Bass, San Francisco, CA.

Southwest Airlines (A-1) (1995) Case prepared by Professor C. O'Reilly, Stanford University Graduate School of Business, Stanford, CA.

Sower, V.E., Quarles, R. & Cooper, S. (2002) 'Cost of quality distribution and quality system maturity: An exploratory study', *ASQ's Annual Quality Congress Proceedings*, American Society for Quality, Milwaukee WI, pp. 343–54.

Stalk, G. & Abegglen, J. (1985) *Kaisha: The Japanese corporation*, Basic Books, New York.

Stalk, G. & Hout, T. (1990) *Competing against time: How time-based competition is reshaping global markets*, The Free Press, New York.

Stewart, G.B. (1999) *The quest for value*, Harper Business, Boston, MA.

Stivers, B.P. & Joyce, T. (2000) 'Building a balanced performance management system', *SAM Advanced Management Journal*, 65 (2): 22–9.

Storey, J. (ed.), (1989) *New perspectives on human resources management*, Routledge, London.

Strategos Institute (2001) 'Building the post-industrial firm', Presentation at the 21st Annual International Conference of the Strategic Management Society, San Francisco, 22 October 2001.

Svendsen, A.C., Boutilier, R.G., Abbott, R.M. & Wheeler, D. (2000) *Measuring the business value of stakeholder relationships*, The Center for Innovation in Management (Simon Fraser University, Vancouver, Canada) and Erivan K. Haub Program in Business and Sustainability (York University, Toronto, Canada).

Sweeney, M. (1991) 'Towards a unified theory of strategic manufacturing management', *International Journal of Operations and Production Management*, 11 (8): 6–22.

Tallon, P.P., Kraemer, K.L. & Gurbaxani, V. (2000) 'Executives' perceptions of the business value of information technology: A process-oriented approach', *Journal of Management Information Systems*, 16 (4): 145–73.

Thakor, A.V., DeGraff, J. & Quinn, R. (2000) 'Creating sustained shareholder value – and dispelling some myths', in Financial Times, *Mastering strategy: The complete MBA companion in strategy*, Pearson Education, Harlow.

Thompson, A.A. & Strickland III, A.J. (1992) *Strategic management: Concepts and cases*, Irwin, Homewood, IL.

Treacy, M. & Wiersema, F. (1993) 'Customer intimacy and other value disciplines', *Harvard Business Review*, January–February: 84–93.

Treacy, M. & Wiersema, F. (1995) *The discipline of market leaders*, Perseus Books, Reading, MA.

Trigeorgis, L. (1997) *Real options*, MIT Press, Cambridge, MA.

Tropman, J.E. (2001) 'The compensation solution: How to develop an employee-driven rewards system', *University of Michigan Business School Management Series*, Jossey-Bass, San Francisco, CA.

Truss, C. & Gratton, L. (1994) 'Strategic human resource management: A conceptual approach', *The International Journal of Human Resource Management*, 5 (3): 663–86.

Tyson, S. (1987) 'The management of the personnel function', *Journal of Management Studies*, 24 (9): 523–32.

Tyson, S. (1997) 'Human resource strategy: A process for managing the contribution of

HRM to organizational performance', *The International Journal of Human Resource Management*, 8 (3): 277–90.

Ulrich, D. (1997a) *Human resource champions: The next agenda for adding value to HR practices*, Harvard Business School Press, Boston, MA.

Ulrich, D. (1997b) 'Measuring human resources: An overview of practice and prescription for results', *Human Resource Management*, 36: 302–20.

Ulrich, D., Brockbank, W., Yeung, A.K. & Lake, D.G. (1995) 'Human resource competencies: An empirical assessment', *Human Resource Management*, 34 (4): 473–95.

Van den Berghe, L.A.A. & Levrau, A. (2000) 'Corporate governance in de privé-sector: Nuttige inspiratiebron voor raden van bestuur in overheidsondernemingen', *Vlaams Tijdschrift voor Overheids-management*, 5 (4): 7–14.

Van der Stede, W.A. (2000) 'The relationship between two consequences of budgetary controls: Budgetary slack creation and managerial short-term orientation', *Accounting, Organizations and Society*, 25 (6): 609–22.

Van Dierdonck, R. & Vereecke, A. (1994) 'World-class manufacturing', in Van Dierdonck, R. & Vereecke, A., *Operationeel Beheer*, Academia Press, Ghent.

Van Dierdonck, R. & Busschop, K. (1996) 'Supply chain management', *Management voor Ingenieurs*, 17: Chapter 3.3.5.

Van Looy, B., Gemmel, P., Desmet, S., Van Dierdonck, R. & Serneels, S. (1998) 'Dealing with productivity and quality indicators in a service environment: Some field experiences', *International Journal of Service Industry Management*, 9 (4): 359–76.

Van Ossel, G. (1998) 'Measuring customer satisfaction', in Van Looy, B., Van Dierdonck, R. & Gemmel, P. (eds), *Services management: An integrated approach*, Financial Times/Pitman, London, pp. 125–48.

Venkatraman, N. & Ramanujam, V. (1986) 'Measurement of business performance in strategy research: A comparison of approaches', *The Academy of Management Review*, 11 (4): 801–14.

Volberda, H.R. (1997) 'Building flexible organizations for fast-moving markets', *Long Range Planning*, 30 (2): 169–83.

Volberda, H.W. (1998) *Building the flexible firm: How to remain competitive*, Oxford, University Press, Oxford.

Waggoner, D.B., Neely, A.D. & Kennerley, M.P. (1999) 'The forces that shape organizational performance measurement systems: An interdisciplinary review', *International Journal of Production Economics*, 60–61: 53–60.

Walburg, J.A. (1997) *Integrale Kwaliteit in de Gezondheidszorg: Van inspecteren naar leren*, Kluwer Bedrijfsinformatie, Amsterdam, pp. 26–9.

Walton, M. (1986) *The Deming Management Method*, Perigee Books, New York.

Weill, P. & Broadbent, M. (1998) *Leveraging the new infrastructure: How market leaders capitalize on information technology*, Harvard Business School Press, Boston, MA.

Wheatley, M. (1992) *Leadership and the new science*, Berret-Koehler Publishers, San Francisco, CA.

Williams, G.A. & Miller, R.B. (2002) 'Change the way you persuade', *Harvard Business Review*, September–October: 64–73.

Wiseman, C. (1985) *Strategy and computer information systems as competitive weapons*. Dow Jones/Irwin, London.

Zech, J. (2001) 'Rethinking risk management: The combination of financial and industrial risk', *The Geneva Papers on Risk and Insurance*, 26 (1): 71–82.

Zeithaml, V.A., Berry, L.L. & Parasuraman, A. (1988) 'Communication and control processes in the delivery of service quality', *Journal of Marketing*, 52 (April): 35–48.

Index

Compiled by INDEXING SPECIALISTS, 202 Church Road, Hove, East Sussex BN3 2DJ. Tel: 01273 738299.
E-mail: richardr@indexing.co.uk
Website: www.indexing.co.uk